W9-ABZ-593

THE LIFE AND DEATH OF

LOUIS XVI

LOUIS XVI IN HIS CORONATION ROBES
Portrait by J. S. Duplessis, 1777. Musée Carnavalet.

THE LIFE AND DEATH OF

LOUIS XVI

By

SAUL K. PADOVER, Ph.D.

Author of "Revolutionary Emperor: Joseph II"
Formerly Research Associate in History
University of California

ILLUSTRATED

D. APPLETON-CENTURY COMPANY
INCORPORATED
New York *London*
1939

PRINTED IN THE UNITED STATES OF AMERICA

TO

RUTH

AND

WILLIAM CHERIN

PREFACE

THE FOLLOWING PAGES contain the first full biography of Louis XVI in any language, based almost entirely on archive materials. Here, admittedly, is the life of a little man, who during his lifetime was overshadowed by a vivid wife and after his death calumniated by a victorious Revolutionary tradition and ignored by generations of historians. The Revolutionary tradition libeled his memory because he was an inescapable and much-needed victim, and the historians neglected him because they lacked imagination to see that the figure of Louis XVI was at the core of the French Revolution. He lost his head and throne precisely because he was the sort of man he was, and had he been something else, the course of the French Revolution (if there had been a revolution at all, which is doubtful) and the direction of Europe might have been measurably altered.

What kind of man was he to whom such memorable things happened? This book tells the story of a man *in* a revolution, without attempting to glorify the one or belittle the other. The man was significant as a vessel and symbol of power, and the Revolution was important because it happened and, in happening, wrecked the man and changed the social system.

Louis XVI's personal tragedy (the emphasis is on the personal, since the author does not believe that any individual is sufficiently important in the general social scheme to be viewed in the light of tragedy) was that he inherited power. What he inherited he could not use, and what he used was not enough to protect his position and his life. The Jacobins shouted, "Down with the Tyrant Louis XVI," but the historian knows that the king was decapitated because he was not a tyrant. If he had had strength of will, or a modicum of necessary ruthlessness, he would have escaped his fate and might have spared France years of agony and decades of bloodshed. But Louis nursed a prejudice against violence.

Even during his life, when his subjects generally liked him and exempted him from their harsh and bitter sarcasms, Louis XVI did not know how to sell himself to his people. The nation cried for a king, and it was given an image of a stout man too shy to play to the galleries. Louis XVI built no bridges between himself and his subjects, and the wonder is that he retained their affections as long as he did. Almost to the very end, Frenchmen were attached to the monarchy, but they demanded something more of the monarch than ritualized inertia. In no way, except intentions, did Louis meet the expectations of his people. This interplay of forces, as expressed by what an aroused nation wanted and a slow-moving ruler did not offer, forms one of the fascinating chapters in history.

One of the curious ironies in the career of Louis XVI is that his death came to be perhaps more important than his life. From the point of view of the Revolutionary reforms, the king's death was unnecessary because it took place after the Revolution had achieved its program; and from the point of view of French history, the decapitation of Louis XVI was a national tragedy because it tore the country from its traditional moorings and cast it into a sea of violence.

The execution of the king opened the flood-gates of anarchy, terror, dictatorship, and international war. Louis XVI was succeeded by Danton, Danton by the mob, the mob by Robespierre, Robespierre ultimately by Bonaparte. For more than two decades aftter the decapitation of Louis XVI France knew no peace. And ever since that time she has been subject to political upheavals revolving about the problem that the French Revolution failed to solve—how to have order without losing liberty. Regardless of what one thinks of Louis XVI, it seems to the author that a constitutional monarchy on the British lines, if permitted to develop without violence, might have gone far to stabilize French politics. The execution of Louis XVI prevented such a development.

Why Louis XVI failed in his functions, and how, is told in this book. Perhaps this is the place to remind the reader that Louis XVI, as a despot, was a good man and like good men of his time he went to the guillotine.

I wish to thank the Guggenheim Foundation for the Fellowship, granted me in 1936, which enabled me to collect data in the archives of Paris, Vienna, and London; and, in particular, Henry Allen Moe for his kindness and interest in my project. I also wish to express my gratitude to those friends who patiently read portions of the manuscript and offered valuable criticisms and suggestions: Mr. Robert Ballou, Mrs. Ruth Cherin, Dr. William Cherin, Professor Louis Gottschalk, and Dr. Leo Rosten.

S. K. P.

CONTENTS

ILLUSTRATIONS

THE LIFE AND DEATH OF

LOUIS XVI

I pause before history. Remember that it will judge your sentence.— De Sèze, concluding his defense of Louis XVI before the Convention.

CHAPTER I

"One should take women only in Saxony"

EARLY in the morning of August 23, 1754, a courier galloped from Versailles in the direction of Choisy, carrying the news to Louis XV that his daughter-in-law the Dauphiness Maria Josepha had just been delivered of another boy. In his hurry to reach the king the reckless courier beat the horse until the animal, whether from pain or protest, threw the rider, who fell into the road with a broken neck. That was the way Louis Augustus, named Duke of Berry and fated to become Louis XVI, was introduced to the world—heralded by misfortune. A bad omen, said some, thinking of the dead courier. Others marveled at the fertile mother. *"Voilà une brave allemande,"* said the king's minister d'Argenson, "who is giving us plenty of heirs to the throne."

⚜

SHE WAS an unusual woman, the Dauphiness Maria Josepha, and should be remembered, though not perhaps commended, as the mother of the last three Bourbon kings of France. At the age of sixteen, in 1747, she had left her native Dresden to come to Versailles to marry Louis the Dauphin, irreverently called Louis the Fat, the only legitimate son of Louis XV. She was then a sapphire-eyed, straw-colored little girl, very earnest and very cool. Her self-possession, so remarkable in a provincial princess, impressed even the elegant Louis XV, who always relished the memory of how, on the wedding night, when he and his court burst into the bridal chamber to bear witness to the consummation, the terrified young dauphin hid his naked body under the blanket while the bride calmly sat up and engaged His Majesty in polite conversation.

Maria Josepha needed all her strength of character and the consolation of religion to keep herself from becoming just another female in the haremized court of Louis XV. Her fat and slovenly husband, whom she regarded, with the eyes of piety, as the "most handsome and most estimable prince in the world," lost no time in telling her that he detested her. He would always love, he taunted, his first wife, a swarthy and voluptuous Spaniard. Often he wept for the dead first wife. Maria Josepha was touchingly humble. "Monsieur," she said to her blubbering husband, "weep freely; I shall not be offended. On the contrary, your tears show what I might expect should I ever be fortunate enough to please you."

Such calm forbearance and loving patience brought its reward. The dauphin, starved for affection and neglected by his royal father, gradually learned to trust his devoted wife. Even the court of Versailles, so gay and artfully corrupt—"dominated by females who are full of the devil and wicked to boot," in the words of the expert Marshal Saxe—esteemed the dauphiness. Her good sense was sharpened by an excellent education. Despite her youth and religious principles, she knew instinctively when it was politic to ignore preferences in favor of advantages—a knowledge which, incidentally, she did not transmit to her sons. One look at the smitten Louis XV as he sat near the blond and regal Madame de Pompadour showed the dauphiness who was the real ruler at Versailles. To please the monarch it was necessary to flatter the mistress. Maria Josepha was gracious to the gratified de Pompadour, and Louis XV was delighted.

What most endeared Maria Josepha to the court, however,

was her matchless fertility. Brought from Germany to supply the French monarchy with heirs, she lived up to the most extravagant expectations. She gave birth to a daughter in 1750, a son in 1751, another son in 1753, still another son—Louis XVI—in 1754; then she filled four more cradles. The courtiers were struck with honest admiration at such fecundity. "Sire," the impressed Marquis de Souvré said to Louis XV, "one should take women only in Saxony, and if none are left, one should have them made out of Dresden porcelain."

But not all Frenchmen, by any means, were delighted. What was to the courtiers a guarantee of dynastic perpetuation merely spelled heavy taxes to the citizens. Already the nation was weary of the monarchical burden, and signs of protest, mild at first, were not lacking. After her third child was born, the sheltered Maria Josepha experienced a shock which foretold the tragedy that was to come. As she and her husband crossed the Seine bridge on their way to Notre Dame to thank the Almighty for a happy delivery, thousands of ragged women blocked the way with cries of "Give us bread, we are dying of hunger!" The twenty-two year old girl from Saxony had never before seen a crowd of hungry people, and the experience was unnerving; white-faced, she fell back in her seat. The dauphin handed a purse to the captain of his guard and directed him to distribute the money. But the poor women, with the scorn that was to make them so decisive a factor in the coming Revolution, shouted, "Monseigneur, we do not want your money. It's bread we want!"

THE DAUPHIN, father of the boy who was to become Louis XVI, was at the time of his marriage a composite of avoirdupois and pedantry. He was neither a libertine nor a spendthrift; on the other hand, he lacked charm and was devoid of royal manners. Contemporaries considered him a mass of dully sentient flesh. "He is extremely stout," d'Argenson described him, "an enemy of all movement and exercise, without passion, even without taste; everything stifles him, nothing stimulates him. If there is still some spark in him, it is a dying one, extinguished by fat and bigotry."[1]

Quietly Maria Josepha took the stout prince into her competent hands. She showed no contempt when her husband, to celebrate the death of a relative, danced under a black canopy. Nor did she, a woman of considerable culture, ever openly resent his boastful ignorance. She had a wise understanding of her husband's shortcomings and was convinced that he was good. Her kindness was unfailing and her patience inexhaustible. She guided his education and, despite frequent pregnancies, was able to maintain a home environment truly middle-class in its solid virtues. An excellent musician—she played the harpsichord and organ—she made her small court a center of artistic gatherings where her husband, in contact with more refined spirits, could improve his own.

The father of Louis XVI thus slowly grew into a dignified prince with a sense of social responsibility. He was not, despite the malodorous reputation of his family, the proverbial Bourbon intransigent. On the contrary, he was a reader of Rousseau and the "new philosophy," and although he resented Jean Jacques' hostility to the Church, he considered *The Social Contract* largely sound. Thinking of his own father's misgovernment, the dauphin said that every ruler should recognize the limits of his authority. "The

[1] Although d'Argenson's judgment of the dauphin is seconded by most contemporaries, a few were more flattering. In a manuscript in the Arsenal Library at Paris, MS 2325, written by a priest close to the dauphin, there is the following description: "Monseigneur the Dauphin was tall and well proportioned. He had a long face but pleasantly formed; the complexion was fine and of the utmost freshness. The eyes were dark and small, but full of spirit and fire; the smile charming, fine and sometimes a little mischievous. His attractive black hair was well kept and reached to his waist. Gentleness, goodness, politeness, affability and the most natural gaiety were reflected equally on his face and in his manners; and no one more than he possessed that *je-ne-sais-quoi* which one feels but is unable to define." The truth, nevertheless, was that the dauphin was generally rude and always fat.

THE DAUPHIN LOUIS

Portrait by Quentin de la Tour. Louvre.

THE DAUPHINESS MARIA JOSEPHA

Portrait by Quentin de la Tour. Dresden Museum.

monarch," he argued, "is nothing but the steward of the state revenues."

In other ways, too, the father of Louis XVI showed that he was conscious of the currents of the age. Neglected by his father the king, the dauphin found pleasure in reading criticisms of all that his parent represented—a form of antiparental revolt common in many an autocratic court. The dauphin eagerly read law and history at a time when Voltaire was composing history for use as a weapon against bigots and despots. "Ignorance," remarked the son of Louis XV, "produces almost as many tyrants in monarchies as does ambition in republics." Here was an echo of Montesquieu, and in truth the dauphin read *The Spirit of the Laws* and memorized many of its passages. These books aggravated resentment against his father who kept him cruelly at a distance. "History," the dauphin said with acerbity, "teaches the children that which they dare not tell the parents." [2]

Father and son were separated by two unbridgeable barriers, morality and religion. The dauphin was brought up by his pious mother Maria Leszczynska, the neglected wife of Louis XV, and he viewed his father's boudoir activities with the eyes of his outraged mother. To him the life his father led was unworthy of a Christian prince. Possibly the dauphin exaggerated his father's immorality, but there could be no doubt about Louis XV's aversion for clerical meddling and his distaste for Church-inspired morality. And the dauphin was, despite some excellent qualities of heart and mind, an excessively religious man who persistently surrounded himself with religious fanatics, as if flaunting them in the face of de Pompadour and her royal lover. Such an entourage Louis XV regarded as nothing less than ill-mannered. The king, moreover, deplored his son's occasional outbursts of rudeness as much as his demonstrative piety. He never for-

[2] Much of our information on the dauphin comes from an interesting manuscript in the Bibliothèque Nationale, MS Fr. 13784, by Abbé Soldini, *Essai sur la vie de Monseigneur Louis Dauphin mort à Fontainebleau le 20ᵉ de décembre en 1765*. Soldini was the dauphin's confessor.

gave the dauphin's remark that de Pompadour's father was a gallow's-bird, and never forgot that the dauphin's intimate friends were zealous priests. "One could get along without Parlements," the dauphin once argued with his father, "but not without bishops." Louis XV told him coldly that fanaticism ill befitted a prince. "My son, you should wish me a long life, for you do not yet know how to conduct yourself."

The dauphin, moreover, was a man of restricted tastes and simple morality, and the waste of his father's government troubled him no end. He had read enough of Rousseau and Voltaire to know that the poor starved to support dandified courtiers and perfumed mistresses, but he had neither influence nor authority to mend matters. He could only pray and wait until he ascended the throne. In the meantime he stayed away from the activities of the court and practised the most rigid economies, so as not to be an additional burden to the state. He lived only for his children, and so boundless was his self-effacement that he gave up a much-desired journey through France because, he said, "my whole person is not worth what it could cost the poor people in taxes."

Such was the father of Louis XVI.

CHAPTER II

"Poor Berry, make a noise"

Louis Augustus, Duke of Berry, the future Louis XVI, was a sickly child despite his mother's Saxon vitality. None of his brothers, in fact, was vigorous, but Berry was so feeble that his parents did not expect him to live. Dr. Tronchin, a Swiss scientist, advised country air and a simple diet. In the country little Louis Augustus grew strong.

Louis, whom everybody called Berry, was the second of four brothers, but except in heaviness of body he resembled none of them and suffered accordingly from a sense of peculiarity. Burgundy, his older brother, was brilliant and pampered, Provence studious, and Artois, the youngest, spirited. Only Berry had no accomplishments. Even as a little boy he felt that every one pitied him for his dullness and mocked his heavy gait. He sought refuge in rough play and outdoor exercise, which strengthened his muscles but not his wits.

No one—not even the clever mother—paid special attention to the shy boy. No one made any effort to develop what good qualities he had or to give him self-confidence. His childhood world, especially his malicious brothers, considered him stupid, and he accepted the judgment of his fellows. It was the boy's misfortune that his mother had a greater knowledge of classic languages than of the mind of a child.

What intensified his conviction of inferiority was the brilliance of his older brother Burgundy, a dazzling sun that eclipsed all lesser luminaries. Parents and courtiers and teachers worshiped him as the shining hope of the Bourbons. His seniority and pride gave him authority over all his brothers, especially the humble Berry who submitted to domination. A haughty little pedant, Burgundy never failed to lecture Berry on his shortcomings. Even on his death-bed—he was fatally injured at play at the age of nine—Burgundy continued to criticize his younger brother for his faults. He read him scrupulously kept lists of sins until Berry would burst into tears and murmur, "Please, that fault, I think I have corrected it."

Burgundy died in May, 1761, and Berry, who was not yet seven years old, became, in the event of his father's death, heir to the throne of France. But the knowledge of his ultimate destiny did not buoy his temperament or exalt his mind. His gait was as furtive as ever, his silences as embarrassing. Even after Burgundy's death he did not dare assert himself over his younger brothers, who, both by etiquette and by law, owed him obedience. Provence was cunning and Artois quick, and Berry knew he was no match for them. The more he yielded to his younger brothers, the more acutely did his self-contempt grow upon him. His strange inarticulateness did not encourage sympathy, and he was convinced that no one loved him, which may well have been true. So deep was his self-depreciation that he was afraid to win at play over his little brothers, even though he excelled them physically.

Asked what surname he preferred, Berry revealed his cherished desire: "I want to be called Louis the Severe." Severity, however, was something he could not achieve. He was as self-effacing as his father and shied from people as bats from light. He was an unhappy child, without joys and without enthusiasms. Once his father's sister Adelaide took pity on the silent creature. "Go ahead, my poor Berry," she said to him, "you are at home here; go ahead, talk, make a noise, yell your head off, break things, do anything!"

She called him "my poor Berry"—even as one day Marie Antoinette was to call him "the poor fellow"—and this pity, which he was quick to sense, strengthened his feeling of inadequacy. In the presence of people he was too unhappy to make a noise. But in the woods and in the shop, where he liked to play with his instruments and tools, he was manly enough. He could shoot with perfect accuracy and use a tool with the precision of a craftsman.

THE DAUPHIN unwittingly fortified his son's timidity. Deeply religious, he wanted his children, the future kings of France, to be honest before men and humble before God. Austerely he forbade amusements. "The man who learns frivolity at play," the dauphin told his sons, "will carry over this frivolity into his work." To impress upon the little princes the vanity of pride, he showed them the baptismal register where their names were inscribed on the same page with those of commoners. "This," the father admonished, "should teach you that the distinctions you enjoy were not given you by nature, which has created all men equal." Thus deeply had penetrated the ideas of the eighteenth-century Enlightenment!

Berry needed no such admonitions. Nothing in the world could make him feel a superior being. Once, when a courtier fatuously complimented him on his cleverness, he replied simply, "No, it's not I who am clever, but my brother Provence." Yes, Provence, the fat little Provence, whose legs were so formed that he could hardly sit a horse and who is known to history as the king who succeeded Napoleon on the throne of France, was praised by Père Berthier, the Jesuit tutor, as having "a head for great affairs." No one ever said such a thing about Berry. The dauphin, who played no favorites among his children, wrote to a friend that his son Berry had a good memory. Nothing else. But he described the brilliance of the seven-year-old Provence at great length.

The dauphin was proud of all his sons and wanted them to make a good impression. There is the curious incident of the meeting between David Hume and the dauphin's sons in 1763, when Berry was nine years old. The Scotch philosopher-historian, much admired by the dauphin as he was later to be by Louis XVI, on his visit to Versailles—where, he said, "I eat nothing but ambrosia, drink nothing but nectar, breathe nothing but incense, and tread on nothing but flowers"—was introduced to the three princelings, who were groomed by their fond father for the occasion.

> What happened last week [Hume wrote], when I had the honour of being presented to the Dauphin's children at Versailles, is one of the most curious scenes I have yet passed through. The Duc de Berry the eldest, a boy of ten [sic] years old, stepped forth, and told me how many friends and admirers I had in this country, and that he reckoned himself in the number, from the pleasure he had received from the reading of many passages in my works. When he had finished, his brother, the Count de Provence who is two years younger, began his discourse, and informed me, that I had been long and impatiently expected in France; and that he himself expected soon to have great satisfaction from reading my fine History....

UNFORTUNATELY for Berry, his father had strange pedagogic notions. With the best of intentions he entrusted the education of his sons, of whom he said proudly that "some day they will rule," to a queer pedant named Antoine Paul Jacques de Quélen, Duke de La Vauguyon. This Breton gentleman was of a type once well known to, and exquisitely satirized by, Molière. La Vauguyon conversed in moral maxims and listened through keyholes—Marie Antoinette once maliciously caused him to tumble into the room by suddenly opening the door. His pompousness was monumental, and when he died—to the articulate relief of his princely charges—Europe laughed at the burial announcement which he himself had prepared.

In conversation La Vauguyon sounded like Don Quixote, in behavior he was a crafty French *petit bourgeois.* He knew how to collect impressive titles and how to get paying jobs. It was said that he procured his position as governor of the princes by bribing one of the dauphin's valets to tell him daily the name of the book his master was reading. He then studied the book and talked to the dauphin about it with casual profundity. The dauphin was impressed by the sound views of the duke.

The other tutors were less pompous. Most modest was Jean du Coëstlosquet, bishop of Limoges, whose learning was praised by the diarist Barbier and virtue extolled by the Academician Marmontel. The bishop was Berry's preceptor and swore an oath to employ all his talents "to bring up the prince in the love and fear of God, to regulate his morals, to develop his mind by a knowledge of letters and sciences." He succeeded: all his life Louis XVI was to fear God and lead a monotonously moral life. The bishop's assistants were two abbés and one Jesuit, the "saintly" Father Berthier. Except for his antipathy for La Vauguyon, Berry showed neither like nor dislike for any of his teachers. If anything, he retained a mild aversion for priests in politics.

Berry had instructors also in calligraphy, drawing, music (harpsichord), dancing, fencing, physics, and mathematics. But he never learned to dance gracefully—his awkwardness was to exasperate Marie Antoinette—or fence skilfully or play music at all. His mother had bequeathed none of her talents to him.[1]

⚜

BERRY was not an apt pupil. Usually he preferred low company, laborers and servants, with whom he could play on common terms. His favorite was Grau, a valet, big as a giant and ticklish as a kitten. Berry loved to tickle Grau, who, contorting like a clown, roared in pleased excruciation. At the

[1] The wages of the teachers varied from 2,000 livres for M. Laval, the dancing-master, to 1,200 for the physics instructor. In the Archives Nationales, o[1] 3785, there is a full account of the expenses of the dauphin's family. The "Dépenses des chambre, garderobe et cassette des Princes" for 1758-1771 totaled 4,418,578 livres. This makes an annual average of 315,612 livres for the dauphin's sons.

The teachers were not always paid regularly, and when the Duke of Berry became King Louis XVI, he made up the arrears (Archives Nationales, o[1] 3785[2]).

spectacle of the laughing colossus, the future king of France howled with delight—and later paid him the not inconsiderable pension of 1,500 livres for his complaisance, 300 livres more than the salary of a professor of physics. After the tickling orgy, Berry climbed on the roofs of Versailles and chased cats.

Returning to his lessons from his unprincely "sports," Berry listened glumly to moral exhortations. The days were full of moral homilies. Berry earnestly wrote them in his copybook again and again, intending to engrave them in his memory. Always he listened with dull fidelity as the tutor droned *éloges* and *panégyriques* of all the great men who had ruled France, from Charlemagne to Louis XV. From the plentiful sack of history the teacher brought forth strange models, especially of ancestors, and urged the little duke to cherish them as heroes. "Son of Saint Louis, imitate your forefather, be like him, kind, humane, accessible, affable, compassionate and generous. Be thou the inheritor of his virtues before that of his crown."

Sometimes the clerical instructors, remembering that their pupil would some day rule France, instilled subtle lessons of intolerance and perverted historical facts. Berry was told never to forget that he was a loyal son of the Church and that the Church had always extirpated heresy with fire and sword. Philip Augustus, a bold medieval Capetian monarch who had respected neither pope nor king, was transformed by the earnest pedagogues into a saint. "The piety and zeal of this prince may be seen from the hatred which he always showed for the enemies of religion. *He gave no quarter to heretics.*"

Of all the ancestors, Berry admired Louis XIV most. Everywhere he turned in the enormous château at Versailles the boy could see portraits, tapestries, busts, statues of his great-great-great-grandfather, and he hoped that he too would be a glorious king. Therefore the young duke treasured the last words addressed by the dying Louis XIV, sick of vanity, to his great-grandson Louis XV:

My dear child, You will soon be king of a great kingdom.... Try to keep the peace with your neighbors. I have loved war too much: Do not imitate me in this.... Take counsel in all matters and follow the best advice. Relieve your people as soon as you can, and do that which I have had the misfortune of being unable to do.[2]

⚜

WHEN Berry was a boy of ten, La Vauguyon addressed him as man to man. He explained that the duties of a Christian king were comprised in four words: Piety, Goodness, Justice, Firmness. The tutor outlined these virtues, and Berry carefully copied them in his notebook:

Piety.—"Your Highness should set a pious example to your subjects by punishing those who reject religion."

Goodness.—"Your Highness should be polite but not familiar, liberal but not extravagant."

Justice.—"You should treat your subjects as your own children."

Firmness.—"As cruelty is the most odious of all vices, so firmness is the most necessary of all virtues. In a prince firmness is a virtue so absolutely necessary that without it all others are as nothing."

After Berry had digested the four virtues, La Vauguyon inflicted moral reflections upon the bewildered lad. "I speak," the tutor said to the speechless boy, "to *a man* whom reason enlightens and who seeks to know the rights of humanity." And painstakingly, laboriously, the ten-year-old man filled many notebooks with maxims about God, Duty, Conscience, Goodness, Morality, and Nature.[3] More than half a century after his death these notes were published under the title *Reflections on My Conversations with the Duke de La Vauguyon.*[4] Of all this awful verbiage one early passage stands

2 The foregoing quotations are taken from a two-volume manuscript of extracts which were used for the education of young Berry; in the Library of the Arsenal, Paris, MS 2324-25.

3 See the MS in the Bibliothèque Nationale, MS Fr. 14715: "Première conversation avec Mgr. le duc de Berry, le 1er avril 1763, et le plan général des instructions que je me propose de lui donner."

4 Louis XVI, *Réflexions sur mes entretiens avec M. le duc de La Vauguyon*, edited by de Falloux (Paris, 1851). Another edition is in the *Œuvres de Louis*

out with sharp pertinence. It is entitled "Concerning My Faults":

> My greatest fault is a sluggishness of mind which makes all my mental efforts wearisome and painful: I want absolutely to conquer this defect; and after I have done so, as I hope to, I shall apply myself without respite to uprooting all the others which have been pointed out to me, and I shall cultivate the good things that are said to be in me. I shall often reread my character in order to judge myself of my progress.

BERRY WAS NOT, however, a hopeless student. Some subjects he learned well, despite his apathy. Among his favorite studies was history, the sort of history that preached by example and bored by precepts. His father wanted him to find warnings against absolutism and waste.[5] Berry learned Latin gladly in order to read Roman history. "I love and admire Tacitus," he said, and to prove it he wrote a sensible schoolboy composition on the Roman historian. He admired most of the Romans, but could not stomach Seneca because he was not moral. Seneca, the boy said priggishly, was a "rogue who did not practise what he preached." "Berry," his father wrote to a friend, "makes great progress in Latin and astonishing

XVI (Paris, 1864; 2 vols.), I, 191-356; the *Œuvres,* however, are mostly spurious and should be used only with extreme caution. The *Réflexions* take up 164 octavo pages in print: 3 pages are devoted to Natural Law, 17 to Piety and Goodness, 52 to Justice, 19 to Firmness, 73 to Judging Character. In short, firmness and character-reading get more than half the attention.

The original MS of the *Réflexions* was offered for sale by a London bookseller a few years ago. See the Catalogue No. 12 of G. Michelmore & Company, 5 Royal Opera Arcade, London.

[5] The historiographer Jacob Nicolas Moreau compiled a special textbook, *Leçons de morale, de politique et de droit public, puisées dans l'histoire de notre monarchie.* It was printed nine years after it was composed, by the Printing Office of the Department of Foreign Affairs (Versailles, 1773; 202 pp. in-8). There are two copies of this rare book in the Bibliothèque Nationale at Paris, one with the arms of Louis XVI's sister Madame Elizabeth and the other with those of Marie Antoinette. The keynote of this textbook was a sharp warning against the evils of absolutism in government. "The chief benefit which you will derive from the study of our history," Moreau wrote in the Preface, "will be the conviction that the most independent monarchy destroys itself with abuse."

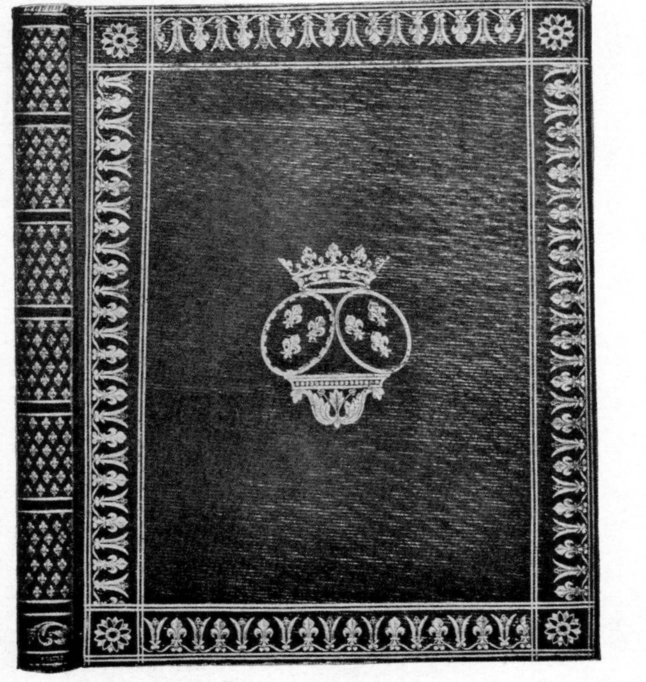

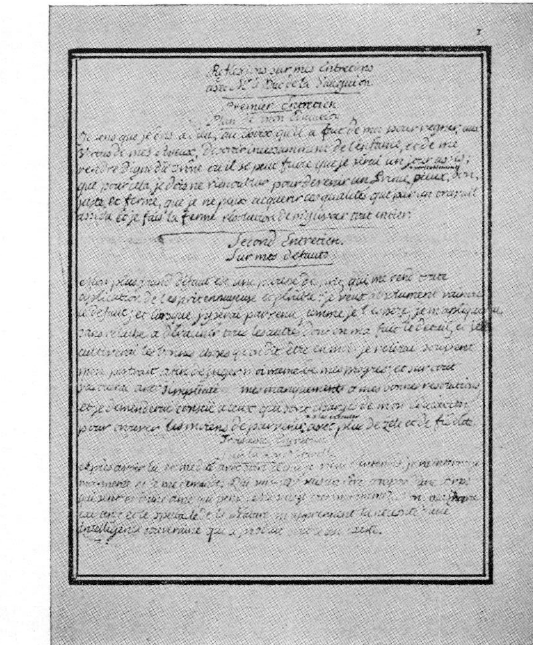

Reflexions sur mes Entretiens
avec M. le Duc de la Vauguyon.

Premier Entretien.

Second Entretien.
Sur mes défauts

COVER AND FIRST PAGE OF LOUIS' MANUSCRIPT "REFLECTIONS"

In the possession of G. Michelmore & Company, London, through whose courtesy these illustrations are reproduced.

advances in history, which he retains factually and chronologically with admirable memory."

Berry was decidedly not an imaginative child. What struck everybody was his cumbrous matter-of-factness, his interest in the concrete and the accountable, his memory avid for minutiae. If he had one intellectual passion in his childhood that he retained in his manhood, it was the earthy science of geography. Like the craft of locksmithing, in which he was to become an acknowledged master (praised by fellow-artisans),[6] geography appealed to his uncomplicated mind. He liked to draw maps and make atlases. At the age of eleven he wrote a *Description of the Forest of Compiègne,* a meticulous and thorough compilation, in the precise style of a time-table. The booklet is in a way terrifying, for it does not contain a single expression of personal opinion: the lad seemed to function like an automaton, registering but not feeling. "This Forest," he writes, "has 32,000 acres of which 5,000 are clearings. It contains Avenues, Large Paths, Large Roads, Squares, Pits, Bridges, Rounds, Wards, Fences, Patches, Hills, Pools, Fish-Ponds, Moats and Boats: it is surrounded by villages and hamlets." [7] Never a word of color or movement. If he had not had the "misfortune of being king," as he phrased it years later, he might perhaps have become a geographer respectable enough to win a seat in the Academy.

FAITHFULLY learning maxims in the study-room and counting Paths and Pits in the open, Berry grew up a vigorous, hard-muscled lad. At the same time his father, once a mountain of flesh, began to lose weight and contemplate his end. In the autumn of 1765, when the rains began to drench Versailles, the gaunt and sallow dauphin was racked with

[6] Authorities such as Quérard believe that the well-known locksmith's manual, *Supplément à l'art du Serrurier* (1789), was the work of Louis XVI.

[7] *Description de la forêt de Compiègne, comme elle étoit en 1765; avec le guide de la forêt:* Par Louis-Auguste, Dauphin (Paris, 1766; 58 pages, in-4). A copy may be consulted in the Reserved Room of the Bibliothèque Nationale.

coughs and spat blood. It was evident that the thirty-six year old heir to the French throne was dying of tuberculosis.

Berry observed simply that "papa coughs again." He was only eleven and unable to realize either the reality of his father's condition or the consequences of his death. There is a letter which he wrote at this period to an unnamed girl, remarkable because it is the only one preserved from his boyhood:

DEAR LITTLE FRIEND:

I have been very sorry to leave you, I will be very glad to see you again. How are you? Everybody is well here. Papa king [Louis XV] has a little cold. Papa coughs again, but he spits blood, which he has not done before. On the sixth [October] he began to take ass's milk and also turtle broth; the day before he ate half a wing of chicken although he was allowed to have two wings. M. de La Vauguyon got a blister on his leg, but they applied a plaster which made it disappear and he hopes that he will not need to lance it. We are very well, for some time we have had very good weather: it was very bad before. I hope that we will see each other. I like you and embrace you with all my heart.

LOUIS AUGUSTUS.[8]

The dauphin was dying. On his death-bed he said hopelessly that "it would require two successive good reigns, one to extirpate the abuses in the realm and the other to keep them from arising again." He knew that the awful burden of reform and reconstruction would fall on the shoulders of his little son, and he groaned at the prospect. Parental affection did not blind the dying father to the realization that the good-natured Berry would never be another Henry IV and would never have the ruthlessness necessary to "extirpate the abuses" which had been accumulating for generations.

[8] British Museum, ADD. MSS 21,509, fol.58. The letter is dated Fontainebleau, 23 October, 1765. I am somewhat dubious as to the authenticity of this letter, although the British Museum lists it as genuine. The handwriting is not Berry's, but it may have been rewritten by a secretary or tutor. What makes me skeptical, however, is the tone of the letter. It is too personal, almost warm. Berry was not the kind of boy to communicate so freely with a girl. He was much too shy. Nevertheless, on the chance that the letter might be genuine, I reproduce it for what it is worth.

The dauphin spent the last days of life preparing elaborate instructions for Berry's education and guidance, and when he had finished, he prepared to die without a last farewell to his family, whom he wished to spare the sight of his suffering. He prayed God to "protect for ever this kingdom," and died.

Louis XV hurried to the apartment of his grandson Berry to tell him of the death of his father. The eleven-year-old boy burst into tears. Calmly the king explained to him that it was necessary to tell his mother. At the door of Maria Josepha's apartment Louis XV said to the usher:

"Announce the king and the dauphin!"

Again Berry—now the dauphin—wept. His mother looked at the tear-stained boy and fainted.

"Poor France," Louis XV murmured, "a king of fifty-five and a dauphin of eleven!"

CHAPTER III

"Long live the dauphin!"

THUS the insignificant and humble Berry, who was not yet in his teens, became the dauphin, the most important person in the realm next to His Majesty the king. Whenever he passed the guards, they stiffened, saluted, cried "Long live the dauphin!" The words brought tears to his eyes.

The widowed Maria Josepha was no less overwhelmed by the turn of events. She had no desire to survive her husband, and only the sternest sense of duty kept her alive. The orphaned princes who were in line of succession to the throne of France still needed guidance. "I live only for my unhappy children," Maria Josepha said.

She appealed to her august father-in-law to help her educate the children, but the easy-going king, absorbed in his amorous adventures, complimented her with the assurance that he considered her sufficiently competent to bring up her own sons. Maria Josepha was left to her own resources and the notes of her deceased husband. Piously she gathered and arranged systematically all the papers he had written on education. Then she made a summary.

"Heaven, my son, is preparing for you the finest crown in the universe; it has given you life in order some day to govern a nation as enlightened . . . as it is attached to its master. May your destiny be brilliant! . . . But it includes duties! It demands knowledge! . . .

"It is not," Maria Josepha concluded, "only a matter of exercising your memory and adorning your mind. What is more important, *it is necessary to teach you how to think.*"

⚜

DURING the following two years the young dauphin made notable intellectual progress under his mother's guidance. She tried to overcome his feeling of inferiority by giving him the deference due to a future king of France. She even made her boisterous younger sons, prone to ridicule their more sluggish brother, respect the person of the dauphin. Louis Augustus gradually developed some dignity and acquired much useful information.

The mother encouraged him in all manner of intellectual activity. Noting the dauphin's bent for classification and systematization, Maria Josepha gave him the idea of collecting the most striking passages from the books he was reading and cataloguing them according to subject. He accumulated a pile of quotations from Bossuet, Fénelon, La Bruyère, and other moralists, and planned to publish them as an anthology under a title which reflected nicely his education as well as his personal preference: *Concerning a Moderate Monarchy.* In the end he decided to print only the quotations from Fénelon's *Télémaque;* he set up a printing-press and invited his brothers Provence and Artois, aged eleven and nine respectively, to help him with the type-setting. Within twelve days the *Maximes Morales et Politiques, tirées de Télémaque*[1] was off the press, and the proud printer-publisher-editor hurried with the first copy to his royal grandfather Louis XV.

His Majesty was slightly disdainful and mildly amused at a booklet dealing with the "science of kings" as compiled by a

[1] Altogether he printed twenty-five copies. The booklet is so rare that the Bibliothèque Nationale possesses only one original copy. In 1814, at the request of the Duchesse d'Angoulême, the only surviving child of Louis XVI and Marie Antoinette, it was reprinted under the title *Etudes du Télémaque, imprimées en 1766 par Louis-Auguste, dauphin* (*depuis Louis XVI*) (Paris: Royez; 55 pp.).

twelve-year-old. "A knowledge of men," the king read in the First Maxim, "is the primary and true science of kings." This was innocuous enough, but other precepts concealed unintended stings. The Twenty-Sixth (last) Maxim made Louis XV frown: "The sovereign is a man; as such he shares with other men the duties of a Christian. But he is a man elevated by the hand of the Creator above all other men; and in this quality he should show himself a model of virtue, of respect for religion, and an example of piety and zeal." Louis XV took his little grandson's innocent compilation as a subtle criticism of His Person. "Monsieur le dauphin," the king said coldly, "you have done enough. Break the plates."

DESPITE his failure as a publisher, the dauphin was growing in earnestness and knowledge. His mother taught him to appreciate memoirists such as de Retz, but she failed to develop in him a sense for poetry or an appreciation of *belles lettres.* One day he was given a book, looked inside, saw it was verse. "What's that good for?" he asked naïvely. He had some difficulty with grammar and vocabulary,[2] although in later years, under the stress of the Revolution, he was able to express himself with fine lucidity. Once he said *"Il pleuva"* and was mocked by his learned young brother Provence: "What barbarism, a prince should know his tongue!" "And you," the dauphin retorted in one of his rare fits of temper, "should know how to guard yours."

Maria Josepha made him learn Italian, German, and English. Leclerc de Sept-Chênes taught him English history, introduced him to English letters, and helped him with a translation of Horace Walpole's essay on Richard II. Years later, when Gibbon's great history of Rome appeared, tutor

[2] In his Journal, begun in 1766, there are such misspellings as *quartres, inquestionnable, indistinguable.* Nevertheless, in his letters I have found few errors, except an occasional omission of letters in spelling, which was customary in that period. He wrote as well as any educated Frenchman of the upper classes.

and royal pupil (then Louis XVI) undertook to translate it; they got along nicely until they reached the chapter in which the mocking English historian treated the historical foundations of Christianity with a manifest lack of reverence. The pious son of Maria Josepha then called a halt: he would not translate a heretic. In 1812 Guizot considered the Leclerc-Louis XVI translation good enough to incorporate, in revised version, in his edition of Gibbon.

Louis' interest in English letters and history continued throughout his life.[3] He was particularly fascinated by the great English Civil War and read and reread the history of Charles I—a foreshadowing of his own fate. Once, when Sept-Chênes read to him the history of the conflict that led to the decapitation of Charles I, Louis said, "As for me, in the place of Charles I, I should never have drawn the sword against my people."

The future was to show that he spoke sincerely.

FROM his German mother the dauphin learned the desirability of methodical and scrupulous accounting. On January 1, 1766, at the age of eleven and a half, he started to record minor activities and events in a diary which he continued, with long interruptions, until July, 1792, his last month as king. This innocent Journal has had a veritable *succès de scandale*. A few words of explanation and analysis are, therefore, in place.

[3] In the Archives Nationales, K163, no.3 [4] et,[5] there is an undated letter addressed in English to Louis XVI: "Few days ago, Your Majesty expressed his desire to know who was the author of Junius' Letters. It was Mr. Fitzpatrick who lived on his comfortable income. He was a private friend to one Mr. Francis a man of parts who was a Clerck in the Court-Offices and from him Mr. Fitzpatrick got his best informations." Attached to this was a French translation, *not* in Louis' hand. This leads me to doubt his mastery of English. Possibly he knew the language well, but had to consult a dictionary frequently. Mercier, on a visit to Louis' library, observed a dog-eared book and examined it: "It was," he relates, "Boyer's English dictionary, and was used like a student's textbook, which shows that it was consulted daily."

The Journal, modeled after Books of the Hunt, was not political. Because the entry under July 14, 1789, the momentous day of the fall of the Bastille, reads *"Rien,"* malicious historians, including Leon Trotsky, have pretended to believe that Louis XVI was a virtual imbecile, ignorant of or indifferent to the most vital happenings. Actually the oft-used *"Rien"* in the Journal always refers to hunting; it means "No hunt to-day," or "Shot nothing to-day."

The entries are not day-by-day, but casual and scattered. For months, and sometimes for years, there are no entries. Between 1766 and 1792 there is an average of about twelve pages per year. There are no ideas, sentiments, or opinions in the Journal—simply dry facts. A characteristic entry reads (August 21, 1766), "I went horse-riding to-day." Louis' first entry as king (December 14, 1774) records, "Laid the foundation stone for the School of Surgery in Paris." Other entries mention illnesses (cold nine times, fever four times, inflammation seven times, hemorrhoids once), horse-rides, accidents, dinners, social visits, expenses. About twenty-three pages record hunting. Food takes up three pages, health six, family six, religion three, reviews two, balls three, theater three, promenades five, gaming five, expenses forty-one. Altogether about one-third of the Journal is devoted to hunting and expenditures—a faithful mirror of the diarist's interests.[4]

⚜

IN MARCH, 1767, the thirty-six year old Maria Josepha, who had for years been spitting blood, received the holy sacraments and called her three sons to her bedside. They knelt by the bed weeping. The mother was most distressed about her oldest son, whose destiny it was some day to rule France and who, none knew better than she, was pitifully unprepared. "Remember your father," she sobbed, "and take him as a model for your conduct." Then she died, and the dauphin

[4] The original copy of the Journal is kept in a glass case in the Museum on the second floor of the Archives Nationales in Paris. It has been excellently edited by L. Nicolardot, *Journal de Louis XVI* (Paris, 1873).

was left with a relic of the true cross which his mother had bequeathed to him in her will.[5]

[5] In her Testament Maria Josepha left some curious items for the dauphin: "I bequeath to my eldest son: The relic of the true cross in a large crystal reliquary set in gold and precious stones . . . ; the relic of St. Louis in a reliquary of vermeil . . . ; a reliquary of vermeil with figures in relief, which is the first my father acquired after his conversion . . . ; all the papers written by the [late] Dauphin, so that my eldest son may profit from the reflections and the example [of his father] in order that he may become himself a benefactor of religion and the state." To the other children she bequeathed similar gifts: two reliquaries each to Provence and to Artois, one reliquary and a picture of the Holy Virgin to her eight-year-old daughter Clotilde, and one reliquary and an ivory Virgin to three-year-old Elizabeth.

CHAPTER IV

"My daughter will love you"

THE ORPHANED DAUPHIN was left alone. He had no friends, and his relatives were interested in other things than a dull boy; this was particularly true of Louis XV, who was too absorbed in his new mistress Du Barry to have any time for a grandson. With no one to guide him, the boy sank into a sort of barbarism, avoiding the society of his equals and spending his time in the forest and the forge.

His appearance and behavior shocked the perfumed courtiers and filled the ladies with consternation. There he was, the future ruler of France, a barrel-chested led with untidy blond hair, grinning at courtiers like a country bumpkin and bursting into loud, offensive laughter at pranks played by his low-born companions. His manners, like his language, were those of a stable-boy. "The fat, ill-bred boy," the usually good-natured Madame Du Barry called him. Others were no less harsh. "He seems to have been born and raised in the forest," said the Neapolitan ambassador. And the Duke de Choiseul told Louis XV that unless the dauphin changed his conduct he would become the "horror of the nation."

But Louis XV was too indifferent to waste time on his successor. Possibly he feared that the boy, reputed to be as pious as his mother and as prudish as his father, would disapprove of his way of life. At his age His Majesty was not going to reform for the benefit of a youngster! He thought it best, therefore, to leave his grandson alone, to keep him at a distance from affection and polite manners. Thus the young Louis was left with his boars in the Forest of Compiègne, and the old Louis remained undisturbed with his mistress in the scented boudoirs of Trianon.

If Louis XV was indifferent to the fate of the heir apparent, the ambitious minister Choiseul was not. Years back, when he was ambassador in Vienna, he had made tentative arrangement for a marriage alliance between Bourbon and Habsburg to fortify the political union of the two families. Now, after Maria Josepha's death, Choiseul began anew his negotiations with Vienna. He was eagerly seconded by his friend Prince Kaunitz the Austrian chancellor, who, for reasons of high policy, wanted to see an Austrian archduchess on the throne of France. To carry through the plan, Kaunitz selected his intimate friend Count Florimond Mercy-Argenteau as ambassador to France.

This Mercy-Argenteau was fated to play the rôle of Polonius in the drama of Louis XVI and Marie Antoinette. He arrived at Versailles at the age of thirty-nine, a tall, lean, cool-eyed Lorraine aristocrat, and settled down in a large palace to a life of dignified diplomacy. When he left France a quarter-century later, he was gray and disillusioned, his world shattered in a cyclone of revolution which he had foretold. He was a man of culture and, despite his enormous wealth, of moderate politics. Yet this handsome and well-meaning gentleman, this discreet bachelor (he had the same mistress, an actress, for twenty-four years), did enough damage to the French monarchy to deserve a kind of immortality. Again and again he appears in every crisis in the royal family, standing behind the throne or in the boudoir and whispering in the ear of Marie Antoinette.

The fastidious Mercy looked upon the dauphin with unutterable distaste, but as a diplomat devoted to the interests of the House of Austria he carried through the appointed negotiations with vigor. By the summer of 1769, when the dauphin was fifteen, an agreement was reached, and Louis XV exerted himself to write a personal letter to Maria Theresa in Vienna:

MADAME MY SISTER AND COUSIN:

I can not delay much longer . . . the satisfaction which I feel about the forthcoming union which we are going to form by the marriage of the Archduchess Antoinette to the Dauphin, my grandson. . . . This new tie will more and more unite our two houses. If Your Majesty approves, I think that the marriage should take place in Vienna soon after next Easter. . . . I shall do here what I can, and so will the Dauphin, to make the Archduchess Antoinette happy.[1]

Neither of the two children—Marie Antoinette was fourteen—was, of course, consulted. They were pawns in a high game played by their elders. To Choiseul the marriage was another tie in the Franco-Austrian alliance. To the Empress Maria Theresa the French crown was the most illustrious in Europe and deserved to be worn by the prettiest of her many daughters. She would have given her most beloved daughter to any French dauphin, even to an idiot dauphin. In fact, so far as she knew, the dauphin *was* a sort of imbecile. At least, so her trusted Mercy-Argenteau reported to Vienna confidentially (only to Kaunitz, but he probably informed the empress as usual) in a letter remarkable for its antipathy and exaggeration:

This monarchy [Mercy wrote in 1769] is so decadent that it would not be regenerated except by a successor of the present monarch who, by his qualities and talents, would repair the extreme disorder of the kingdom. . . . But one should rely very little on this resource, less because the heir apparent to the throne is being educated by an incompetent and vicious man [La Vauguyon], than that *nature seems to have refused everything to the Dauphin*. This prince, by his face and his talk, shows only an extremely limited intelligence, much clumsiness.

[1] June 4, 1769; Haus- Hof- und Staats-Archiv, Vienna: Frankreich Hofcorrespondenz, fasc.7, no.357. Maria Theresa's reply is in fasc.8, no.148.

THE MARRIAGE CONTRACT between Louis Augustus, Dauphin of France, and Marie Antoinette Josepha Jeanne, Princess Royal of Hungary and Bohemia, Archduchess of Austria, was signed by proxy in March, 1770, at Vienna. As dowry Marie Antoinette was to receive from her mother and her brother, Emperor Joseph II, 200,000 silver florins in cash. In addition to the money the bride was to take with her to France about 200,000 florins' worth of rings "and other jewels." The contract stipulated that the dowry constituted the price paid by the court of Vienna for the relinquishment on the part of Marie Antoinette of all her rights, privileges, and prerogatives as a princess of the House of Habsburg.

She left Vienna early in the spring, a high-spirited little girl of fifteen, happily going to her destiny as dauphiness of France—the luckiest girl in all Europe, as her mother told her. She knew nothing about her betrothed except that he was born to wear the crown of France and that his name was Louis, to be the XVIth Louis on the throne of the lily. On the way to Versailles she received a letter from her exhortatory mother, reminding her of her lofty duties in her new estate:

MADAME MY DEAR DAUGHTER:

You are going whither Providence has destined you to live.... You are the luckiest of all your sisters and of all princesses.... About the Dauphin I say nothing. You know my delicacy on this point; a woman is submissive in everything to her husband and she ought to have no other occupation than to please him and do his bidding. The only true happiness in this world is a happy marriage. If I may say so, all depends on the woman, if she is obliging, gentle and amusing....[2]

All the way to Strassburg, through territory over which floated the flag of her proud house, Marie Antoinette was splendidly fêted; everywhere she was received with flowers and songs and gay dances. At Strassburg she entered the land that she was some day to rule. It was spring in the

[2] May 4, 1770; Vienna Archives: Frankreich Hofcorrespondenz, fasc.8, no.301.

Rhineland, and spring was in the heart of the "luckiest" girl who was going forth to join in wedlock the most august prince in Christendom.

THE DAUPHIN was not excited at the coming of his bride. While Versailles buzzed with rumors about her beauty, Louis Augustus went his daily rounds, calmly forging locks and shooting boars. Though almost sixteen and very vigorous, he was still immature: women were nothing to him, not even a subject of conversation.

Just before Marie Antoinette's arrival the dauphin received a letter from Vienna which caused him some bewilderment:

> Your wife, my dear Dauphin, has just been separated from me. As she has been my delight, so I hope she will be your happiness. I have brought her up for this, because for a long time I have foreseen that she would share your destiny. I have inspired in her a love for her duties toward you, a tender attachment, and the ability to know and practise the means of pleasing you. . . . *My daughter will love you,* I am sure of it, because I know her. . . . Adieu, my dear Dauphin, be happy, make her happy. . . . I am all bathed in tears. Your tender mother,
>
> MARIA THERESA.

He did not reply. On the subject of wives he had no opinion, but he was told that it was his Christian duty to marry.

THE COURT met the Austrian archduchess on the highway near Compiègne. Marie Antoinette gracefully threw herself at the feet of Louiv XV, and His Majesty, touched by such a spontaneous tribute from a charming young girl, raised her gently and looked her over with approval. The king saw that she was good to look at and moved her to tears with a gallant compliment: "You are already a member of the family, Madame, for your mother has the soul of Louis XIV."

Then Louis Augustus, clad in brilliant silks, was introduced to his bride. He seized her hand almost roughly and kissed

MARIE ANTOINETTE AT THE CLAVECIN
Portrait by François Hubert Drouais. Imperial Palace, Vienna.

it with gusto. She reddened. He looked at her with naïve admiration, impressed by her slender figure, the bright blond hair, the dazzling skin—a "mixture of lily and rose," as one observer called it. His inarticulateness kept him from speaking his admiration.

His Journal that day had a laconic entry: "Interview with Madame the Dauphiness." In her letter to her mother she wrote: "All that has taken place has been like a dream."

The court talked about nothing but her charm and grace. Her blue eyes were so vivacious and her tongue so pleasingly ready that people forgot that her nose was too aquiline, her lower lip too "Austrian," and her forehead too high. Only Madame d'Oberkirch, the well-known memoirist, was keen to observe that her mouth was "already slightly disdainful." And she walked with the grace of a dancer.

⚜

AT NOON on May 16, the dauphin, followed by his two brothers, entered the king's cabinet at Versailles where the bride was waiting. The stout bridegroom was dressed in the gold-meshed robe of the Order of the Holy Ghost. Marie Antoinette appeared "delicate and pretty" in white. The young couple bowed to each other and then walked hand in hand to the royal chapel.

They knelt on a hassock at the foot of the altar.[3] Near-by Louis XV knelt on his *prie-dieu*. On each side of the altar was a cordon of thirty-five white-clad ladies. Solemnly the Archbishop of Rheims, whose historic function it was to crown and wed the kings of France, blessed thirteen pieces of gold and one gold ring. The customary sacrament was completed under a canopy of silver brocade held by two bishops.

[3] One of the medals struck to commemorate the event shows the head of Louis XV and on the reverse side the dauphin and Marie Antoinette kneeling before the altar and holding hands. Incidentally, these medals were rather costly. Altogether 1,780 medals—554 of gold and 1,226 of silver—were distributed at a cost of more than 72,000 livres (British Museum, Add. MSS. 20707, p.136). The total cost of the wedding festivities was 9,000,000 livres.

⚜

In great crowds the people from Paris came to Versailles to celebrate the wedding of the heir to the throne, but a rainstorm which lasted all night converted the gardens into mud pools. Nevertheless, the "good people of Paris" could not be denied their fun. Since under the old régime it was the inalienable right of every Frenchman to enjoy fireworks, the government prepared a grandiose display in Paris on the Place Louis XV (soon to become the Place de la Révolution), the present-day Place de la Concorde.

In the center of the vast square, near the statue of Louis XV (where the obelisk stands to-day), the architect Ruggieri erected a Temple of Hymen, which contemporaries lauded as a veritable *chef d'œuvre*. Inside the Temple were piled boxes of fireworks which, at the proper hour, were to blaze forth into the sky in augury of a joyful event.

The great square had only one opening, the rue Royale, through which crowds, on foot and in wagons, kept pouring in. Along this street workers had been excavating for a new building, and in the excitement of the occasion they had forgotten to cover their work, leaving a gaping pit which had filled with rain-water. Neither the lieutenant of police nor the municipal authorities had taken any precautionary measures.

Hours before the celebration was to begin, the square was already packed, tight as a full bottle. Suddenly the piled-up fireworks in the flimsy Temple of Hymen, ignited by a wayward spark, burst into blinding flames. Temple and fireworks went up into the air in roaring flashes, raining blazing cinders on thousands of exposed heads. Every living creature was stampeded into blind panic. The terrified, shrieking crowd, madly searching for an escape, rushed for the rue Royale, where the deep excavation lay open and rain-filled. Hundreds fell in, choked and crushed to death.

Next day grief-stricken Parisians mourned hundreds of dead, and wondered—as Russians years later once wondered after the catastrophe attending the celebration in honor of Nicolas II—whether the heir to the throne was born under an evil star. Those who believed in omens remembered that a tragedy had occurred also at the dauphin's birth.

At the news of the accident the dauphin sent 2,000 livres to the lieutenant of police for distribution among the poor survivors of the victims. That was his pocket-money, and he had no more. With the gift went his first public letter:

> I have learned of the misfortune which took place in Paris on my occasion; I am moved by it. I have just received the sum which the king sends me every month for small expenses; I have nothing else, and I am sending it to you. Help the most needy. I have, Monsieur, much esteem for you.
>
> LOUIS AUGUSTUS.

⚜

THE MASS TRAGEDY that took place on the Place Louis XV did not loom so large in the eyes of the young couple as their marital frustration. On their first night and on every subsequent occasion for seven years the dauphin was unable to acquit himself of his duties as husband.

Even a boy of sixteen, especially one ridden with a feeling of intellectual inferiority, does not like to face the conviction of masculine inadequacy, and Louis Augustus was no exception. The honeymoon was wrecked in defeated hopes and physical pain, and the consequences were lasting. The fifteen-year-old-bride developed a grudge, privately nursed and not always subdued, against the husband who painfully failed to be a man. He, on the other hand, sustained a permanent sense of guilt in the presence of his wife, the lifelong result of which was to be an alternation of escape and submission.

In his inarticulate way he did everything else to please her, and she, an avid little egoist, took advantage of his "complaisance and gentleness," as the surprised Mercy described it. Within a few short weeks, Mercy observed, the "Dauphiness governs her husband in all small things, without his making the slightest objection." In fact, he seemed to relish her fussing and meddling. When at the dinner-table Marie Antoinette took away his plate of pastries, which he was in the habit of eating until he groaned with stomach-ache, he laughed good-naturedly. One little victory sharpened the taste for another. She wanted to cure him, in those early weeks, of his habit of excessive hunting, which made him come home late for dinner, smelly with sweat and too tired to bathe and dress. "You are leading a savage life," she told him; "the outdoors is coarsening your manners. If you continue you will end up by destroying your health and by making yourself detested." He blushed and begged her to forgive him, and continued to hunt as before.

One day the dauphin was talking with his brother Provence when Marie Antoinette entered in fine rage and scolded him for his "savage life." The dauphin quickly left the room. Marie Antoinette followed into the corridor, her tongue loud and crackling. He burst into tears. She too began to cry. Then the boy and the girl embraced tenderly and promised to be good to one another. They returned to the room arm in arm, and Provence asked if they had made up. "Lovers' quarrels," Louis laughed happily, "don't last long."

Lovers' quarrels? He was no lover. He was kind, to be sure, but kindness was no substitute for potency. She may not have understood the full meaning of his escape to the forest and the smithy, but always she resented the affront. What she did not know, what few suspected, was that despite appearances his "impotence" was not altogether physiological or irremediable. The doctors who secretly examined him assured him, truthfully enough, that there was nothing unalterably wrong with him. A slight malformation caused pain, but a little courage and a minor operation might yet make it possible for him to become a father.[4]

[4] Report of the Spanish ambassador Aranda to the Spanish king: "La consumacion de su matrimonio aun se duda . . . Suponese que en la ropa de ambos principes hai manchas que manifiestan el acto, pero no falta quienes las atribuyen a expulsion del Delphin, sin acabar de penetrar, no por debilidad, sino por mortificarles algun dolorcillo en la punta al insistir su introduccion. Apoyase da completa operacion, en que de tiempo a esta parte manifiesta mas apego a la Delphina; pero el estar en duda un asunto tan interessante que se huviera publicado con aplauso, puede inclinar mas bien a que no se ha consguido aun el fin principal."

⚜

SHARP ORDERS reached Marie Antoinette from Vienna: You must do so and so; you must love your husband and you must respect the king's mistress; you must never interfere in politics and you must look out for Austria's interests. The young girl was bewildered by so much pressure and always in fear of her imperious mother.

Louis Augustus was lord of his own behavior, but Marie Antoinette had to obey instructions from Vienna. If she did not, she knew that her confessor, the Abbé Vermond, who was paid by Maria Theresa, would report her; should the abbé fail, Ambassador Mercy was certain to write one of his long and sometimes insidious dispatches. From these Arguses, who did not hesitate to look through keyholes and examine her bedclothes, Marie Antoinette was never to escape. Often she envied—and silently hated—her husband who had neither imperious mother nor interfering confessor and who was not sufficiently sensitive to mind gossip. For eighteen years Marie Antoinette's husband never so much as exchanged a word with her confessor, and as for the noble ambassador from Austria—he was just another stuffed courtier.

How did the young couple spend their time together and apart? The dauphiness submitted a time-table account to her mother in Vienna:

> I rise at 9:30 or 10, say my prayers, and after breakfast I visit the aunts,[5] where I generally meet the King. At 11 I go to the coiffeur and then dress in public; I put on rouge and wash my hands before everybody; then the men leave and the ladies remain. At noon we go to mass with the King. If the King is not with us, I dine alone with my husband; we finish by 1:30, for we eat very fast, my husband and I. Then I go to the Dauphin's apartments, and if he is busy I return to my own rooms where I read, write or work; for I am making a jacket for the King, which does not advance at all, but I hope that with the help of God it will be finished in a few years.
>
> At 3 in the afternoon I visit the aunts. [Abbé] Vermond comes to see me at 4 and the music teacher at 5. At 6:30 the aunts again.

[5] Madame Adélaide (1733-1800) and Madame Victoire (1733-1799), known as *Mesdames*. They were the daughters of Louis XV, hence the aunts of the dauphin.

You must know that my husband always accompanies me there. We play from 7 to 9, but when the weather is good we promenade. At 9 we dine, either with the King or with the aunts. We always wait for the King until 10:45; I sleep on the couch until he comes. When he does not arrive we go to bed at 11.

But my sole pleasure is to write to my mama.

THEIR LIVES gradually froze into a sterile routine, and the months gave way to years and the years saw no fruit of the union. Louis' conviction of inferiority increased with every day of his marriage. It was an awful humiliation to realize that his wife's prolonged childlessness was a public confession of sexual deficiency—on his part. Their sterility was the gossip of Europe. Marie Antoinette, he knew, suffered shame and anguish. She told him that her mother constantly upbraided her, and he could not face her alone.

The dauphin and his wife slept apart one night. Abbé Vermond was informed and immediately reported to Mercy, who promptly wrote to Maria Theresa, who impulsively seized a quill and scribbled an angry sermon to her daughter on her marital duties. Then the empress wrote another letter to her ambassador ordering him to tell Marie Antoinette how to behave. The delicate Mercy, a bachelor, went to Abbé Vermond and urged him to speak bluntly to the dauphiness. This the confessor did with a "zeal which is beyond praise."

Marie Antoinette in turn badgered her husband, but the futility of remonstrances and recriminations grew with the years. Marie Antoinette came to dread her tireless mother as much as the dauphin feared his wife—a curious chain of familial irritations which produced no pearls. But the vigorous old busybody in Vienna would not rest; she could not understand how any child of hers could be barren. It was sacrilege, almost *lèse majesté*. Seriously alarmed lest her childless daughter be divorced from the dauphin and thereby lose the finest throne in Europe, Maria Theresa drove her henchmen in Versailles into doing something to remedy the desperate situation. Every morning snoopers (pages, chambermaids, lackeys) searched for results. Not even the couple's bedsheets were free from prying eyes. In the end the blunt Maria Theresa concluded that her august son-in-law was not fully a man and seriously urged an operation.

> The coolness of the Dauphin toward a pretty woman [Maria Theresa wrote with eighteenth-century forthrightness] is inconceivable to me. Despite all the assertions of the faculty [of medicine], my suspicions about the physical constitution of this prince keep increasing, and I almost count upon nothing else but the intervention of the emperor [Joseph II], who, on his arrival in Versailles, will perhaps find the means to engage this indolent husband to acquit himself better of his marital duties.

THE YOUNG COUPLE faced the bitter prospect of seeing others' children occupy the positions that should rightfully belong to their own. Provence, the dauphin's fat young brother with the deformed hips, married a swarthy and extremely ugly princess of Savoy, whose thick eyebrows and black mustache made her look like a lady of the circus, but who, nevertheless, had temperament. On the night of their marriage, so the sixteen-year-old Provence boasted to the delighted and appreciative Louis XV, he was "four times happy" and she enjoyed it "marvelously." To the chagrin of the pretty Marie Antoinette, who despised her sister-in-law's looks and comparatively low birth, the swarthy Savoyard, in time, gave France an heir. Even the phlegmatic dauphin was vexed to see a stupid and homely woman carry off the honors that belonged, by birth and seniority, to beauty. When Provence asked him maliciously, "How do you like my wife?" the dauphin replied, "Not too well; I would not care to have her for my wife." Provence said ironically, "I am sure that you have one to your own taste."

The dauphin, indeed, could not compare with his brothers. And yet, as the often dejected Marie Antoinette admitted, *malgré tout* he had his qualities. Unlike his brothers, he was honest and kind, incapable of any type of treachery. Observing that Provence was sly and insincere and that the rude

Artois was a gambler and roué,[6] Marie Antoinette consoled herself with the thought that a dull husband was preferable to a dishonest or immoral one.

"He has," Marie Antoinette said of her husband when he was nineteen, "a decided bent for justice, for order and for truth, also good sense and propriety in his own way of seeing things. But I fear the effects of his nonchalance, his apathy, and finally that failure of will without which one can neither think nor feel keenly enough to act effectively."

PRODDED by Mercy, who insisted that the dauphin stood in need of "further development," Marie Antoinette made sporadic efforts to "elevate the soul" of her husband.

"You do not," she said to the dauphin, "make the best use of your time. You must show yourself more intellectually flexible. Your manners are still rude, like your exterior."

Louis listened humbly and promised to reform. Alternately scolded and cajoled by his pretty wife, he did indeed change somewhat his mode of life. He still hunted excessively, but with moderated recklessness, for sometimes Marie Antoinette accompanied him, not so much to see the fun as to keep him, who was short-sighted, from riding wildly and breaking his neck. On their first hunt she observed with some admiration, "He shoots marvelously and with great care; he has killed forty animals, which proves that he is not so short-sighted as one would believe from looking at him."

She had little else to be proud of besides his prowess as a Nimrod. It was a happy day in her life when, in a sudden outburst of urbanity, her husband said *bon jour* to courtiers. In time, she hoped, he would learn to behave like a king. The chief difficulty was to wean him away from his extraordinary passion for manual work—his one genuine passion. A

[6] In 1820 Artois succeeded Provence (Louis XVIII) as king of France under the names of Charles X; ten years later a revolution drove him from the throne. As the *Encyclopædia Britannica* (14th ed.) remarks with British finality, "The best that can be said of Charles X is that, if he did not know how to rule, he knew how to cease to rule."

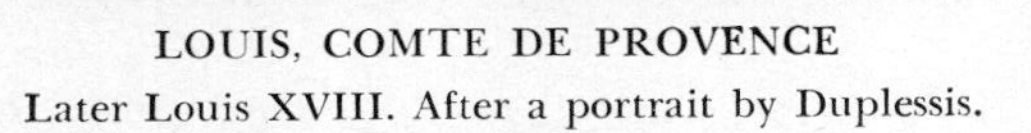

LOUIS, COMTE DE PROVENCE

Later Louis XVIII. After a portrait by Duplessis.

CHARLES, COMTE D'ARTOIS

Later Charles X. After a portrait by Vanloo.

born craftsman, his capable hands itched for expression, which, alas, all the world combined to discourage and to ridicule.

"Despite her efforts," a contemporary reports, "the Dauphiness is unable to make her husband control his unusual taste for all that concerns construction, such as masonry, carpentry, and other such things. He always finds something new to fix in his apartments; he works himself with the laborers in moving materials, girders, paving-blocks, and devotes whole hours to this toilsome exercise. Sometimes he comes home more tired than any laborer who is obliged to do such work for a living."

He would enter his apartments bathed in dirty sweat, his clothes grimy and his hands greasy, and would be received with sneers from an outraged wife. Contritely he would admit his faults and beg her forgiveness, but despite the sincerity of his protestations, the pull of manual labor was irresistible. Every time he could escape his wife's tongue-lashing—which was beginning to be so scandalous that Mercy urged her to scold him with less "vehemence and acidity"—he rolled up his sleeves and joined the laborers.

AND WHAT about this dissatisfied young wife, who was to have so baleful an influence on the history of France in the next two decades? She herself was victim of a bad education and no help to her husband. Like her mother Maria Theresa,[7] Marie Antoinette had no education beyond the elementary R's; her only attainment was a mastery of French, which she spoke flawlessly despite her rather eccentric spelling. As though she were a proverbial Bourbon, this mentally incurious girl never learned anything. While in later years her plodding husband was earnestly cramming his head with history, law, and literature, Marie Antoinette either played cards

[7] For an account of the life and character of Maria Theresa, see the present writer's biography of her son, *The Revolutionary Emperor: Joseph II* (London and New York, 1934).

for stakes higher than a queen could afford or read pornographic romances.[8] Lest any reader think that her education was typical of upper-class women of the period, he should recall such women of culture as Voltaire's mistress Madame de Chatelet, Madame Necker, Madame du Deffand, and finally Maria Josepha, whose learning was as solid as that of any man at Versailles.

Moreover, Marie Antoinette developed none of the gracious attributes that made so many women in high position become patrons of art and culture. Her mother-in-law Maria Josepha, for example, had acquired at her father's court in Dresden a love for art and serious music, and when she came to Versailles, she continued the tradition of encouraging artists and making valuable art collections. But the daughter of the pious Maria Theresa of Austria had no mature artistic tastes or interests. Like so many frivolous society women, she liked to show her splendid plumes at the Italian operettas and French comedies. Often, indeed, she displayed her fine figure on her own little stage to a select group of friends. But all this was merely a way of killing time when not dancing or playing cards.

The Habsburg princess was not a devout daughter of the Church. In view of her background and education, this lack of piety is astonishing, but also characteristic. In her mother and mother-in-law, for example, faith (no matter how intolerant) was an expression of mental stability and solidity of character. In Marie Antoinette the lack of faith meant precisely the contrary, a fear of boredom and a dislike of any discipline that might hamper her quest for pleasure or thwart her will. She went through all the motions of prayer and confession, to be sure, but God was not one of her heroes. Once, in fact, she wanted to meet and chat with the notorious

[8] Marie Antoinette kept her favorite books in the boudoir of her "hide-out" in the Petit Trianon. The "Catalogue alphabétique des 'Livres du boudoir' de la reine Marie Antoinette," in the Bibliothèque Nationale, MS.n.a.Fr.1699, lists 198 amazing titles: *Amusements of a Septuagenarian, Anecdotes of Conjugal Love, Memoirs of a Young Virgin, Confidences of a Beautiful Woman, Impudences of Youth.* In all this pile of trash and triviality there were hardly six serious books.

Voltaire, but her scandalized husband, a faithful son of the Church, was adamant where his Christian conscience was concerned, though he rarely checked his wife in other things.

With no tradition of culture in her home background and no intellectual equipment, Marie Antoinette was impelled by a vast boredom into frivolous amusement. It should be remembered that during her most impressionable years she had no children to occupy her time and no love for her husband to keep her contented. Temptations surrounded her during every waking hour. Life was easy, brilliant, dazzling; but it never had any inner meaning because it lacked faith and love. In the later period, when tried by misfortunes, she had nothing to fall back upon but family pride. She never understood what was going on outside her egocentric little world. And meanwhile the day of glory, when she would rule France through her meek husband, was coming close.

TIME was rolling inexorably, and the dauphin was doing little to prepare himself for the unavoidable task of kingship. And yet upon this boy, whose character and education were unknown to most Frenchmen, the nation, then still overwhelmingly and perhaps unanimously monarchical, centered all its hopes. Misgoverned for decades and crying for reform, France ardently hoped that the aging king, considered both a burden and a disgrace to the nation, would give way to the dauphin as soon as possible. A new broom, Frenchmen were saying, sweeps clean, and there was a lifetime of cleaning to do. When in the summer of 1773 the dauphin and his wife made one of their rare visits to Paris, they were almost mobbed by joyous crowds who hailed their future rulers with delirious enthusiasm. Marie Antoinette was touched. "What has moved me most," she remarked, "is the tenderness and eagerness of these poor people who, despite the taxes which overwhelm them, were transported with joy at the sight of us."

The dauphin, usually so diffident, was warmed by so much enthusiasm. He smiled and waved, and even made a few short speeches to the people whom he let into the garden of the Tuileries. Simple prince that he was, he believed that this outburst of popular affection was for him personally because he was so well intentioned. If he liked the people, why should they not like him also? That evening the royal couple went to the Théâtre Français, where the audience roared with approval at one line spoken on the stage:

"In his prince the Frenchman likes to see a brother."

CHAPTER V

"Le roi est mort, Vive...!"

YET FORTY DAYS and Nineveh shall be overthrown."

Such, in the spring of 1774, was the text of a sermon with which Bishop Jean Baptiste de Beauvais broke the clerical conspiracy of silence in regard to God's anointed, the Most Christian King of France. The bold bishop electrified his flock by pointing a trembling finger of accusation at the court of Versailles.

"Sire, my duty as a minister of the God of Truth commands me to tell you that your people are wretched, that you are the cause of it, and that you are kept in ignorance of it."

Yet forty days and the words of Jonah were fulfilled.

The stroke came like lightning. Dallying in the Trianon, the sixty-three year old Louis XV, who was fat and tormented by dyspepsia but who refused to heed his physicians' advice to give up the rosy-skinned Du Barry, suddenly collapsed. Upon being revived, he complained of headache and pain in the kidneys. He was carried across the park to the château, where a medical council, after weighty conferences, decided that His Majesty was suffering from "catarrhal fever" and needed to be bled. The doctors quickly reduced the patient's resistance by twice taking from his slowed-down arteries four big vials of blood.

Within two days skin-deep purplish pustules broke out over the patient's body, and the council of bewigged medicine men at last recognized the symptoms. When they pronounced the dread word *smallpox,* Louis XV murmured, "At my age one does not recover...."

The putrescent royal body filled the apartment with a fetid smell. Terrified courtiers, who dared not leave so long as the king was alive, spread the rumor that the pestilential air would kill all who breathed it. There was hasty packing; carriages were kept ready, waiting for the moment when His Majesty should depart for a cleaner world. Ten awful days passed, in fear and nausea. Much of the time the king was unconscious.

At the other end of the château the dauphin was alone with his wife in her apartments; they were not allowed to come close to the patient. Fear of the pestilence and the even greater dread of the imminent responsibility facing them haunted their days. Menaced with kingship, the dauphin fervently hoped that His Majesty would not die. He was one of the few persons in all France who wanted Louis XV to live. When early in the morning of May 10 the doctors gave up hope, saying that the king had only a few hours to live, the desperate dauphin wrote a hasty note to the Director of Finances: "Monsieur Comptroller-General, I beg you to distribute immediately 200,000 francs to the poor of Paris in order that they pray to God for the king; and if you find that this is too expensive, keep the balance for the Dauphiness and me." He wanted to avoid being king, but thought that two hundred thousand francs was perhaps too much to pay for the divine favor.

The prayers did not help. In the afternoon of May 10, 1774, Louis XV died in agony.

At the expiration of the last royal breath the good news spread with telegraphic celerity among the long-suffering courtiers. Shouting in an ecstasy of relief, they stormed into the apartments of the dauphin, crying hysterically, *"Le roi est mort! Vive le roi! Vive le roi! Vive la reine!"*

At these cries, so wild and so sudden, the dauphin—instantaneously become Louis XVI—turned pale. The world came crashing down on his head.[1] On his knees, his face lifted to heaven, he exclaimed in anguish, "O my God, what misfortune! O my God, help me!" And the sobbing Marie Antoinette, kneeling beside her husband, cried, "O God, guide us, protect us, we are so young!"

As fast as horses and carriages could move, the courtiers left infected Versailles. There was no time for ceremony, for the stench in the royal apartments was sickening; even the valets deserted the body they had once obsequiously tended. The gangrened corpse of the sometime great lover was decomposing with such rapidity that something had to be done quickly or not a living being would remain in the château to do the last pitiful honors to the dead. A leaden coffin was brought in and filled with a mixture composed of lime, vinegar, and camphorated spirit of wine. But no courtier, no relative, no servant could be induced to shroud the dreadful body and put it into the coffin. A few poor laborers, heavily remunerated, did the gruesome job. One of them was said to have died from retching. The soldered coffin was quickly transported to the monastery of the Feuillants near the Tuileries in Paris, where the monks were to pray for the royal dead; thence, in the night, what was left of Louis XV was silently and unceremoniously removed to St. Denis and deposited in the damp crypt. On the way people mocked, "There goes the ladies' pleasure, ladies' pleasure."

In this ignominious way the man who had misruled France for over half a century passed from the stage, but not from Frenchmen's memory. With Louis XV was buried absolute monarchy, although his successor, the young and innocent Louis XVI, did not realize it. Had the new monarch been alert, he might have observed with trepidation the way the

[1] This is his own expression. "They are all under inexpressible affliction," British Ambassador Stormont reported to London on May 11, 1774, "and none more so than the King and Queen, who all along expressed the greatest anxiety for their grandfather's Recovery, and the utmost apprehension of the Load which His Death would throw upon them and which their Youth and inexperience made them so little able to bear. One of the Dauphin's expressions was *Il me semble que l'Univers va tomber sur moi.*" Public Record Office (London), SP 78/292.

people celebrated the death of the autocrat. There was widespread public rejoicing, and the pent-up hatred of the régime, if not yet of the dynasty, broke forth in a rash of stinging lampoons. On the church of St. Denis were posted some cruel, and not unjustified, epitaphs:

Louis "Well-Beloved" lies here interred,
He was the second—as we have heard—
Who bore that name.—Save us from a third.

Here lies Louis the dull,
His life one deep mire,
Flee thief, flee trull,
You have lost your sire.

Lewd jokes and jests he had heard in scores,
He liked to drink deep, and he filled his station
To the great satisfaction of charlatans and whores!
Let that be his funeral oration.

By good fortune the blessèd pox
Put Louis XV in the funeral box.
The "small" has done in quicker stages
What the "great" could not in many ages.

LOUIS XVI was hardly twenty years old when, by the grace of God and the smallpox, he became king of France.

His physical appearance was not kingly. In height he was rather average—some five feet six inches—but his waist was too bulging and his powerful shoulders sloped. He waddled on chubby legs, with the rhythm of a duck. There was no force either in his walk or in his face. The mouth under a hooked and fleshy nose was small, full, almost cupid-shaped, suggesting gluttony rather than sensuousness. Behind the lips there were irregular, discolored teeth. From the nape of the neck through the receding forehead down to the double chin, the head formed an almost perfect circle. Everything about Louis, in fact, tended toward rotundity—a greased ball, his brother once called him. To this indecisive moon of a face no illumination was added by gentle and rather faded blue eyes which were so myopic that they could not distinguish between a chambermaid and a duchess.

In mind and character Louis was not remarkable either. He was Good, Pious, and Just, to be sure, but he was not Firm. He had a knowledge of two or three languages, a reasonable familiarity with French history, and a mastery of geography. His intelligence, although hampered by inarticulateness at this time, was not mediocre; rather, it was practical, understanding, and very retentive. All these good qualities, however, though useful in a parish priest or storekeeper, were dispensable in a monarch. A king of France, bearing the powers and prerogatives of absolutism sanctioned by religion, had to be firm and ruthless when necessary, and self-confident always; but the timid Louis XVI feared violence and distrusted himself.

⚜

THAT AFTERNOON of the king's death, Louis was a prey to anxiety as he and Marie Antoinette drove to Choisy to set up their temporary court. For a long while they rode in silence; but the May air was too exhilarating for gloom, and the young couple unexpectedly burst into joyous laughter. They laughed long and loudly, for no reason at all, except that it was spring and they were the absolute masters of France.

Louis knew nothing of what was facing him. From his late father and from other reliable persons he had often heard that much was wrong with conditions in France. But his grandfather the king had told him nothing and taught him nothing, as if ruling a great country were something that anyone could do automatically, like breathing.

Vaguely the king who still lacked three months of being twenty knew that the court was full of intriguers and immoral persons (such as the Du Barry clique—but he would get rid of them right away), that the administration was hampered by dishonesty, and that in the country there were people who went hungry. He was sure he would have to do something about all this, but he had no idea what.

The laughter subsided, and Louis again began to brood. He wondered, for he was devoid of vanity, how he, a simple boy without gifts or experience, could ever rule a great nation. From now on he would no longer be allowed to avoid people and evade all social responsibility; on the contrary, he would be forced to meet the world, to face people, mingle with people, command people. Tears welled into his eyes, for all his life he had been afraid of strangers. The prospect was intolerable, but there was no way for a Christian, particularly a Christian prince, to avoid his duty. For Louis had been brought up to believe that God had selected him for the trials and tribulations of ruling his fellow-men, and although he doubted himself, he never doubted his position.

THAT NIGHT, his first as king, he shut himself up in his room in the large hunting-lodge at Choisy and studied a long manuscript composed by his late father, entitled "List of various persons recommended by the Dauphin to that one of his children who shall succeed Louis XV." To the bewildered Louis XVI, faced with the need of selecting a new cabinet and appointing a corps of new officials, this testament of his father was a sacred beacon. How else, indeed, was he to know who among twenty-five million Frenchmen was honest and who was virtuous? Thanking the Almighty for a saintly and farseeing sire, the boy, his head heavy in his palms, read and memorized:

Maurepas—"A former minister, now in disfavor . . . , has retained the true principles of politics . . ."

Aiguillon—"His principles in the matter of royal authority are pure . . ."

Machault—"Harsh but honest . . . ; the clergy detest him . . ."

Nivernois—"Has spirit and grace; can be employed in embassies . . ."

Castries—"Good for the army . . ."

Muy—"He is virtue personified . . ."

MM. St. Priest—"The younger one may become useful . . ."
Broglie—"Has spirit and energy . . ."
Vergennes—"Has a sense of order; sagacious and capable . . ."

Louis read until late into the night, making notes in his tiny cramped handwriting on small scraps of paper. Then he drew up a list of honest men in the kingdom—practically everybody recommended by his father was sooner or later appointed to an important position—and put it in his pocket, where he kept it for consultation. The list was not very long.

⚜

IN THE MORNING of his second day as king his grandfather's ministers sent Louis the first official document for consideration: it contained a series of questions to which His Majesty was to give answers. His replies were short and to the point, as usual,[2] and are of considerable interest as being his first royal decisions. For the first time in his life he experienced the unforgettable sensation of knowing that his word was literally law.

To the question whether for the time being the old officials should continue in office, he simply replied *Yes*. To the question whether "the bishops, commandants of the provinces, and the intendants should return each to his place," he answered, "After I have seen them." When should the ministers who had visited the late king's sick-chamber present themselves before the new king? "After nine days," Louis XVI wrote.

QUESTION: "Does the same apply . . . to all other functionaries?"
LOUIS: "The same."

QUESTION: "Royal orders, are they to be signed merely *Louis* or *Louis Augustus?*"
LOUIS: *"Louis."*

QUESTION: "If Your Majesty is not going to see your ministers, does he not think it desirable that they should form a committee for foreign and internal affairs?"

[2] His laconic tone surprised everybody. On June 7 he gave his first reception to the *corps diplomatique*, and Ambassador Stormont reported to London: "He uses few Words, but His answers are very precise and pertinent."

Louis' significant reply to this was: "If anything important comes up, the matter should be sent to me."

⚜

HIS SECOND royal act that day was characteristic of his upbringing but was not a credit to his heart. He had always disliked his grandfather's good-natured mistress Du Barry, to whom he had frequently been rude and for whom Marie Antoinette had a violent aversion, and now was his chance to punish "that impertinent creature" who had lived out of wedlock with the late king.

> Monsieur [Louis wrote to the minister of the royal household], in the frightful trouble of yesterday I have not been able to send you my orders on the subject of Madame Du Barry. Since she knows many things, it is necessary that she be confined sooner rather than later. Send her a *lettre de cachet* to enter a provincial convent and command her to see nobody. I leave to you the choice of the place and the pension which I am giving her (so that she may live like an honest woman) out of consideration for the memory of my grandfather.

This, one may say, was hardly a way of showing consideration for the memory of one's grandfather, and the court resented the young king's harshness. In transmitting his command to the weeping Du Barry, the pained minister begged her to forgive him—"I am forced to execute the orders of the king." But Marie Antoinette was revenged for the slighting remarks the beautiful Du Barry had made about her looks. "The king," Marie Antoinette wrote exultingly, "has sent away that creature to a convent and has driven from court all those who bear her scandalous name." [3]

[3] This happened on May 12, when a special order exiled the whole Du Barry family. Concerning Count Jean Du Barry, a brother-in-law of the royal mistress, the king wrote with unaccustomed vehemence: "One should redouble the zeal against this scoundrel who trafficked with his sister-in-law and robbed her at the same time. Is it not the height of indignity and scandal, this traffic in vice of such a woman by men like this Count Du Barry and their set?"

⚜

THE FRENCH, with their usual realism in such matters, considered the exile of the Du Barrys not so much a victory of virtue over vice as a resounding uxorious triumph. Courtiers as well as the informed public knew that kings of France had always been ruled by women, and they saw no reason to assume that Louis XVI would be an exception. From the first hour of his accession, Louis was regarded as a nonentity, and all the seekers for position and influence concentrated upon Marie Antoinette. The court swarmed with wily flatterers and glib intriguers anxious to gain the ear and eye of the girl-queen whose vanity was well known and precisely evaluated. Louis, the shy and self-effacing, was not being flattered.

All the numberless Cabals and Intrigues [Ambassador Stormont reported to London one day after the death of Louis XV] have this one common Object, to attempt to gain the Favour of the present Queen, from a Persuasion that she will have the greatest weight with the King her Husband. . . . If it is just, if the Queen has that decided Influence, this conclusion I think is clear–She will, for some time at least, be chiefly directed by the advice of Her Mother.[4]

But Louis surprised everybody. The courtiers were pained to discover that the king for whom they had so little regard showed no inclination to consult his wife in matters political. It was shocking to hear him say, with more bluntness than regard for the possible feelings of his queen, that "what has always ruined this country has been women, whether legitimate wives or mistresses." He had but few strong convictions, but two of them he took seriously: the evil of "petticoat rule," as his brother-in-law Joseph II of Austria called it, and the undesirability of foreign interference in his (France's) affairs. Marie Antoinette was both a "petticoat" and a foreigner who, he knew although he did not say it, was surrounded by a faction devoted to Austrian interests; and for Austria, curiously enough, he had an ineradicable dislike. Every time Marie Antoinette showed a disposition to linger in the cabinet

[4] Public Record Office, SP78/292, no.38 ("Secret").

where Louis was working on state papers, he said gently, "Madame, I have business to attend to." Sometimes when she entered suddenly, he quickly covered up the papers on his desk.

Marie Antoinette was surprised at his attitude of distrust. But her astonishment was nothing compared with the shock she received when her husband greeted the exiled Duke of Choiseul, who was the chief of the so-called "Austrian faction" and a candidate for the prime ministry. Louis had two good reasons to detest Choiseul (who, incidentally, had been his "match-maker"): the duke was an ally of the Austrians, and he had been a bitter enemy of the dauphin, the king's late father. When Choiseul was presented, Louis addressed just one caustic sentence to him: "Have you not lost your hair since I last saw you?" As the duke flushed, His Majesty abruptly turned his back on him. Marie Antoinette also changed color. "I am extremely glad to see you, sir," she said loudly to the mortified duke; "I shall ever remember with gratitude the obligation I owe you for the share you had in the negotiation of my marriage, and shall never forget that it is to you in part I owe my happiness."

Louis showed himself so jealous of his personal authority and so suspicious of his wife's friends and relatives that Marie Antoinette could hardly bring him to the point of writing a courteous letter to Maria Theresa. He finally added a few stilted lines as a postscript to Marie Antoinette's letter to her mother, and the queen had to apologize in a post-postcript: "I know well that it would not have been too much for him to write a special letter; I beg my dear mother to excuse him, in view of the great number of business matters with which he occupies himself much, as well as his timidity and natural embarrassment."

And so the court learned that, for the moment at least, Austria would not rule France and there was no petticoat behind the throne. But contemporaries were smilingly skeptical of the durability of the king's independence. Would he resist his wife after she had succeeded in making him a father? Lord Stormont commented with British whimsy: "If Time should call forth those Talents, which have hitherto lain concealed . . . , Her Influence will be great and her Charms and Address irresistible; but it will be trifling, if Nature has made Him Proof against all Her Charms."

CHAPTER VI

"The king barricades himself with honest men"

THE GREAT WORRY was, Who should guide him? The bewildered boy stood alone on a pinnacle facing a whole nation, and he was frightened at the awful responsibility. He had never before had to make decisions or take action. Always there had been somebody mastering him—father, mother, brother, wife; but now he was king and absolute lord of the realm, and all the world expected him to rule and command. Yet he did not have the remotest idea of his specific functions, or any knowledge of finance and legislation, or any awareness of the complex problems that waited solution. He knew how to sign papers submitted by ministers and was of course conscious that his signature implied sanction and compelled obedience. But his distrust of all his grandfather's ministers and functionaries was too deep to allow them to remain in office.

At court there was no one in whom he had confidence. Yet it was essential that he find one man to whom he could entrust himself and the destinies of the state; such a man could serve as prime minister, as royal tutor, and even as a sort of parent-substitute. But where was the king to find such a mentor? He had virtually no contact with prominent men, and some of the persons recommended in his father's list—Maurepas, for example—had not been at court in Louis' lifetime.

Immensely worried, Louis consulted the one woman he

trusted, his clever and haughty Aunt Adelaide, who was his father's sister and who knew everybody. Together they scanned the late dauphin's list of recommendations until by a process of elimination there remained only Machault and Maurepas, both of them past their allotted span of years. But Madame Adelaide was a pious woman, and when her nephew asked her what she thought of Machault, she replied that the former minister of finance, although honest enough, was a Jansenist and therefore a heretic. Louis, accordingly, decided against him. Thus only Maurepas, equally ancient and presumably equally wise, was left in the field. In this way the king chose a minister who was to shape his reign during his most impressionable years and who was destined to leave a permanent mark on the course of his life.

> In the genuine grief which overwhelms me [Louis wrote to Jean Frédéric Phélipeaux, Comte de Maurepas], and which I share with the whole kingdom, I have large duties to fulfil. I am king, and this word comprises all my obligations; but I am only twenty years old, and I do not possess all the knowledge which I need: Moreover, I can not see any minister, all of them having been with the king during his last illness. The certainty which I have of your probity and your profound knowledge of affairs, induces me to pray you to aid me with your counsels. Come, therefore, as soon as possible and you will give me great pleasure.

THE MAN who read this boyish letter from his monarch was a slender little wrinkled flower of the old régime, an aristocrat and a wit. A quarter-century before Louis XVI was born, Maurepas was already an eminent minister and a boon companion of Louis XV, with whom he shared everything except women. Agile and frivolous, the effeminate Maurepas always talked wittily and never listened. A good conversationalist, he took delight in the play of his own razor-edged tongue. An epigram meant more to him than a fact, and a *bon mot* was worth a whole library. His irresistible penchant for ridicule, in fact, had cost him his office and the friendship of Louis XV. He had—over a quarter-century before—become jealous of de Pompadour and devoted his not inconsiderable talents as a mocketeer to flooding Versailles and Paris with rhymed poison about the beautiful lady, who was his rival, and her crowned lover, who was his friend.[1] In danger of being laughed "out of court," de Pompadour went to war against the bright-eyed little rhymester who, she explained vehemently to the king, was the author of such scurrilities as

'Tis said that Her Excellency
The sultana of Choisy
Continues her quadrille
With our great Sophi,
And he is in hopes
Of producing a little Mamamochi . . .

Louis XV had laughed at the silly rhymes. Once, after reading a libel on himself and his ministry, Louis XV remarked to the Duc de Richelieu, "Strange that every one is attacked except Maurepas." "That," the duke replied ironically, "is not surprising; it's he who wrote it." In the end Louis XV was convinced that his scintillating crony had written all those *vilaines chansons* that were making him ridiculous and permanently exiled him to his estates. Even this blow—after thirty years of service—did not subdue the irrepressible fellow. "The first day in the country," he joked, "I was nettled; the second day I was consoled."

Such was Jean Frédéric Phélypeaux, Comte de Maurepas, a gentleman in his seventies, whom the young Louis XVI selected to be his guide and minister.

The sprightly exile, full of glee and a sense of belated victory and vindication, wasted not a minute in hurrying to Versailles to obey the summons of his king, the grandson of

1 Some of the verses attributed to Maurepas may be found in Lefèvre d'Amécourt's manuscript journal, *Journal des principales époques du règne de Louis XVI,* in the Bibliothèque Nationale, n.a.Fr.22111, p.7-13. A fair sample of anti-Pompadour verse is the following:

This little bourgeoise,
Brought up as a merry wench,
Reduces all to her own level
And makes the court a dirty slum.

Louis XV, despite his scruples,
For her coldly burns.
And his ridiculous love
Makes all Paris laugh. . . .

COMTE DE MAUREPAS
After a portrait by Dupin.

JACQUES NECKER
After a portrait by J. S. Duplessis.

his late royal friend. For twenty-five years Maurepas had not shown his grinning face at court, and a new generation had grown up which did not know him. Early in the morning of May 13 he presented himself to the king.

From the first interview Louis XVI fell victim to the seductive tongue of the nimble old courtier.

"I come," Maurepas said smoothly, "to thank Your Majesty for having named me prime minister."

"Prime minister!" Louis was taken aback. "I don't need any."

"Eh bien," Maurepas replied imperturbably, "I shall then teach Your Majesty how not to need a prime minister."

The king burst out laughing.

Louis XVI had a weakness for old people, or rather perhaps a distrust of young ones, possibly fearing their competition. With old men he always felt safe—and Maurepas was seventy-three. And so, from the first day they met, the king put himself in the paternal shelter of the quick-witted old rhymester who was inclined to solve difficulties with an anecdote.

MAUREPAS immediately settled at court, and Louis felt relieved enough to begin work in earnest. He devoted eleven to twelve hours a day to reading state papers and making conscientious replies. Always he consulted the clever Maurepas, whose poise was a tonic to the king's gnawing self-doubts. Earnestly Louis studied his *métier,* in order, he said, "to make my people happy." Within the first few months he wrote no less than sixty letters on policy to his minister of foreign affairs. These and other letters—"incorrect in style, but true and forceful," as the historian Moreau described them—were widely cited as proof of the young monarch's zeal.

Mostly Louis occupied himself with finances; he plowed through figures and balance-sheets, but sank gradually into a morass of incomprehension. For hours he and the Abbé Terray, the comptroller-general, were closeted in the cabinet, pouring over account books. "I hand him reports on all branches of my administration," the financial abbé told his friends; "he reads them with me, summarizes them, asks me questions. If he follows my advice, in three months he will know as much about finances as I do."

This may have been Gallic irony, for Abbé Terray did not know much about finances. The net impression Louis gained from the dismal figures was that taxes were too high, governmental income too low, and that economy was a crying need.

Insulated though the king of France was from his subjects, there was no doubt in Louis' practical mind that money-saving was a virtue, and one which Frenchmen deeply appreciated. From his gloomy sessions with Comptroller-General Terray, and after consulting Maurepas, Louis emerged with a gift for the nation. It was customary for a new monarch to impose a tax, the *Joyeux avènement,* upon his accession to the throne. This tax amounted to some forty million livres. In a memorable edict which swept through France like a breath of hope, Louis XVI relinquished his right to the "joyous accession" and promised at the same time to stabilize the finances by paying the national debt as well as to relieve the nation of its tax load by drastic economies.

This—"the first edict emanating from my royal authority" —was hailed by the nation with transports of delight. For the first time in years Frenchmen faced the prospect of reduced taxes, and they greeted their young monarch as a savior.[2]

[2] Hearing of the effervescent enthusiasm of the nation for the young monarchs, the shrewd old Maria Theresa in Vienna said that it contained too much danger, since the people might come to expect miracles from an inexperienced king. She advised Marie Antoinette to tell Louis to "establish definite principles and not to deviate from them." Marie Antoinette echoed her mother's words: "I am disturbed by this French enthusiasm and its consequences. The little that I understand of politics makes me realize that they are very difficult and perplexing. It is admitted that the late king had left things in a very bad state; minds are divided and it will be impossible to satisfy everybody in a country whose vivacity is such that it demands that everything be done in an instant. It is quite true what my dear mama says: establish principles and do not deviate from them. The king will not have the same weakness as his grandfather. I also hope that he will have no favorites, but I fear that he might be too soft and easy."

And when Marie Antoinette likewise renounced her tax privilege known as "the Queen's Girdle," the joyful nation knew that at last a new day had come. The pretty queen was greeted with a graceful compliment:

You renounce, charming sovereign,
The largest of your revenues;
But what need you the Queen's Girdle
When you have that of Venus.[3]

ON THE TENTH DAY of his kingship Louis assembled his first Council of State.[4] This was the first time he met face to face the five ministers he had inherited from his grandfather. Louis was embarrassed and stammeringly read the speech he had prepared, but he did not flinch when he came to the passage declaring that he intended to rule by himself and that the irresponsible days of his grandfather were over.

> I want each one of you [Louis concluded] to hold himself in readiness for the time I shall indicate to render a clear and exact account of his department and to take my orders. . . . Since I wish only to occupy myself with my kingdom and the happiness of my people, it is only by your conformity to these principles that your work will have my approbation.

This was a strong hint to the elderly gentlemen to prepare their books and make ready to get out.

TO THE FRIVOLOUS COURTIERS, who stood like an impregnable wall between the king and his people, Louis' zeal and activity began to look serious. From the first week of the reign the court combined to defeat the king, for such, indeed, was

[3] *Vous renoncez, charmante souveraine,*
Au plus beau de vos revenues;
Mais que vous servirait la ceinture de reine
Vous avez celle de Vénus.

[4] The Council of State was not unlike the modern cabinet; it met twice weekly under the chairmanship of the king. No prince of the blood, not even a dauphin, was admitted to any of the sessions.

the tragic function of the royal court. Princes and high dignitaries who made up the royal entourage were not allowed, by law and custom, to participate in active administration; and it was inevitable that they should try to gain power, income, and prestige through intrigue. Inevitably, also, cliques formed around certain prominent individuals, and all were engaged in an undercover, but nevertheless deadly, battle for position. In this permanent struggle around the throne no reputation was sacred and no weapon was despised. The courtiers fenced the monarch off from the nation, and no one could approach him except by gaining the favor of some one at court. Moreover, the king was shackled by iron traditions (which it was to the advantage of the courtiers to keep alive) and the slave of a ceremonious life almost primitive in its symbolism. It required extraordinary courage and unusual persistence to break through the many walls that hedged in a king of France.

Louis was hopeful in those early days of his kingship. He was a curiously sad figure in that cesspool of a royal court–one might almost say a tragic figure, had he possessed more diginity. For this stolid, phlegmatic boy towered morally above his entourage, including his brothers. In a court which for over a century had been the concentrate of cynicism and the very essence of *raffinement,* the king had the transparent honesty of a child and a simple man's distrust of underhandedness. He disliked the courtiers and was sure that the way to solve political problems was to keep these dishonest people out of office. It must be admitted that his chances of winning the political race in competition with the most cunning and feline characters in Europe were not substantial.

His Majesty [the acute Ambassador Stormont wrote to London] wishes to place Himself out of the Reach of all Intrigue. This, however, is a vain Expectation, and the Chimera of a Young, inexperienced Mind. The Throne He fills, far from raising him above Intrigue, places Him in the Center of it. Great and Eminent Superiority of Talents might, indeed, crush these Cabals, but as there is no Reason to believe Him possessed of that Superiority, I think, He will be a prey to them and find Himself more and more entangled every Day.[5]

THE EAGERNESS of the boy-king, so well-meaning and yet so clumsy, touched even so hardened a cynic as Maurepas (who, after all, knew Voltaire and had been a friend of Montesquieu). The old minister had been at Versailles, the most corrupt court in Europe, for a generation, and though another generation had intervened since then, he knew what pitfalls were strewn in the path of an honest man. He recalled also that Louis XV too had been sincere in his youth, much like this grandson of his. Maurepas knew that since Henry IV no Bourbon had had the ruthlessness necessary to dominate the court and that every effort made to break the inner "ring" was wasted. No single individual, whether king or minister, seemed able to destroy the politico-social machine with its etiquette, its bribers, its permanent office-holders, its job-sellers, its social profiteers and political racketeers. It did not, therefore, much matter who was appointed to what office, since, to Maurepas at least, the system seemed to be beyond repair. A bad minister could not do much more harm, a good one little good.

In this spirit Maurepas guided the king's appointments, and Louis, eager to have ministers as honest as himself, unhesitatingly accepted the old man's recommendations. And to Maurepas' credit it must be said that he did a good job in selecting ministers.

MOST CONSPICUOUS among the new ministers were Vergennes the cautious and Turgot the radical. Vergennes remained longest in office and affected the destinies, not of France, but of those English colonies beyond the Atlantic which were, with French money, to become the United States of America.

When Louis appointed him minister of foreign affairs,

[5] June 8, 1774; Public Record Office, SP 78.

Charles Gravier, Comte de Vergennes, was a tall, florid man of fifty-seven, with thirty-four years of diplomatic service behind him. He had learned the intricacies of his craft at the four corners of Europe, in Portugal and Germany, Turkey and Sweden, and there was not much he did not know about diplomacy. A moderate monarchist, full of conventional tact, Vergennes was suspicious of innovations and was inclined to look upon his colleague Turgot with alert distrust. In his political principles he was the conservative Frenchman of the upper classes, urbane in manner and class-conscious in conviction. Among his prejudices were a dislike of Austria and a hatred of England, but his dread of violence (in which he resembled Louis XVI) was usually stronger than his antipathy for enemies. A cultivated and rather humane gentleman of the Voltairean age, Vergennes regarded war as the culmination of all evils, and he never failed to tell Louis that a monarch could find true glory only in peace. He violated this maxim only once in the thirteen years of his office.

Thomas Jefferson, who as United States ambassador to France had occasion to meet Vergennes, thus described him:

> He is a great minister in European affairs, but has very imperfect ideas of our institutions, and no confidence in them. His devotion to the principles of pure despotism, renders him unaffectionate to our governments. But his fear of England makes him value us as a make weight. He is cool, reserved in political conversations, but free and familiar on other subjects, and a very attentive, agreeable person to do business with. It is impossible to have a clearer, better organized head; but age has chilled his heart.

Vergennes was an almost perfect minister for Louis. Their relationship was cemented by that most durable of all solders, common weaknesses, although the feebleness of the king was inherent and the vacillation of the minister was a matter of occasional strategy. Louis appreciated Vergennes' caution, and the minister sympathized with the monarch's timidity. Neither liked adventure. The king favored inaction, and the minister believed in compromise; the one hoped to preserve the prestige of France without undue exertion, and the other strove to maintain the balance of power. The glove, in brief, fitted the hand.

Almost immediately upon entering office, Vergennes composed a long picture of the international situation for the guidance of the inexperienced king, and Louis was deeply impressed by the sentiments of the foreign minister. A few passages follow:

> The absolute contempt of the principles of justice and decency which characterizes the conduct and enterprises of some contemporary powers [6] ought to be the pressing subject of serious reflections and even of precautionary measures.... If might is right, if expediency is a claim, how can states feel secure in the future? If immemorial possession, if solemn treaties... no longer serve as a brake on ambition how can one protect oneself against surprise and invasion? If political brigandage perpetuates itself, peace will soon be nothing but an open barrier to perfidiousness and treason.

Having relieved himself of his indignation at the successful rape of Poland on the part of Prussia, Austria, and Russia, Vergennes sharply criticized the foreign policy of Louis XVI's Austrian in-laws and implied that an honest Frenchman should treat those unscrupulous Viennese—especially Emperor Joseph II—with caution. Louis heartily agreed.

Of England, France's "mortal" enemy, Vergennes wrote: "On our flank we see a restless and greedy nation, more jealous of the prosperity of its neighbors than of its own welfare; powerfully armed and ready to strike at the moment when she shall find it expedient.... England regards with envious cupidity the prodigious treasure of our plantations in America and our industry in Europe...." [7]

Louis nodded vigorous approval as he read.

[6] Prussia, Russia, and Austria, which, in 1772, dismembered Poland.

[7] Archives Nationales, K164, no.22. Part of this long document has been reprinted in Doniol's *Histoire de la participation de la France à l'établissement des États-Unis d'Amérique* (1886), I, 15*f.*

⚜

At the age of forty-seven Anne Robert Jacques Turgot, Baron de l'Aulne, a tall and handsome patrician, had a reputation as wide as France and even beyond. Louis XVI knew little about him except that he was reputed to be an economist with ultramodern ideas—an eighteenth-century New Dealer, so to speak—but the king took Maurepas' word that the ex-intendant of Limoges was a man whose ability was matched only by his honesty.

> Inform M. Turgot immediately [Louis wrote to the minister of the royal household] that I appoint him Comptroller-General of my finances. I place the greatest hopes on this choice for the welfare of my people, whom the disastrous administration of Abbé Terray has so much alarmed. Let M. Turgot come to see me tomorrow morning and bring with him the memoir on grains....

Punctually next morning Turgot presented himself to His Majesty and without circumlocution explained his program. Rigid economy, free trade in grain, stable finances—above all, economy, Turgot stated tersely. Louis had never before heard sentences spoken with such precision and so much austerity.

"As for the generosity of kings," Turgot spoke almost contemptuously, "you must... reflect whence comes this money which you distribute among your courtiers.... Compare the misery of the people, from whom taxes are extracted by force, with the position of the persons who have claims on your liberality."

Louis was impressed. Those were the sentiments he himself felt but had never formulated. The word *economy* had a pleasing sound, particularly from the lips of a minister, for Louis never forgot the words of his father that a "king is the steward of the nation's finances."

The king eagerly promised Turgot his whole-hearted support and loyal coöperation.

"It is," the proud Encyclopædist informed His Majesty, "to the honest man, to the just and good man, rather than to the king, that I offer my services."

Turgot's appointment to the most important office in the

government caused a minor sensation. Intellectual and liberal circles were convinced that the comptroller-general held the keys to Utopia, while the privileged classes frowned upon the radical (somewhat atheistic) innovator. In reality, however, Turgot took over the worst job in the realm, the one position it was impossible to fill with even a modicum of honesty without disturbing hoary privileges and creating a host of relentless enemies.

And Turgot was not at all the man for the position, despite the eulogies that later historians have heaped upon him. The cynical Maurepas, who had brought about the comptroller-general's appointment, could have warned him (but, out of impish irony, did not) that he would be a failure from the start, because there was not a millimeter of the courtier in Turgot's make-up. Upright and inflexible, Turgot was as unfitted for court politics, the politics of backstairs intrigue and feline clawings, as a New England puritan. Reserved, sometimes disdainful and always abstemious, the comptroller-general had many fine qualities, but none that were useful for a successful minister. Never doubting the immutability of his convictions, he did not know the meaning of compromise. He was a reformer with One Idea and a worshiper of Reason, in which he believed religiously. No sooner had he entered upon his duties than he began to waste his great energies and fine gifts in trying to crash through walls rather than going around them, and Frenchmen, with their unfailing gift for the phrase, were saying, "Turgot does good things badly, Terray did bad things well."

Louis, no diplomat himself, saw nothing wrong with Turgot's blunt tactics and gave him full freedom to go ahead and do what he thought needed doing. If there was any doubt in the king's mind, it was on the subject of the comptroller-general's reputed irreligion. Louis demanded assurance from Maurepas. "Tell me," the king asked his mentor, "what kind of man really is this Turgot whom you have given me?"

Maurepas, tentatively: "Eh, sire, he has a sense of justice and a heart of a citizen; he observes the laws, respects morals . . ."

Louis: "That's very fine, but he never goes to mass."

Maurepas, delicately: "Sire, I don't know much about that. But they tell me that Abbé Terray, his predecessor, used to go every day."

⚜

"THE KING barricades himself with honest men." In these words the Swedish ambassador characterized the first months of Louis XVI's reign. Other observers were likewise favorably impressed. One of the clearest accounts of those early days was written by Lord Stormont, the British ambassador to France. His confidential report, taken from his secret dispatches which are preserved in the Public Record Office in London, still makes good reading:

> I will confine this letter to such topics, as could not properly find place in an official Dispatch: The most important of these, is the Character and Sentiments of the present French King. . . .
>
> His Most Christian Majesty did by no means . . . betray the least impatience to reign; but on the contrary . . . a real apprehension of being raised so early to the Throne. . . . He speaks of His Inability, Inexperience, and total Ignorance, in a manner which . . . does him honour, and gives room to hope that he will endeavour to learn. . . . The number of Letters which he has wrote with his own hand to the Princes of the Blood, and to his several Ministers show that he is capable of Application: the Style of those Letters, and the clear precise Manner in which He answered the questions put to him by His Ministers, indicate an aptitude to Business, and tho' those Questions were not very material, carry marks of a good, plain, natural Understanding. . . .
>
> The strongest and most decided features of this King's character are a Love of Justice, a general desire of doing well, a passion for Œconomy, and an abhorrence of all the Excesses of the last Reign. He heard much whilst he was Dauphin of the consequences of those Excesses . . . , is strongly bent upon correcting those abuses, and sets about it, with the eager Impatience of a parsimonious Son who succeeds to a prodigal Father. He is eternally repeating the words Œconomy, Œconomy, and begins already to enter into the minutest details. . . .

As to the present French King's political Principles . . ., my own opinion is that as to foreign Politics, they are as yet unformed. . . . I have indeed heard it surmised, that he was not favourably disposed towards England. . . . His passion for Œconomy, and dread of Expences, give room to hope that he will not wantonly, and hastily, plunge into a war with England. . . .

He certainly does not consult the Queen openly, and he has been heard to say more than once, that Women ought not to meddle with Politics. Were she to attempt to take a decided lead, she would probably lose all her Power, but she is too wise, and too well advised to take so unguarded a step. She will I imagine employ the much surer Arts of Insinuation and Address, attempt to guide him by a secret line, and try to make him follow, whilst he thinks he leads.[8]

[8] Public Record Office, SP 78/292; no.42: Supplement, "Most Confidential."

CHAPTER VII

"The violet on the throne of the lily"

THE TEAM of honest ministers needed an expert and decisive driver, but the king had neither a formulated policy nor a strong will. Like the nation itself, the cabinet was divided and uncertain of its goal, and Louis XVI, born to autocracy, was expected to lead and at the same time to satisfy clashing expectations. A generation of wits, critics, and scholars had undermined ancient loyalties and disintegrated sacred beliefs, and at the time when Louis XVI ascended the throne, France was in a state of indecision and perplexity, not sharply aware that it had already broken with the past and unsure of the future. Altogether too much power had been concentrated in—perhaps more correctly, seized by—the hands of the monarch during the last two centuries, and if the throne failed to exercise this immense social-political-economic power in the interest of the majority, then a revolutionary situation was bound to develop.

For more than half a century the French people had been groping for a formula that would satisfy at once the need for authority and the desire for liberty (of economic action), but neither king nor ministers had any just appreciation of public opinion.

Already, as some observers felt, it was too late for mild reforms. What had been a mere rivulet of national aspirations under Louis XV became a good-sized stream of demands under Louis XVI; and it was not difficult to foresee that it would go on swelling until it would burst its banks and inundate the land. Popular, or rather group, claims were as yet incoherent and vague, but real none the less. The most urgent demand, on which the nation was virtually unanimous, was a reduction in the tax burden, which caused real want among the poor and which hampered business. In the provinces the great mass of the peasants, though materially better off than they had been a century earlier, yearned for more land and sullenly eyed the plethora of acres that belonged to the barons and the bishops. In the cities there was deep and often forcibly articulate resentment of royal wastefulness (a reaction acutely felt in the last years of Louis XV's reign) and governmental inefficiency: intracity trade was hamstrung by a thousand untouchable "privileges" and senseless regulations which dated back to the middle ages. But what most galled the proud city-folk, both businessmen and artisans, was that the fine-feathered ladies and high-born gentlemen lived in idle luxury on the taxes extorted from the working people and that those wastrels also enjoyed all political privileges and social immunities. Throne, noblesse, and clergy had, between them, a monopoly of rights, offices, privileges, prerogatives, and powers. To the bourgeoisie, better educated and more skilled than the aristocracy and clergy, this situation was becoming insupportable.

Louis, of course, had no idea of the real needs and demands of the various classes of his subjects. Hitherto, as duke and dauphin, he had had little if any contact with common people, and to him their aspirations and wants were written in hieroglyphic. And no decipherer stood at the elbow of the crowned boy who was the personification of the absolute power of the state.

Willy-nilly Louis was in conflict with the nation almost from the first day of his accession. This is not to say that either crown or commonalty wanted to fight or was activated by hostility toward the other; on the contrary, Louis was sincere in his "love" for the people, and the latter felt only dutiful affection for their young monarch. But the nation nursed grievances which only the crown could alleviate and fostered aspirations which could be satisfied only at the expense of the absolute monarchy.

The first skirmish between king and people started quietly enough with the question of the so-called Parlements. The story must be told in some detail, for it was a portent of things to come.

French *Parlements* were not Parliaments. They were courts of law of superior jurisdiction. At least half of these Parlements (there were twelve altogether[1]) dated back to the middle ages, and all bore a curiously medieval character. They differed from ordinary courts in that they claimed to be independent of the absolute royal authority, although in legal theory the king was the fountain-head of justice. In the course of the centuries, for example, the Parlement of Paris had become a sort of national Supreme Court (by tradition rather than legal force) and arrogated to itself the right of registering royal edicts before they could become the law of the land. As a rule, king and Parlement worked together well enough—that is to say, the monarch decreed and the Parlement obeyed—but the magistrates were always a potential source of opposition, the one group of functionaries in the realm over whom the crown had no unchallenged power.

Only a few years before Louis XVI ascended the throne, his grandfather had come in conflict with the Parlement of Paris and, in a fit of autocratic assertiveness, had exiled the obstinate magistrates and appointed his own obedient judges under Chancellor Maupeou. That act of royal arbitrariness had not merely deranged the judicial system but had shocked

[1] In Paris (founded in 1302), Toulouse (1302), Grenoble (1431), Bordeaux (1460), Dijon (1476), Aix (1501), Rouen (1515), Rennes (1553), Pau (1620), Metz (1633), Besançon (1676), Douai (1686). All the Parlements were founded by the kings of France.

a politically alert nation, which saw in the justices the last barriers against unbridled despotism.

Now the nation, encouraged by Louis XVI's reputed susceptibility to reforms, clamored for a recall of the exiled Parlement. This demand was a more or less conscious test of strength between the people and the crown. To force the king's hand the folk of Paris stoned and reviled the incumbent magistrates until the "usurper" Maupeou and his justices resigned in disgust (secretly, however, they got pensions). The matter was now entirely up to the king.

What would Louis do? He had been on the throne only a few weeks, and although the subtleties of the politico-legal struggle were somewhat beyond him, he sensed well enough that his divine-right authority was challenged. To appoint a new Parlement in Paris would be acting as arbitrarily as his grandfather—and creating the same resentment. To recall the exiled Parlement meant to insult the memory of Louis XV and to defeat the principle of absolutism. Would he have the courage to restore to office magistrates whom Louis XV had treated as rebels? The king, who had just celebrated his twentieth birthday, faced his first test of statesmanship.

"The king," Maurepas told a friend, "abhors the Parlements. He is even more opposed to them than his grandfather." By education and background, from his conception of kingship and his religion, Louis was indeed hostile to an independent judiciary; but he was also king of France and determined to be fair to his subjects. He was torn between sentiment and duty.

The whole court was riven by the struggle. On the side of the king in his antipathy for an independent judiciary were "all the serious minds," as a contemporary phrased it—Provence, most of the clergy, the Jesuits, the archbishop of Paris, many of the peers, the old ministers of Louis XV. But the "serious minds" could not drown out the clamor of the people, especially since a powerful faction at court favored the recall of the exiled judges. Among the pro-Parlement people were two who counted for most, Marie Antoinette and Maurepas. The queen was dragged into the dramatic conflict by her emotions: those who favored the exiled magistrates were gay and enlightened, and intuitively the spirited queen sensed that this was a fight between old and new, between stuffed shirts and unpowdered hair. She liked the novelty of "modernism." Vanity also drove her to court national popularity. "A monarch who will recall the Parlements," she heard Maurepas tell the king, "will be worshiped as a friend of the people."

Louis himself was almost like an inanimate object buffeted by violent forces. His instinct for self-preservation, not yet deadened, impelled him to oppose any restoration of the independent magistrature. Even an inexperienced autocrat could see the danger to his position in being challenged and overruled. Was it not the simplest logic that a free judiciary meant the end of absolutism? Either the king had all the power, in which case the courts should be subservient, or the judges were independent, in which case the crown was not absolute. Short of revolution this dilemma could not be solved.

Bedeviled, Louis listened to everybody. He was no fanatic and was usually amenable to reason—or to the last argument. When his brother Provence talked, he agreed. When Vergennes talked, he agreed. When Maurepas talked, he agreed. All the arguments were good, and everybody sounded convincing. Vergennes warned Louis: "The old Parlements are rivals of royal authority. To restore them is to uncover a precipice which will destroy the monarchy." Another said: "The magistrates will return gentle as lambs; once on the benches they will become lions." Louis' brother Provence argued hotly: "If you restore the exiled Parlements, France will soon see republican senators, comparable to those of the senates of Geneva, Venice, or Berne, and the king will become hardly more than a doge."

Gently Louis replied: "My brother, we are as yet too young to trust much to our own judgment, and therefore should lean upon the wisdom and experience of others."

Maurepas had the final word. He argued persuasively that it was no longer a question of whether His Majesty did or did not like the Parlements, but whether he could afford to antagonize the nation. Louis was at the beginning of his reign, Maurepas said, and dared not sow "seeds of discontent." "Without Parlement," the old minister repeated, "no monarchy." Whether motivated by fear or apathy or desire for popularity, or even all together,[2] Louis yielded to Maurepas. In November, 1774, Louis XVI recalled the magistrates whom Louis XV had exiled as rebels. The exultant nation had won the first round with the crown.

To staunch monarchists the splendid *Lit de Justice* which the king held in order formally to reinstate the justices was a mockery. They were all there for the "Bed of Justice," the noblest and the highest of the realm, resplendent in their garments and bitter in their hearts. It was evident that the monarchy had given itself a blow, even though Louis assumed a severe tone in addressing the magistrates. "I recall you to-day to your functions; appreciate my goodness, and do not ever forget it.... Do not occupy yourselves with anything but the response to my wishes."

There was a faint trace of mockery in the reply of d'Aligre, the president of the pardoned Parlement: "The reign of Your Majesty will be in the annals of history a lesson for posterity..., an epoch of glory...."

Throughout France the upholders of absolute monarchy were anxiously wondering whither their king was leading them. They circulated a pamphlet which asked some pointed and unanswerable questions:

2 Contemporaries speculated on the causes for Louis' action—it seemed so incomprehensible and contrary to monarchical self-interest. Ambassador Stormont wrote to London: "I am still inclined to think that the principal, if not only Motives, were M. de Maurepas' old and hereditary Partiality to the Parliament, the desire of destroying at once all the latent Seeds of National Discontent, and of distinguishing the young King's Reign by an Act which carried the appearance of great Goodness and Moderation, and was sure to be attended with the popularity of which His Majesty seems very ambitious. Your Lordship well knows that all Countries, and all Ages, afford numerous Instances of essential Interests sacrificed to momentary Applause." Stormont to Rochford, 16 November, 1774; Public Record Office, SP 78.

Will the nation not be right in believing that it ought to obey the Parlement rather than the king?

The Parlement once restored, will the king be master in France?

The Parlement, may it not do everything against the king?

The king, can he do anything against the Parlement?

If there is no answer to these questions, is it not clear that we shall have a Parlement but no king? [3]

⚜

IN THE FIELD of economic legislation trouble was piling up high. The king had accepted Turgot's three-point program—"no bankruptcy, no increase in taxation, no loans"—and stood by his minister loyally; but there was no feeling of sympathy between the two. King and minister stood so far apart that their very coöperation of the moment was an act of arbitrariness.

The reforming economist minced no words when he told His Majesty that he despised the whole royal tradition. "The traditions of the past have often been the worst guides for princes . . . ; the experience of the past has never been indispensable, and the barbarous centuries should not serve as a rule for the needs of the present." What mattered to Turgot was efficiency based upon ability and not birth: he implied that absolute monarchy was outworn.

Louis was not shocked. "One has no need to be a scholar," he replied, "to understand that M. Turgot tends toward nothing less than the overthrow of the whole monarchy." He defended warmly the monarchical system, which he considered best for man and ordained for that purpose by God. His conception of the monarch was, in general, that of a benevolent father who does what he can for his children and is always just and kind to them, even when provoked. To Louis no other system of government was conceivable. In his argument with Turgot he asked jestingly if the minister thought that the period of Richelieu and Louis XIV was barbarous. "Turgot's system," Louis concluded, "is a fine

[3] The pamphlet is in the Bibliothèque Nationale, MS n.a.Fr. 6967, p.241.

dream. It is another one of those utopias which comes from a man with good views but which would overthrow the present state. M. Turgot's ideas," he added as an afterthought, "are extremely dangerous."

Louis was convinced that his minister's ideas were dangerous, but he nevertheless permitted him to experiment—for that was what it amounted to—with economic legislation novel and drastic. Either the king did not see the implication of Turgot's economic regulations or he thought them beneficial, which was likely; but whatever the reason, he approved Turgot's revolutionary decree establishing free trade in grain. This decree, a classic expression of *laissez faire* dear to Turgot, was designed to ameliorate a famine situation (due to a bad harvest), but the consequences were not those the minister had expected. The abolition of grain restrictions deprived thousands of municipal and provincial customs officials of their revenue, and they formed a powerful army of enemies determined to sabotage the acts, and thereby destroy the prestige of the radical comptroller-general. Curiously enough, the poor people also turned against the minister, for the price of bread went up—always a portent of trouble in France—because rich speculators cornered the now free grain market and created a lucrative monopoly. Neither Turgot nor Louis was at fault, but almost universal blame fell on the comptroller-general, who kept on adding to his growing legion of enemies by abolishing such medieval dues as the *corvée* (which deprived nobles of free labor), limiting the powers of the ancient guilds (which angered the skilled craftsmen), and sharply restricting the expenditures of the court (which aroused the fury of the courtiers). As Emperor Joseph II said, it was impossible to do anything serious in France without causing everybody to "combine to prevent it, because every one hopes to derive advantages for himself." Within a few months, Turgot, the sincere reformer, was the best-hated man in the realm, and much of the hostility was secretly aimed also at the king.

⚜

Reaction to Turgot's reforms came with frightening rapidity. In the spring of 1775 there occurred a strange shortage of grain in the *halles* of the big cities and phenomenal pillaging in the country. Bands of well organized men suddenly fell upon bakeries, sacked mills, plundered river vessels carrying flour to market. The outburst resembled a forest fire in unexpectedness and rapidity.

Versailles was in panic. Courtiers openly accused Turgot of having aroused the temper of the canaille by his reforms, and Maurepas, who in the seventy-four years of his life had never witnessed even a minor revolt, lost his head altogether. Louis, too, was alarmed. Only Turgot kept cool. He explained to His Majesty that the riots were not spontaneous but incited by enemies of the crown, and that it was necessary to remain firm and hang the ringleaders. Louis was impressed by such decisiveness and promised his loyal coöperation. "Such crimes," he wrote to Marshal Biron, the commander of the troops in Paris, "should be repressed, checked, and quickly punished."

Turgot acted energetically. He strengthened the police, called out the gendarmes, and mobilized the army; to every trouble-center he sent detachments of regular troops. He himself went to Paris and kept in hourly touch with the king at Versailles. Louis was very much excited, but remained firm. He directed activities exactly as Turgot had told him.

> I have just received your letter [Louis hurriedly wrote to Turgot in Paris], Versailles is attacked. . . . I am going to confer with Marshal du Muy. . . . Count on my firmness. I am going to order the guard to the market-place. I am very much satisfied with the precautions you have taken. . . . You will do well to arrest the persons about whom you have spoken to me; but, above all, when they are held, no hasty action. . . .

Two hours later Louis wrote to Turgot again:

> The musketeers have received instructions to keep ready in Paris. . . . The Intendant told me that he has no fears for the Upper-Seine and the Marne. . . . As for Versailles, we are entirely peaceful. . . . M. de Beauveau has questioned the rioters; most of

ANNE ROBERT JACQUES TURGOT

By J. A. Houdon. Boston Museum of Fine Arts.

LAMOIGNON DE MALESHERBES

By J. A. Houdon. Louvre.

them said that they had no bread, that they had come to get it, and showed pieces of barley bread which was very inferior. . . . The markets were ordered open and everything came off well. Things were bought and sold as if nothing had happened. Then the rebels left. . . . I am not going out to-day, not out of fear but in order to keep everybody tranquil.

In Paris the police were probably unable and perhaps unwilling to prevent disorders, and Turgot, outraged at the violence which threatened his whole legislative program and which he considered a personal insult, ordered Biron's troops to use their guns. There was shooting and clubbing, and two of the ringleaders were promptly hanged. Such severity against hungry people, exercised by a statesman of known liberal principles, left a painful impression on the nation. Even Marshal Biron, who had only obeyed orders, was under stigma, contemptuously dubbed *General Wheat*.[4]

To Louis the repressive measures of his minister were extremely distasteful. He had been brought up to consider himself the father of his people, and a parent does not shoot his children, even guilty offspring, with a clear conscience. What upset him most of all was the fear of having been unjust. Perhaps the rioters were hungry, after all! Turgot, however, convinced the king that such was not the case, that far from being an outbreak of hungry people, the riots were due to a remarkable plot to overthrow the government.

The plot theory was not altogether spurious. Large sums of money, Turgot explained, were found on the arrested leaders. Where, the comptroller-general asked, did poor people get so much money, and if they had money, why did they break into food shops to obtain bread? Moreover, some of these men carried royal patents and wore royal orders to

[4] *Général Farine* was the title of a sarcastic song against Biron:

Biron, tes glorieux travaux
En dépit des cabales,
Te font passer pour un heros
Sous les piliers des halles.

De rue en rue, au petit trot
Tu chasse la famine;
Général, digne de Turgot,
Tu n'es qu'un Jean-Farine.

convince the people that they spoke in the name of the king. Who, Turgot wanted to know, was behind them?

Furthermore, although for days the capital seethed with rumors of revolt, only two priests had urged their flocks to remain peaceful and orderly; the rest, including the archbishop of Paris, gave no sign of life. And, most unusual of all, ecclesiastical property and church granaries were not touched by the rioters. That looked very much like a clerical conspiracy.

Finally, the police everywhere were strangely inactive. Turgot knew the reason. The edict establishing free trade in grain had deprived the police officials of their income as supervisors of the markets. In their resentment they did nothing to prevent disorders. They actually may have provoked them. And, Turgot explained to a bewildered Louis, all the enemies of His Majesty who hated reform—rich monopolists and profiteers—combined with the police to undermine the government.

In these circumstances it was dangerous to be lenient. His Majesty, Turgot argued, must assert his authority or lose prestige. Louis quietly agreed. Le Noir, the lieutenant of police of Paris, was summarily dismissed. Commander Biron was instructed to "repel force with force" if troubles should start again. But the price of bread continued to rise, and here and there sporadic outbursts of violence occurred; at Château-Thierry the green wheat-fields were cut down and trampled. Turgot, secretly worried, told Louis to keep calm.

CHAPTER VIII

"Crown you yourself this king..."

THERE WERE other things to worry about. For months the court had been preparing for the coronation ceremony at Rheims, as law and custom required, but the Bread Riots disturbed public tranquillity and frightened the government. Was this a time to flaunt a gorgeous spectacle in the face of a nation threatened with a food-shortage? Would not the colossal cost of the ceremony outrage public sentiment? Timid folk like Maurepas urged the king to postpone the coronation, and Louis, no hero, nodded agreement. But Marie Antoinette protested. What! the haughty young Habsburg asked angrily, would a king of France show fear before a craven mob? "Such petty fear," she exclaimed, "would make us the laughing-stock of Europe."

Louis sympathized with the queen's point of view, but his conscience troubled him. He told his wife that he doubted whether the treasury could afford the cost of a coronation. The queen summoned Turgot, and for once the comptroller-general showed himself a diplomat. He agreed that for the prestige of the monarchy it was important that the coronation take place on the scheduled date, and ventured a mildly humorous remark: "Although it is always a pleasure for a comptroller-general to postpone spending money, this matter is so important the money will be found at any cost."

Louis was not happy at the prospect of spending millions

on a ceremony for himself when hundreds of victims of the recent riots cried for help.

> I feel [he wrote to the minister of the royal household] that the unfortunates who have been pillaged have the right to be at least relieved. . . . All this will cost lots of money, and more than ever it will be necessary to economize. . . . One must, if it is possible, reduce the cost of my coronation; I also want to retrench on the projected celebrations. . . . You will also inform the Provost of the Merchants of Paris that I want no festivities there and that the money rather be spent to relieve the poor.

The burden of scraping together the necessary funds—for the reparation of the roads to Rheims, for transportation, housing, medals, gifts, charities, robes—fell on the harassed Turgot. Louis, despite good intentions, was too vacillating and indecisive to be helpful. This was a Church-*cum*-state occasion designed scrupulously so as to please at once God, the courtiers, and the nation, and the king was in no position to play the miser. He always found it difficult to say *No* to anybody, especially to those who surrounded him. When high functionaries appealed to him to pay their traveling expenses to Rheims—carriages rented for as high as thirty-three livres a day—he did not have the heart to refuse. He also permitted his brothers to go to Rheims with a suite of forty-two persons, which in itself cost a small fortune. Every one took advantage of his weakness. The patient Turgot, troubled by intrigues and racked by the gout, made vindictive enemies but managed to keep the expenses down to about one million livres.[1]

EARLY in June, 1775, while bands of marauders roamed the countryside and broke into granaries, Louis set out for Rheims to be crowned as his ancestors had been for centuries. To his

[1] Some of the expenditures included:

Robes for the king, princes, and peers..........	148,183	livres
Church vestments and medallions..............	159,692	"
Gifts and medals..............................	134,654	"
Repairs, construction, etc.......................	249,122	"
Carriages	54,196	"
Lighting, music, ceremonials....................	24,962	"

delight he was everywhere received with spontaneous demonstrations of affection. From far and near thousands upon thousands of humble and hopeful folk had come and lined the highway to catch a glimpse of their good young sovereign, to wish him happiness and prosperity. Louis was happy to observe that the Bread Riots were not a spontaneous outbreak of the people but, as Turgot had told him, the work of a handful of agitators. Marie Antoinette was likewise pleasantly surprised.

> It is astonishing and at the same time fortunate [she generalized in a letter to her mother] to be so well received two months after the revolt and despite the high price of bread, which unfortunately still prevails. It is a surprising aspect of the French character to let itself be carried away by bad influences and then to return immediately to the good.

AT THE GREAT DOORS of the Gothic cathedral, packed inside with the élite of France (twenty-two dukes, nine princes, eleven marshals, ten archbishops, twenty bishops), His Very Christian Majesty was received by the master of the sacred ceremony, the second hero of the day, Charles Antoine de la Roche-Aymon, cardinal and archbishop of Rheims. Before this proud man of God the king of France fell on his knees and bowed his head. When the humble monarch rose, the cardinal pronounced a speech of welcome in which he reminded the king that the mitre was older than the crown.

The king, seemingly taller than usual in his red-heeled violet-satin boots, gravely entered the cathedral and received a thunderous ovation from the nobles and clergy of the realm. Even the staid bishops applauded, a liberty which they permitted themselves also when Marie Antoinette walked in among the guests (the king only, and not the queen, was being crowned). The tension was high, and at the sight of the earnest boy in his violet lily-embroidered cloak of majesty, and the slender young woman so pale and lovely in her silks, many prelates burst into tears.

The choir sang: "O God, who knowest that the human species cannot subsist by its own virtues, accord thy succour to Louis thy servant whom thou hast put at the head of thy people in order that he may himself aid and protect those who are subject to him."

Louis knelt on a velvet cushion at the feet of the Cardinal de la Roche-Aymon, who sat upon the throne. Perspiration poured down the king's cheeks, for the dazzling coronation vestments were heavy. Underneath the violet-velvet cloak with its cape of ermine he wore a satin *dalmatique* and underneath that a satin *camisole*—all air-tight; the garments were decorated with golden fleurs-de-lis and lined with silks and hung with tassels. The air in the cathedral was stifling. In a daze the kneeling king looked up at the coronation ornaments and was glad that he did not have to carry them all the time. It would soon be uncomfortable enough to have the *couronne de Charlemagne* on his head. He saw the golden sword of Charlemagne, the violet belt, the golden scepter (five feet ten inches long), the gold-ivory Hand of Justice, the golden *agrafe* that looked like a fleur-de-lis, and his shoulders drooped in anticipation of the burden.

The cathedral was very still, and one was conscious only of the flicker of the candles. The cardinal-archbishop raised his hand and slowly lowered it; his right thumb touched the holy balsam in a golden paten. With the holy balsam he made the sign of the cross on the king's head and said: *Ungo te in regem de oleo sanctificato, in nomine patris, et filii, et spiritus sancti.*

Amen, every voice rang out.

And the sign of the cross on the chest.

Amen.

And between the shoulders, and on the right arm, and on the left arm.

Amen.

The choir sang the anthem: "The priest Sadoch and the prophet Nathan crowned Solomon in Zion, and approaching him, they said to him with joy: Long live the king unto eternity!"

Amen.

The cardinal-archbishop lifted high the crown of Charlemagne so that the rubies, sapphires, emeralds, caught the candle-light in a cascade of rays, gently put it on the king's bowed head, and then sat down on his episcopal throne. On his knees the crowned king began to pray:

"O Christ, crown you yourself this king..."

On the day following the coronation the king went to the park of the abbey, showed himself to the people, and touched hundreds of scrofulous patients. Afterwards he pardoned seventy-nine prisoners in the local jail.

CHAPTER IX

"Only Turgot and I love the people"

THE BREAD RIOTS having failed to dislodge the comptroller-general because of the king's loyal support, Turgot's enemies joined forces and lined up behind the queen, who was cynically selected as a battering-ram. King and minister soon faced a formidable coalition, composed of the courtiers who feared a slash in expenditures, high functionaries who saw themselves threatened in their extralegal incomes, tax-farmers who profited from a corrupt administration, and financiers who disliked the radical minister's budgetary reforms. Such a combination of powers had more than once broken a powerful minister.

The first sharp clash in which Marie Antoinette figured prominently—she had hitherto remained in the background, as Mercy advised her, on account of Louis' pronounced hostility to female meddling—was over the appointment of a minister of the royal household (practically a minister of the interior). Since this official was in charge of the king's purse, Turgot considered it essential for his reforms to appoint one whom he could absolutely trust, and he proposed Councillor Lamoignon de Malesherbes, president of the *Cour des Aides* attached to the Parlement of Paris. Louis did not know Malesherbes, but he had heard of him as a man of unimpeachable integrity, and he eagerly offered him the office. To the king's surprise, the philosophical councilor smilingly refused a post which he frankly considered much too dirty for an honest man.

At this point—and for the first time—Marie Antoinette intervened. She wanted the ministry of the royal household to go to her henchman Sartine, whom Turgot regarded as an avowed enemy. The queen summoned Maurepas and told him imperiously—*"je désire et exige"*—that Sartine must have the job. Maurepas stammered that he was helpless, that His Majesty had some one else in mind, and Marie Antoinette walked out in a huff, muttering veiled threats. The perturbed old minister hurried over to Turgot and told him that neither of them could afford to antagonize the queen, for Louis was took weak to be relied on for any length of time.

Turgot decided upon a strange move. He invited Ambassador Mercy to dinner and frankly told him what was taking place in the *coulisses.* Without an honest and loyal minister in the royal household, Turgot added, he would be unable to carry through his program, and Sartine, whom the queen proposed, was hostile to reforms. It was extremely regrettable, the forthright minister concluded, that Her Majesty should interfere in politics, which were no concern of hers.

Mercy was embarrassed. He was a foreigner and a gentleman and knew well that the queen, also a foreigner, was doing things that might become dangerous. He said cautiously that as a foreign diplomat he could not advise a minister of the crown what to do, but in his opinion it was expedient to try to win Her Majesty's confidence.

Turgot returned to Versailles and told Louis to try Malesherbes again, and the king wrote the councilor a letter in which he practically begged him to become his minister, even if only for a short while. "I believe that your acceptance is absolutely necessary for the good of the state." Despite his better judgment, Malesherbes accepted the position provisionally, for six months, in order to help his friend Turgot. When Marie Antoinette heard of it, she stormed into the king's cabinet and upbraided him hotly. Louis listened, silent and awkward as usual. As a "compensation" she demanded that Sartine be given a seat in the Council of State. Louis hastily acquiesced.

But Marie Antoinette never forgave Turgot.

THE COURT laughed at the rotund Lamoignon de Malesherbes with his black gown and magisterial wig. He was so funny, the round, chubby little jurist with his merry smile, that the hostile queen melted and laughed, the courtiers laughed, even the king laughed. Malesherbes, too, grinned, for he loved a joke and relished laughter even if he had to produce it by occasionally putting a piece of burning paper under the nose of a sleeping person. He was famous for his *camouflets.* On the bench he once brusquely interrupted a garrulous lawyer: "Morbleu, Maître, when are you going to stop boring us?"

A friend of the Encyclopædists, a skeptic, a scholar, full of eighteenth-century virtues, Malesherbes did not like the job his friend Turgot had thrust upon him. He soon found that his doubts were justified, for the courtiers among whom he was to work were not only dishonest but devoid of brains, too lazy to work and too cynical to serve. But he had promised to stick to the job for six months, and he did so with high good humor, despite a multitude of vexations. To please the king, for whom he developed a genuine affection which was to last throughout Louis' life, the skeptical minister even went to mass. But, good philosopher that he was, the conviction grew upon him that he and Turgot were wasting their time. When Mercy asked him how the ministry was getting on, he replied jestingly, "Maurepas does nothing, Turgot doubts nothing, I doubt everything."

LOUIS liked his two talented ministers and signed the decrees they submitted, including such acts as the freeing of many prisoners in the Bastille, amelioration of the treatment of prison inmates, and the abolition of the penal regulations against the Huguenots. But the king, as Maurepas had warned Turgot, did not possess the strength of character to resist the intrigues of the court, and the violently unpopular comptroller-general did nothing to help the situation. Instead of placating opponents and winning adherents, the inflexible minister pursued his straight path of economic legislation and financial economizing, paying attention to neither imprecations from the Right nor the curses from the Left (the price of bread being still high). He made enemies by the hundred, not wilfully but thoughtlessly.

To speculate on historic alternatives is an idle game. Could a Turgot have saved the French monarchy, and the head of Louis XVI, had he been given a chance to carry through all his reforms? Had Louis XVI continued to support Turgot, would the French Revolution have been avoided? Did Turgot have the necessary talents to reform the state? Was his program just the thing the nation needed? Affirmative answers would be as dogmatic as negative ones; but it is possible to assert in general terms that there are good and bad ways of doing things, right techniques and wrong ones—whatever the ultimate consequences. And Turgot rarely solved a problem (even when he had the right answer) in the right way. This is particularly injurious in the realm of politics, where, in the absence of certitude, the correct evaluation of imponderables is essential and the careful handling of human beings (even as "forces") not only necessary but an end in itself. Turgot always dealt with timeless principles, rarely with mortal men.

A smile here, a favor there—even at the expense of a cherished principle—and Turgot could have made loyal friends and collaborators; but he was incapable of compromise, even for a kingdom. Nobody appreciated inflexible virtue which paraded a bit too self-righteously. Stormy scenes took place in the minister's cabinet, but, instead of warning, they only strengthened the comptroller-general's obstinacy. One day came Louise Julie Constance Yvonne Bretagne de Rohan-Guéménée, Duchesse d'Elbeuf, Comtesse de Brionne, and petitioned for a continuation of her pension. Probably the pension was not deserved, but it was a small matter compared with the value of such friendship as the influential duchess had to give. What did Turgot do? He ignored the obstinate reality that in feudal France a Rohan was close to the angels and a Rohan-Guéménée next to God, and turned down the petition with a sneer: "Know, Madame, that the rule of females has passed." Rohan-Guéménée drew herself up in all the pride of twenty generations of blue blood and snapped: "Yes, Monsieur, but not that of impertinents." A legion of insulted Rohans and Guéménées and Elbeufs and their relatives sharpened their knives.

No doubt Louis should have shielded Turgot from the venom of the court, but the king's intentions were stronger than his will. Psychologically it was difficult for him to identify himself with the minister against the court, for the court was always around the monarch and the minister only a few minutes daily. Nor was Louis proof against ridicule. The queen and her feline friends took every occasion to mock the stiff and puritanic comptroller-general, who, to be sure, was devoid of humor. Willy-nilly Louis occasionally joined in the laughter against Turgot. Once, when Turgot refused to grant a pension of six thousand livres to Duchesse Jules de Polignac, the queen's favorite, the outraged lady wrote him a sarcastic letter which she first showed to Maurepas. "If you are ever dissatisfied with me," the malicious old man told her, "I wish that you would rather slap my face than write me such a letter. But it would be nice to amuse the king with it. Show it to the queen." Marie Antoinette laughed uproariously at Polignac's gibes, and Louis joined her. A king with character, it goes without saying, would have sent these meddling females to the kitchen. "My darling," Marie Antoinette said to her *amie,* "you shouldn't post this letter; I will write another one for you." And while Louis guffawed, the queen composed one even more biting which her friend copied and sent to Turgot.

The comptroller-general did not laugh. Not merely because the letter was not funny, but because the prevailing conditions did not encourage laughter. Everything was going wrong: the treasury was losing money on Turgot's experiment in public transportation, designed not merely to reduce fares but also to increase efficiency; the price of bread continued to climb; speculators were hoarding grain; the ministers and high officials were sabotaging the government. Even Maurepas was beginning to grumble against his colleague, who antagonized everybody. Turgot, worn out and ailing, put his hopes in the king.

A CHANGE came gradually over Louis himself. In the first flush of kingship he had worked ten to twelve hours a day, but after the novelty and the fear of responsibility had worn off, he began to shirk his job and devote more time to the chase than to business. The change may well have been physiological for already Louis was growing excessively heavy. Almost noticeably a strange sluggishness was conquering him, and although his intentions were still good, every decision cost him an effort. And Turgot, a relentless worker, was making life difficult for himself and the king. It required more energy than Louis was able or willing to exert to ward off the blows that were continually falling upon the comptroller-general. "You at least," the king said wearily to Malesherbes, "have no enemies like your friend Turgot." The minister of the royal household replied jestingly that if he fulfilled his position as well as Turgot did his, he too would have a host of enemies. "Then," Louis said, "you would be like the comptroller-general, who can never be liked."

What Louis should have said, had he realized the seriousness of the conflict, was that *no* honest comptroller-general could ever be liked by the court. Between a minister of finance and a royal court there was bound to be unremitting war, for the duty of the former was to economize so as to avoid state bankruptcy, and the function of the latter was to spend in order to give glamour to the crown. Turgot was worrying himself into ill-health thinking up ways and means of reducing expenditures, especially those of the royal household, which reached the colossal sum of thirty-six million livres a year—about one-sixth of the national budget.[1] In the meantime Marie Antoinette, with that recklessness which aroused all France against her, did everything to make Turgot's life miserable by squandering money as if there were no limits to her husband's resources. That Louis did not discourage her may have been due to his feeling of guilt at having failed in his marital duties: it was a way of placating the furies. And Marie Antoinette, who was essentially a decent woman, thoughtlessly surrounded herself with a gang of idlers and gamblers whose greed knew no bounds.

Paradoxically enough, it was precisely during the ministry of the economizing Turgot that Marie Antoinette developed her most extravagant habits and gave her most magnificent balls. In the *Journal* of Papillon de la Ferté, the intendant in charge of royal amusements, one reads of balls given by the queen (Louis hardly ever participated) every two weeks in which the gilded plumes alone cost a fortune. "These days," Papillon writes under the date of March 25, 1775, "I have been going over the accounts of the queen's balls. I am much grieved at this expenditure [for the month] which exceeds 100,000 livres, because of the quantity of gold embroidery which was used for the gowns and the quadrilles."

In the eyes of Marie Antoinette and her friends of dubious reputation—Louis despised most of them—the realm of France was a special preserve set aside by a generous Providence to produce wealth for the amusement of the elect. All she had to do was to scribble her name on a scrap of paper and lo! . . . the gold flowed. Turgot winced at these slips of paper, the pile of which grew higher and higher, each almost

[1] The expenditures for the year 1776 amounted to 214,001,233 livres. Of this sum, approximately 36,000,000 livres went to the support of the court, 5,703,300 to buildings, 16,498,411 to the sinking fund, and 61,221,456 to the army and navy. The armed forces (including pensions) thus consumed a little under one-third of the budget. From the account in the Bibliothèque Nationale, MS n.a.Fr.21206, 1-4.

like a personal blow. For the comptroller-general, who had no respect for divine-right monarchy, was primarily a patriot, a servant of France and not of the throne; and he saw no justification for a foreign girl's extravagance at the expense of French working people. Marie Antoinette, for her part, tried in every way to show that she did not approve her husband's sou-pinching minister, but her ordinary weapons were ineffective against Turgot. At one reception she hoped to crush him by receiving him in icy silence, but he was so unsusceptible to girlish whims that he could not differentiate between a frigid reception and a hearty one, and told friends afterwards that the queen had been pleasant as usual!

THE COURT was an octopus whose tentacles could not be broken.[2] Malesherbes was the first to give up. Although he was sorry for the well-intentioned king, the ex-councilor of Paris told His Majesty that it was impossible for him, a mere lawyer and scholar, to cope with intrigantes, wastrels, and obstructionists. And anyhow, Malesherbes said with appalling irony, he was losing prestige among his fellow-jurists for being a minister of the crown. Louis did not feel the awful sting of those words, for he could not imagine with what contempt French intellectuals and educated bourgeois viewed the political system of which he was head. So deep had the monarchy fallen that a judge was apologetic for being a minister! Louis begged him to reconsider. "Your obstinacy, my dear Malesherbes," he said pathetically, "distresses me. Sully never quitted Henry IV when that prince needed his lights. You

[2] The court was composed of about 886 officials and servants whose wages ranged from 300 to 4,000 livres a year (excluding board). There were: 15 gentlemen-in-waiting, 7 bookkeepers and secretaries, 6 chaplains, 1 reader, 8 doctors, 8 ushers, 8 chambermaids, 2 maîtres d'hotel, 48 kitchen workers (4 cooks, 8 bakers, etc.), 7 yard workers, 29 valets, 2 couriers, 3 sedan-chair carriers, 14 Swiss, 7 servants for the pages, 4 riding-masters, 9 coachmen, 22 postillions, 20 stablemen, 4 heyducs, 47 musicians (29 singers, 6 violinists, 2 flutists, 2 cellists, 2 bassists, 5 trumpeters, 1 instrument carrier), 8 architects, 11 gardeners, 10 gentlemen-cadets with 23 servants, 30 bodyguards, 56 hunting staff. Each member of the royal family also had his small court. Bibliothèque Nationale, MS n.a.Fr.21206.

are, if you will permit me to say so, somewhat egoistic in your virtue."

Turgot was left alone now, unsupported in the ministry and less and less protected by the king, for Louis too grew discouraged. "Turgot," the Swedish envoy de Creutz wrote, "finds himself the butt of a most formidable coalition composed of all the grandees of the realm, all the Parlements, all the financiers, all the women of the court and all the zealots." The comptroller-general made a determined effort to warn the young king against the "disastrous consequences" of permitting an unscrupulous court to seize the important posts in the government. But Louis, agreeing with the minister in his heart but not having the strength to carry on the fight, kept guiltily silent. Stiff and pale after the interview, Turgot went home and wrote the king a letter brutal in its frankness:

> Sire, I do not wish to dissimulate to Your Majesty how profoundly hurt I have been at the cruel silence with which you listened to me last Sunday, after I have pointed out to you in detail . . . my position, your own, the dangers facing your authority . . . , the impossibility of my continuing to serve you if you do not aid me. You have not deigned to reply. I cannot believe, Sire, that you would light-heartedly consent to sacrifice your reign and the welfare of your people.

Then Turgot warned the king that, surrounded as he was by dishonest men and intrigants, he was standing before a precipice:

> You lack experience, Sire; I know that at twenty-two and in your position you do not have the resources which the habit of living among equals gives to individuals to judge men, but will you have more experience in eight days, in one month . . . ? You have no personal experience, but to realize the dangers of your position, do you not have the recent experience of your grandfather?
>
> I have painted to you all the evils which have been caused by the weakness of the late King. I have traced the course of the intrigues which gradually degraded his authority. I dare to beg

you to reread that letter and to ask you if you want to run the risk of the same dangers, I should say even greater dangers. . . .

Never forget, Sire, that it was weakness that put the head of Charles I on the block. . . .

You are considered weak, Sire. . . .

Louis winced at the letter, reread it, then sealed it and put it carefully away—too ashamed to show it to anybody. He refused, or was afraid, to see his comptroller-general, who—curious man that he was!—did not believe that Louis could turn against an honest minister. But Turgot counted without that intransigence of a weak man which always has a quality all its own. Louis was not simply obstinate, he was guiltily obstinate, a coward made by his conscience. The royal door was brutally, repeatedly shut in Turgot's austere face. And the comptroller-general refused to resign, despite studied insults. "What do you want?" Louis said harshly to Turgot, who was waiting patiently in the anteroom. "I have no time to talk to you." The minister considered his work for France too important for personal offense, and he came back again and again, several times in the same day. Finally the doorman refused to let him in.

On the morning of May 12, 1776, the king's secretary arrived at Turgot's apartments with a royal order demanding his resignation. Turgot canceled his dinner invitations for that night and immediately began to pack. "I have nothing more to do in Versailles."

⚜

THE COURT was jubilant, not only because it had rid itself of a dangerous enemy, but mainly because the queen had won an important victory. Every one was convinced that the dismissal of Turgot was Marie Antoinette's first great political triumph. It was also her husband's greatest defeat, in more ways than one. Subtly she had poisoned Louis' and Maurepas' minds against the comptroller-general, and now she reaped the reward in redoubled adulation on the part of the courtiers, who said that the queen had the power henceforth to "remove any one who displeases her." Louis sulked in his cabinet, beaten and unhappy. "Only Turgot and I love the people," he murmured.

IN THIS the third year of his reign, Louis XVI was left without a competent minister and without a program. Governmental corruption reappeared, the grain edicts were not enforced, the tax burden was not lightened. Like a rubber band, conditions snapped back to "normal," and the twenty-two year old king, who had started out with glowing hopes of reform, let the ancient Maurepas persuade him that the best policy was to do nothing. The seventy-five year old minister, now that Turgot was gone, became the real ruler of France (subject to the queen's whims), and his attitude is revealed in an anecdote which has a flavor all its own.

The Duke of Manchester was at a reception given by Maurepas and observed a youth to whom everybody paid court.

"Who is that?"

"It is the king, my lord," Maurepas replied seriously.

"Why this sarcasm?" his lordship asked in a hurt tone.

"My lord," Maurepas replied, "I never use sarcasm. I tell you again he is the king. I see that you need proof, and here goes. He sleeps with a cousin of mine, Madame de Montbarey, who rules Madame de Maurepas; the latter does with me as she pleases, I lead the king, so you see that gentleman reigns."

A MAN named Clugny was appointed to take Turgot's place, and everybody at court was happy, for Maurepas' underling did not have a reputation for virtue. He opened the sluices of the treasury.

Clugny died five months after he took office, and Maurepas picked a burly, heavy-featured Swiss banker named Jacques Necker as director-general of finances. He was, as Madame d'Oberkirch wrote, a "true bourgeois from Geneva," stiff, pedantic, and disagreeable. His wife was a lean, cadaverous, learned female, dominated by one demoniac idea—the success of Monsieur Necker. The task of the Protestant banker was to shepherd the straying French finances.

> Here [a lady in Versailles wrote candidly to a friend] everything goes as it pleases God; common sense, right reason, the welfare of the public and the individual are unknown.... A king who means well but has neither the force nor the light to achieve it; a minister [Maurepas] who was frivolous and feeble at forty and whom old age has enervated even more, and who does the strangest things and mocks at public opinion; a St. Germain [3] who has upset everything ... ; Vergennes, who is a worthy man, whom I like but whose feeble and timid character cannot resist Maurepas; Sartine whom I still like but who, though minister of the navy, does not know a ship.... That's where we are. The queen goes ceaselessly to Paris, to the opera and the comedy, makes debts ..., wears plumes and topknots, and ridicules everything.

[3] Count Charles Louis de St. Germain, appointed by Turgot minister of war in December, 1775, was another drastic reformer whose activities antagonized as many people as did those of Turgot. St. Germain was an old soldier, trained in the harsh Prussian military school under Frederick the Great, and he tried to introduce Teutonic methods and tactics into the French army. He abolished the privileged corps, suppressed the aristocratic military schools, tightened discipline, introduced economies into a notoriously wasteful army administration. But he caused almost a revolution when he ordered soldiers to be flogged as a disciplinary measure. The French were outraged at such Prussian brutality, and in September, 1777, St. Germain was forced out of office—the last of the reform ministers.

CHAPTER X

"Louis XVI was not impotent: a stammerer is not a mute"

Maurepas was impotent,
The king made him omnipotent;
The grateful minister said, Sire,
All that I can possibly desire
Is to do the same for you.

CENTURIES of inoculated respect for the crown prevented the French conscience from criticizing the king; but there was no divinity that hedged a queen, and public opinion veered sharply against Marie Antoinette. She was an ideal scapegoat, a convenient object of accumulated hostilities. In every possible way she outraged the French: she was as extravagant as an oriental despot, a foreigner who associated with people of no character, the wife of a faithful husband whom she henpecked. Thrifty bourgeois resented her gambling, devout women suspected her piety, submissive husbands hated her domineering habits. Everybody, in short, had a grievance against the queen, particularly since she was unable to fulfil her function in life by providing the French monarchy with heirs.

That, indeed, was a national scandal and a continued domestic tragedy. Years passed and there was no dauphin. Louis spent hours on horseback, shooting deer and boar;

Marie Antoinette, starved for masculine love, read trashy or pornographic romances and developed passionate friendships for women. In moments of exasperation she referred to her husband as *un homme de bois.*

Marie Antoinette got into the habit of joking at her husband's expense, and the court was encouraged covertly to sneer at the king's impotence, although he was really vigorous and sound.[1] "My tastes," the queen joked in a letter to an Austrian courtier, "are not those of the king, who loves nothing but the chase and mechanical labor. You must admit that I would not look attractive near a forge. I would not like to be Vulcan, and the rôle of Venus would displease him much more than my present tastes, which he does not disapprove." There was an evident bitterness underlying the witticism, and though it may have been justified privately, nothing was served by laundering unclean linen in public. Courtiers enlarged upon the queen's *bons mots,* which were considered good enough to make the rounds of Europe. Marie Antoinette's recklessness, more in word than in deed to be sure, alarmed her mother in Vienna. One letter that Maria Theresa wrote to her daughter was a veritable whiplash, and for over a century and a half the Austrian archives refused permission to publish it.[2]

1 Ambassador Aranda to the king of Spain: "Quien dice que el frenillo sujeta tanto el prepucio que no cede a la introduccion y causa un dolor vivo en el, por el qual se retrahe S.M. del impulso que conviniera. Quien supone que el dicho prepucio esta tan cerrado que no puede explayarse para la dilatacion de la punta o cabeza de la parte, en virtud de lo que no llegua la ereccion al punto de elasticidad necessaria.

"Si fuera lo primero, a muchos ha sucedido lo mismo y aun acaece regularmente en los primaros ensayos; pero como suelen estar con mejores ganas de las que tendra S.M. por su temperamento o inocencia, con el acaloramiento, un quejido y una buena resolucion se rasga el frenillo del todo o lo que basta para la continuacion del uso, que insensiblemente despues deja corriente el acto; pero quando son timidos, entra el cirujano con una pequena incision y liberta del inconveniente.

"Si fuera lo segundo, seria operacion mas dolorosa y grave en su edad, por que exige una especie de circumcision, pues sino se redondease el corte de los labios, quedarian imposibilitando el uso."

2 The Vienna copy is the only one known; Marie Antoinette seems to have destroyed the original. It was written on July 30, 1775.

MADAME MY DEAR DAUGHTER:

I cannot dissimulate that a letter which you wrote to Rosenberg has thrown me into the greatest consternation. What a style! What frivolousness! Where is the heart so good, so generous of that archduchess Antoinette? I see nothing but intrigue, low hate, a spirit of persecution, persiflage; intrigue like a Pompadour or like a Du Barry, but not worthy of a queen, a great princess, a princess of the house of Lorraine and of Austria, full of goodness and decency. Your too quick success and the flatterers have always made me tremble for you ever since that winter when you threw yourself into pleasures and ridiculous head-dresses. These courses of pleasures without the king, when you know that he takes no joy in them and that he accompanies you out of complaisance and lets you do everything, all this has aroused my deepest anxieties. . . .

What language! The poor man! Where is the respect and the gratitude for all his kindnesses . . . ?

Your happiness might change radically and precipitate you, through your own fault, into the greatest misfortune. This is the effect of that terrible dissipation in not applying yourself to anything. What reading do you do? And you dare, after intervening in the most important affairs, to decide upon a choice of ministers? What does the abbé [Vermond] do? What does Mercy do? It seems to me that they have become disagreeable to you, not being flatterers, loving you to make you happy and not to divert you or profit from your weaknesses. Some day you will appreciate them, but too late. . . .

THE "MAN OF WOOD" overcame his shyness and submitted his muscular body to a faculty of physicians, who decided that there was nothing basically wrong with him and that his shortcoming went by the name of *phimosis*. All that was needed was "to cut the string." But Louis shuddered at the thought of an operation, and even Marie Antoinette, whom he could refuse practically nothing, could not move him to submit to the knife. He tried to make up for his "voicelessness," as one doctor called it, by showering his wife with gifts and gold—eagerly he paid the queen's gambling debt of half a million livres, although he hated gambling—and on a rare occasion she rewarded him with a "very tender night." Such nights, however, were fruitless.

The marital crisis was brought to a head by Vienna. Maria Theresa talked the matter over with her son Joseph II, the incurable "fixer" and world-improver, and the emperor decided to go to Versailles and set things right. He would tell his sister how to behave, he would urge his brother-in-law to undergo an operation, and—being a Habsburg—he would try to reap some political benefit in general.

⚜

THE AUGUST BROTHERS-IN-LAW met for the first time in the queen's boudoir in Versailles. Louis, who was very reserved, noticed that the emperor resembled Marie Antoinette, especially in their lower lips and the arrogance of their eyes. Joseph in turn surveyed his sister's husband, whom for years Ambassador Mercy had portrayed as a sort of half-wit, and was astonished to see a normal-looking young man, quite stout, with a nice smile but rather flabby cheeks. "For two hours," the emperor recorded in his diary, "we conversed with the king. Then he showed me all his rooms."

Joseph was an immediate success with everybody he met, but he was too vivacious for the slower Louis, who could not shake off his suspicions that there was something behind it all: no one would pour out so much charm just to be charming. But Louis would have done well to accompany his brother-in-law on some of his visits to Paris, for the contrast between the two monarchs—the one so approachable and inquiring, and the other isolated and sedentary, never showing any interest in his capital or his subjects—was too startling to escape unpleasant comment.

Inevitably Louis nursed a quiet feeling of jealousy of his brother-in-law, and he remained cool to the emperor's blandishments. For days Joseph attacked that smooth wall of indifference. He spent much time with Marie Antoinette (whose frivolous life he criticized so sharply that she often broke into tears), he flattered Louis' family, he attended the theater with the king, he went hunting with him (even though Joseph disliked the chase), he even showed up for the *lever* which he thought ridiculous.[3] In the end Louis succumbed and opened his heart.

The brothers-in-law took a long walk through the park, and Louis, his diffidence melting with the exercise, talked as never before. He talked about the administration of the country. He explained the complicated political problems. He made sensible observations on the character of the French. And Joseph listened in silent amazement as the young king talked not merely factually but with characteristic French logic. Occasionally Louis halted, sought for the right expression (being unaccustomed to long speeches), but always he found the precise word. So *this,* Joseph thought, was the fool whom Mercy had been deriding for years!

Words poured and poured. His wife, Louis said with unexpected warmth, was a lovely, virtuous, and tender woman, a worthy queen and one of whom he was proud. It was not her fault, he said reddening, that she had no children. The fault was his. What could he do? Should he or should he not submit to the operation?—a subject which Louis had never dared discuss with any man. Joseph, his senior by thirteen years, was sympathetic and understanding. He firmly advised, *"Il faut couper le filet."* The operation, the emperor explained, was not dangerous. Louis was so grateful for the encouragement that, as Joseph said, "If I had asked him, he would have shown me the most secret papers of state."

From Joseph's candid letters one gets a sharply etched flash of Louis and his court.

> This man [Joseph wrote to his brother Leopold] is a little weak, but not an imbecile. He has ideas and a sound judgment,

[3] To the iconoclastic emperor the *lever* of the French monarchy was a survival of medieval vulgarity, and he described it in mocking words: "In the presence of everybody the king pulled off his trousers, stockings, and shoes which he had put on in the morning, whereupon other persons were called in, and now he was putting on the shirt; all this while all sorts of persons were presented to him, and never did he speak a word. . . ." Vienna Archives: *Reisen S^er Majestät nach Paris und durch die Schweiz von 1777, Journal,* p.94.

MARIE ANTOINETTE'S BEDROOM IN THE PETIT TRIANON

but his mind and body are apathetic. He converses reasonably, but he has no taste for instruction and no curiosity. The *fiat lux* has not yet come; the matter is still without form. . . .

The queen's relation to the king is peculiar; she drives him by force to do things which he does not wish to do. . . . At the court there rules an aristocratic despotism. . . . The king is but an absolute lord in order to succeed from one slavery to another. He can change his ministers, but he can never become master of his business. . . . Petty intrigues are treated with the greatest care, but important affairs . . . are completely neglected. . . .

The king is badly brought up, his appearance is against him, but he is honorable, possesses some knowledge, yet he is weak in the presence of those who know how to intimidate him. . . . The queen is a very beautiful and charming woman, but she thinks only of her pleasures, has no love for the king . . . ; she does not fulfil either the duties of a wife or of a queen. . . .

SOMETIME in the summer of 1777, shortly after Joseph left, Louis submitted to the operation. It was successfully performed by Dr. Lassone, the queen's physician, and on his twenty-third birthday Louis "exercised his rights and duties of husband."

His joy at the "diversion," as he called it, was so great that he proved his new-found manhood repeatedly, and he gaily told his aunts how much he regretted not having tasted it all these years.[4] Marie Antoinette, quietly happy, informed her mother by special courier: "This is the happiest moment of my life. It is eight days now since my marriage has been perfectly consummated; the test has been repeated, yesterday even more completely than the first time. . . . I am not yet pregnant, but hope to be from moment to moment. . . ."[5]

Anxious days followed, and Louis, like his wife, alternated

[4] Ambassador Aranda to the king of Spain, August 25, 1777 (in cipher): "A mas de esto es cierto que el Rey lo contò a una de sus tias, diciendole con mucha naturalidad que le gustaba mucho la diversion y sentia no averla conocido en tanto tiempo. Esta S.M. mucho mas alegre que antes y la Reina frecuentemente con ojeras, que nunca se le avian observado, diciendose que el Rey menudea el entretenimiento."

[5] August 30, 1777; this letter also was kept secret in the Vienna Archives until a few years ago.

between hope and dejection. The hopeful king wrote to Joseph, "It is to you that we owe this happiness," and the emperor replied, "Continue the same—." They continued, and at last, in the spring of 1778, Marie Antoinette was with child.

Louis was beside himself with joy and became an unbearably attentive husband. He was ready to lay his life and his kingdom at the feet of his wife, and she promised him to reform. "Henceforth I want to live otherwise than heretofore. I want to live as a mother, nurse my own child, and devote myself to his education." Louis could occupy himself with nothing but his wife; ten, fifteen times he visited her apartments daily, bringing her gifts, loading her with attentions.

⚜

EARLY in the morning of December 19, 1778, the queen was in labor, and her bedroom, following an ancient custom, was filled with princes and princesses who surrounded the bed and gloated with morbid curiosity over the pain-convulsed woman. Her *accoucheur* was, characteristically enough, a political appointee (a brother of Abbé Vermond) and almost killed both mother and child. It was a girl—Maria Theresa Charlotte, known to history as Madame Royale and the only child of this union to survive an outrageous fortune.

The happy father overwhelmed the clumsy *accoucheur* with presents, gave him a pension of twelve thousand livres, and hung on him the Order of St. Michael. The court was treated to a *fête* which cost a hundred thousand livres. For a week after the confinement Louis would not leave his wife's apartments; he could not take his eyes off the tiny creature that was indubitably his.

But not everybody was happy. Louis' own brothers, seeing themselves deprived of their chance for the throne, were not above besmirching their dynasty by circulating doubts as to the child's paternity—the implication being that His Majesty was not capable. During the baptism, as the king held the infant at the font and the Grand Almoner, in the course of the ceremony, asked what name to give her, Louis' older brother cut in with loud sarcasm: "But that isn't where one begins: the first thing is to know who are the father and the mother—"

THE CONFINEMENT had been so perilous, or rather so clumsily managed, that Marie Antoinette was frightened at the thought of another pregnancy. Nevertheless, the king, the nation, and above all the court of Vienna clamored for a male child. France must have a dauphin, and Louis assured the nation that one would be forthcoming.[6] Almost three years passed before the promise was kept. On October 22, 1781, Marie Antoinette gave birth to a boy—Louis Joseph Xavier François. The king wept with joy and stammered like a man who had lost his head from excitement. The reality was too wonderful to be believed. "My son, the dauphin!" Louis kept on repeating: "my son . . . !"

The enchanted father had the infant brought to his own cabinet, and had him washed and dressed under his unutterably tender eyes.

But the cynical court did not believe that Louis XVI had produced an heir. Nasty couplets surreptitiously made the rounds and informed the gossips that the dauphin was a bastard:

D'un Dauphin la naissance
Enchante tout Paris;
Sa subite existence
Trouble le Paradis:
"Qui diable l'a produit"
Dit le Verbe en colère?
C'est quelque coup du Saint-Esprit,
Car jamais personne n'a dit
Que le Roi fut son père.

. . . .

. . . .

[6] His proclamation announcing the birth of the girl contained the words: "This visible mark of Providence makes me hope for the complete accomplishment of my desires and those of my people, by the birth of a Dauphin." Dec. 19, 1778. Archives Nationales, K161, no.13[12].

Dit le comte d'Artois
Si j'en eus voulu faire,
J'aurais pu prononcer
Cette race bastarde,
Mais, pour le bien de mon enfant,
J'allais tranquillement
Baiser ma Savoyarde.

CHAPTER XI

"To-day we pay dearly for our enthusiasm for the American war"

IN THE YEARS intervening between Turgot's dismissal and the birth of the dauphin Louis had permitted himself to be drawn into an adventure which was to have grave and far-reaching consequences. The whole story fitted nicely into the pattern of Louis XVI's destiny.

From the very beginning of the conflict between England and her colonies on the other side of the Atlantic—the mother-country imposing certain economic legislation and the colonies objecting to it—Louis took the position that in a family quarrel a foreigner had no business to interfere. Nevertheless, he was disturbed by the unrest in North America and feared that England, victorious or vengeful, might seize what was left of France's colonial empire in the New World.[1] One year before the American Declaration of Independence, Louis

[1] Despite her losses in the Seven Years' War (1756-63), France's colonies in America were still rich enough to tempt any aggressive naval power. The French West Indies were particularly rich in sugar and annually supplied the mother-country with considerable wealth. In 1773, for example, 700 ships brought to France the following products from the West Indies:

2,043,386 pounds of indigo
3,993,430 " " cotton
84,965,973 quintals of sugar-loaf
70,446,122 " " unrefined sugar
58,560,193 " " coffee
1,285,316 pounds of cocoa.

From the confidential report of Ambassador Stormont, March 20, 1775; Public Record Office, SP 78.

wrote to his ally the king of Spain that it was necessary to be on guard:

> I know Your Majesty's aversion for war and I sincerely share this sentiment. Perhaps there has never been a time when the appearances of war with England were less probable, not the slightest dispute between them and us, but the unfortunate policies of that country are such that one cannot count upon it. England is much occupied with her American colonies and although I do not believe that they will ever come to terms with the mother-country, nevertheless England might try to go to war with us in order to escape her present difficulties. I think, therefore, that we should pay all our attention to preparations . . . in order to avoid war.[2]

FRANCE was overwhelmingly on the American side of the struggle, which in itself was a curious phenomenon of antiroyalism. Stormont, the British ambassador in Paris, was struck by this wave of sympathy for those whom every good monarchist should have regarded as "rebels."

> Our Wits, Philosophers and Coffee House Politicians [Stormont wrote disdainfully] who are all to a Man warm Americans, affecting to consider them as a brave People struggling for its Natural Rights and endeavouring to rescue those Rights out of the Hands of violent and wanton Oppression . . . With what Complacency the French talk of what they least understand, making up in Petulance what they want in Knowledge.[3]

There was, of course, good reason for this pro-American feeling. Ever since the Seven Years' War, when France lost to England most of her overseas empire, Frenchmen had smarted at the defeat and hoped for revenge. And as the war between the British and the colonists finally broke out, France was seized with a frenzy of excitement. Patriots now saw the beginning of the destruction of a hated rival; liberals regarded the colonial war as a fight for liberty against despotism. It became so fashionable to be "American" that even Marie

[2] August 7, 1775; Archives Nationales, K164, no.3, 1775.
[3] December 7, 1774; Public Record Office, SP 78 ("Most Secret").

Antoinette and her entourage embraced the cause of the colonies.

The Americans, moreover, were superb propagandists even before the marvelous Benjamin Franklin came to Paris and made the feminine hearts flutter. Silas Deane, one of the American agents, was surely not a provincial when it came to practical diplomacy, and his clever suggestion to his home government was worthy of the great cause he represented.

> The queen [Deane wrote] is fond of parade and, I believe, wishes for war, and is our friend. She loves riding and horseback. Could you send me a fine Narragansett horse or two? The money would be well laid out. Rittenhouse's orrery, or Arnold's collection of insects, a phaeton of American make, and a pair of bay horses, a few barrels of apples, walnuts, cranberries, and butternuts would be great curiosities.

Louis was one of the two or three important persons in France who remained unaffected by the war fever. "War ought to be shunned as the greatest of misfortunes." Turgot used to say to him, and Louis strongly agreed. France, he well knew, could not afford an international conflict; the monarchy, it was clear, had no business helping rebels. However strong his political dislike for Britain, Louis had no antipathy for George III, who was a fellow-king and in trouble. As Emperor Joseph II aptly put it when asked his opinion of the American Revolution, "It is my métier to be a royalist." All this thoughtless enthusiasm for the Americans, this chatter about liberty, was vaguely disturbing to Louis XVI.

THE KING, however, trusted his ministers to shape policy, and it was Vergennes, the strong Anglophobe, who worked out a subtle scheme whereby Britain would be harmed without danger to France. Vergennes collaborated with Beaumarchais, the brilliant author-adventurer, in subsidizing a large commercial company which was to supply the Americans with munitions and materials, on the basis of private commercial exchange. The French government would not be involved formally, and therefore the British could have no excuse to attack France. So careful was Louis XVI's foreign minister to preserve the appearance of neutrality that his letters to Beaumarchais were written by Vergennes' young son, whose handwriting no one would be able to trace. The confidential letter in which Vergennes outlined his project to Beaumarchais (April, 1776) has a very "modern" flavor:

> It is necessary that in the eyes of the English government and of the Americans the operation should have essentially the aspect of an individual speculation to which we [France] are strangers. . . . We will secretly give you one million. We will try to obtain an equal sum from Spain. . . . With these two millions you will establish a big commercial house, and at your risk and peril you will supply the Americans with arms, munitions, equipment, and all other things that they will need to maintain the war. Our arsenal will deliver to you arms and munitions, but you will either replace them or pay for them. You will not demand money from the Americans, since they do not have any, but you will ask in return the produce of their soil which we will help you sell in this country. . . .

That Vergennes should have been able to win over the virtuous Louis to a scheme of such dubious morality was due to the plausible argument that if the American colonists could be quietly helped, the war would be prolonged until England, already tottering as he believed ("England is at the point of despair," Beaumarchais reported after a trip to London [4]), would be totally exhausted. "Two or three millions," so ran the argument advanced by Vergennes and Beaumarchais, "may save us our sugar islands worth three hundred million." In this way France would permanently dispose of a great danger to herself and cripple a powerful enemy without the cost of a war. Louis approved the scheme of invisible intervention, without realizing that precisely the path he had chosen led to armed conflict.

[4] May 2, 1776; Archives Nationales, K164, no.3, 1776 no.9.

⚜

THE PLAN worked well, so well, in fact, that even the Americans, plentifully supplied with powder, rifles, shoes, were in ignorance as to the money that paid for the generous supplies. Frenchmen were likewise unaware that their government was helping the American "rebels" against their lawful sovereign. For Beaumarchais was an almost detective-story conspirator and as hard to hook as a round ball. Consider, for example, the circular path described by the million livres from Spain. The Spanish ambassador deposited the money with the French treasury and got a receipt. He gave the receipt to Vergennes. The foreign minister handed it to an agent, who brought it to Beaumarchais, who then presented it to the French treasury, which exchanged it for cash.

One of the few people who were not fooled was Lord Stormont, the British ambassador, who employed excellent spies. But His Lordship was helpless. He cursed and fumed and called names, but he could not ruffle the suavity of Vergennes.

> No tone I can take [Stormont reported to London indignantly], no Endeavours I can use, will produce any great change . . . on the general Conduct of this Court. . . . With the Duplicity of France even Walsingham could not contend. . . . They do not wish at least in the present Moment, to plunge into actual War . . . , but they have a fixt invariable purpose to do us all the secret Mischief they can.

His lordship loudly protested to Vergennes: "In the history of the world there is no example of aid given to rebels of a country one professes to be friendly with."

Vergennes replied calmly, "We cannot stop smugglers."

Stormont shouted, "Do smugglers go in fleets, sir?" [5]

[5] American privateers, helped by France, had become so menacing to British commerce that 114 Merchant Traders and Ship Owners of London protested to the Secretary of State that if these raiding practices "are not immediately put a Stop to, they must sap the Vitals of this Kingdom." The petition is in the Public Record Office, SP 78: 24 November, 1777; see also Stormont's despatch of November 5, 1777, in *ibid.*

⚜

THEN Benjamin Franklin arrived in France and caused a sensation. Everywhere the smiling old philosopher was received by enthusiastic crowds. The French lost their heads over this fur-hatted colonial, whose poise and simplicity recalled the sages of ancient Greece. Ambassador Mercy described him as "cool-headed, modest, thorough." Intellectuals found him profound, ladies courtly, and everybody witty. *Le docteur* Franklin became the fashion, and his portrait was on every mantelpiece.

The handsome old man, with his bearskin and walking-stick and steel-rimmed spectacles, presented a living picture of a republican and a scientist: simple, neat, dignified—a veritable triumph of character. Yet Franklin's apparent guilelessness concealed one of the shrewdest brains of his time, not merely a scientific brain but a diplomatic one. The way this seventy-year-old gentleman played the ladies, who, he knew, ruled France socially and (indirectly) politically, was a masterpiece of adroitness. To be frank, he loved the ladies, and they, to his humorous delight, loved him.

> Somebody, it seems [he wrote], gave out that I lov'd ladies; and then everybody presented me their ladies (or the ladies presented themselves) to be embrac'd, that is to have their necks kiss'd. For as to kissing of lips or cheeks it is not the mode here, the first, is reckon'd rude, & the other may rub off the paint. The French ladies have however 1000 other ways of rendering themselves agreeable; by their various attentions and civilities, & their sensible conversation. 'Tis a delightful people to live with.

Ladies and all, Franklin was intensely busy. He saw the ministers secretly, at night, and had long conversations. His impression was, "The cry of this nation is for us, but the Court views an approaching war with reluctance." He set out to "please the Court."

⚜

FRENCH ARMS and munitions were of invaluable help to the Americans, and when they defeated Burgoyne's army, it became apparent that England could be beaten. The American cause looked brighter than ever before, and even Louis XVI, who had nursed doubts about the efficacy of the Vergennes-Beaumarchais scheme, was now hopeful of the outcome.

> America is triumphant [Louis wrote to the king of Spain] and England beaten, but still having a great naval force which is untouched.... Lord North himself has promised in full parliament a plan of pacification to be ready for the first session and they are working on it energetically.... By various means they will reunite with America and will not forget our ill services; they will fall upon us with as much force as if the civil war had never happened.... After having taken the advice of my counsel ... I thought it just and necessary ... to begin to treat with the insurgents and to prevent their reunion with the mother-country.[6]

It was Franklin who subtly spread the notion that the Americans might make peace with England and then the latter would be free to revenge herself on France, and it was Louis XVI who swallowed the fear-baited hook. On February 8, 1778, the French government and the representatives (Franklin, Deane, and Arthur Lee) of the thirteen United States signed two treaties, one of friendship and commerce and the other (kept secret) of a defensive-offensive alliance. Louis XVI explained this momentous act in a letter to the king of Spain:

> Knowing that England was working for a reconciliation with her colonies, that which I have foreseen has just happened. England has announced her projects for a conciliation with America, the nation applauded it and all that was lacking was the consent of the latter.... I hope that the measures which I have taken will thwart those of England.... The dignity and honor of the crown induced me to order my ambassador to issue a declaration in London which should tend to sustain the courage of America and subdue the audacity of England.[7]

As soon as the outraged British government heard of the treaty, it commanded Ambassador Stormont "to quit Paris without taking leave."

[6] January 8, 1778; Archives Nationales, K164 no. 3, 1778 no.1.
[7] March 9, 1778; Archives Nationales, K164 no.3, 1778 no.2.

Thus had Louis XVI been dragged step by step along a path that led inevitably to a war which he feared.

⚜

Louis was not very warm to the plenipotentiaries of the newest republic at their formal reception on March 20. The king spoke only a few cool words: "Assure the United States of America of my friendship; I am very satisfied with your conduct in my kingdom." Then he left the room.

"The king," Arthur Lee tells, "had his hair undressed, hanging down on his shoulders; no appearance of preparation to receive us, nor any ceremony in doing it."

Marie Antoinette, however, was gracious. That evening she invited the American envoys to the *Jeu de la Reine,* where the royal family was playing cards around a large table. The queen paid special attention to the handsome Franklin—he had exchanged his brown coat for a black-velvet one, cotton for silk stockings—and did him the honor of asking him to stand behind her during the game. Marie Antoinette was fond of his nickname, *L'Ambassadeur électrique.*

⚜

Louis was singularly sensitive on the score of aiding rebels against their lawful sovereign; his conscience, moreover, was uneasy because he felt that his policies had goaded England into war. Hence he felt the need for a public justification, particularly in the eyes of his fellow-kings in Europe, and encouraged Vergennes to compose an "Exposé of the Motives of the King's Conduct in Relation to England," in which Europe was asked to judge "which of the two sovereigns is the real author of the war which afflicts their states." [8]

The fascinating thing about this pamphlet is not its propaganda aspect, not the conscious attempt to influence public opinion, but the king's own marginal corrections in the

[8] *Exposé des motifs de la conduite du roi, relativement à l'Angleterre* (Paris, Imprimerie Royale, 1779), 14 pp.

LOUIS XVI BEFORE THE REVOLUTION

Engraving from a drawing by D. A. M. Raffet.

manuscript before it went into print. These rare comments are like the light of a match against a face in the dark, revealing in a flash the fleeting shape of the thought—for generally Louis hardly ever took the trouble to outline his opinions. The marginal corrections also show, by the way, how much keener was the king's appreciation of political events than was generally supposed. There was, indeed, nothing wrong with his thinking; it was his resolution that was at fault.

Vergennes' draft read:

> France has not made herself the judge of the quarrel between Great Britain and her colonies: independence has come without her aid. If the king of France took up arms to-day, it has been to free the seas of British tyranny. This power has respected nothing, not even the person of the king of France with her invectives. The British government has always been the same—without faith, without principles. . . .

Louis commented in the margin:

> Vergennes is wrong to deny that we have acted for the independence of the United States; we have done more, we have judged them free people, we have given them existence as a nation, and this existence . . . could not have taken place without the recognition of foreign powers. This act of recognition is our deed and it should be proved just and legal. It is England's tyranny on the seas that is the sole and true cause of France's conduct. . . . For the rest, I should not attribute to the king of England my having been personally abused. . . . The king of England cannot . . . inveigh against anyone; there everything falls on his ministers. . . . These words, *degraded, infamous, perfidious, dissimulation,* which M. de Vergennes uses repeatedly, are expressions which hardly go with French politeness or that of all the courts. . . .
>
> It will be difficult to persuade Europe, and England, that France has not taken part in the troubles of the English colonies; it would be better not to touch upon this particular point, because whether true or false it is a controvertible subject. . . . It would be more appropriate to bring out in evidence English animosity. . . . Seeing my subjects flogged in India, France and Europe will say unanimously . . . that the time has come . . . to chastise England. It is well known how the spectacle of two ears which

the Spaniards cut off an English fisherman stirred up the people of London.[9]

This shows a level-headed appreciation of the use of atrocity propaganda. Louis continued his gentlemanly criticism of Vergennes' composition by objecting to the mention of certain unpleasant historical incidents, which might set a bad example:

> As for the assassination of King Charles I and of Marie Stuart, these are crimes for which England blushes even a hundred years after. . . . Furthermore, the house of Hanover is a stranger to these *attentats*. . . . Such a remark could authorize England to help openly the malcontents in Brittany . . . , our French Protestants, and all discontented Frenchmen. . . . It is not for France to set an example. . . . I would prefer to strike out the word *Cromwell* . . . ; as it is, the English reproach us enough for having recognized the government of that odious man. . . .

Finally Louis summarized his observations on the American war:

> It is quite evident that we have not been neutral. In general it is necessary to . . . point out the grave disadvantages for the public safety in permitting Great Britain to take the tone which she arrogates for herself against all the maritime and Continental powers. It is necessary to show that she has abused her power.

⚜

Louis was not happy in his American adventure, which was dragging along indecisively and pulling France deeper and deeper into a morass of debt. Criticism began to be heard at court. Louis' brother Provence spoke of the war as a "punishable rebellion," and Marie Antoinette, incited by Vienna (Britain's friend), urged the king to give up the insurgents. Vergennes, too, was losing hope, especially since Spain, France's ally, gave but "sorry aid" and France had to bear the whole burden alone. A prolonged war, Vergennes told the king at the end of the first year of hostilities, might

[9] The reference is to the so-called War of Jenkins' Ear, which broke out between England and Spain in 1739.

"entrain the ruin of your navy and even your finances."[10] Necker, the director-general of finances, likewise objected to pouring France's wealth across the Atlantic in a dubious adventure, but the irresponsible government was already so deeply committed that the reluctant Vergennes and the cynical Maurepas drove the banker from Geneva to some desperate financial juggling. Instead of antagonizing public opinion (Necker always played to the galleries) by levying fresh taxes, the director-general of finances piled up foreign loan upon foreign loan, so that the nation did not—yet!—feel the burden of the war.

"Credulous people," cried Mirabeau, to whom no one paid attention, "hasten to admire Necker, for some day your children will curse him!"

Louis was immensely worried—nothing upset him so much as debts and the payment of interest—but indecision together with a sense of honor kept him from ending hostilities until 1782, when the Americans made separate peace with England. It was not, in the code of international ethics, a "gentlemanly" thing to do, but Louis was not angry at his selfish allies. He was actually so relieved that when the news reached him, he is said to have got out of bed in his nightshirt and sung a vulgar ditty which was popular in the *halles* in the time of the peace of 1735:

> *L'empereur dit à Louis* [*XV*]
> *Ne reviens plus dans mon pays,*
> *Baise mon . . . la paix est faite,*
> *Turlurette*
> *Turlurette*
> *Lantanturlurette!*

In September, 1783, Louis also made peace with England. "My joy," he informed Joseph II, "is most keen."

[10] December 5, 1778; Archives Nationales, K164 no.3, 1778 no.12. In September, 1780, Vergennes informed the king: "The condition of the finances is truly alarming and seems to leave no other resource than peace." *Ibid.*, 1780 no.3.

FRANCE had gained absolutely nothing except the independence of the United States of America. Apart from the vast cost of keeping the navy and the army on a war footing, Louis XVI had given America the following sums in cash:

1775-1778	3,000,000	livres
1779	1,000,000	"
1780	4,000,000	"
1781	4,000,000	"
1782	6,000,000	"

Apart from this sum of 18,000,000 livres in cash, the United States wanted to borrow another 25,000,000 to maintain an army of thirty-two thousand, but even Franklin had to admit that the "resources of France are limited."

The total cost of the war to France amounted to about a billion livres, and it drained the French treasury beyond recovery. From 1782 on the financial and political life of France slid toward the abyss with increasing speed. Thus, in a direct sense, the financing of one great revolution—on the part of an absolute monarch—led to another, a much greater one. It was not long before the truth of this dawned upon the throne. In 1789, when the Bastille was already a heap of yellow-stoned ruins, Marie Antoinette said bitterly, "To-day we pay dearly for our infatuation and enthusiasm for the American war."

Clouds were now gathering on the horizon, growing large and black.

CHAPTER XII

"This anarchy must give place to some catastrophe"

THE WAR and fatherhood had wrought a change change in Louis. He gave less time to the chase and more to books, but reading, unfortunately, did not inspire greater exertion. His tendency towards gormandizing increased with the years, and the more he ate the less he worked. As a result he became Chestertonian in proportions though not in wit. "Where a barrel sufficed for Louis XV," old courtiers said, "a hogshead is necessary for Louis XVI." He could not, in truth, ever resist the sight of food, and he ate with a gusto so unrestrained that Buffon, the naturalist who observed apes and kings with the same detachment, once remarked that Louis XVI's eating reminded him of a monkey in the zoo.

A normal lunch, sometimes prepared by Louis himself, consisted of four cutlets, a fat chicken, six eggs *au jus,* a slice of ham, and a bottle of *vin ordinaire*. Often he gorged himself until his faculties ceased to function and he had to be carried, inert, to bed. This gave rise to nasty rumors of drunkenness. Except for small bottles of wine with his meals, however, Louis XVI drank little. Moderate in everything else, his immoderation in food sapped his will and reduced his dignity. He was sometimes heard to emit *"un bruit très suspect"* after a heavy meal, and disgusted courtiers privately named him *un gros cochon*. The solid structure of his body expanded, filled like a balloon of flesh. "The doctors," a contemporary writes, "make him drink Vichy water to arrest, if possible, an excessive and dangerous *embonpoint.*"

Curiously enough, his stoutness did not impair his health. On the contrary, he developed tremendous strength. Contemporaries commented upon the extraordinary fact that, in an age of epidemics and divers mysterious illnesses, Louis XVI was hardly ever sick and never took a drop of medicine. France d'Hézecques, who was a page at court, tells in his *Souvenirs* that the king liked to show off his enormous strength by putting a small page-boy on a heavy shovel and lifting it with arm extended. He was proud of his mighty blacksmith's muscles.

The flesh and the muscle, however, were a grave drain on his capacity for exertion, and he frequently sank into prolonged fits of lethargy. From all descriptions it would seem that there was something radically wrong with Louis' glands. After an eating orgy he was incapacitated for hours and, according to Mercy, "deprived of reason." He would then use words of slop-pail grossness—and feel dreadfully contrite afterwards. In such a drugged state—dressed in one red shoe, one black shoe, an unbuttoned dressing-gown, hair disheveled—he once received King Gustave III of Sweden.

The heavier he grew the less he acted, and the less he acted the more he read. He became, in fact, as prodigious a reader as he was a gormandizer and achieved a thorough familiarity with the laws and history of France. His memory remained as fresh as in his boyhood, and what he read he retained. While Marie Antoinette was gambling or playing theatricals in the Petit Trianon, Louis, with his shortsighted eyes, read with an intensity as if his life depended upon it. When something interested him, he took precise, meticulous notes and digested the materials with slow thoroughness.

Among his favorite journals was Linguet's *Annals,* a political periodical which was forbidden in France but which

His Majesty read as if it were a catechism. "I never read with as much interest," he admitted, "as when I read Linguet." He also read a number of European, including English, periodicals. The journalist Mallet du Pan tells that on the eve of the Revolution he visited Louis' private library in Versailles:

> I saw many English books, travel, history, science, the *English Review,* the *Annual Register,* etc. . . . There were collections of newspapers from Leyden, Amsterdam, the Lower Rhine, the *Journal de Paris, Affiches, Gazette de France,* the *Statutes at Large* of the English Parliament for several years. The king reads a lot and, with the exception of the *Encyclopédie,* all the books in his library have passed through his hands. He prefers English books to French ones. He has read the whole great English Universal History in translation.

THIS FAT and learned king was rapidly losing his usefulness as a monarch because, with the best of intentions, he seemed physically incapable of bestirring himself and in a crisis he showed himself as helpless as a paralytic.

This time it was Necker who was battling with financial difficulties and steadily losing ground. Louis could not help him any more than he did Turgot. The king was the victim of a system which required him to spend over 6,000,000 livres a year on the royal table and about 1,500,000 on furniture.[1] His personal *dépenses particuliers* averaged around 500,000 annually,[2] and his Civil List ran into the millions.[3] His family and their retainers never let go of the treasury which they regarded as an ancestral money-box to be dipped into whenever any kinsman needed a few millions. The king's younger brother Artois, a notorious gambler, piled up an enormous debt of 11,000,000 livres in 1779 and asked

[1] Between 1775 and 1791 the expenses of the *garde-meuble* amounted to to 20,544,955 livres.

[2] Approximately 4,346,000 livres between 1776 and 1784.

[3] At least 1,500,000 of this fund was secretly invested abroad, especially in London, about three years before the Revolution: it was to be used for bribery and propaganda during the Revolution. There may have been much greater sums invested abroad, but I have found no other evidence.

His Majesty to pay it. Louis, who occasionally behaved like a king, refused, and Artois said bitingly that his brother's title should not be *Roi de France et Navarre* but *Roi de France et Avare.* It was a clever pun but undeserved. Louis replied, "I am *avare,* in effect, because I have only the well-being of my subjects in mind." But in the end the "avaricious" monarch paid his brother's debt.

Necker struggled desperately with the budget, but it was like trying to save money and to satisfy all the habitués of Monte Carlo at the same time. The court, in fact, was like a casino, despite the king's aversion for gambling. "It's stupid to gamble," he reiterated; but sometimes Marie Antoinette wheedled him into a little game. The really high stakes usually began after midnight when the king was in bed. Once Louis surprised the party in the gaming-room and angrily swept the stacks of gold and notes off the table, ordering that the money be given to the poor. But, as one courtier remarked, "nothing can reform the gamblers."

Necker, a curious mixture of banker, careerist, and idealist, did everything to postpone bankruptcy. He made colossal loans abroad, which only staved off disaster, for the notes were bound to fall due—with a crash. Meanwhile interest kept piling up and devouring the national income. The director of finances hoped to increase the tax income by reducing the number of tax-collectors ("farmers-general") and to economize by suppressing more than four hundred officers of the royal household. Then a hail-storm descended upon the minister's head, and he was lashed as brutally as once was Turgot. The enraged court and politicians combined against the luckless Geneva banker. "I know you have many enemies," Louis said to him, "but you can count upon my firmness." Louis had said that to Turgot, too.

Suddenly Necker precipitated a crisis by publishing a booklet which fell upon France like a bomb. It was the famous *Compte Rendu,* the first public statement of the receipts and expenditures (not altogether accurate) of the treasury, which immediately became a "best seller." The

Compte Rendu was selling at the rate of thirty thousand a week, and France talked about nothing but Necker and finances. The country cried that the banker from Geneva was a savior, a *vrai patriote;* but neither king nor country was able to withstand the courtiers and politicians. Necker's life was made unbearable, and he got out of office. Louis locked the letter of resignation in a special drawer.

It was the end of any pretense to reform or "good government" in France, and the country felt it. As for Louis, his hands had willy-nilly slipped off the tiller, especially since the death of Maurepas (in 1781). The queen and her clique were running things—and heading straight for the rocks. Amidst financial anarchy Louis approved the appointment of the middle-aged Charles Alexandre de Calonne, whom Maurepas had recommended before his death and whom Mercy described as "not being endowed with extraordinary talents." Louis disliked Calonne, treated him with rudeness and contempt, and refused to coöperate with him. Calonne was supported by the queen and the court, and he repaid them for their backing with "unprecedented squandering and extravagance," to quote a contemporary. Calonne's administration of the finances became a national scandal. The country, moreover, had lost all hope of reform coming from a court dominated by *l'Autrichienne,* the most hated figure in France. So long as the present clique ruled, there would be no relief from poverty and no improvement. The nation turned away from the throne (although Louis was personally spared criticism), and intelligent observers were convinced that a crash—the long-heralded deluge—was imminent. Early in 1786, more than three years before the Revolution, Mercy, who was a conservative aristocrat, wrote:

"There is a cry of misery and of terror... The present government surpasses the last one in feebleness, disorder, and rapacity, and it is morally *impossible that this anarchy continue for long without giving place to some catastrophe."*

⚜

Knowledge of his weakness gave Louis a sense of self-contempt, which further enfeebled his will. He grew morose and uncommunicative and lost much of his *bonhomie*. Mallet du Pan tells that during a chase in the woods of Verrières he watched Louis get off his horse and stand under a tree waiting for the rain to pass. "During the half-hour he stood there he never opened his mouth once." But in his sluggishness there was on occasion a certain obstinacy and flash of independence which even Marie Antoinette could not overcome. This was particularly true in matters of foreign policy. Despite his fatal complaisance in all things concerning his wife, Louis never forgot that Marie Antoinette was a foreigner. His French patriotism was stronger than his love for his Austrian consort, as Marie Antoinette discovered when she tried desperately to enlist the aid of France for Austria's war against Holland.

On that occasion the queen wrote a strange confession to her brother Joseph II:

> It is necessary to know him well in order to judge how few resources and means his character and prejudices offer me. He is naturally untalkative, and often it happens that he does not talk to me about important affairs even if he does not intend to conceal them from me. He answers when I ask him, but he never informs me beforehand; and, when I learn one-fourth of an affair, I need adroitness to get the rest out of the ministers by making them believe that the king has told me everything. When I reproach the king for not having talked to me about certain matters, he is not angry, he has a somewhat embarrassed air, and sometimes he replies in a natural tone that he had not thought of it.... His natural distrust had been fortified by his tutor. Since before my marriage, M. de La Vauguyon frightened him on the subject of the domination which his wife would want to exercise over him, and his [La Vauguyon's] black soul delighted in scaring his pupil with all the phantoms invented against the house of Austria.... M. de Vergennes follows the same plan.... I have clearly spoken about it to the king, and more than once. Sometimes he replied with temper, and, since he is incapable of discussion, I have not been able to persuade him....

In personal matters, however, Louis was unfailingly generous to his wife, particularly after she had given birth, in March, 1785, to a second son, the Duke of Normandy, who was destined to die as dauphin in the prison of the Temple. On that occasion Louis spent six million livres to buy her the château of St. Cloud as a personal gift. The annual bill for the upbringing of the three royal children amounted to two million livres.[4] Louis groaned when the Duke d'Harcourt, the governor of the princes, asked for this staggering sum. "I don't blame you," the king muttered to the apologetic duke, "but rather the system."

⚜

Louis' financial worries were momentarily forgotten in the excitement of an amazing story which became the scandal of the age. The tale of the Diamond Necklace, a mystery tailored to fit Hollywood, involved a queen, a cardinal, a mysterious adventurer, a high-class courtesan, and above all the reputation of the French throne. Louis XVI himself was but an innocent bystander, but in his desire to punish the traducers of his wife he committed one of the great blunders of his life.

The central figure of this fantastic affair was the Cardinal de Rohan, prince bishop of Strassburg and Grand Almoner of France, a handsome libertine whose loose morals shocked even eighteenth-century French society. Marie Antoinette, no prude, refused to speak to him. The cardinal pretended to be in love with the queen, and in his boundless fatuity he thought he could become her lover. That was the motivation in the drama.

The plot itself was woven by another bizarre figure, an Italian soothsayer, magician, alchemist, mystery-monger, fortune-teller, seducer, named Cagliostro. It is a commentary on French upper-class morals and manners on the eve of the Revolution that a charlatan like Cagliostro, whose means of support were as obscure as his origins, was an adored figure

[4] Archives Nationales, K161, no.41[2].

in society, so much in demand by duchesses and countesses that he had to barricade himself in his house. He was short, stocky, bull-necked, a thorough bull dressed in blazing polychromatic garments which had a fascinating attraction for the cows. He talked perpetually and obscurely in a special gibberish consisting of Italian, French, and Arabic words. His loud voice boomed about the sky, the stars, the great arcanum, Memphis, hierophants, transcendence, alchemy, giants, and African cities ten times the size of Paris. In the midst of this cascade of heavenly discourse he would interrupt himself and turn around to pinch caressingly Madame de Lamotte—his current mistress who was used as the instrument in the Diamond Necklace affair—and in his thundering voice call her his *biche,* his dove, his swan, his gazelle.....

The gazelle and the soothsayer easily caught the cardinal in their net. They knew how eager the dissolute Rohan was to meet the queen *tête-à-tete* and easily persuaded him that Madame de Lamotte was an intimate friend of Marie Antoinette. De Lamotte pretended to be the go-between—she even arranged a little scene in a thicket where a chambermaid impersonated the queen—and the fatuous cardinal believed he was making progress in his courtship. The upshot of this extraordinary intrigue was that Rohan, having received a forged order supposedly from the queen to buy her the gorgeous diamond necklace (worth 1,600,000 livres) which the jewelers Boehmer and Bassenge had long been trying to sell, acquired the ornament by making a down-payment and confidentially informing Boehmer that he was acting in the name of Her Majesty. Rohan showed the jeweler an order which contained the signature "Approved, Marie Antoinette de France." Both cardinal and jeweler presumably acted in good faith. Boehmer entrusted the precious necklace to Rohan, Rohan handed it over to de Lamotte, de Lamotte was to give it to Marie Antoinette. And the necklace disappeared as if dropped into the ocean!

Sometime later Boehmer, believing that Marie Antoinette had received the precious ornament, went to Versailles to

VISE USED BY LOUIS XVI
Musée Carnavalet.

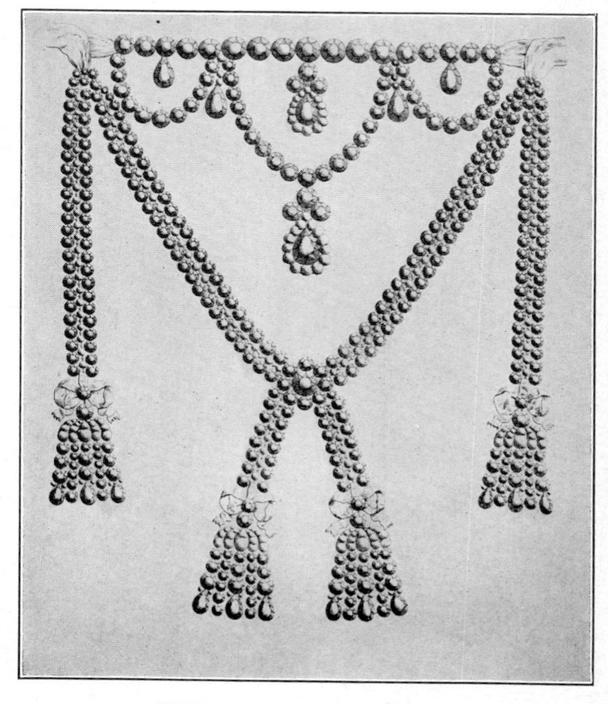

THE DIAMOND NECKLACE
Reduced one-half.

get a further payment. Then the whole fantastic story broke into the open.

The furious Marie Antoinette informed her husband immediately, and Louis promptly ordered the arrest of Rohan (which was in itself a sensation, for cardinals were not as a rule subject to arrest in the ancient régime), de Lamotte, Boehmer, Cagliostro, and all their accomplices. The cautious Vergennes warned the king not to precipitate a dangerous scandal but to hush up the affair, for the tribe of Rohan was too powerful and the queen's reputation could not afford such publicity. But Louis made the mistake of letting his anger overcome his judgment and decided to have the affair threshed out in the open.

⚜

Louis offered Rohan the choice of being tried by the Parlement of Paris or of admitting his guilt and being judged by the king. This was a tactical mistake, and Rohan quickly took advantage of it by demanding a Parlement trial. The Rohan family had powerful friends, and the counselors of the Parlement were not friendly to the throne. There was no crime, indeed, for which a Rohan could be condemned in pre-Revolutionary France. Abbé Georgel, the imprisoned cardinal's secretary, wrote frankly to one of Rohan's friends:

> Stop worrying about our dear cardinal.... His health holds up in prison, the rigors of which are moderated: and his soul is at peace, as much as can be that of an illustrious accused who foresees that he will *never be condemned*.... The history of France shows seven cardinals accused by our kings: not one was condemned.... The Lord Privy Seal and Vergennes ... are our friends; the same views, the same aversions.... We will triumph completely.

Rohan did triumph. The only results of the trial were the condemnation (since a scapegoat was needed) of de Lamotte —public whipping, branding, and lifelong imprisonment— and the besmirching of the queen's reputation. Rohan, the *grand seigneur,* was vindicated by a court which cynically ignored all evidence against him. The queen, to be sure, was declared innocent, but she had figured in a scandalous trial, and her name was dragged in over and again to make a French holiday. Moreover, she received a direct blow when the Parlement declared the cardinal not guilty and thereby told the country that every one was free to insult the queen (and, by the same token, the king). Mercy states flatly that the elderly justices were openly bribed by the Rohan family —which was probably true.

The judgment of the court outraged the king. Marie Antoinette burst into tears. But the one would not and the other could not do anything about it. Louis curtly ordered Rohan to give up his decorations, relinquish his offices, and retire to the country. But the damage was done: the prestige of the monarchy had suffered an almost fatal blow, and so had French justice.

The country was electrified by the astounding outcome of the whole affair, since every one assumed that Rohan was a dissolute high-born scoundrel and de Lamotte only a poor woman working for a living in her own devious way. Yet the noble-born wretch was freed and the working woman was whipped, branded, and imprisoned. Justice was a cynical mockery.

Libels and lampoons and mocking verse flew about from hand to hand. No one and nothing was spared. Typical was the satire on the Parlement:

If this sentence of the cardinal
Appears to you too illegal,
Then remember that finance—
Oh hell!
Runs everything in France.
—You understand me well!

Most widespread satire was one which impaled the whole government and which such an informed judge as Mercy described as "perfectly rendered after nature":

In France one suffers in patience
Miromesnil's ignorance,
De Castries' insufficience,
Ségur's dull existence,
Brusque Breteuil's arrogance,
Vaudreuil's high impudence,
The minister of finance's
Squandering and indecencies,
So many others' impertinences;
Vergennes with indifference
Silently watches this evil sham,
He does well, for Louis doesn't give a damn.

But how long, people asked, would France suffer in patience?

⚜

BY SOME strange magic which seems to hedge crowned heads, Louis himself remained a popular figure, liked for his unpretentiousness and respected for his honesty despite diamond scandals and financial disorders. He was the sort of man who generally appeals to Frenchmen anyhow: a stout *bonhomme,* a hearty eater, and personally frugal withal. If he had had the energy to exert himself and the force to carry out his intentions, he might have been one of the beloved kings in French history. As it was, his disillusioned subjects exempted him from attack. In their sharp criticism of the government, the people separated the king from his ministers and the ministers from the system. The king was good, the ministers corrupt, the system rotten. This trichotomy struck deep roots and helps one to understand much that is perplexing in the Revolution. To the very end Louis XVI was liked by Frenchmen.

Louis himself did not know the extent of his popularity. Not until June, 1786, the month when the scandalous necklace trial ended, did the king realize how deeply his person, as a symbol of paternal kingship, was rooted in the affections of the nation. With the exception of the coronation trip to

Rheims, he had never traveled anywhere in France and had never seen anything of the country he was ruling except the royal châteaux and woods. The absolute lord of France lived as far removed from Frenchmen as if he were moored on a raft in mid-ocean. He lived, it is no exaggeration to say, in a sort of mythical eighteenth century created on a Hollywood set, complete with gowns, costumes, uniforms, and routines, all precise copies of the "period." It was, therefore, a tremendous revelation to Louis when he left the "set" and was jubilantly received by the outside world. The court may have thought him a fool and his wife may have called him a poor fellow, but to his subjects he was a king!

In the summer of 1786 Louis left his "royal prison" and took a short trip to Normandy as far as Cherbourg, where he was to inspect the magnificent port. The journey was carefully planned by the court, every meter of the way inspected, measured, and prepared.[5] They wanted him to travel like a horse with blinders, looking neither to the right nor to the left but only straight ahead, from Versailles to Cherbourg through the richest section of France. The deliberate intention of the ministers was to keep the king from seeing, in the words of a contemporary, "the unhappy state of the interior provinces where misery reigns and where the tax devours the bread of the people."

The trip proved a personal triumph (Marie Antoinette did not accompany him), and the delighted Louis admitted that the nine short days constituted the happiest period of his life. All along the way Frenchmen turned out by the hundreds of thousands to give a warm and sincerely felt reception to their king and to see what he looked like—this kindly victim of a dissolute wife. *Ah, comme il est gentil,* maidens sighed, and felt sorry for him because he was married to that *misérable Autrichienne.* Louis wrote happily to his wife at Versailles: "The love of my people has resounded to the

[5] Archives Nationales, KK 1085: *"Mémoires et plans pour servir au voyage du roi en Cherbourg,"* contains a detailed itinerary.

bottom of my heart; judge if I am not the happiest man in the world."

He was as delighted and light-hearted as a prisoner released from bondage, and he showed, in the fine Norman summer air, an unexpectedly youthful gaiety. The Normans might have changed the course of events had they abducted the king and kept him among themselves—to reign, a simple man among humble folk. In one small town a young woman broke through the crowd and fell on her knees before the king, looking up to him worshipfully. "All that is lacking to make me happy," she cried, "is the chance to kiss a prince so dear to the nation." Louis laughed and beckoned her. After she had kissed his hand, he said with a grin, "Now it's my turn, Madame," and gave her a loud smack on the neck. The people burst into joyful cheers.

"Why," Louis pathetically asked his courtiers, "do I receive here such testimonies of love to which I am not accustomed elsewhere?"

He answered himself: "I see it: they must have given me a bad reputation in Versailles."

But he was wrong. It was not that "they" gave him a bad reputation, but that he was, in the fullest sense, a prisoner of Versailles, victim of a system which he had inherited and not made.

At Cherbourg he was inspecting the works in the port aboard the vessel *Patriote* when the wind suddenly shifted. "Where would the wind take us?" he asked. "To England, Sire," the captain replied. "Oh, I would gladly go there; the English would not receive me badly, and in that country they do not deceive kings."

Everywhere the people cried, "Long live the king," and he replied heartily, "Long live my good people."

His good people put up statues and monuments to him throughout France. At Dôle in Franche-Comté an equestrian statue in the principal square bore the simple inscription To Louis XVI. Another statue stood in Rennes. At Vendre in Roussillon a hundred-foot-high marble obelisk, surmounted by a globe and fleur-de-lis, was set on a plinth on which bronze bas-reliefs proclaimed the four epochs of Louis XVI: "Servitude abolished in France," "America made independent," "Commerce protected," "French navy revived."

Louis XVI was "a king well beloved."

CHAPTER XIII

"The unfortunate reality of the deficit"

IF IT HAD not been for the pressure of money, or rather the lack of it, things might have gone on drifting indefinitely, possibly until Louis XVI had reached old age. But the deficit grew, from a hundred to a hundred and twenty million livres annually, and the national debt assumed Alpine proportions. During the five years of his ministry, Calonne was said to have piled up a debt of nine hundred million livres, much of it devoured by the court. In 1786 the national debt stood at the colossal figure of from four to five billion livres—which, at a rough estimate, may be compared to some forty or fifty billion dollars in modern purchasing value. France, to be sure, was the richest country, in resources and industry, on the Continent, but no nation could forever live under such a load, particularly since the people got no compensations for the burden they bore.

Possibly the situation was not so alarming as these figures indicate, but Comptroller-General Calonne did not know how to manage without new loans and additional taxes. Calonne was a man of no principles but of great charm. He was witty, graceful, a splendid talker and keen debater, possessing a dangerous facility for words and an equally dangerous ignorance of the state of public opinion. His eloquence, according to Mercy, was "all-bewitching," but there was a limit to the dialectical susceptibility of hard-headed bankers, who, seeing no improvement in the finances of the government, would grant no more loans. Calonne could think of no way out other than new taxes, but it seemed certain that the Parlement of Paris would refuse to "register" any tax edict that did not have the consent of the nation. And to get the advice of the nation—however it would be done—meant to open wide the flood-gates of pent-up demands and indignations.

How does an absolute monarchy go about consulting the people who have had no voice in the government? In France there was neither Parliament (not to be confused with Parlement, which, to repeat, was a court of justice) nor political party nor popular cabinet—in short, no machinery for the expression of the national will. Voting of any kind was out of the question, for there was neither instrument nor precedent for it. Calonne was convinced that the one possibility was to consult the Notables.

Notables? Most Frenchmen did not know what the term implied. The majority of the nation had never heard that in France there was at one time a governmental instrument known as the Assembly of Notables, which, as the name indicated, consisted of the most notable personages of the realm—nobles, bishops, magistrates—meeting for the purpose of advising the king on policy (or demanding privileges). The Notables had not assembled for one hundred and fifty years, and the institution seemed as dead as the middle ages which had created it. Louis XVI for one, who knew the history of France as few men did, disliked the idea of reviving a corpse which he was sure his ancestors had permanently buried. For, however conservative the Notables were (representing only the upper classes), they were a challenge to monarchical absolutism. The king, however, was not proof against Calonne's "all-bewitching eloquence," and in the end he agreed to the idea—which struck everybody as ludicrous—that the Notables should be dug up, revived, reconstructed, and reassembled at Versailles to help His Majesty pass certain economic legislation.

⚜

AT THE END of the year 1786 royal invitations went out to twelve dozen Notables, summoning them to appear at Versailles in the latter part of January, 1787, "in order to communicate my views concerning the alleviation of my people."

Among the round gross of invited Notables were seven archbishops, seven bishops, seven marshals, ten dukes, thirteen counts, six marquises, twelve councilors and maîtres des requêtes, thirty-eight magistrates, twelve provincial deputies, twenty-five municipal officers. The common working people were not invited.

The Notables were to meet in the Grand Trianon at Versailles (a palace which Louis XIV had built for his mistress Maintenon and where Louis XV entertained his *amies*) and were informed to be prepared to discuss:

Reform of various laws
Form for the promulgation of edicts
The administration of civil and criminal justice
The administration of finances
The national assets and liabilities
The management of the domains and the *gabelles* (salt tax)
A territorial tax
Customs and excise barriers
Provincial assemblies
Abolition of mortmain
Civil status of the Protestants
A permanent loan fund

In brief, the Notables were to debate a reform plan of such magnitude that it would have changed the face of France. This was so sudden and so ambitious that, after centuries of misrule and disillusionment, the common people did not believe that the government was sincere. When the invitations to the Notables were made public, Paris responded with satiric placards:

"The little comedians of M. de Calonne will give the first presentation of *FALSE APPEARANCES*. His Majesty will honor the spectacle with his presence."

⚜

THE NATION was right to be skeptical, for the Assembly of Notables did not turn out to be even a good spectacle. From the start it was badly managed. The opening was postponed for more than a week, for at the last moment it was found that the Grand Trianon was too small to hold twelve dozen noble personages, and the Hôtel des Menus-Plaisirs across the park had to be hastily prepared. When the Notables finally did assemble to hear what the government had to say, they were disappointed at the king's general speech of welcome and his silence on policy. Louis left the proposals to Calonne, who had had several months to work out a detailed program. But Calonne had neither marshaled facts nor prepared plans, and when he got up to speak, he immediately antagonized the haughty lords with his sneering tone and vague generalities. The Notables had come to Versailles prepared to discuss policy, not to be commanded and insulted. And now Calonne, with incredible levity, told them, in a tone which hardly concealed its contempt, that His Majesty was resolved to carry through the projects anyhow but had simply invited the Notables for the sake of form!

This "crazy and shameless" speech was greeted with a storm of rage. *Fou, insolent,* the lords and gentlemen cried, and united to destroy the minister. And as if insulting the Notables was not enough, Calonne also went out of his way to sneer at his predecessor Necker and to accuse him of having mismanaged the finances. The vain Necker, who had an enormous following among the non-privileged classes, angrily struck back in a pamphlet which the king had expressly forbidden him to publish.

While the nation seethed with excitement and hurled imprecations at Calonne, the latter lost his head and found the pen. Hoping to defend himself from the attacks of powerful enemies, Calonne took to authorship and hotly wrote *Advice to the People,* a combustible pamphlet in which he castigated his opponents, especially the clergy and nobility. Not satisfied with the quill, the comptroller-general decided also to use the dungeon. In the midst of this war of words and hates,

L'ASSEMBLÉE DES NOTABLES.

Citoyens assemblés par un Roy Citoyen,
Conseil de la Patrie, et son noble soutien,

Vous ne trahirez point l'attente généreuse,
D'un Roi qui veut par vous rendre la France heureu

La Lettre de convocation, écrite
par le Roi
aux divers Membres, conçue en ces termes:

M

Ayant résolu d'assembler des Personnes de diverses conditions et des plus qualifiées de m état, afin de leur communiquer mes vues pour le soulagement de mes peuples, l'ordre de mes fi nances et la réformation de plusieurs abus, j'ai jugé à propos de vous y appeller.

Je vous fait cette Lettre pour vous dire que j'ai fixé la dite Assemblée au 29 du mois d Janvier 1787 à Versailles, et que mon intention est, que vous vous y trouviez le dit jour à son ouverture, pour y assister et y entendre ce qui sera proposé de ma part: Je suis assuré que je trouverai en vous le secours que je dois en attendre pour le bien de mon Royaume, qui en est l'objet. Sur ce je prie Dieu qu'il vous ait en sa sainte garde.

A Versailles, ce 29 Décembre 1786.

A Paris Chez | C rue St. Jacques No. 9
| Mlle Lesclapart Libraire, rue du Roulle.

THE CONVOCAT

A conte

IE NOTABLES

venir.

Calonne asked Louis to sign twenty *lettres de cachet* for the imprisonment of that many Notables. It was like pouring gasoline on fire, and Louis thought that the comptroller-general had gone crazy. Early in April, 1787, the author of the plan to invite the Notables was dismissed. Meanwhile the Notables continued to squabble furiously.

WITHOUT a responsible minister, Louis was lost. To make matters worse, Vergennes suddenly died. The minister of foreign affairs had served the king loyally for about a dozen years, and Louis had always trusted him. "I have lost," Louis wailed, "the only friend on whom I could count, the only minister who never deceived me." Louis was only thirty-three, but his former friends and ministers—Turgot, Maurepas, Vergennes—were all dead. He felt himself alone and helpless, while the nation was clamoring excitedly for reform. Marie Antoinette, disturbed by the storm that the Calonne-Notables conflict had created, suggested that Necker be recalled.

But Necker had made the mistake of publishing his attack on Calonne in contravention of the king's direct order, and when the queen showed Louis a printed copy of the pamphlet, she had an unusual chance of observing how roaringly mad a good-natured fat man can sometimes really be. Louis cursed up and down the cabinet and swore that by God he would exile that conceited so-and-so from France. Marie Antoinette was not accustomed to such language, especially from an ordinarily meek husband, and she burst into a tirade of her own; she shouted that His Majesty must indeed have gone mad to think that in the present state of the public mind he could with impunity persecute a man of Necker's reputation. Louis' rage cooled, but it continued to smolder, and on the following day he exiled Necker from Paris.

Gloom and discouragement settled over Versailles. Louis shut himself off from everybody, helpless as an invalid, while a tempest of opinions raged all over the country.

The king means well [Louis' young sister Elizabeth wrote to a friend]. The queen is very pensive; sometimes we are alone together for hours without her saying a word: she seems to fear me. Ah, but who, however, could take a more lively interest in the welfare of my brother than I? Our opinions differ: she is Austrian, and I am Bourbon. . . . I have a presentiment that all this will turn out badly. . . . Intrigues fatigue me. . . . I love peace and repose. But when the king is unhappy it is not the time for me to separate from him.

Louis spent hours in his wife's boudoir, weeping inconsolably. What caused the shock was not the acrimonious dispute unleashed by Calonne and the Notables, but the revelation of the deplorable state of finances. Louis had known in a general way that things were bad, but he had never been told the extent of the evil. For years both Necker and Calonne had kept the truth from him, probably because they did not want to discourage him. But in the course of the triangular Calonne-Notables-Necker battle—which was aired in public—it had come out that the national debt was a mountain of four or five billion livres. That such a debt (or at least a large part of it) could pile up during the short reign of a monarch who prided himself upon his frugality and economy was a blow to the ego from which Louis found it hard to recover. Because the king was such a frugal, simple-living man, he laid undue stress upon financial difficulties; and because he was an honest man, he suffered deeply at the realization that he would never be able to pay the gigantic debt that had been incurred in his name. Louis sobbed that he was a discredited bankrupt, that as king he had lived beyond his means, and that now public confidence had fallen to the point where the bourse was deserted and no honest broker would even touch government bonds. The queen told him that only Necker could restore public confidence, but Louis shook his head with the sort of obstinate hopelessness she knew so well.

After long brooding, Louis shook off his lethargy and

called together another meeting of the Notables, who had in the meantime been amusing themselves with intrigue and political throat-cutting. Louis addressed them solemnly, urging the need for financial legislation and implying that only new taxes could save the state.

> I do not wish to dissimulate the unfortunate reality of the deficit [the king said]; it must appear frightful at first glance. ... I know that the best means to abolish the deficit is to establish economies, which I am firmly resolved to do. Already I have decreed many retrenchments and others are being considered. It is essential to act with celerity; the evils which have been unveiled are great and have caused disquiet among the public. ... I am assured that you will give me new proof of your zeal and fidelity.

But the Notables saw no reason whatever for sacrificing anything for king or country. The aristocracy had lost all sense of social responsibility. During the generations they had enjoyed unchallenged social-economic privileges, the lack of competition deadened the sense of self-preservation and blunted all feeling of class interest. A ruling élite that has no competition must sooner or later decay, and the Notables were a glaring illustration of this principle. The position of the French aristocracy had been so long established and unchallenged that it seemed inconceivable that things could ever be otherwise than they were. The Notables failed to realize sharply enough that as a privileged class it was tied to the monarchy; any wound inflicted upon the crown was bound to cause bleeding in the body of the aristocracy. And when Louis asked them for coöperation and some sacrifice (such as permitting the nobility and clergy to be taxed), the Notables thought the king's demand either stupid or frivolous. Instead of getting together upon some practical program, the Notables enjoyed themselves in maliciously digging out examples of Calonne's wastefulness and graft. One noble, the Prince de Conti, accused the dismissed comptroller-general of having embezzled eighty million livres; others showed how he had enriched his friends. Still others burrowed into the treasury figures and proved triumphantly that the deficit which Calonne had claimed to be only one hundred and fifteen million amounted to one hundred and forty million. The Notables saw no reason for more taxes to enrich grafters, but they were unwilling to do anything about the grafters.

When the Notables coldly informed the king that Calonne had minimized the deficit, Louis seized a chair and smashed it in rage. "That scoundrel of a Calonne! I should have him hanged!"

⚜

FROM chair-smashing and cursing Louis fell into heavy fits of melancholy, and for weeks he brooded over the appointment of a new financial magician. There were only two possible candidates, Necker and Loménie de Brienne, archbishop of Toulouse. But Louis disliked the one and distrusted the other. A pious man, the king thought that a priest's place was in the church, not in politics. *"Je ne veux ni neckrailles ni prêtrailles,"* he said in a fine phrase—"neither neckerhood nor priesthood." Toward Loménie de Brienne he had a special aversion, for the archbishop of Toulouse was known to be a lover of women and a disbeliever in the Deity. Years before, when Brienne, a friend of Turgot and of Malesherbes, was proposed for the archbishopric of Paris, Louis had refused the appointment with a rare flash of wit: "But surely the archbishop of Paris should at least believe in God!"

Marie Antoinette, however, was convinced that there was no better candidate for the comptroller-generalcy than Brienne, and she persistently urged the king until, out of weariness, Louis put the archbishop into an office that had broken men like Turgot, Necker, and Calonne. "The archbishop," Mercy wrote to Vienna, "is a creature of Her Majesty." Brienne, indeed, considered himself such: no sooner was he appointed than he went to the Austrian ambassador and thanked him for his office!

The archbishop, if not pious, was certainly frank. He told

the king that he knew little about finances and asked that Necker be appointed his assistant. Louis replied obstinately, "I don't doubt Necker's talents, but now that I have you I can get along without him."

Now that he had another minister of the finances, Louis thought he could also get along without the futile Notables. They had become, he said, "tiresomely importunate." At the end of May, 1787, after three and a half months of fruitless squabbling, the Notables were dissolved and sent home. Calonne's thoughtless move had achieved nothing but further damage to the royal authority. Assembling the Notables after a century and a half of oblivion had set an unforgettable precedent. So quick-witted and intelligent a nation as the French did not fail to see the true significance of the gesture: that the absolute monarch who, like his ancestors, wielded absolute power had confessed himself incapable of exercising it and had called in outside help. The Assembly of Notables had, by very reason of its existence, torn the veil off the imposing front of absolutism, and the foundations that Louis XIV had built were seen to be unsound. It required only audacity to topple the whole gilded structure. Louis XVI had taken the first halting steps towards consulting with *some* representatives of the nation—even if these were only the upper classes—and logically there was no reason to stop there. On the contrary, there were millions of Frenchmen—especially the members of the bourgeoisie, merchants, intellectuals, artisans—who felt that the real representatives of the people (meaning themselves) could do better than the bishops and the aristocrats. Let the king consult them! It was a portent of things to come when the Marquis de Lafayette, a thirty-year-old noble recently returned from the American war with memories of a popular Congress fresh in his mind, spoke of an Estates-General for France. Gradually but insistently the voice of the nation rose in criticism, swelled in demand. "It is unbelievable," Mercy reported to

Vienna with unconcealed bitterness, "with what freedom the nation allows itself to criticize, complain of, condemn the slightest operation of the ministers."

Louis, whose appetite remained so ravenous that he always ate gargantuan meals which put him to sleep at moments when critical decisions were necessary, did not coöperate with Brienne. But like Turgot and Necker, Brienne started out with sincere intentions of retrenching and economizing. He would apply the paring-knife to the octopus court, and his first bold step took the form of reducing the royal stables from three thousand horses to a mere two thousand seven hundred; with one voice the personnel of the *écurie* cried that it was being robbed. Brienne then tried to cut down the huge sum of ten million livres that was spent annually on buildings and grounds, but Director d'Angiviliers vigorously objected and blocked the move. Marshal Ségur, the minister of war, flatly refused to chop more than eight million off his budget of one hundred and ten million, although it was pointed out to him that a much larger army under Louis XV was better equipped and maintained for only seventy million livres. At every step Brienne met with almost insuperable obstacles, for the king, who had the right to command, did not have the strength to fight. The little that Brienne was able to achieve in the way of economy was like scraping a barnacle-encrusted hulk with a finger-nail. With no master to crack the whip, each minister was an absolute lord, a despot in his own domain, fighting tooth and claw against any encroachment upon his income or prestige. The government was in a virtual state of anarchy, and the country reflected the government. "In France at the present moment," one writer remarked in the summer of 1787, "there is neither legislation nor legislator."

Unable to carry through economies, Brienne followed the path beaten by numerous predecessors—that of imposing new taxes. But the day of such arbitrary impositions had passed.

The Parlement of Paris, which exercised the functions of a supreme court, refused to register the tax laws, on the ground that they were invalid without the consent of the nation. Let the Estates-General, that is to say a congress representing the various classes ("estates"), be assembled and vote upon taxes—so argued the Parlement of Paris. The session of the Parlement was marked by violent words. Louis' brother Artois, speaking for the crown, cried that the English, whose fashions everybody imitated, also had the kind of tax that the government proposed. To which one Robert St. Vincent, whose mordant wit had earned him the nickname *Robert le Diable,* flashed back, "Monseigneur, we ought not to imitate the English. You should recall that they have dethroned seven of their kings and cut off the head of an eighth."

Millions of Frenchmen rolled the phrase on their tongue.

When the obstinacy of the Parlement, the same Parlement that Louis had restored to office a dozen years earlier and had then warned that it must be absolutely obedient, was reported to the king, he cried that he would "break it like glass." His temper suddenly flared up because he was frightened by the possibility of a conflict with the judicial authorities. He summoned the Parlement of Paris to Versailles and held a *Lit de Justice,* which was a legal institution under which the justices of the crown were compelled to "register," that is approve, whatever laws the king decreed. This was a clever trick, worthy of Brienne who had advised it, but it was no longer effective. No sooner had the justices returned to Paris, a Paris bursting with excitement, than they publicly declared that they had acted under constraint and therefore the tax laws were null and void.

Even a weak monarch could not afford to ignore such a direct challenge to his authority, and Louis angrily exiled the Parlement of Paris to Troyes. His grandfather Louis XV had acted in the same way, and Louis XVI knew with what painful results. But he had no choice, his ministers having pushed him into a position from which he could not retreat.

All France was tossing as if in fever. From the English Channel to the Mediterranean the air was filled with cruel, sultry words. "The Frenchman," one writer observed sadly, "is incapable of cool deliberation."

⚜

CARTOONS and *pasquins* burst upon the land, "pullulating like a pestilential wind," in the words of a contemporary. In no country in the world, "not even in the most independent republic," a foreigner observed, was there a press so unbridled as that of Paris. The walls were plastered with angry demands and incendiary appeals. In Toulouse, Rennes, Bordeaux, and numerous other cities orators fanned the "flames of revolution," as the Duke of Orleans called it. Everywhere stinging words fitted biting pictorial art. A cartoon showing the king and the queen at table was captioned, "The king drinks, the queen eats, the people weep."

Louis was troubled and frightened, particularly since his notorious cousin the Duke of Orleans, who was soon to play the part of a revolutionary hero, wrote him a stern letter of warning that unless he recalled the Parlement and dismissed the discredited ministers, France would burst into a "fatal conflagration which will be hard to extinguish." [1] In his bewilderment Louis took a step which he had always refused to consider—that of appointing a prime minister to bear all responsibility and make decisions. For premier he chose the ailing and elderly Brienne and informed the cabinet suddenly that "the situation demands that there be among the ministers one to whom the others may report." [2]

Promptly the ministry resigned. Castries left the navy, Polignac retired from the bureau of posts, Lamoignon laid down the privy seal, Ségur gave up the war office. No minister wanted to obey a master. The governmental structure was cracking at the top . . . all around Louis XVI.

1 Arsenal MS 6316, p.65-68.
2 Archives Nationales, C220, 160 142, no.6.

⚜

In the provinces mass-meetings were held in defiance of royal authority, and government officials were refused obedience. The country was in a mood of insurrection, and everywhere was heard the "obstinate and unanimous" cry for the convocation of the Estates-General. The Estates-General had not met for almost one hundred and seventy-five years, but at one time, from the middle ages to the year 1614, it was a sort of national parliament in which the people were represented by classes—clergy, nobility, commoners. Whatever its shortcomings, the Estates-General had been more or less representative of the nation at large, as against absolute monarchy; now Frenchmen were clamoring that this long-dead assembly, killed by the ancestors of Louis XVI, should be revived to cure the ills from which the nation was suffering.

Louis might have continued to ignore the turmoil had not the financial situation been growing really desperate. There was no money in the treasury, and no new taxes could be imposed since the Parlement of Paris had refused to "register" the edicts; even if the tax decrees were issued arbitrarily, it was certain that, in the inflamed state of public opinion, collecting the taxes would be an impossibility. But the treasury was so depleted that, as Mercy confidentially reported to Vienna, "from day to day they do not know how to meet the slightest expenses." A loan was imperative, but confidence in the government was so shaken that the cautious bankers would advance no more money without the consent of Parlement. So Brienne, the ailing and broken archbishop who believed he would succeed where Turgot had failed, persuaded Louis to confess himself beaten and recall the exiled Parlement. It was a terrific humiliation to the king personally and a crashing blow to the monarchy, but Louis saw no choice.

The people celebrated their victory with frenzied joy. In Paris intoxicated crowds burned effigies of Calonne and of Madame de Polignac, the queen's favorite. Only the timely intervention of the police prevented the burning of the effigy of Marie Antoinette herself, so deep was the resentment against *l'Autrichienne*. But the police could not drown out the mocking cries: "Madame Deficit!"

On the walls of Paris laughing voices read:

Le parlement est fou, je pense,
Car il a perdu son latin
De vouloir regler la dépense
D'un ivrogne et d'une . . . putain.

In such an atmosphere of excitement the king invited the restored Parlement to Versailles for a *Séance Royale*. A "Royal Session," it should be explained, differed from a "Bed of Justice" in that debate was allowed in the presence of the king. This Royal Session was assembled in order to register one edict for a loan of four hundred and forty million livres and another granting civil rights to Protestants—the latter a compensation for the former. In the course of his address, Louis uttered a few words that electrified the country. "Only I have the right to decide on the usefulness of the Estates-General," he said. Which implied that he might decide to assemble the Estates. This was the first time such words had passed the king's lips.

But the Parlement was not so easily bribed. The Royal Session turned into a desperate struggle where opponents and proponents of absolute monarchy battled each other. The debate on the loan lasted seven passionate hours, during which time Louis listened in silence, heavy and brooding. Finally, in fear that the vote would be adverse, Louis ordered the keeper of the seals to register the edicts on the ground that they had a majority vote. Then something unforeseen occurred which shocked the hall into breathless silence.

From among the peers and dukes arose the stocky figure of the king's cousin, the Duke of Orleans, who in a trembling voice—scared at his temerity—asked His Majesty a sarcastic question: "Is this, then, a Bed of Justice?" The implication was clear: only in a Bed of Justice did the king have a right to issue decrees without a vote.

Louis, never quick-witted, stammered, "No, it's a Royal

Session." Which was an admission that he had no right to command the registration of edicts without a vote.

"Nevertheless," Orleans sneered, "I see nothing that does not bespeak a Bed of Justice," and added that the king's procedure was manifestly illegal.

In the tumult that followed this verbal exchange, the humiliated king, never before challenged in person, lost his presence of mind and quickly left, almost fled, the hall, without taking the trouble to dissolve the Royal Session, which continued its turbulent debate. In his frustration Louis took out his rage on the Duke of Orleans, whom he exiled to his estates in Villers-Cotterets—and thereby made a national hero. More and more the king, incited by the baffled Marie Antoinette, inclined to solve problems with exile. Meanwhile the Parlement returned to Paris and countered the king's move with an *arrêt d'objection*—repudiating the tax edicts as illegal. The war between crown and people was well under way.

⚜

So ENDED the year 1787, the fourteenth year of Louis XVI's reign, with the monarchy everywhere in retreat, the state bankrupt, and the country on the verge of insurrection. The strain began to tell on the rulers. Brienne began to cough blood. Marie Antoinette, full of anxiety and forebodings, took to her bed. Louis came down with erysipelas. Up on the throne there was neither will nor light nor decision. "From day to day," Mallet du Pan writes, "they change political systems. No rules, no principles. The sun does not rise three days at Versailles on the same counsels. Uncertainty of weakness and total incapacity."

A disinterested observer coming to France from the outside world would have been startled by a spectacle of chaos and anarchy—the experience of a nation in the process of breaking with its past—by a scene of decay above and of ferment below. One such observer, Baron Philip von Alvensleben, a cool-headed Prussian diplomat sent to France at the end of 1787 to investigate conditions, wrote a devastating account of what he saw:

> The queen is more hated and more powerful than ever. She has left her frivolous society and occupies herself with politics. Since she has no head *à système* she goes from caprice to caprice. . . .
>
> The principal minister is a mediocre fellow who will hold his place only so long as the queen wishes and so long as he is weak. . . . He has arrived by intrigue and will maintain himself by intrigue. . . .
>
> Count Montmorin [3] lacks not so much the will as the ability to do evil. . . . The Comptroller-General is, so to speak, null. . . . Baron de Breteuil could perhaps act with a certain energy, but the queen will have nothing of him, since he is too much of a man.[4]

Alvensleben then remarked that the government "lives only from day to day" and expressed his doubts as to whether reforms would do any good: it was hopeless to try to do anything about the situation.

> It is as impossible for France to put order into her affairs and consequence into her plans as it is for water to go against the current. . . . If credit were revived, the squandering, the disorder, the magnificence of attire, the abuses, and the arrogance of conceit will go on with head raised and the people will be more ground down than ever before. . . . France is like a young man whom one cannot free of his debts, because the more money he has the more credit he gets, and the more credit he gets the more he squanders. . . .
>
> To regenerate this nation, or rather the government, it would require a king who has capacity, will, force, and, above everything, perseverance; but how can one ever get such a king of France?

Was there any hope in the people? Alvensleben did not think so. To the Prussian diplomat the French nation was

[3] Armand Marc de Montmorin succeeded Vergennes in the department of foreign affairs. Like Brienne, he was a creature of the queen. Mercy described him: "About forty years old, with a small insignificant figure and unpleasant face. No wit or natural eloquence, of a quiet, taciturn character, cold in the presence of strangers;" Bibliothèque Nationale, MS n.a.Fr.6968, p.366.

[4] Louis Auguste de Breteuil (1733-1807) was the minister of war.

egoistic and shallow. Rulers and people, the Prussian concluded, were cut on the same pattern.

> Everything here is in ceremony, in formal dress, in veneer, in phrases, in national *gasconnades,* in tinsel, in intrigue. . . . Substance always gives way to form. Twenty-five million united egoists, and vain of their union, despising all other nations . . . , and everybody up in arms if any attempt is made to remedy the evil and destroy the abuses.

CHAPTER XIV

"Frenchmen, gather your forces!"

Become ye, O French people, the model of Europe!
Of Europe? Nay—of the whole world!
The world has its eyes fixed upon you,
It is ready to burn incense before you.
O Frenchmen, terminate your slavery!
Recover your courage—gather your forces! [1]

IN THE MIDST of violent agitation Louis permitted himself to make the mistake of trying to reform the judicial system. At a time when the nation applauded the Parlement of Paris as a champion against absolutism, the king, with that fatal lack of timing which was one of his basic characteristics, issued a sudden decree reducing the Parlements to their original functions of mere courts of law and depriving them of their right to pass upon political or financial questions. The reform in itself was not bad, but the time chosen was deplorable.

Instantly the country reacted. Everywhere the royal reform act was greeted with spontaneous and overwhelming protest, in some cases insurrectionary. At Rennes, for example, the Breton provincial assembly, abetted by the officials of the province, flatly rejected the new measure and for-

[1] Archives Nationales: K 160, no.7 [41]: from a pamphlet, *Le Second Coup de Vêpres.*

mally stigmatized as "infamous" all those who accepted positions in the new courts. This was revolution.

Louis sent an army to Rennes. The Bretons countered with a deputation to Versailles to protest against the royal troops. This questioning of his authority enraged Louis still further. "You came here without my permission," he shouted. "I ought to punish you. I alone have the right to give the law to my subjects." He clapped the deputation into the Bastille and ordered thirty thousand more troops to Brittany.

Royal soldiers kept the fires down in Brittany, but they could not extinguish spontaneous flames elsewhere. It was the ancient city of Grenoble that set the tone for and voiced the demands of the whole country. Here the Notables of Dauphiny gathered and challenged the king:

"Sire, no one has ever made a more terrible use of arbitrary orders. . . . Sire, in thus multiplying acts of harshness, did your ministers hope that fear would reduce us to silence? They have very badly estimated our courage. . . ."

Then Dauphiny spoke in the name of France and made a series of demands which became the national program:

> All the suppressed tribunals to be restored.
> Dauphiny to make common cause with other provinces.
> No taxes be paid without the consent of the Estates-General.

FROM Grenoble the cry for a national parliament rang out and reverberated throughout all the cities, towns, and hamlets of France. The fever was so infectious that even highborn aristocrats became advocates of parliamentarism. When the Duke de Luynes was asked which side he intended to take, he replied, "I am for the nation rather than the king." Other nobles, among them such blue-blooded ones as the Duke de Rohan-Chabot and the Marquis de Lafayette, signed a popular petition in favor of the imprisoned Breton deputation. Montmorency, another duke of ancient lineage, strode up and down his chamber, slapped his thighs and roared, "We'll see how the sorry king will extricate himself this time!" The chasm between crown and aristocracy was widening rapidly.

And the "sorry king"? He was very unhappy. Agitation always upset him, and the use of force caused him physical revulsion. Only the promptings of what he considered his duty made him employ violence at Rennes. But the thought of repeating the experience sickened him.

Brienne, at the point of resignation, told Louis that there was no alternative to further violence except the Estates-General.

Estates-General? The two words echoed and reëchoed throughout the land, but neither king, nor ministers, nor subjects knew precisely what kind of institution the Estates-General was. Some thought it a Parliament like the British, others an upper-class debating society like the Notables. For a hundred and seventy-four years the Estates-General had not met, and its composition, membership, procedure, jurisdiction, function, method of election, all were hidden in the obscure past. Curious, the power of words! All France was clamoring for something of which no one had any knowledge.

Louis agreed to revive the Estates-General—but how does one revive something about which one knows nothing? Common sense dictates that one should study the subject and decide upon a specific course of action. But instead of doing this, Louis committed the mistake of inviting the nation to tell him about it. "His Majesty invites all the scholars and informed persons in his realm, and particularly the members of the Academy of Inscriptions and Belles Lettres, to send all the information on the subject of the Estates-General to the Keeper of the Seals."

THE CALL for the Estates-General, issued in the summer of 1788, galvanized the nation but disquieted the king's friends. From the point of view of absolute monarchy, it was a dangerous step, fraught with incalculable consequences. For, once the representatives of the nation were invited to give advice, there was no way of quieting them, quashing their demands, keeping them in check—unless the monarch was firm in his leadership and knew exactly what he wanted. This was what the sixty-seven-year-old Malesherbes told Louis in an urgent interview. Malesherbes went to see Louis and pointedly reminded him that Charles I had lost his head because he was weak.

> You read much, Sire [Malesherbes said], and you are well instructed, but reading is nothing if it is not accompanied by reflection. I have recently gone over the life of Charles I in Hume's *History of England.* Do reread it carefully: your positions are similar. Charles I was virtuous, attached to the laws, and yet he perished on the scaffold. And this is the reason, I believe: He lived at a time when the nation disputed the prerogatives of the crown; he dared not yield those prerogatives for fear of humiliating himself.... It is the same in France to-day.

Louis squeezed Malesherbes' arm approvingly, and the ex-minister continued:

> The softer manners of to-day, to be sure, reassure you against the violence of those times [!], but the people will wrest from you by degrees many of your prerogatives. It is up to you to have a clear-cut plan of concessions you are ready to make for the general good. On your firmness will depend the success of such a plan. Without such firmness—perhaps you will not meet the fate of Charles I, but there may be excesses....

Louis assured his friend that he would be as firm as Henry IV. Then he formally announced to a jubilant nation that the Estates-General would meet in the coming spring—April, 1789.

"Now," Louis' faithful valet Thierry said, "the king will be much happier."

⚜

MEANWHILE the country was impatient with a government which was palpably drifting without aim or will. Unfavorable economic conditions added to the confusion and insecurity.

On the bourse shares were dropping and in the markets the price of bread was rising—a formidable combination. A scapegoat and a savior were badly needed. Inevitably the country cried *Down with Brienne! Long live—Necker!*

Even the court was convinced that only Necker could save the country in the interim. Marie Antoinette wanted the banker from Geneva to became the assistant of the helplessly floundering Brienne, but the bourgeois idol of the nation refused to be anybody's subordinate. Brienne had to go. Then Louis reluctantly appointed Necker, whom he ardently disliked, dictator of the finances.

It was a sad day for the monarchy and a triumph for the people. Louis, knowing the appointment to be a self-inflicted defeat, shut himself up broodingly in his cabinet. Marie Antoinette sensed likewise that the step had dangerous possibilities. "This day," she wrote tearfully to her brother, "has affected me.... One can no longer hesitate.... It is very urgent. I tremble to think that it is I who brought Necker back. My fate is to bear misfortune. If internal intrigues will make Necker fail again..., they will detest me even more."

Paris celebrated riotously. The commune formally declared "execrable the memory of Loménie de Brienne because of his well-known crimes" and decreed that he be burned in effigy. So deep had the monarchy fallen that a minister of the crown was publicly branded a criminal by the government of the nation's capital! On the Place Dauphiné in front of the statue of Henry IV, where pyres flamed, crowds went wild and attacked the guards with shouts of *Vive Necker!*

Provincial assemblies asked that Necker be crowned with a civic crown; the Estates of Dauphiny solemnly declared him the savior of the nation. "The nation was in alarm, on the verge of ruin, when a just king recalled you. *That event alone was a great revolution.*" [2]

[2] Bibliothèque Nationale; MS n.a.Fr.6619, p. 15.

⚜

MARIE ANTOINETTE AND HER THREE CHILDREN

Portrait by Vigée Lebrun, 1787. Musée de Versailles. Left to right the children are: Madame Royale (1778-1851); the second dauphin, Louis XVII (1785-1795); the first dauphin, Louis Joseph (died June, 1789).

A MORE PROFOUND revolution in the mind of France was caused by the nation-wide discussions on the subject of the proposed Estates-General. For months nobody talked about anything but the Estates-General. The country was flooded with pamphlets, typical of which was perhaps Sieyès' *What Is the Third Estate?* and his bold answer, *Everything!* Louis did not agree with the response, but he read and studied much that appeared on the subject.

From pamphlets and resolutions it appeared that in general the nation wanted the Estates-General to be a moderately democratic parliament, more or less like the British. There was a universal feeling that only the representatives of the people could understand the needs of the people and alleviate their suffering, which was uncommonly great.

For in the autumn of 1788 and the winter of 1789 the economic situation was grave. Floods and hail-storms had in many places reduced the harvest by about half. The price of bread was steadily rising: in 1761 a pound of bread cost one and one-half sous and in 1789 five sous—a catastrophic increase. Unemployment reached disastrous proportions, especially in the larger towns. In Abbéville twelve thousand out of fifteen thousand people were out of work; in Lyons twenty thousand out of fifty-eight thousand had no employment—Arthur Young has described their distressing conditions. Paris, a city of six hundred thousand inhabitants, had one hundred and twenty thousand unemployed, and numerous people from the distressed provinces kept streaming into the capital to find bread, if not work, thus adding to the mounting misery and unrest.

WITH Louis' approval, Necker worked out a plan whereby the Third Estate (the common people) was to be given the same representation in the forthcoming Estates-General as the other two orders combined. The Third Estate, to be sure, formed the overwhelming majority of the French nation and by right of numbers should have been granted control, but the Estates-General had never been a democratic parliament in the modern sense. Even so, Louis' concession was a victory for the commons, since it gave them—for a start!—equality vis-à-vis the two privileged orders.[3]

The king's resolution was announced at the end of December, 1788, a New Year's gift to the delighted country. One month later Louis sent out the epoch-making royal letters to the governors of the provinces informing them how the representatives to the Estates-General, to open at Versailles at the end of April, were to be chosen. The novelty in the royal letters was not in the surprisingly democratic method of election—granting the suffrage to all tax-paying males over twenty-five years of age[4]—but in the request that the nation draw up lists of grievances for the deputies to take along. This was a request either of matchless generosity or of unexampled stupidity, for at one blow, without the slightest preparation, France was made a democracy by being granted the basic democratic privilege, that of free expression of opinion.

Louis' request electrified the nation. Immediately the king

[3] There are no accurate figures as to the number of persons in the two privileged orders. The general population of France was approximately 25,000,000. Of these, according to estimates made by Taine, 140,000 were clergy and about 30,000 families were noble; others have estimated the noble families as high as 100,000. Only a fraction of these nobles, however, had the privilege of attending court—some 649 families (the list is in the Archives Nationales, Registres MM 810-816). At the very most, the two privileged classes were made up of about three-quarters of a million persons—or three per cent of the population.

[4] The elections were indirect. Louis Gottschalk, *The Era of the French Revolution,* 104-05, thus describes the method: "The district of the *bailliage* or the *sénéchaussée* was used as the electoral unit. On a given day, the *bailli* was to call the clergy of his *bailliage* or bailiwick together. Each clergyman . . . was to represent himself in person or by proxy and to be eligible to the Estates-General. . . . On the same day, the *bailli* was to call the nobility together, and they likewise, by direct representation, were to choose their deputies to the Estates-General. But the Third Estate chose its deputies by two and sometimes by three separate steps. In the country districts, the villages elected their deputies to the bailiwick assemblies, while in the cities the guilds . . . chose representatives to the municipal electoral assembly that, in turn, sent representatives to the bailiwick assembly; and there only did the bailiwick assembly elect its deputies to the Third Estate. Paris and four other large cities were given direct representation."

was hailed, in that bitter-cold and hungry winter, as a self-destroyer of tyranny, a champion of liberty.

O Louis! O roi populaire!
Il brise le sceptre arbitraire!

The nation was in near-hysteria with its exclamations: "Our good king!" "The king our father!"

But Louis asked for a *cahier* and got an avalanche. For centuries grievances had been accumulating, economic grievances and political, social and personal grievances, grievances of the soil and the shop, of the merchant and the worker, parish grievances and city grievances—and now His Majesty suddenly asked his good subjects to come and tell him their troubles! Louis XVI's request became a national psychoanalysis, a course of treatment lasting two stormy decades.

A good example of grievances and demands was the *cahier* of the Third District of Paris (Feuillants and Louvre), drawn up by the famous astronomer J. Sylvain Bailly. Within half a year Paris was to head the upheaval and Astronomer Bailly was to head Paris, and so this *cahier* was the advance voice of the Revolution.

Paris demanded:

Liberty of the press
Abolition of the *lettres de cachet*
Abolition of lotteries
Responsibility of the royal ministers
Alienation of the crown domains
Admission of commoners to all offices, ranks, and employment
Secrecy of letters confided to the post-office
Reform of civil and criminal justice
Free election of municipal officers
Internal freedom of commerce and the suppression of monopolies
Suppression of feudal justice, of asylums and privileges
Construction of four hospitals in Paris
Abolition of the *Mont-de-Piété* (municipal pawnshop).

CHAPTER XV

"Twenty-five million united egoists"

IN THE SPRING of 1789 the rents in Versailles sky-rocketed as excitable deputies from the most remote reaches of France began to arrive. They came, those French curés, nobles, lawyers, merchants, summoned to adjust the finances of the realm, some unwitting heralds and others conscious makers of a new order. The fateful moment had arrived, but Louis did not know that it portended a change deeper than anything Europe had ever dreamt. He had been out walking in the Marble Court when his artisan's curiosity prompted him to climb a scaffolding on which laborers were working; suddenly he lost balance and would have fallen forty feet to his death had not a worker quickly grabbed his coat-tails. The grateful monarch granted his humble savior a pension of one thousand two hundred livres on condition that the worker should not change his station in life.

Though Louis still thought in terms of permanent social status and was not aware of the temper of the nation, other observers were. Early in April, Mercy wrote frankly that he feared a revolution was imminent. "We are in an abyss which makes us face with terror the moment of the Estates-General; they portend disastrous reverses for royalty. My dispatches . . . give but an incomplete idea of the *revolution which is brewing in this monarchy.*"

Already Paris was tossing in fever. In the proletarian Faubourg St. Antoine, where towered the gloomy Bastille which was bitterly cursed as a rocky symbol of tyranny, the workers defied the police, assembled nightly, formed ominous *attroupements,* and burned effigies. These were curtain-raisers, so to say, experiments designed to test the vigilance and potency of the police. The police did not come off well, a fact which the workers were quick to observe and remember. Hourly the baited lieutenant of police reported to the king at Versailles, and in the faded words of the manuscript letters one can still read the palpitation of an agitated official: "I hasten to inform Your Majesty that the French Guards dispersed the mob; no one was hurt." At 6 P.M.—"The evil makes surprising progress every second; the audacity and temerity of the people are carried to an extraordinary degree; the crowd is big." Later—"Calm continues to reëstablish itself; in the Faubourg St. Antoine only a few groups remain." [1] The police mind was frantic, but all this was child's play.

ON THE FIRST of May, heralds, superbly clad in violet velvet embroidered with golden fleurs-de-lis and riding white chargers, proclaimed by mouth of silver trumpet the formal opening at Versailles of the Estates-General—an event which had not taken place for one hundred and seventy-five years. On that day Louis received the deputies of the three estates and tried to impress them with the majesty of his position. The reception was time-honored and ritualistic, but already somewhat dated. First came the order of the churchmen, 309 of them, in the king's private cabinet; afterwards His Majesty received the 285 aristocrats in the same chamber —a mark of confidence and intimacy. Lastly came the 599 commoners, who crowded into the long Hall of Mirrors (where the Treaty of Versailles was signed a hundred and thirty years later); Louis did not greet them with effusion, and many sensitive plebeians were hurt.

[1] Reports of de Crosne to Louis XVI, April 24-28, 1789; Archives Nationales, C221, 160 [146], nos.48-57.

Then a heavy rain fell, and Louis kept thoughtfully looking out of the windows wondering whether on the morrow the ground would be dry enough for tapestries to be laid on the way to church.

It cleared in the morning, and at ten o'clock the regally dressed king left his apartments surrounded by the princes of the blood and entered the royal carriage which was drawn by prancing white-plumed horses. Slowly the gilded procession rode toward Notre Dame de Versailles, there to meet all the deputies of the nation. A curious incident occurred on the way. In the respectful crowd that sardine-packed every foot of the route, Louis suddenly espied a familiar face—the captain of his greyhound bitches. His Majesty brusquely stopped the procession, leaned forward, and loudly told the man not to waste his time gawking but to go back to his kennels.

Mild exclamations greeted Louis at Notre Dame. Applause for the queen was noticeably chilly. The royal carriages stopped while the waiting deputies fell in line to march to the church of St. Louis; the way was guarded by two rows of troops which were hardly able to hold back the milling crowd. Through this life-lined path the élite of France marched slowly and with impressive dignity. Never had France seen such a solemn cortège.

At the head of the march were the curés of the churches of Versailles, and behind them, in two parallel lines, ambled the deputies of the Third Estate, representatives of the common people, all in black with gleaming white cravats, flowing hair covered with the curious tricornered hats later made famous by Napoleon. They were solemn as penguins. In their midst there towered a craggy head, hewn like arrogant rock but chipped with deep pock-marks: it was a monstrously ugly head, but the most impressive, most explosive, most eloquent head in France—Mirabeau. Wave after wave of thunderous applause greeted the black-clad representatives of the Third Estate—and Mirabeau.

Behind the commoners walked the noblesse, also in black,

wearing white-plumed hats *à la* Henry IV, cocky and colorful. At their appearance the applause died sharply; it was briefly resumed only for the popular Duke of Orleans, the future Philip Égalité, a "friend of the people." Silence fell again as the clergy passed by carrying the Holy Sacraments. The king and his family marched immediately behind the Sacraments. Louis was cheered, Marie Antoinette was greeted icily.

Inside the church of St. Louis the bishop of Nancy preached a dull sermon on "Religion Is the Strength of States, the Only and Inexhaustible Source of Their Prosperity." Mirabeau, sitting in the rear of the church with the other deputies of the Third Estate, muttered contemptuously that the good bishop's homily was awfully stupid, "without plan, without ideas, without style, without effect." Everybody was bored, but at one passage the audience sat up. "And it is in the name of a good king," the bishop cried, "of a just and sensitive monarch, that the miserable exploiters of the people exercise their barbarities." Peals of prolonged applause greeted these words.

Vives pierced the dignified church at every mention of the "good king."

On May 5 the three estates met in the Salle des Menus-Plaisirs, a gilded and colonnaded hall one hundred and twenty feet long with an exquisitely painted oval in the ceiling and an elevated platform for the king at the extreme end. The deputies began to arrive at nine in the morning, but it took the combined efforts of three masters of ceremony two hours to seat each in his proper place.

They made a large splash of color—the nobles in their silks and white plumes, the cardinals in their red hats, the bishops in their violet cassocks, and the commoners in drab black, penguin-necked. All were nervous and, while the roll was called, waited impatiently for the king.

Agitated sighs of relief greeted His Majesty's arrival at noon. Louis was dressed in the mantle of royalty, and with fattish dignity he ascended the gilded throne on the platform. The deputies rose, clapped, *Vive le roi!* Politely they cried *Vive la reine!* as Marie Antoinette seated herself on her husband's right.

As the applause died, Louis rose, ceremoniously raised his plumed hat in greeting, and firmly read the speech from the throne:

> Gentlemen—This day which my heart has awaited a long time has finally arrived, and I see myself surrounded by the representatives of the nation which it is my glory to *command*. . . .
>
> The debt of the state, already immense at my accession to the throne, has increased even more during my reign; a costly but honorable war has been its cause; augmentation of taxes has been the necessary consequence. . . .
>
> A general uneasiness, an exaggerated desire for innovation, have seized upon the public mind, and we hurried to allay matters by assembling wise and moderate counsel.
>
> It is in such confidence, messieurs, that I have brought you together. . . .
>
> I have already decreed considerable retrenchments in expenditures . . . ; [2] but despite the resources which the most severe economies may offer, I fear, gentlemen, not to be able to relieve my subjects as promptly as I should like. I shall lay before your eyes the exact condition of the finances. I am assured . . . that you will propose to me the most effective means of reëstablishing them and to strengthen the public credit. . . .
>
> May a happy understanding, gentlemen, reign in this assembly. . . .[3]

The brief speech was greeted warmly enough, but mainly by the Third Estate. The two privileged orders were rather cool; among them were carping erudites who commented

[2] Despite these claims the budget of the royal household still stood at 25,000,000 livres. This colossal sum was thus distributed:

The queen's household	4,600,000 livres
Table	2,500,000 "
Stables	3,500,000 "
Guards	4,000,000 "
Buildings	2,500,000 "
Pensions	3,000,000 "
The king's aunts	1,600,000 "

[3] Archives Nationales, ADI 98, v.I.

OPENING OF THE ESTATES-GENERAL AT VERSAILLES

A Dutch engraving of 1794 after a drawing by J. Bulthuis.

drily upon a rhetorical slip the king had made. He had said, "The nation which it is my glory to *command,*" instead of "the nation which I *govern.*" For, the aristocratic purists said, one *commands* individuals but *governs* a nation.

The deputies of the Third Estate were satisfied with the king's friendly tone and hoped that his ministers would be more specific about proposals. What concerned the commoners most was the question of voting, whether by head, which would give the Third Estate ultimate control, or by body, which would perpetuate power in the hands of the two privileged orders. But on this basic question king and ministers were eloquently discreet.

With minor reform proposals the government was more generous. Barentin, the keeper of the seals, promised changes in the criminal code, liberty of the press, redistribution of taxation. The deputies applauded politely and waited for more. Finally Necker rose to speak. Perhaps he, the vaunted tribune of the bourgeoisie, would say something to justify the great occasion. But the fatuous Genevese banker droned on for three awful hours, traveled over eighty (printed) pages, covered miles of figures, and left the audience limp and bewildered. From the torrent of words the bored deputies disentangled three simple statements: that the income stood at 475,294,000 livres, the expenditures at 531,444,000, and the deficit at 56,150,000. As a matter of fact, the deficit was well over 150,000,000 livres. Necker concluded by asking for a loan of 80,000,000 livres.

The deputies looked at each other in surprise. Was that what they were invited for—to vote more loans?

In the afternoon the Third Estate muttered about the need for a democratic constitution, a thorough political reform. There was much excited talk about where political power should rest. Marie Antoinette said sarcastically, "Are the Estates-General the masters of the king, or will the king remain master of the nation?"

⚜

THE STRUGGLE for power began in earnest on the following day. While Louis was conferring with his ministers, the deputies of the three estates met in separate rooms, and the first two orders began to verify credentials. At this point the Third Estate, regarding itself as *the* representative of the nation, took up the challenge and started a revolution.

The vital question that came up was how the Estates-General should vote. If the Third Estate accepted the principle of voting by body, then, regardless of the number of its deputies, it would always be outvoted by the other two estates. If, however, the vote were by head, then the superior numbers of the Third Estate would give it equality for the present (600 *vs.* 600) and assured victory for the future. It took no political genius to realize what was involved, and as a matter of fact the Third Estate included many experienced lawyers with a keen sense of reality, and at least one man endowed with unusual political generalship—Mirabeau. The commoners, moreover, were fired with an élan that comes from a conviction of the justice of one's cause, while the other two orders were divided as to their self-interest (the poor, low-born parish priests had little love for the rich aristocratic bishops) and uncertain as to their position. The two privileged orders were on the defensive and in half-agreement with their critics. Furthermore, the insecurity of their position was aggravated by the king's known unreliability. Traditionally, to be sure, clergy and nobility had always stood by the throne, which was an amalgam of a trinity —crown, miter, sword. Historically the special privileges and position of the upper orders derived from the monarch, and they in turn gave the king their selfless devotion and loyalty. Such was the theory and foundation of monarchy.

Now, in a crisis, the two upper classes felt they were without support from the crown, for Louis XVI had an almost unbroken record not only of vacillation but also of what the aristocracy considered unroyal liberalism. They felt they could not trust him to fight for their interests. From hour to hour no marquis or bishop was sure of Louis' support. Any moment a courier might arrive from the château with the news that His Majesty had decided to back the claims of the Third Estate against the other two.

In the struggle about the voting everything depended upon the king's decision. Louis' popularity and authority were still so great that he could have imposed almost any moderate program upon the Estates-General—if he had had a program. Unfortunately his advisers were mediocre and his talent for leadership somewhat less than adequate: he could not make up his mind whether to espouse the cause of the common people or of the privileged people. The sensible thing for him to have done was to transform the Estates-General into a parliament on the British model, with the first two orders forming one upper chamber and serving as more or less of a check upon the lower chamber. But only one man, the bishop of Langres, timidly made such a proposal, which Louis ignored. As usual, Louis hoped that something would happen, and so he did little to soften the acerbity of the conflict among the deputies. The sharp class feelings that were thus permitted to be generated lived on for years.

A conciliation committee appointed by the estates to straighten out the question of voting labored across a canyon of misunderstanding for four weeks. Finally Louis resigned himself to some sort of action. He wrote a letter to the Estates-General offering to mediate between the three orders. But Mirabeau, distrusting the king's intentions, shouted *A trap!* Let His Majesty, the pock-marked deputy cried, mind his own business and stay out of the quarrel!

"A mediator such as the king," Mirabeau argued, "can never leave any real freedom of action to those whom he desires to conciliate. The majesty of the throne alone would be sufficient to enrapture them. We have not given him the slightest pretext for intervention. . . . It is a trap, a snare. . . ."

Instead of accepting Louis' offer, the Third Estate, following the advice of the shrewd Mirabeau, decided to send to the king "an address full of love" and fidelity for the throne. The honeyed words covered a clever proposal, namely, that the king should combine with the people against the upper classes. Louis was reminded that in French history there had always been a "natural alliance between throne and people against the aristocracies."

Louis was taken back by this sudden manœuver on the part of the despised commoners. He was not only unprepared for such a démarche but also temperamentally unreceptive. His reply was non-committal. "All the orders of the realm," he said, "have an equal right to my goodness, and you may count upon my protection and my good-will."

Thus Louis XVI missed his first big chance to ally with the Third Estate and set himself at the head of the popular movement.

⚜

INEXORABLY events took their course, without the king. An accident complicated matters and had curious consequences. While the estates were locked in their struggle and the commoners were trying to win over the king, the royal family was suddenly bereaved by the loss of the dauphin. The child, hardly eight years old, died of tuberculosis, according to the autopsy, his left lung entirely destroyed. Louis broke down under the shock, and Marie Antoinette's hair whitened. The parents shut themselves in their apartments and refused to see any one, at a time when matters of vital importance to the state were shaping. When a deputation from the Third Estate came to offer condolences and insisted upon being admitted, Louis, his lips trembling, said, "Is there no father among them?"

The consequence of the dauphin's death was this: The mourning court moved from Versailles to Marly, and there, away from the active political stage, Louis fell under the influence of the extreme right wing led by his wife and his brother Artois. Stiffened by them to resistance against the detested Third Estate, Louis began to scold the commoners and reprimand them for their various presumptions. What he resented particularly, he wrote, was the plebeians' attack on the two privileged orders, even, in fact, the very use of the word "privileged":

> I disapprove of the repeated expression, "privileged classes," which the Third Estate employs to designate the two first orders. These obsolete expressions serve only to maintain a spirit of division absolutely contrary to the advancement of the public good. . . . I am convinced that the more the deputies of the Third Estate will give me marks of confidence and attachment, the better will their actions express the sentiments of a people whom I love and by whom it will be my happiness to be loved.[4]

Thus the Third Estate conceived that it had no friend in the king and that it was unwise to depend upon him. On June 17, about six weeks after the opening of the Estates-General, the impatient Third Estate took matters into its own hands and declared itself *the* National Assembly of France. The idea was that those who liked might join—and the lower clergy kept trickling in by the dozen—and those who did not could go and tell the king about it! It was a challenge to the crown to do battle with the representatives of the common people. What would Louis XVI do? Louis XIV would have clapped the impudent plebeians into the Bastille; Louis XV would have exiled them. And Louis XVI?

To Marly hurried the archbishop of Paris with harrowing tales of impending doom if the defiance of the commons was left unpunished. The archbishop of Rouen seconded his Parisian colleague's plea for action. On their knees the two princes of the Church painted a picture of the awful dangers that faced the monarchy, how the commoners were planning and plotting to gain control of the army, place it under the command of the Duke of Orleans, and seize power from the king.

Louis was really scared. Hastily he called a council of his ministers and advisers and asked for opinion. There was a division of minds. Necker and three other ministers advised the king to accept gracefully the action of the Third Estate. But the other ministers and the princes of the blood urged

[4] June 16, 1789; Bibliothèque Nationale, MS Fr.13713.

severe measures against the impudent canaille. Outvoted in council, Necker's friend St. Priest, the minister of the royal household, said bitterly: "You talk about maintaining the old constitution at any price, but you ignore the horrible consequences to which this may lead.... Your Majesty has an army, it needs to be paid, but the royal treasury is empty."

Unwilling to take drastic action against the Third Estate and afraid not to, Louis compromised by postponing his decision. A special meeting of the Estates-General was to be called three days later, and then His Majesty would explain his intentions. In the meantime the meeting-place of the Third Estate was to be locked up and made ready for the royal session.

By a curious and, as it turned out, fateful oversight the king failed to inform Bailly, the long-nosed and sad-eyed president of the so-called National Assembly, that there would be no meeting for three days. And so, on June 20, when the deputies of the Third Estate arrived in the morning for their usual session, they were astonished to find the hall under guard and repairs going on inside. To the tense and nervous commoners, who for weeks had been under strain and always expecting trouble, this looked like a trick on the part of the government, a lockout, to prevent them from holding their meetings. Rebelliously they adjourned to an indoor tennis-court near-by, talking excitedly as only Frenchmen can in a political crisis and working themselves into a frenzy against the diabolical machinations of the court. Heads were quickly inflamed, took fire from one another, and gave way to an emotional conflagration. Suddenly a startling oath was proposed.

Upon a table rose the lean figure of President Bailly and solemnly read words that electrified the deputies. Each one of them repeated the so-called Tennis-Court Oath:

> The National Assembly, inasmuch as it was called to establish a constitution for the realm, effect a regeneration in the public order, and establish the true principles of monarchy, nothing can prevent it from continuing its deliberations *in no matter what*

place it is forced to establish itself, and that finally *wherever its members are joined together there is the National Assembly.*

All members of this Assembly swear immediately a solemn oath never to separate and to reassemble wherever circumstances demand until the constitution of the kingdom be established.

Among those who signed this veritable declaration of independence were Mirabeau, Robespierre, Barnave, Bailly, Camus.

The French Revolution had begun.

Louis paid no attention to the Tennis-Court Oath and its revolutionary implications. He failed to see that the oath, promising a constitution to the people of France, challenged his very existence as an absolute monarch and that the only way to meet the defiance was either to imprison the rebellious deputies or grant their claims. Louis did neither. The oath had been taken on a Saturday, and over the week-end the king was busy working with Necker on his speech to be given at the promised royal session on Monday or Tuesday. King and minister behaved as if nothing had happened and as if mere words were effective weapons with which to fight revolutionary demands. When Montmorin, the minister of foreign affairs, suggested mildly that the king yield to the *Tiers* because the nation was behind it, Louis shrugged his shoulders.

All Versailles turned out to hear the king's speech on Tuesday. Even on this solemn occasion the government could not refrain from insulting the Third Estate by keeping the deputies out of the hall—Salle des Menus-Plaisirs—until the first two orders were seated. The king spoke in hushed silence.

The Estates-General [Louis said in his well-modulated voice] have been open almost two months and they have not been able to come to an agreement on the preliminaries of their operations. A perfect understanding should have been born from love of the fatherland alone, and a fatal discord throws alarm into everybody. I want to believe, and I like to think, that the French people have not changed. But to avoid making reproaches to any of you, I consider that the revival of the Estates-General after such a long period, the agitation which preceded it, the purpose of its convocation, so different from that for which your ancestors were summoned, the restrictions of powers, and various other circumstances, all have necessarily led to conflict, debates, and exaggerated claims.

I owe it to the welfare of my realm, I owe it to myself, to put a stop to these fatal divisions. It is as the common father of all my subjects, it is as the defender of the laws of my realm, that I come to recall to you the true spirit and to repress the blows which have been aimed. . . .

Then Louis proposed his concessions "for the public good" and explained, with evident pride, that "never has a king done so much for any nation," immediately adding, "but, then, what other nation could have merited it more than the French!"

The deputies leaned forward tensely to hear what the king offered to the nation:

No new taxation without the approval of the representatives of the people.

The budget to be published annually.

Each governmental department, including the royal household, to have a fixed budget.

No privileges or distinctions in the imposition and collection of taxes.

Abolition of the *lettre de cachet*.

Liberty of the press.

Provincial diets—half the membership of which was to be made up of the Third Estate—to be given self-administration (hospitals, prisons, finances, forests, roads).

Liberty of commerce within the country.

Reforms in the administration of justice.

Permanent abolition of the *corvée*.

Suppression of the mortmain.

Thus Louis offered to return to the nation many of the rights wrested by his ancestors. For himself he proposed to retain the "army, as well as all authority over the police, such as the French monarchs have always enjoyed." It was a sound reform program and acceptable to the Third Estate;

but there was a catch to it, hidden, like the lash of a scorpion, in the tail. Louis concluded:

> Reflect, gentlemen, that none of your projects, none of your proposals, can have the force of law without my express approval. I am the natural guarantor of your rights.
>
> I command you, gentlemen, to separate immediately and to come to-morrow morning, each to the chamber allotted to your order, to resume your sessions.

In other words, the king ignored the Tennis-Court Oath and refused to recognize the Third Estate as *the* National Assembly. He still spoke in terms of three separate orders.

Applause from the benches of the nobility and clergy; silence from the Third Estate.

The commoners remained in the hall in a rebellious mood. They agreed with the king's statement that never had a monarch offered so much to his subjects as Louis had done that day, but, they said, he should have thought of that two months ago. To-day it was too late; they, the deputies of the Third Estate, had traveled a considerable distance in the last eight weeks. They had taken an oath not to disband until France had a constitution, and they were determined that France should have a constitution. Twice they had defied the king with impunity, and they felt they could do it again. Louis had shown no disposition to fight.

The master of ceremonies told the commoners to leave the hall, as the royal session was ended and king and aristocracy had long left. Mirabeau shouted a defiant *No.* President Bailly cried that no one had a right to give orders to the nation, and the Third Estate was the nation, its deputies the National Assembly. In this mood of defiance they voted unanimously that the "person of each deputy is inviolable" and that he—whether king or official—who harmed a member of the National Assembly should be declared "infamous and traitor to the nation, and guilty of a capital crime." Brave words, these, but legally devoid of value, for the Third Estate had no right to vote on such matters, let alone to vote without the other two orders. Still, the resolution set a precedent, and it was up to the king to accept or reject it. The deputies fully expected to be thrown out of the hall by the king's officers, but to their delight and surprise nothing happened. Louis, tired out by his long speech, refused to take the doings of the Third Estate seriously. When a messenger told him that the deputies were still squabbling in the hall, the king shrugged wearily. "*Eh bien,* let them stay!"

⚜

Louis thought that now, after he had offered his reform program, the people would be grateful for the favors and go quietly home. In this he did not even miscalculate: he simply did not calculate at all. It is no idle figure of speech to say that the temper of the people, especially the people of Paris, was like that of water heated to the boiling-point, with no one making an effort to turn off the heat. Thrice the monarchy had been defied by the Third Estate, and every time His Majesty had ignored the challenge—a political lesson that no fool could miss. Since the beginning of his reign Louis had had a reputation for kindliness; no Frenchman actually imagined him ruthless enough to use force. People remembered that only once in his fifteen-year-long reign, under the prodding of the late Turgot, had Louis shown a disposition to employ violence. And though few of the common people had ever seen or met Louis XVI in the flesh, none believed him cruel or capable of severity, all thought him a good man victimized by crooked ministers and deceived by a scandalous wife.[5]

They had come, the people of Paris, by the thousands to exert pressure on the Estates-General, as well as to encourage their own delegates. The popular heroes at this time were

[5] The attacks on Marie Antoinette never let up. The printed libels against the queen gained in virulence and number, a mounting spout of sewage. One pamphlet addressed the king in the following tone: "One favor which the people hope and expect from Your Majesty, Sire, is the perpetual banishment of this Messalina, whose scandalous excesses dishonor the court and whose infamous avarice prepares the ruin of the throne." Another pamphlet speaks of her as "the ruin of France, a spouse *often* separated in body and *always* in interest from His Majesty Louis XVI." Archives Nationales, AD I 75G.

HONORÉ GABRIEL RIQUETI, COMTE DE MIRABEAU
Portrait by Joseph Boze. Louvre.

Necker and Louis XVI. No one doubted that in his heart the king was with the people. He might be misled by wife and counselors, but the people were there to make him correct his course, by direct action where necessary.

So now the people took matters in hand, cautiously feeling their way. On the day after the king's speech the carriage of the archbishop of Paris was surrounded by a threatening crowd, the windows smashed, and His Eminence bespattered with mud. This was a mild hint that the archbishop's well-known lack of sympathy for the populace was heartily reciprocated. On the following day Versailles overflowed with tumultuous crowds from Paris. Mobs ran through the streets, carried torches at night, shouted *Vive la Nation! Vive le Roi! Vive Necker!* The crowds were harmless, all they intended was to terrorize the upper classes and to remind the king that the people were alert. These terrorist tactics were successful. Within two days after the king's speech in which he "commanded" the three estates to meet separately, more than half the clergy had gone over to the National Assembly.

Thus inexorably the Estates-General was transforming itself into a one-chamber parliament, despite the king's wishes and intentions. Panicky courtiers warned Louis that unless he exerted himself quickly he would lose the throne. "The state," Comte Talleyrand said to the king, "is menaced by a total revolution." Barentin, the keeper of the seals, bluntly warned Louis against tolerating the "apparent contempt" which the people were showing him and said that only force could save the royal authority. Artois, the king's brother, urged that troops be called out to suppress the Assembly. Louis did not budge. On June 27, four days after his now-ridiculous "command" to the estates to meet separately, the king yielded to the people and instructed the two upper orders to unite with the Third Estate to form the National Assembly.

The people celebrated jubilantly. Louis and Marie Antoinette had to come out on the balcony, bow, and even try to smile. *Vives* rent the air. Folk embraced and wept and sang and danced. In Louis' heart there was fear, and in Marie Antoinette's bitterness.

In the Salle des Menus-Plaisirs, where the Assembly held its sessions, one lone aristocrat refused to compromise with his conscience, despite the king's orders. Baron de Lupé, a little atrabilious man from Auch, went daily to the hall of the noblesse and spent several hours holding meetings by himself. He was the last true aristocrat of the *ancien régime,* the Baron de Lupé of Auch.

On the same day Louis secretly dispatched troops to Paris, for no reason except that the die-hards at court such as the Queen and Artois urged it. Breteuil, the minister of war, boasted, "If it's necessary to burn Paris we'll burn Paris."

CHAPTER XVI

"Lo, the fire of revolt!"

BEGINNING with July, 1789, the populace of Paris was king, Louis XVI its amazed and reluctant subject. From this point forward history moves on two levels—what the populace did, how the monarch reacted. The biography of Louis XVI merged with the life of the people of Paris.

The city on the Seine was the largest metropolis on the Continent, with one thousand three hundred streets and boulevards, fifty-two government buildings, forty-eight parishes, thirty markets, twenty-nine hospitals, twenty-four colleges and seminaries, fifteen parks, fourteen bridges, nine prisons, and eight big palaces. It had a population of about six hundred thousand, one-fifth of whom were unemployed at this time, and a revolutionary atmosphere as manifest as the marvelous hues of its shifting cloud-speckled sky. What gave Paris (and still gives, for that matter) its air of excitement, political and other, is hard to define. Since time immemorial it has been a gay, restless city. An historian is not privileged to speculate, but he has observed that Parisians smoke incessantly and are inveterate wine and apéritif drinkers. And as an artist who has lived in the French capital for years remarked to this writer, "The Parisian is hardly ever drunk and never quite sober."

On the day when Louis ordered the two estates to join the National Assembly, the court fell into a state of hysteria. Marie Antoinette was weeping, and everybody behaved as if he were insane, so Mercy relates. Queen and courtiers scared the passive Louis with wild talk about Necker's plans to set himself up as dictator and the Duke of Orleans as commander-in-chief of the army. Crazily they talked about running away from France, declaring war on the National Assembly, burning Paris....

The hotheads goaded the king into sending an army of some forty thousand to Paris. It was a stupid show of strength, futile because it was unnecessary and dangerous because it was provocative. The king had no intention of doing anything with his mercenaries, yet the appearance of the royal army in Paris had the effect of the proverbial red rag on the bull. The Parisians instantly defied the royal authority, not by attacking the troops, but by breaking open the prisons. On the last night of June a crowd of several thousand rushed to the jail of the Abbaye St. Germain and liberated fourteen members of the French Guard who had been imprisoned for radicalism. The soldiers were carried to the Palais Royal and fêted amid scenes of emotional intoxication. To add irony to the insult, and by way of showing the close connection between the people of Paris and the National Assembly at Versailles, the crowd asked the Assembly to demand of the king clemency for the freed Guards.

Perhaps this was a test to see how far Louis would tolerate the violence of the Parisians. If so, it was successful, for the king was disposed to forgive. To the delegation he said, "I hope that everything will go well. I shall let you know my final intentions."

His final intentions were expressed in a letter which he wrote to the National Assembly. The letter, forgiving the Parisian rioters, did justice to his heart but did not enhance his authority.

> The violence used in the liberation of the prisoners from the abbey [Louis wrote] is infinitely condemnable; all the orders, all

the corporate bodies, all honest and peaceful citizens have the greatest interest in maintaining the laws for the public tranquillity. Nevertheless..., I shall yield to a sentiment of goodness and I hope never to have to reproach myself for my clemency, since it has been invoked by the Assembly of the nation for the first time.[1]

No longer did Louis and the people, at least those of Paris, speak the same language. The king clung to the old-fashioned notion that violence was altogether deplorable and that it was his duty, as chief of the state, to uphold the laws (but not by force); the people, on the other hand, felt that the laws must be drastically changed, forcibly wherever necessary. It came down to this: Could a ruler who abhorred violence maintain himself against those who employed it as a deliberate technique?

And yet, because Louis was unable and unwilling to employ force against those who defied him, he constantly encouraged further disorders. A sort of guerrilla war existed between the mercenary troops and the people; even the democratic French Guards provoked the foreign soldiers—despised hirelings of monarchy—into fights. The concentration of the royal troops in Paris destroyed the peace and inflamed the temper of the people. Something had to be done to allay the fears and furies that obsessed the city. But what? Louis could have ordered his troops ruthlessly to enforce order in the capital, in which case a civil war might well have been the result; or he could have withdrawn the army, which would have meant a public confession of defeat. The clever lawyers in the National Assembly were quick to see the trap into which the king had been manœuvered, and under the stirring eloquence of Mirabeau, now the idol of the populace, the Assembly passed a resolution asking His Majesty to withdraw the army from Paris.

This time Louis was prepared with an intelligent answer. He told the deputation that the army was necessary to main-

1 July 2, 1789; Archives Nationales, C220, 160 142, no.13; Louis wrote and corrected the letter himself in an unsteady hand.

tain order because of the "scandalous scenes which have taken place repeatedly," and explained, not without malice, that the troops were also necessary to protect the National Assembly from the mobs.

Then he added cleverly: "If, however, the necessary presence of the troops in the environs of Paris still gives umbrage, I shall . . . transfer the Estates-General to Noyon or Soissons, and then I shall move to Compiègne in order to maintain communication–." [2]

From the point of view of the monarchy, that was an astute idea, for Noyon or Soissons was not so close to the menace of the proletarians of Paris as was Versailles. But the National Assembly was too clever to fall into the little trap. Far from the brawny arms of the Parisians, the Assembly would have been helpless vis-à-vis the king. Thank you, the deputies told Louis in effect, we prefer Versailles.

ON SATURDAY July 11 there was an angry scene between Louis and Necker. The king accused his minister of intriguing against him and of having aroused the popular beast against the monarchy. Necker defended himself with dignity, but Louis told him brusquely to pack up and get out of the kingdom as quickly and as unobtrusively as possible.

Necker went home and wrote a note to the king in a hand that trembled so that drops of ink fell on the sheet: "Your Majesty is losing the one man in the world who was most tenderly devoted to him. . . . I shall depart alone, without going through Paris, without opening my mouth to any one, and I urgently ask the same secrecy of Your Majesty." Then he ate dinner and drove off towards the Swiss frontier without seeing a soul. The most popular minister in France was fleeing the country at night like a thief.

As Paris awoke next morning, July 12, and heard the news of Necker's banishment, the already heated temper of the populace became incandescent. Promptly stocks fell on the

[2] July 10; Bibliothèque Nationale, MS Fr.13713, p.32.

bourse and the price of bread rose. Grim folk sought the streets and squares, formed processions and marched by the thousands, carrying likenesses of their heroes, Necker and the Duke of Orleans. They packed the vast garden of the Palais Royal, property of Orleans and the rookery of the revolutionists, and listened to firebrands haranguing them from chairs and tables, lamp-posts and tree-tops. Again and again came the terrible cry *Aux armes, citoyens, aux armes!* From the windows women fed the fires by throwing down *chapeaux* and feathers and ribbons. *Aux armes, citoyens, aux armes!* Nervous fingers were tearing the hats and ribbons and making cockades. *Aux armes!*

"I said to myself," a clerk from the Châtelet recorded in his Journal, "lo, the fire of revolt!"[3]

A riotous crowd marched to the Place Louis XV (Place de la Concorde), where a troop of Swiss mercenaries and dragoons barred the way to the Champs Élysées. The mob goaded the soldiers, who, terrified by the frenzied shrieks, drew their sabers. Piles of rock used for building a bridge across the Seine lay at hand, and as the steel flashed on one side, rocks began to fly from the other. Furious, Commander Lambeth ordered the troops to charge. They fell on the screaming populace, broke some heads, safely reached the garden of the Tuileries. Only one man was knocked out with a saber.

The revolution had its first martyr, had tasted its first blood.

Through the night and through the following day and night Paris seethed and boiled. Theaters closed, the stock-market closed, the markets closed. The gates at the Faubourgs St. Antoine and St. Honoré were burnt down. Torch-lighted crowds, armed with sticks and stones, poignards and pikes, roamed through the city, yelling and singing. They threatened to pillage the rich homes of "our common ene-

[3] This and the subsequent account is taken from a MS in the Bibliothèque Nationale, Fr.13713: *"Journal des événements survenus à Paris, du 2 avril au 8 octobre 1789 . . . , par un clerc du procurer au Châtelet."*

mies," but the bourgeois marchers restrained their proletarian allies; they were united against the crown, but not for plunder of private property. The armories of the prisons and the Hôtel de Ville were raided; guns and cartridges quickly passed into the muscular hands of the cockaded *soldats de la patrie.*

At the convent of the Lazarites—a delightful find: fifty-two wagon-loads of grain. Ah, the cowled wretches hoarding food while the poor were starving! In the cellars were fine wines and liquors. The grain was sent to the public *halles,* the wines were consumed on the spot. Trembling monks hid underground.

At the Hôtel de Ville citizens set up a new municipal government and created a bourgeois guard to preserve order and protect property.

In Versailles Louis was having his usual *lever.* Thither came the Duke of Orleans, the hero of the Paris mobs, to offer his services to his royal cousin and to show that he really had not instigated the populace. As Orleans approached with the shirt—as was his privilege, being a prince of the blood—Louis snapped, "What do *you* want?" Orleans said, "I come to take Your Majesty's orders." "I want nothing of *you,*" the king shouted, "return to where you belong." Orleans, the high-born master and puppet of the Paris mob, flushed and vowed vengeance on the royal family.

ON JULY 13 the court knew that Paris was virtually in the hands of the revolted people. The National Assembly begged the king to remove the troops from the capital, arguing that the presence of the army served as a constant irritant. Paris, in fact, ascribed all manner of fiendish machinations to the court, convinced that the king's friends were planning a St. Bartholomew of the patriots. Hence the terrible cry of *Aux armes!* in the streets of Paris. But the people were only partly right: some members of the court, particularly Artois, urged the king to shoot the rebels, but Louis could not bring himself to do it.

"I have thought it over," Louis told his brother. "To resist at this moment would be to expose the monarchy to peril; it would lose us all. I have retracted my orders; our troops will quit Paris. I shall employ gentler means. Do not speak to me about a *coup d'autorité,* a mighty act of force. I believe it more prudent to temporize, to yield to the storm, and above all to bide my time, for the awakening of the men of good-will and the love of the French for their king."

But just as Louis ordered the troops to leave Paris, the people took matters into their hands once more. Throughout the 12th, 13th, and the 14th of July the people had been collecting arms. Most of the muskets, cannon, and powder, however, was kept in the Bastille, a yellow-stone eight-towered fortress at the mouth of the Faubourg St. Antoine, in the heart of the workers' section. Thither, on July 14, a detachment of popular guards and some five thousand armed citizens went to obtain weapons. De Launay, the governor of the fortress-prison,[4] intended at first to resist, but was persuaded to capitulate. The Bastille was taken and De Launay killed. For days and weeks afterwards the Bastille was being demolished as an awful symbol of tyranny. But July 14, the day of its seizure, remained forever after a republican holiday.

That night La Rochefoucauld-Liancourt entered the king's cabinet and described the exciting events of the day. "It's a riot," Louis exclaimed.

"No, Sire," the nobleman cried, "it's a revolution."

Later, about eleven o'clock, a delegation from the National

[4] Legend had made out the Bastille to be a dreadful dungeon full of prisoners, but when it was taken in July, 1789, it had only nine inmates. Throughout the whole reign of Louis XVI the Bastille took in 287 prisoners, each averaging some six months' detention. Many of these prisoners, some 77, were put there by Turgot. It was in no way a terrible prison; its rooms were rather comfortable, in fact. In the reign of Louis XVI at least twelve prisoners went there voluntarily.

Assembly told Louis that the Bastille had fallen. The king's lips trembled. "You tear my heart with your recital. . . ."

⚜

Louis passed a restless night, and in the morning he decided to speak to his people through the National Assembly. He harbored no ill-feeling for those who had broken the peace in Paris, but he regretted their misbehavior. His wife and brothers wanted him to shoot the rebels, but Louis said that they were only children and he was their father, and he must go to them, tell them that they had been misled.

On the morning of July 15, while Louis was dressing for his visit to the Assembly, the deputies were debating how to receive him. Mirabeau had just finished one of his vehement speeches against the court, and many deputies said, Let us receive the king in silence, to show him that we are mourning the events of yesterday. Others said, No, each must act as he pleases, but with calmness and dignity.

If he had planned it consciously, Louis could not have made a more moving appearance. He was accompanied only by his two brothers—no guard, no cortège, no ministers. There he stood at the door, solitary, without the trappings of majesty, rotund, earnest, very sad. A spontaneous *Vive le roi!* burst forth in the hall. And it was sincerely meant.

Facing the whole Assembly, Louis spoke quietly:

> Gentlemen, the chief of the nation comes with confidence to its representatives to give evidence of his grief and to invite them to find the means to restore order and calm. I know that unjust accusations have been made; I know that some have dared proclaim that your persons were not safe. Is it necessary to reassure you in the matter of such criminal rumors, belied in advance by my known character?
>
> Well, it is I now who entrust myself to you. Help me to insure the safety of the state. Counting upon the love and fidelity of my subjects, I have ordered the troops to move away from Paris and Versailles.

The Assembly warmly applauded this capitulation on the part of the monarch and thanked him for his confidence.

THE BASTILLE

An engraving in Mirabeau, *Enquiries Concerning Lettres de Cachet, etc.* (London, 1787).

ARRIVAL OF THE KING AT THE HÔTEL DE VILLE

July 17, 1789. Note the time, 2:30. After an engraving by J. L. Prieur.

Then the radical Marquis de Sillery made a speech in which he praised Louis as the "best of kings" but denounced his ministers as "public pests." Sillery concluded with a phrase which winged its way through France:

"The French, Sire, worship their kings, but they never want to have to fear them."

So moved was everybody by the speeches that when Louis left the hall all the deputies spontaneously followed him as an honorary escort to the château. Crowds joined on the way, crying *Vive le roi!* It was a genuine tribute to Louis' humanity—or weakness. Even the queen was greeted when she and the dauphin (the second) came out on the balcony to watch the king's triumphant homecoming.

⚜

WHEN the deputies returned to the assembly, Joseph Barnave, a twenty-eight year old lawyer from Dauphiny with a handsome face and romantic eyes, made a motion that the king be warned that "none of his present ministers will ever obtain the confidence of the people." Immediately the cabinet resigned, and Louis humiliated himself by writing to Necker, "I invite you to return as soon as possible to resume your place near me." Necker accepted.

⚜

IN THE MEANTIME Paris had created two new heroes. Sylvain Bailly, the long-faced, long-nosed, long-bodied astronomer, was elected mayor of the city. Lafayette, a young aristocratic veteran of the American Revolution, was appointed commander-in-chief of the bourgeois militia (which soon became the National Guard).

Mayor Bailly invited Louis to come to Paris to show himself to his good people. The king dared not refuse. Marie Antoinette stood on a balcony and watched her husband's departure with tears in her eyes. She was not sure that she would ever see him again. Weeping, she said to Mercy that if they kept the king prisoner in Paris, she would take the dauphin and flee with him to Belgium. Louis was not certain of his fate either, but he went bravely, showing an impassive face to the *Vive*-shouters.

As the royal carriage rolled toward Paris, Mayor Bailly and his municipal councilors were arguing the question of how to receive the king. Traditionally the monarch was received by his subjects on their knees, but Bailly, a distinguished scientist and an honorary member of three French academies, swore that nothing in the world would induce him to deliver his welcoming speech in any position other than an upright one. His intransigence, however, may have been due to a less lofty cause than revolutionary idealism.[5]

At the gates of Paris the astronomer-mayor, preceded by two aldermen carrying the keys of the city on a vermilion cushion, coolly received His Majesty. Bailly elongated his lean scholar's body, handed the keys to Louis, and spoke a few but startling words:

"Sire, I am bringing to Your Majesty the keys of the good city of Paris; they are the same that were presented to Henry IV. He reconquered his people; here it is *the people who have reconquered their king.*"

Louis made an involuntary gesture of surprise at the double-edged words. He was not reassured when he watched the armed militia surround his carriage, nor did he feel himself master of his destiny, let alone that of France, when he observed guards flanking the road all the way to the Hôtel de Ville.

Inside the throne-room at the Hôtel de Ville was a streamer whereon bold letters reminded the king that he was LOUIS

[5] In 1779 Bailly lost his government job as custodian of paintings, and in a letter of protest written on August 6, 1779, he complained bitterly that the position was rightfully his because it had been held by members of his family for more than a century: "Thus, Monsieur, the descendant of a family attached to the king's service for 116 years, I filled for 25 years this position which you believe to-day I ought not to occupy. . . . To be sure, my studies have turned in the direction of science rather than painting, but this position does not demand the talents of a painter: I am not altogether ignorant of this *genre,* and I do not at all resemble that librarian who was put in the midst of books which he could not read." *L'Amateur d'Autographes,* 1862, p.222. He did not get his job back, and became an ardent revolutionist.

XVI, FATHER OF THE FRENCH AND KING OF A *FREE PEOPLE*. As he read the words and wished that he, too, were free like his people, Bailly handed him a cockade. Louis took this symbol of the revolution graciously, put it on as a token of democratic fellowship. Then he listened quietly to orations about Liberty and made a speech himself: "My people can always count upon my love." He showed himself from the window, and the immense crowd below thundered *Vive le Roi!*

Having thus impressed the king with its power, Paris this time let him go home to his family in Versailles.

"To-day, gentlemen," Necker said to the National Assembly, "it is in your hands that the salvation of the state lies."

CHAPTER XVII

"The baker, the baker's wife, and the baker's little apprentice"

STEP BY STEP the National Assembly was voting itself the royal powers which Louis' unsure hands had let fall—powers pertaining to legislation, taxation, war and peace—while the common people throughout the land, in cities and in villages, were hastening the process of disintegration by direct action. This chaos hurt Louis more than the loss of many of his royal prerogatives. He had been brought up to regard himself as the father of his people, and he was convinced that he was a kind parent. He had denied his children nothing; he had never been harsh or unjust. Why were they doing this to him, these misled children of his? Why were they smashing furniture, breaking windows, tearing down walls, and even flaunting him, their good father? He wrote to the bishops of the realm "publicly to implore the help of divine Providence," and he appealed to his children to "entrust themselves to my protection and to my love." Nobody listened to him.

Louis' brother Artois, who had wisely left France because he frankly disliked the canaille in power, sneered at such shilly-shallying, such unroyal timorousness. What the mob needs, the future Charles X wrote to his irresolute brother, is a whip—not prayers. And Louis was upset by his brother's arrogant strictures.

> You [the king wrote to his brother] speak of courage, of resistance, of will. My brother, you are not king. Heaven, in placing me on the throne, has given me a feeling heart, the sentiments of a good father. All Frenchmen are my children; I am the father of a big family entrusted to my care. Ingratitude and hatred are arming against me; but the eyes are merely clouded, the minds misled, the heads troubled by revolutionary torment. . . .
>
> I could have given, to be sure, the signal of carnage, and thousands of Frenchmen would have been slain. . . . I have done my duty and I can say openly: I am not responsible for any blood spilled. . . . I have the clear conscience of having done good. . . . Stop, my brother, stop accusing me: the times, the circumstances, and a thousand other causes have produced the misfortunes of France. It is too cruel to reproach me.

But even in irresoluteness Louis could not be resolute, for incessantly the court goaded him out of his passivity. The courtiers, to be sure, had fled pell-mell after hearing the shots fired at the Bastille, and they did not stop until they reached the frontier; but enough die-hards remained at Versailles to keep the wavering king in a constant state of vacillation. Chief of the intransigents was Marie Antoinette, lonely, sad, often in tears, but determined to save what she could for her two children. Convinced that her lethargic husband was not the man for a crisis situation, she constantly interfered, gave orders and shaped policy, always blunderingly. For the impulsive queen, full of pride and courage, had no capacity for reflection. At no time did she reveal even a glimmer of comprehension of what the "shooting was all about," to use a felicitous colloquialism.

She brushed aside her timid husband and took matters in hand. She had hardly ever conversed with an educated Frenchman, and yet she passed contemptuous judgment on the National Assembly (which one aristocrat said contained "all the talents, all the energies, all the spirit of France"), calling it a collection of rabble-rousers and traitors, and the people who supported the Assembly bestial mobs incited by scoundrels. Although Marie Antoinette never spoke the notorious words about eating cake, they well expressed her attitude; and the common folk of France instinctively felt their queen's aversion for them and reciprocated, a millionfold, with fear and hate. The same popular instinct exempted Louis from the hatred that overwhelmed his wife.

In all fairness it should be admitted that Marie Antoinette was a victim of circumstances, selected as the most succulent scapegoat for all the grievances that the nation had accumulated against the throne in the course of centuries. As Professor Harold Lasswell once acutely remarked, "All revolutions are ruptures of conscience"; and the sense of guilt (engendered by the break with authority) prevented Frenchmen from directing their animosities against the king, whom since childhood they had been taught to revere and who, moreover, was a Frenchman like themselves. For psychological reasons Louis had to be spared, although in his person resided all autocratic authority against which the nation was fighting. But the queen was ideal as a symbol of hostility—not unlike the Jew in Nazi Germany. She had all the characteristics of a successful "goat": she was conspicuous, she was in power, she was in a minority, she was notorious, and above all she was an outsider. And so she bore the brunt of the hatred of a nation which had been repressed for centuries, and ultimately this hostility was to affect the king also.[1]

As THE EXCITEMENT was beginning to subside, Marie Antoinette thought the time opportune to do something to regain some of the lost royal power. In September she persuaded

[1] In September, 1789, an anonymous pamphlet denounced the queen as *The Iscariot of France:* "The Austrian agent, ruler and tyrant of France, fruit of one of the most licentious concubinages, is made up of heterogeneous materials, fabricated from several breeds. . . . This Persephone wears the redoubtable head-dress of the Fourteenth Apostle, of the same character as Judas. Like him, she dips her claws into the plate to steal and squander the treasures of France: her hard eyes, traitorous and blazing, breathe only flame and carnage . . . ; her nose and cheeks are pimply and purple-colored from the tainted blood which is discharged between her flesh and her hide which is already leaden, and her fetid and infected mouth harbors a cruel tongue."

the reluctant king to bring mercenary troops (the Flanders Regiment) to Versailles. It was an incredible repetition of the blunder committed by the court in the early July days, since Versailles and Paris were comparatively quiet. Every one immediately suspected a sinister plot.

Warning came from an unexpected quarter. The Comte de La Marck, a moderate royalist and a friend of Mirabeau, suggested to Marie Antoinette that it would be wise to win over the great orator, who was needy and ready to serve. The queen said haughtily, "We shall never be unfortunate enough to be reduced to the painful extremity of having to resort to Mirabeau." Nevertheless, Mirabeau told La Marck urgently to warn the king against concentrating troops at Versailles. "The king and queen will perish," Mirabeau shouted. "You will see! The populace will thrash their cadavers!" La Marck's face showed repugnance at this gross expression, but Mirabeau repeated vehemently, "Yes, yes, they will thrash their cadavers! You don't understand the danger they're in! You must warn them."

The court did not heed the warning, and the temperature at Versailles and Paris rose to boiling-point. On October 1 a banquet was given in the palace for the officers of the Flanders Regiment, toasts were drunk to the king and queen, and in the midst of intoxication the red-white-blue cockade of the revolution was torn and trampled.

This destruction of the symbol of revolution started a train of frightful rumors, delirious and combustible. *Treason! treason!* revolutionary leaders cried. In the streets of Paris the sick and twisted Marat thundered, "O Dead! Awaken!" Tense crowds filled the Palais Royal garden where Orleans' money was being effectively distributed. Hunger coöperated with the agitators. For several days the transports of wheat to the capital had been unaccountably held up at Senlis and Lagny, and thousands went without bread. Early in the morning of October 5, a crowd of several thousand hungry women began to march from Paris to Versailles to force the government to feed them. Among the gaunt hunger-marchers on that wet and soggy day were persons with a grim purpose other than bread.

⚜

THE DAY and the night and the day after were wet and altogether crazy. Delirium was in the air, nightmarish doings which seemed to be purposeless in the dripping mist but which were taking shape through all the whirl, as if some hidden brain were directing a fantastic spectacle.

Louis was hunting at Meudon. He had just finished saying to his page, "Go and tell the *braconniers* that they are going too far, they might wound somebody," when a chevalier came running up. "Bands of assassins," he gasped, "are marching toward the château." "I thank you, sir," Louis said calmly, "but I have no fear. You must be tired. Get into one of my carriages and it will take you back to Versailles." At that moment Marquis de Salvert, the queen's equerry, arrived with a letter from Marie Antoinette urging the king to return immediately. Louis got into a carriage and hurried back to Versailles.

As the king's horses were galloping toward the château, the spearhead of the Parisian women marchers entered the hall of the National Assembly. *"Du pain!"* they cried, *"du pain!"* Mounier, the president of the Assembly, told them that the king was making arrangements to supply Paris with bread. "That won't do," shouted Maillard, the male leader of the hunger marchers. The women demanded to see their idol Mirabeau—"Our little mother Mirabeau!" "Our darling Comte de Mirabeau!" He was not there, but his fat younger brother, "Barrel" Mirabeau, reaped the glory for the family and kissed those among the Parisiennes who were good-looking. Then President Mounier and a deputation of twelve women started off for the palace through the mud.

Night had fallen when Mounier and the deputation were led into the château. Half-defiant, half-abashed, the twelve weary women huddled together in the lofty, gilded chamber, waiting for His Majesty. He had had no time to wash or change. As the stout unwashed and serene gentleman entered the chamber, the women dumbly pushed forward the prettiest among them, an art student named Louison Chabry, to speak for them. But the pale girl, overwhelmed by the presence of Majesty and perhaps because she was hungry, was only able to stammer, *"Du pain, Sire,"* and reeled in a fainting-fit. Louis caught her in his arms, had her attended to, and when she was revived he kissed her heartily. "It was well worth the trouble," he laughed.

To the women he said earnestly: "I am greatly touched by the insufficiency of food in Paris. . . . I have given most positive orders for the free circulation of grain on all the roads."

THAT was not the end. The women left the château but did not go home. Most of them remained through the night in the cold wet square in front of the palace, and the king refused to order the troops to disperse them. To appease the people he informed the Assembly that he had changed his mind about the Declaration of the Rights of Man which he had refused to sign the day before—"I accept purely and simply the articles and the Declaration." This was at eight o'clock in the evening. But the women did not move away; ominously they continued to squat outside in the rain. In a moment of panic Louis thought of flight. He could not have known it, but this was actually his last chance to escape the maw of the Revolution. Sleep deserted the palace. At midnight, to the king's immense relief, Lafayette arrived with an army of thirty thousand National Guardsmen and went through the reassuring motions of placing guards here and there throughout the château.

Still no one went to sleep. Before sunrise a group of men somehow broke into the palace, possibly with the connivance of Lafayette's National Guard, and ran murderously towards the queen's apartment. Alarm, screams, clang of steel against steel! Several bodies, especially of the king's Bodyguard, lay in pools of blood on the stairs and in front of Marie Antoinette's bedroom—loyal Swiss had saved her life with theirs. By a secret passage the queen just barely escaped into the king's room.

During the night, as if sprouting with the rain, the crowd had grown tremendously, and the château, in the bleak hours of the morning, looked as if it were under siege. They wanted the king. Lafayette brought him out on a balcony, accompanied by the queen and the two children. "Long live the king!" but not a word for the queen. With quick presence of mind Lafayette knelt beside the pale Marie Antoinette and kissed her hand. This tribute from the popular commander-in-chief of the National Guard aroused a response from the populace: "Long live the queen!" "Long live the general!" Marie Antoinette, white-faced, withdrew to a corner, and Louis stood bleakly alone on the little balcony. Suddenly a voice roared, "The king to Paris!" The populace, the army, the National Guard, the men and the women, took up the cry—"To Paris!"

Lafayette and Louis held a short consultation. Then the general stepped on the balcony and shouted above the uproar, "The king will go to Paris."

Louis spoke down from the balcony: "My children, you want me to follow you to Paris; I consent, but on condition that I shall never separate from my wife and children."

"Oui! Oui! Oui!"

"—My children, I demand safety for my Bodyguard."

"Long live the Bodyguard!"

The Bodyguard put on the revolutionary cockade.

Frantic cries of joy greeted the announcement that the royal family would leave for Paris at one o'clock in the afternoon.

⚜

WHERE thou goest, O Louis, there go we! The National Assembly sent a deputation to the palace to inform the king that it had unanimously decreed that the "person of the monarch is inseparable from the representatives of the nation." Louis replied, "It is the wish of my heart never to be separated from the Assembly."

At one in the afternoon of October 6 Louis and his family took their seats in the carriage in full view of the milling populace. Pale and still, the royal family sat for an hour, waiting for the deputies of the National Assembly and the National Guard. Then began that strange procession toward Paris, moving slowly, to keep pace with the multitude on foot and to give the thrilled populace a chance fully to relish its victory.

Never had France seen such a spectacle. A motley crowd of men and women, singing and dancing, preceded the National Guard with cannon on which men rode affectionately. Fifty wagonloads of flour, seized at Versailles, rolled along in the wake of the artillery. Surrounding these precious flour-sacks was a pretorian guard of hard-bitten *poissardes* waving branches of poplar. The carriage of the royal family followed the flour-sacks, symbol of monarchy in time of revolution, and Louis and Marie Antoinette faced a bizarre forest of swinging branches and bobbing pikes on many of which were impaled the ghastly heads of the Guards killed in the morning. Immediately behind, to underline the humiliation of the crown, straggled pell-mell the Swiss Guard and the disarmed Flanders Regiment.

Strands of hair hanging over their faces, the women sang ribald airs and conversed obscenely with meaningful gestures, all the while winking in the direction of Marie Antoinette. They grinned cynically and pointed to the wagons of grain and then to the royal carriage—"We'll no longer lack bread: we're bringing the baker, the baker's wife, and the baker's little apprentice."

⚜

Louis was impressed by the "grotesque saturnalia," as the *Moniteur* journalist called it. He was thinking of something very grave—the fate of Charles I of England. Recently he had read Clarendon's *History of the Rebellion and Civil Wars in England,* and every detail of that revolution was etched in his memory. "I am menaced by the same fate," he murmured; "the only way to escape from it is to do the opposite of everything that unfortunate monarch did." He recalled that Charles I had opposed the revolution sword in hand, so he was determined not to fight.

At seven in the evening they reached the outskirts of Paris, and Mayor Bailly, not without irony, handed the king the keys of the city. "It is a happy day," the long-nosed mayor said, "when Your Majesty comes to his capital with his august spouse and a prince who will be good and just.... Under the reign of Louis XVI the king will be powerful through his people and the people happy through their king."

Louis, holding the little dauphin on his knees, said, "I always find myself with pleasure and *confidence* amidst the citizens of my good city of Paris."

They drove to the Hôtel de Ville, where a platform was set up in front, facing the packed and torch-lighted square. Slowly the royal family ascended the platform and was applauded by the multitude.

Bailly addressed the populace: "His Majesty said to me that he always finds himself with pleasure amidst the inhabitants—"

Marie Antoinette sharply interrupted, "And with *confidence—"*

Louis added, "Say with *confidence,* M. Bailly."

Bailly: "The king has said it, gentlemen, you've heard him...."

And salvos of *Vives* rumbled through the night.

⚜

AT TEN they were conducted to the Tuileries, a huge palace flung across the garden, one façade facing the Louvre and the other the Champs Élysées. It had not been occupied for decades, and no preparations had been made to receive the royal family. Everything was in a state of dilapidation: the tapestries had rents in them, the furniture was in disrepair, the floors needed fixing, the sconces held no candles. A few candles could not dispel the viscous obscurity inside the prison-like château. In the gloom and chill of the night, without a flicker of light in the hundreds of windows, the palace of the Tuileries looked like a menacing dungeon.

"It's very ugly here, mother," the dauphin whispered.

"My son," Marie Antoinette murmured, "Louis XIV lived here once and found himself comfortable."

CHAPTER XVIII

"We are prisoners here"

THOUSANDS flocked to the gardens of the Tuileries and imperiously demanded to see Their Majesties. All day long Louis and Marie Antoinette showed themselves on the balcony and were greeted jubilantly by the victorious multitude. Even the queen, trembling with fatigue, received ovations. The palace too was crowded, wide open like a fair, and hectic with a carnival spirit. Louis hardly opened his mouth, and Marie Antoinette wept.

Paris was king and caused Louis' title to be changed from "... by the grace of God king of France and of Navarre" to "... by the grace of God and the constitutional law of the state, king of the French."

In the next few days Louis' sanguine temperament began to assert itself, and he came to believe that as soon as the effervescence had subsided, things would become normal again, so that he and his family would be free to move about and do what they pleased. Marie Antoinette, however, was convinced that she and her husband were prisoners of the Paris mob and that the Tuileries was nothing but a glorified jail. This conviction never left the queen, and for the next three years she based her whole political course upon it. Louis refused to share his wife's pessimism.

> We have left the cradle of our childhood [Louis' young sister Elizabeth wrote from Paris]. What do I say—left! They abducted

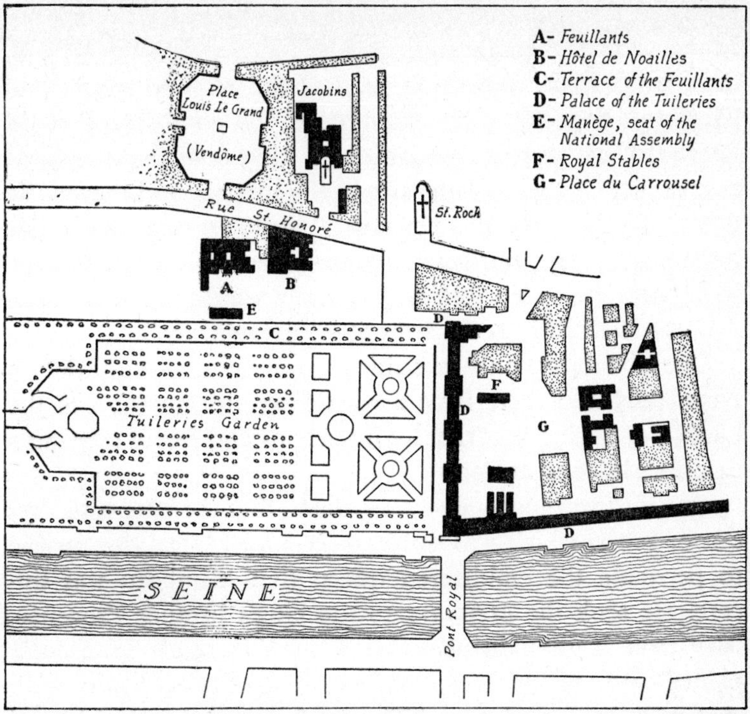

A- Feuillants
B- Hôtel de Noailles
C- Terrace of the Feuillants
D- Palace of the Tuileries
E- Manège, seat of the National Assembly
F- Royal Stables
G- Place du Carrousel

GROUND PLAN OF THE TUILERIES

us! What a journey! What frightful scenes! Never, never will they be effaced from my memory. . . . What is certain is that *we are prisoners here*. My brother does not believe it yet, but time will show him. Our friends are here; they agree that we are lost.

OTHERS thought the same way. Mirabeau said to his friend La Marck, "The king and queen are lost if they do not leave Paris. I am working on a plan. Would you be in a position to go and assure them that they can count upon me?"

A few days later the former firebrand of the revolution made his bid for royal confidence with a long and statesman-like *Mémoire*.[1] The country, Mirabeau reasoned, was at the

[1] The text is given in Bacourt, *Correspondance entre le Comte de Mirabeau et le Comte de La Marck* (Paris, 1851), I, 364-82.

mercy of the mob and on the verge of chaos; for the sake of France and of the dynasty it was imperative that the king escape from Paris. Where to go, was the vital question, and Mirabeau dissected every alternative. To go abroad "would be to declare war on the nation: a king does not flee from his people." To go to some city in the interior and there rally the nobles was equally perilous. "Justly or not, the whole nation has long regarded the Gentlemen as its most implacable enemies. . . . To join the noblesse would be worse than to throw oneself into the arms of a foreign army."

One possibility only remained. Louis was to withdraw to Normandy and there issue a reassuring proclamation to the nation, declaring his friendly intentions and freely offering a democratic constitution.

The idea was good—always assuming that the king could get out of Paris, which was dubious—but La Marck was unable to persuade the embittered queen that Mirabeau was sincere. He took the *Mémoire* to the king's brother Provence, who read it thoughtfully and shook his head. Louis, the prince said, would never accept it. Then he added with extraordinary mordancy: "The weakness and indecision of the king are beyond all description. To give you an idea of his character, imagine *oiled ivory balls which you vainly strive to hold together.*"

⚜

In the Tuileries life was not unhappy. Outside the walls the people were taking over power and were bending the National Assembly [2] to their capricious and sometimes brutal will; but within the palace Louis was free to play king. He was, in fact, expected to do so.

The routine of the king and queen was much like that of Versailles. No one interfered with the royal receptions, the *levers* and *couchers,* or the comings and goings of the aristo-

[2] On November 9 the National Assembly moved into the Salle de Manège in the garden of the Tuileries, a few minutes' walk from the palace. The Manège no longer exists. It stood opposite where the Hotel Meurice is to-day, 228-230 rue de Rivoli.

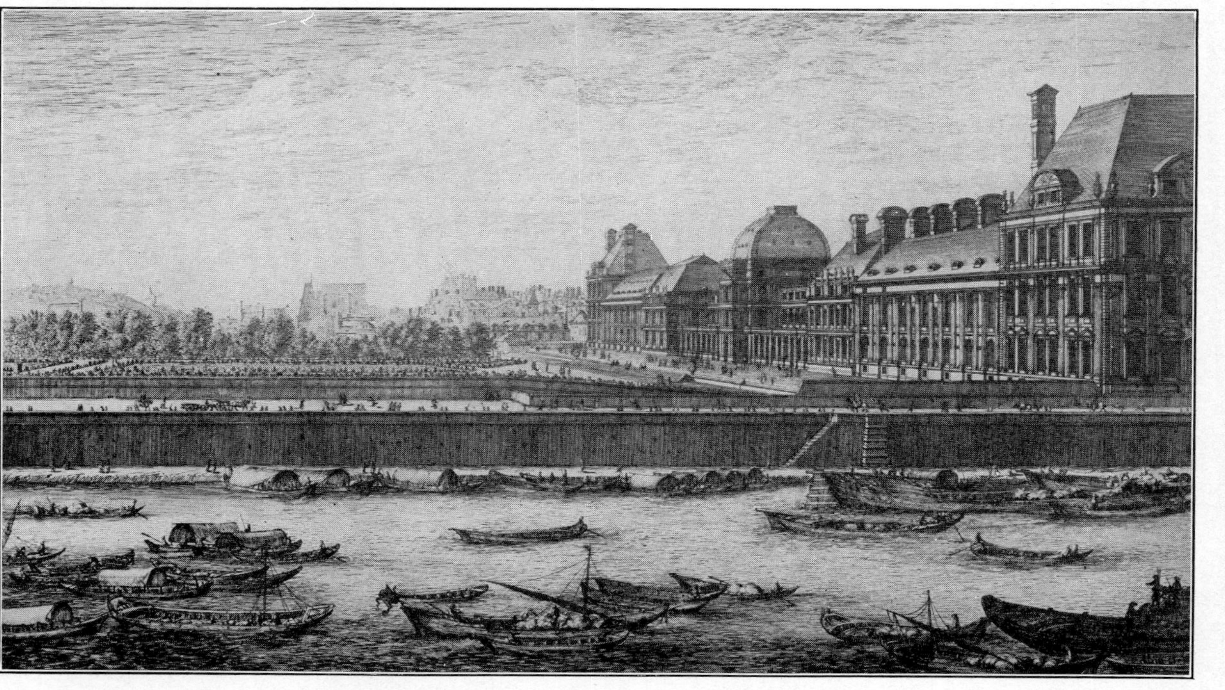

THE PALACE AND GARDENS OF THE TUILERIES

Engraving by Israel Silvestre, 1670. Louvre.

crats who contemptuously refused to buy the national cockades that were being sold outside the gates of the Tuileries. Marie Antoinette seemed to lead the life of a normal wife and mother; she spent time with her children, occasionally played an innocent game of lotto, and sometimes did needlework. Louis, too, followed his ordinary habits. He rose early, prayed, dressed, then joined his family for breakfast. Afterwards he wrote letters in a private room, or met people with whom he liked to talk. In the afternoon he read and played with the children, especially the bright-eyed little dauphin whom he adored. After supper the king watched the games in the salon or in the billiard-room but rarely participated. The revolution had taken over the royal responsibilities, and Louis had much free time on his hands.

One radical change took place in the king's habits: he no longer hunted. For exercise he merely strode up and down his apartment, an exertion which did not keep him from growing excessively stout. This caused uneasiness lest his health deteriorate, for the king was regarded as a useful institution. Lafayette urged Louis to go hunting in the near-by Bois de Boulogne. The king, no admirer of turncoat aristocrats, said ironically, "Have you not assured me that you would be responsible for my person in Paris, but not outside?"

"Sire, I should have the honor of accompanying Your Majesty with the élite of the National Guard."

"I do not wish to disturb such a large number of useful citizens."

UNDERNEATH the seeming peace of the Tuileries there was considerable secret activity. Marie Antoinette had never accepted the revolution; she had merely bowed her head and waited for the storm to pass. In the meantime she was laying the foundations of a great counter-revolutionary conspiracy with ramifications extending to every European court. She started out, in the autumn of 1789, by asking the king of

Spain for money to help finance an uprising in the country, and ended, in 1791-92, by appealing to the monarchs of Europe to invade France. In general Louis did not discourage his wife.

The die-hards did not leave the king alone; they mocked his spinelessness and censured his complaisance. "Will you never dare act by yourself? Do not abdicate your authority ignominiously." [3] But Louis had no means to fight the revolution, even if he were inclined to do so. The army was no longer loyal to him, and the National Guard was the creation of the people. Nor was there enough money in the treasury to finance a counter-revolution; even the National Assembly had difficulty collecting taxes.

Louis also felt that force was no answer to grievances; the nation was on the march, it demanded certain rights and was getting them, too. Despite Marie Antoinette, the king thought it safest to go along with the revolution, work with the people and offer his coöperation. On February 4, 1790, he suddenly appeared before the Assembly and in an extraordinary speech declared himself the leader of the revolution. Paris and France, all Europe, rocked with the sensation. One staunch aristocrat angrily broke his sword in the Assembly, crying that the king had broken his scepter.

That winter and spring Louis was the hero of the nation. Monuments were erected and medals struck in his honor. Lyons took up a collection for a statue of the king with the inscription, "Restorer of French Liberty." A similar monument in Marseilles was to bear the words, "Benefactor of his Subjects." The city of Paris struck a *medaille patriotique* which showed the head of Louis XVI surmounted by an invocation, "Long live for ever the best of kings"; underneath was an eloquent tribute—"Restorer of French Liberty and the true Friend of his People." [4]

[3] *Un petit mot à Louis XVI, sur les crimes de ses vertus* (1789), a pamphlet by F. L. Suleau.

[4] The medal is displayed in the *Musée* of the Archives Nationales in Paris.

⚜

IN THE SPRING of 1790 Marie Antoinette overcame her aversion for the thundering Mirabeau and asked Mercy to approach him with an invitation to serve the monarchy. She was then neck-deep in counter-revolutionary plots abroad, trying to raise fifty million livres in Switzerland and attempting to stir up the king of Sardinia against France; but she needed expert advice within the country, and Mirabeau was best able to give it.

"What Mirabeau will do for us," Louis said to La Marck, "must remain a profound secret from my ministers."

Mirabeau agreed to serve the monarchy secretly, and on May 10, 1790, he sent the first of his confidential letters to the Tuileries. It was a confession of monarchical loyalty and an offer of coöperation: "This letter will forever remain my sentence or my witness. I pledge myself to serve the true interests of the king with all my influence." He promised to see to it that the king should be granted full executive powers in the constitution which was then being shaped by the Assembly.

"My moves," Mirabeau concluded, "will be imperceptible, but each day I will take one step. A quack promises a sudden cure and kills; a true doctor diagnoses, prescribes a diet and a dose, and sometimes cures."

Louis was extremely pleased with Mirabeau's letter and offered to pay his huge debts. He handed La Marck four notes of a quarter-million livres each and said, "If M. de Mirabeau serves me well, as he promised, then at the end of the session of the Assembly you will give him these notes for one million. Henceforth I shall pay his debts."

All parties remained loyal to the agreement. Mirabeau got paid regularly, and regularly he supplied the Tuileries with memoranda on political tendencies and letters on policy.

"TO FORESTALL PLOTS," Lafayette advised Louis in the spring of 1790, "you should neglect no means of gaining popularity." The general suggested that the king make himself popular by reviewing the National Guard, give free horses to the chiefs of divisions, democratize the presentation at court, order the demolition of the Vincennes dungeon. Louis took the advice and set out to court the people. He and his wife showed themselves in public, inspected workshops such as the Gobelins, distributed money among the poor. Everywhere the royal couple were received with simple cordiality. "How good the people are when one goes to seek them out," Marie Antoinette impulsively remarked at one particularly warm reception. "They are not so good when *they* go to seek you," a sardonic voice reminded her.

Despite evidence of popular affection for the monarchs and despite the comparative tranquillity in the country, the intransigent queen wrote to her brother Emperor Leopold II, who had recently ascended the throne in Vienna, "I do not speak to you of our present position; it is too heartrending, it ought to affect all the sovereigns in the world."

In the middle of May Louis went horse-riding in the Bois de Boulogne, for the first time in almost eight months—so great was his sense of security. Like a simple citizen, the king wore a gray coat and rode without a retinue; after all, he was the "leader of the revolution." A few people recognized him and said heartily, *"Tiens, tiens,* there's our good king." Further up the road he passed a stone-cutter who, observing a stout good-natured gentleman riding comfortably on his horse, exclaimed, "Now there's an honest fellow!" Louis was delighted at being called *un brave homme* and told the incident to his family with great good humor.

The National Assembly showed its appreciation of the king in a more concrete fashion. As "chief of a great nation" Louis asked the Assembly to grant him a Civil List of twenty-five million livres for himself and four million for the queen. Promptly and unanimously the Assembly voted the money amidst exclamations of *Vive le roi!* At that moment Marie Antoinette was secretly trying to borrow two or three millions in Vienna, Madrid, and Naples. Some of the money that Louis received from the nation went to his brother Artois, the arch-plotter abroad.

ON JULY 14, 1790, Paris frenziedly celebrated the first anniversary of the fall of the Bastille, and Louis was cheered as the visible symbol of national unity and the restorer of liberty. To the nation's delight, the erstwhile autocrat of France spoke the language of the revolution when he addressed the National Guardsmen who had come from all over France to participate in the glorious holiday:

> Defenders of the public order, friends of the laws and of liberty: Remember that your first duty is to maintain order and to submit to the laws, that the benefits of a free constitution should be equal to all. . . . Repeat to your fellow-citizens that their king is their father, their brother, their friend; that he can be happy only in their happiness, great only in their glory, strong only in their liberty, rich only in their prosperity. . . . Repeat my words, or rather the feelings of my heart, in the humble cottages and lodgings of the poor. Tell them that, if I am not able to go with you to their homes, I want to be among them with my affection and the laws which protect the weak; to watch over them, to live for them, if necessary to die for them.[5]

It was a fine speech and everybody was happy.

The jubilant celebration took place on the Champ de Mars—an unforgettable demonstration of that fervor which has been aptly called the religion of patriotism. Louis and the royal family sat in a raised pavilion at the extreme end of the "field" and looked down upon the vast amphitheater spreading before them, while waves of *Vives* rolled over the massed humanity. Back of the king's seat was an enormous streamer proclaiming THE NATION, THE LAW, THE KING. And when Louis rose to take the Civic Oath, and Marie Antoinette held the dauphin aloft, a wild torrent of acclamation burst from hundreds of thousands of throats. Can-

[5] Archives Nationales, AD I 74, July 13, 1790.

"CA IRA"

Manuscript of the air and variations by Gervais François Couperin, 1790.

non boomed salvos, and the people sang, for the first time, an intoxicating revolutionary song-hit, *Ça ira, ça ira,* whose melody was so gay that Marie Antoinette used to play it as a *contredanse* on the harpsichord.[6]

Ah, ça ira, ça ira, ça ira,
Le peuple en ce jour sans cesse répète:
Ah! ça ira, ça ira, ça ira,
Malgré les mutins, tout réussira.

A little later the couplets grew in number and the words took on the salty taste of blood, but the melody still retained a bitter cheer:

Ah! ça ira, ça ira, ça ira,
Les aristocrates à la lanterne.

[6] The British Museum possesses a song composed by Marie Antoinette, the first stanza of which reads:

Amour, fui loin de moi,
Tu cause seul ma peine.
Je veux briser ta chaine,
Contente toi des voeux,
Que l'on offre à Cythère,
Et laisse vivre heureux,
Le reste de la terre.

Ah! ça ira, ça ira, ça ira,
Les aristocrates, on les pendra,
La liberté s'établira;
Malgré les tyrans tout réussira.[7]

[7] The words *Ça ira* are said to be Benjamin Franklin's favorite expression, possibly a translation of "It'll be all right." The music was taken from Bécourt's *Carillon national,* a country-dance. In the course of the revolution, new improvisations were constantly being made.

CHAPTER XIX

"You have an armed tyranny to deal with"[1]

BY THE END of the first year of the Revolution Louis' personal situation was not unfavorable. He was deprived, to be sure, of most of his prerogatives and much of his liberty, but he had lost little of his popularity. The great majority of the people, including those of Paris, was still attached to the monarchy and to Louis in person. Revolutions, however, do not stand still—they pause, gather strength, and then sweep on with greater violence; and those in a prominent position must either swim with the torrent or be drowned.

Louis inclined to be passive, but as the winter approached, the political situation was becoming complicated again, and it was necessary for the king to take some line of action. "Four enemies," Mirabeau warned the court in vivid language, "arrive at redoubled pace: taxation, bankruptcy, the army, winter." He should have added that there was anarchy in the provinces and no executive authority in the country, for the Assembly had lost power and influence. The national economy, moreover, was disrupted, because tens of thousands of rich *émigrés* were taking their cash and valuables out of the country and numerous families were thrown out of employment by the revolution—six hundred people, for example, lost

1 Edmund Burke to Comtesse de Montrond, January 25, 1791: "You have an armed tyranny to deal with, and nothing but arms can pull it down." Burke also regretted that he was not in power to help the counter-revolution in France.

their jobs when Louis gave up hunting.[2] The administrative machinery was out of gear, and the government, what there was of it, could neither collect taxes nor ensure the free movement of grain. To ameliorate the grave economic situation, and incidentally to head off lower-class criticism, the king bequeathed to the nation most of his inherited real property (except the Louvre, the Tuileries, Versailles, Fontainebleau, Compiègne, Saint-Cloud, Saint-Germain, Rambouillet—all of which are national museums or parks to-day), but thanks to the confiscation of Church lands the market was swamped with real estate and Louis' gift had only a symbolic value. On top of all these difficulties, the armed forces of the nation began to show grave symptoms of revolutionary fever. A mutiny broke out among the sailors at Toulon and an even more serious rebellion in the garrison at Nancy. France seemed on the brink of civil war, but General Bouillé, the king's friend, kept the Nancy fire from spreading by stamping it out with blood.

Louis praised General Bouillé's severe conduct in Nancy.

[2] In 1790 the king received numerous petitions from artisans, craftsmen and small shopkeepers complaining that the revolution had ruined them and asking for aid. The following is a sample showing some of the economic consequences of revolution:

"Sire: We have suffered without murmur all the scourges which great changes bring in their wake; our patience has equaled our hopes, while they talked to us about happiness, liberty, equality. . . . We take the liberty to present to Your Majesty . . . a picture of our frightful position; the total disappearance of specie, the price of food which is increasing daily, the diminution of individual fortunes . . . , the proscription of luxury, the absence of the nobles whose pleasures and caprices fed commerce and the arts . . . , the rupture of our relations with foreigners, and the loss of our colonies, will soon reduce us to unemployment and to the most frightful poverty.

"Is this the fruit of so many sacrifices, the fulfilment of such fine promises? . . . Liberty and equality are chimeras which have broken all social ties, confounded all authority, destroyed order, disseminated discord, invited anarchy. . . . We have arms, they are at the disposal of the supreme chief of the realm. We implore you to use all your powers . . . to remedy the abuses, to reëstablish a balance between the price of food and wages, and above all to dissipate and punish those seditious persons who in the name of being friends of the constitution are its most cruel enemies." This petition was signed by eighty men—painters, masons, woodworkers, tailors, binders, shoemakers, dyers, sculptors, and jewelers. The document, and many others like it, are in Archives Nationales, C184, 115, nos.248, 249, 250, 251, 252.

"You have saved France," the king wrote confidentially. "Continue on the same road, cultivate your popularity, it may be very useful to me and to the kingdom.... I regret very sincerely the worthy men who perished in that distressing but very necessary affair."

Louis ate heartily and digested well and refused to bestir himself. When some harebrained aristocrat would come with a scheme for flight or for destroying the revolution, the king would sometimes shout obscenely, *"Le premier b... qui me parlera de conspiration ou de départ, je lui f... mon pied dans le ventre!"* Lafayette, too, annoyed Louis with his boring warnings against flight (Paris was full of rumors, he said), and once the king banged the door in the general's face: *"Allez vous faire f...!"*

Marie Antoinette, up to her neck in counter-revolutionary conspiracy abroad, had to apologize for the king's indifference to plots and schemes. In a ciphered letter [3] to her brother-in-law Artois (October 15, 1790) the queen wrote:

> I have at last deciphered your letter, my dear brother, and it was not without difficulty: there were many mistakes.... There is another item in your letter which distresses me: It is the manner in which you have condemned the two letters of your brother. You know his heart and his soul.... No, he cannot be and he is not at variance with you, and nobody forces him to write the private letters which he does write you. But *he sees his position differently from what it is.* If he is obliged to refuse you, it has never been without motives.... It is not distrust, but prudence.

The revolutionists themselves, however, finally forced Louis to abandon his passive attitude. They demanded that the king dismiss his ministers because of their royalist sympathies. Louis refused to let them go. "I have always seen in

[3] Marie Antoinette's secret correpsondence in cipher has been published by Alma Söderhjelm. Her first book was *Fersen et Marie-Antoinette* (1930), and the second, *Marie Antoinette et Barnave. Correspondence secrète (juillet 1791-janvier 1792)* (Paris, 1934).

you," he told the cabinet, "the friends of the people, of order, and of the laws." Then the revolutionists, led by Danton, made a demonstration before the Tuileries and loudly threatened the queen's life. "Save me," Louis cried, "from that mad rabble!" The National Guard locked the gates, and the *"canaille enragée"* dispersed. But Louis heeded the warning of the "rabble" and gloomily accepted a new ministry named by Lafayette. The quick-witted Parisians, who were fast forging an effective technique of coercion, drew the obvious conclusion. "The king," they said cynically, "is a good patriot only when he is frightened; the queen is never a good patriot."

And so, after a year of being more or less a prisoner of the people of Paris, Louis at last began to realize his true position. He had coöperated with the Assembly and had given up his power with small reluctance; the least he expected was that he should be free to function within the limits prescribed for him in the constitution. But to no avail. The canaille threatened him in the Tuileries, and the organized people of Paris (with the consent of the now-enfeebled Assembly) forced him to accept ministers in whom he had no confidence. Since the populace recognized no restraints and lived up to no agreements, a king without an army and without a loyal guard was in a perilous position indeed! He must do something—as the queen had been insisting for more than a year. And Louis, so slow and so ponderous, now adopted his wife's counter-revolutionary politics with a heavy heart. On November 26, 1790, he took the fateful step, his first covert act against the revolution, and appointed the Baron de Breteuil his secret agent and informal ambassador to the Courts of Europe.

I have chosen you [Louis' credentials to Breteuil read] to confide to you the interests of my crown. Circumstances do not permit me to give you instructions on specific subjects, nor to keep up with you a regular correspondence. I am sending you this letter to serve as *plein pouvoir* and authorization vis-à-vis the different powers with whom you would have to negotiate for me.

You know my intentions and I leave it to your prudence to make use of them when you believe it necessary for the good of my service. *I approve of everything you will do to achieve the aim* which I propose, namely, the reëstablishment of my legitimate authority and the happiness of my people.

JUSTIFICATION for Louis' counter-revolutionary orientation was not long in coming. On the day after the king wrote his letter to Breteuil, the Assembly passed a decree which opened an old sore. A few months before, the Assembly had voted a series of laws (Civil Constitution of the Clergy) which transformed the religious organization of the country by making priests elective officials paid by the state. At that time Pope Pius VI secretly warned "Our Very Dear Son" Louis XVI not to fall victim to "captious and illusory arguments." "If you approve the decrees," the pope threatened, "you will lead into error the whole nation and precipitate your kingdom into schism and perhaps into a cruel war of religion." Louis agreed with the Holy Father. "I regard it as one of my finest titles, that of being the eldest son of the Church . . . , and my feelings in these matters do not weaken in the midst of difficulties which surround me."[4] But despite the pope's warnings and despite his own conscience, Louis had approved the Civil Constitution of the Clergy for the sake of peace and harmony. He had then hoped that the revolutionary ecclesiastical legislation would not change the essentials of doctrine and discipline. Actually the Civil Constitution of the Clergy had torn at the conscience of France and led to a minor civil war among the clergy. Now, on November 27, the Assembly aggravated the situation by decreeing that nonjuring priests—that is, those who refused to take the oath to the Constitution—would be dismissed from office.

The king's friends urged him not to approve what was to them an outrageous law. Elizabeth, Louis' pious sister, tear-

[4] The correspondence, July 1790, is in the Archives Nationales, C183, 108, no.23 and no.24. These letters were later used as evidence against the king at his trial in 1792.

fully begged him not to sign a law which would deprive thousands of innocent priests of their livelihood for no other reason than their inability to compromise with their conscience. Marie Antoinette pleaded with her husband to fight it out with the Assembly. The clergy appealed to the king to act like a true Christian and "eldest son of the Church." Some one, probably a priest, slipped a stinging accusation into Louis' *Book of Hours:*

> You are a slave, Sire, you cannot dissemble it from yourself. And if you are still alive, you owe this good fortune, if such it be, to nothing but the contempt which you inspire in those who have destroyed your power.... It is your weakness that has saved you.
>
> You have without any difficulty sanctioned all the blows directed at your royal authority.... Step by step you have sacrificed to your masters your God, your crown, your noblesse, your parlements, your ministers, your defenders....

The indictment hurt like a dart in the flesh, and Louis grew somber and silent. For a month he refused to sign the decree. But the Assembly never relaxed its pressure. Louis wearily signed.

⚜

In January, 1791, a change was observed in Louis. He lost his gloom and whistled gaily. One of his tunes was *Je suis democrate, moi, Je suis democrate.* The royal "democrat" had come to a decision to run away from the overzealous attentions of his plebeian fellow-democrats; he promised his energetic wife not to oppose preparations for flight from the revolutionary capital. Ambassador Mercy wrote to Vienna for "precise and positive orders" about the projected flight and added that Marie Antoinette was arranging the whole thing. "I have never had anything directly to do with the king; the conversations which I have had with this monarch always took place in the presence of the queen. All comes from her and everybody addresses himself to her."

First step in the royal migration was taken by Louis' two

fat aunts, Adelaide and Victoire. *Mesdames les tantes* escaped one night a few hours before a mob from the faubourgs came to stop them; but the elderly ladies were arrested before they reached the Italian frontier, and all France buzzed with the scandal. Louis pretended he knew nothing about his aunts' escape, but argued that they were free to do what they pleased. "My aunts being mistresses of their persons," the king wrote to the municipality of Paris, "may travel wherever they wish like all other citizens." The National Assembly was appealed to by the aunts and was compelled to grant them permission to leave the country; otherwise it would have been a public admission that the royal family were prisoners. "There is no law," the Assembly decided reluctantly, "that prevents the king's aunts from traveling freely." The two spinsters went to Rome and there handed the Holy Father a letter from Louis:

"My aunts, more happy than I, have gone to seek a moment of happiness and repose near Your Holiness."

Two of the Bourbons had escaped, and Paris was determined that no more should get away. The revolutionists now redoubled their hostile vigilance over the Tuileries. Inside the palace, however, the royal inmates continued their elaborate preparations for flight. Despite heartbreaking obstacles, great lapses in time between letters to and from abroad, constant peril from exposure, the queen pursued the task with remarkable single-mindedness.

Cash was collected, money was deposited abroad, and an inventory was made of the royal jewels, buckles, medals, diamonds, rubies, emeralds, topazes—worth altogether some ten million livres—which were carefully packed.[5] The queen sent La Marck to Metz to consult with General Bouillé about keeping a loyal army in readiness at the frontier. Bouillé was not encouraging. "They," he said of his soldiers, "are all

[5] The inventory of the jewels, which were ultimately confiscated by the government, is in Archives Nationales, C183, 112, no.124 *bis* and no.124 *ter*.

THE ROYAL FAMILY AT MASS IN THE TUILERIES

Painting by Hubert Robert des Ruines, 1792. Henri Loyer Collection, Paris.

gangrened with the revolutionary spirit." Emperor Leopold II in Vienna was not optimistic either. "We are too weak," he said, "to do anything for France now." [6]

To meet the persistent rumors of the king's imminent flight, deliberately disseminated by the revolutionary clubs, Arnaud de La Porte, the intendant of the Civil List, proposed a million livres for propaganda and bribery. "Money and opinion," he wrote, "precipitated France into the abyss; the remedy must be effected with the same means." [7] Mirabeau was encouraged to break with the Jacobins and was offered by the court "an assured income for the future, either a government annuity or real estate." [8] The indefatigable de La Porte also renewed contact with an old friend, Charles François Dumouriez, one of the ablest generals in the revolutionary camp. "He has spirit, character, much intelligence," La Porte recommended the general to the king; "a man of his mettle can be either very useful or very dangerous."

In the meantime the extreme wing of the revolution, led by the Jacobins, intensified its attack on the monarchy and thwarted every effort of the court. Not only were the revolutionists more intelligent and ruthless than the crown, but the monarchy was poorly prepared for the sort of battle that the radicals offered it at every turn and with demoralizing surprise. Louis was not inclined to defend himself or able to build systematic fortifications around the throne. In emergencies he would display a shocking equanimity. When action was imperative, Louis sat in his study and calmly read journals and newspapers, about twenty a day. No matter how agitated the day may have been, when night came the king went to bed alone and immediately fell into the profound sleep of innocence, snoring heavily. Only one thing could upset him, the sight of violence and bloodshed.

[6] Leopold to Mercy, February 4, 1791; Bibilothèque Nationale, n.a.Fr.6968, p.415-16.

[7] Archives Nationales, C219, 160 [135], no.21.

[8] Archives Nationales, C187, 133, no.7.

An example of this lack of direction on the part of the crown and of suspicion on the part of the revolutionists was the case of the so-called *chevaliers du poignard,* "knights of the dagger," who gathered in the Tuileries—to abduct the king, the watchful radicals said. But these chevaliers of the Order of St. Louis, some four hundred of them, were guilty of hardly more than swagger and irresponsible talk. In any case, Louis had nothing to do with their harebrained "conspiracy." But as soon as they assembled in the Tuileries, the revolutionists summoned the National Guard, beat down the chevaliers, and jailed them. The battle in the Tuileries so shook the king that he fell gravely ill. For a week he tossed in fever and coughed blood.[9] As soon as he recovered, the Assembly gave him a Constitutional Guard, presumably to protect him but actually to keep him under strict surveillance.

That same winter of 1791 the throne suffered another blow when Mirabeau unexpectedly died. Moderate elements, including the king, considered Mirabeau one of the few effective checks on the extreme revolutionists. So widespread, indeed, was the conviction that the dead man had been the last brake on the rising Jacobins that it was said that his dying words were, "After my death the factious will quarrel over the tatters of the monarchy." Mirabeau did not say that (his last words expressed the desire to die washed, shaven, and perfumed), but the prognosis was correct.

ON EASTER the Parisians showed a nasty temper toward the crown and, incidentally, proclaimed to Europe what Marie Antoinette had been insisting for a year and a half, that the king was a prisoner. The royal family had been planning to spend Easter at Saint-Cloud, the summer home near Paris, and on the day before leaving (April 17) Louis slipped into the chapel to receive communion from the Grand Almoner. This in itself was no crime, but it happened that the Grand

[9] *Bulletin du Roi du 8 mars 1791 (jusqu'à 16 mars)*; a copy may be obtained in the Reserved Room of the Bibliothèque Nationale.

Almoner was a nonjuring priest and had no legal right to exercise his religious functions. What was, at most, a tactical error on the part of the king promptly turned into a political blunder of moment. Vigilant spies in the Tuileries reported the incident to the revolutionary quarters, and immediately Paris was galvanized into action. Riots were staged in the streets, and the king's guards mutinied in the Tuileries. Lafayette persuaded the so-called Constitutional Guard to go back to their posts, but they continued to growl and mutter. On the following morning the fountains ominously played in the garden of the Palais-Royal—a long-agreed upon signal of insurrection. Placards proclaimed the king a lawbreaker. Grim folk, heavily armed, assembled on the Place du Carrousel in front of the Tuileries.

The royal carriages were waiting, and so was Lafayette with a troop of cavalry to serve as escort to Saint-Cloud. The populace was strangely quiet. Silently the king, the queen, and the children came out and entered the carriage. Lafayette's horsemen surrounded it. Suddenly, as if the whole thing had been stage-managed and perfectly timed (as it probably was), the crowd burst into terrifying yells and brandished ugly weapons. Louis leaned forward, his face sickly.

The National Guardsmen, whom Lafayette had brought to protect the royal family, drew sabers and . . . attacked the royal postilions. One guardsman, sword in hand, rushed at Louis: "You are a breaker of the law because you give asylum to priests who did not take the oath." Louis was stirred to rare anger: "Wretch, get back! Who made you judge of my conscience?"

Shocked at the behavior of the Guard he commanded, Lafayette rushed in to protect the king. The commander of the National Guard, hitherto the hero of Paris, ordered his men to desist, pleaded with them, shouted, finally in exasperation threatened to resign; but the Guard laughed and ironically applauded his threat. A great revolutionary reputation, and incidentally a legend in the making, was being destroyed by laughter.

Mayor Bailly was no more successful than Lafayette. The second popular hero of the revolution was fading away under mob mockery. An invisible authority, probably emanating from the revolutionary clubs (on the previous day Louis was publicly denounced at the radical Cordeliers Club), had given the order that the king was not to be permitted to leave Paris.

For two hours the crowd shouted, the guardsmen brandished sabers, Lafayette and Bailly pleaded, and the royal family was heaped with insult and humiliation. Finally Louis decided to get out of the carriage and reënter the palace. As he stepped out and helped Marie Antoinette, who was white and sick, a powerful voice thundered, "We like our king, we forgive him his weaknesses, but let him not repeat them often, because we believe in the inviolability of the king as little as in the infallibility of the pope."

Back in the palace, the king muttered resentfully, "I know well that they want to murder me like Henry IV, but a better crown awaits me beyond."

⚜

Louis went to the National Assembly and indignantly complained of the violence offered him by the mob. "It is important for the nation," he cried, "to prove that I am free; nothing is so essential for the sanctions and acceptances which I have given to your decrees." The president of the Assembly replied sincerely, "Our hearts are with you," but every one knew that the deputies of the nation were as helpless as the king. The mob was monarch of Paris, and Paris gave the law to France. No amount of pretense could cover up the unpleasant fact that the National Assembly, duly elected by the people of France, was a puppet of the populace and that the king was a prisoner in his capital. The king was now eager to flee from Paris.

> The events that have just taken place [Marie Antoinette wrote in cipher to Mercy] confirm us more than ever in our project. The Guard which surrounds us is our greatest menace. Even our lives

are not safe. We must give the impression of yielding, until we are able to act, and our captivity will prove anyhow that our actions are not voluntary. But before doing anything, it is essential to know if you can, under any pretext whatever, transport 15,000 men to Arlon and Vitron, and as many to Mons.

Mercy, who lived in Brussels and who had orders from Vienna to help the royal family with every means at his disposal, promised to place the desired number of Austrian troops at the Franco-Luxembourg frontier. He warned the queen to be sure of every detail before taking such a desperate step as flight from Paris. "One trembles to think of the horrors that will take place if you are betrayed and arrested."

⚜

ON THE MORROW of the riot on the Place du Carrousel, incendiary placards, printed in irregular capital letters, were distributed throughout Paris:

THE KING IS A TRAITOR, LAFAYETTE A COUNTER-REVOLUTIONIST, THE NATIONAL ASSEMBLY IS ALL CORRUPT.

The city was under the strain of a vague sort of terror. Rumors, maliciously spread, were as thick as flies on a carcass. *On dit que*—Lafayette is going to set up a dictatorship. ... The king is running away. ... Orleans is preparing to become regent. ... Austrian armies are massing on the frontier. ... On and on. The safety anchor of authority had snapped off the chain, and people's judgment had gone with it. Distrust and fear gnawed at the public life. The National Assembly distrusted the National Guard, the Guard feared the municipality, the municipality suspected the revolutionary clubs. Target of these accumulated fears and suspicions and hates was the handsome Renaissance palace in the garden of the Tuileries where the queen spent sleepless nights and the king sometimes wept.

The palace was guarded as if it were an arsenal: sentinels stood before the gates, the sentry-posts, the doors, the ground windows; on the terrace along the Seine a sentry beat one hundred paces back and forth, back and forth. Inside the palace, in the corridors, in the antechambers, in the passageways, before the royal apartments, stood silent guards with fixed bayonets. And the guards, who did not know whether they were the king's protectors or jailers, were suspicious and worried.

The bewildered Lafayette thus described the situation in France to his American friend George Washington:

> The émigrés line our frontiers and intrigue with all the despotic cabinets; our army is composed of aristocratic officers and undisciplined soldiers; the license of the multitude is not easily repressed; the capital, which gives the tone to the country, is tossed about by different parties. The Assembly is tired from its long labors.

To Louis and Marie Antoinette caged in the Tuileries, with the populace crouching outside, life had become unbearable. Everything depended upon flight, and both the king and queen were determined to *"risquer le tout pour tout"* without delaying much longer. Voices of warning were not heeded. Prince Kaunitz, the Austrian chancellor, was strongly against the court "daring to try to escape." [10] Mercy was also dubious of the whole scheme. Most ominous was the warning sounded early in June in Marat's *Ami du Peuple:*

"You are imbeciles not to forestall the flight of the royal family. Parisians, foolish Parisians, I am tired of repeating to you: lock up the Austrian woman, her brother-in-law, the rest of the family."

THE PLAN of escape hinged on General Bouillé who commanded the French army at Metz. Bouillé, who had fought with Washington in America, was a moderate monarchist and a man of unusual honesty. For months he was in secret contact (by means of cipher letters) with the royal family, whom he pointedly reminded that his own army was unreliable—that is to say, not royalist—and that everything depended upon the Austrian troops in Belgium and Luxembourg. The

[10] Bibliothèque Nationale, n.a.Fr.6968, p.427.

general plan, as agreed upon by Bouillé and the queen, was that the royal family should go to Montmédy, a fort closest to the Belgian frontier, and thence be escorted into the Low Countries. General Bouillé was against the idea of the whole family's escaping at one time, suggesting that the king and queen travel separately; but Marie Antoinette would not hear of it. She feared that should the king be arrested without her, she would never be allowed to rejoin him. For good or for ill, she would share the fate of her husband. Bouillé then urged the use of two small cabriolets, which would have the advantage of inconspicuousness and speed, rather than one large vehicle which was certain to attract attention. For some reason the queen ignored this sensible advice.

In June the final arrangements, such as they were, were completed. One and a half million livres in cash, as well as the queen's diamonds, were sent by special messenger (the Abbé Louis) to Mercy in Brussels. This fortune, by the way, was to be paid to Count Axel Fersen, a handsome Swedish nobleman who lent the king one million livres and was otherwise active in the plans of escape, because, it was widely believed, he was fatally in love with Marie Antoinette. Whatever the truth about this much-bruited romance (in view of Marie Antoinette's inclinations, it was most probably a platonic relationship), it seems that Fersen was cheated out of his money, either by Mercy or by the Austrian government.[11] Fersen supplied vehicles and horses. Simolin, the ambassador

[11] Thereby hangs a real mystery story. The known facts are as follows: On June 20, 1791, the day of the flight from Paris, both Louis and Marie Antoinette put their signatures to the following order: "We beg Count Mercy to remit to Count Fersen all the money he has from us, close to 1,500,000 livres, and we beg Count Fersen to accept it as a testimony ... of our gratitude and as a compensation for all that he loses." Apparently Mercy never gave the money to Fersen, for on August 31, 1794, after the death of Louis and Marie Antoinette, the Swedish nobleman appealed to Thugut, the Austrian prime minister: "My rights are incontestable; it is a clear and precise donation, signed by Their Majesties, of money which belonged to them." In proof of his claim, Fersen submitted the above-mentioned order. He explained that the money in question was not altogether a gift from Louis XVI and Marie Antoinette, but the repayment of a loan of 1,000,000 livres which he had made to the king and queen. Thugut replied, whether sincerely or not, that he knew nothing about the whole

of Catherine II of Russia, provided the passports filled out in the name of Russian citizens.[12]

On the Belgian side, near the French frontier, an army of twelve thousand Austrian troops stood under arms, ready to receive the king and queen of France. Beginning with Chalons, which was half-way between Paris and the frontier, detachments of loyal (to the throne) French cavalry were to guard the road all the way to Montmédy. At the same time the king of Spain proposed to the government in Vienna that they form a *"cordon respectable"* of troops on all the French frontiers in order "to overawe, distract, and curb the revolutionists." The whole plan seemed fool-proof.

DURING the day of Monday, June 20, Louis shut himself in his cabinet and, in his meticulous handwriting, composed a long and precise account of the events since the outbreak of the revolution, his vain attempts to coöperate with the new order, the violence done to his person and his family, and finally his virtual imprisonment. He wanted all France to appreciate his motives for the step he was about to take. The *Déclaration du roi adressé à tous les françois* was to be handed to the Assembly on the day after his escape, so that the nation could judge between the king and the radicals.[13]

So long as the king could hope to see order and happiness reborn in the realm, no personal sacrifice was too great for him.

matter. At this point a curtain of obscurity falls upon the question. Whether Fersen did or did not collect will probably always remain a mystery.

12 The Russian ambassador's letter to Foreign Minister Montmorin, requesting passports, read as follows: "The undersigned . . . has the honor of requesting 2 passports; one for Madame the Baroness de Korff, a lady's maid, a valet, 2 children and 3 lackeys; the other for Madame the Baroness Stegleman, her daughter, her lady's-maid, 1 valet and 2 lackeys—who are leaving for Frankfort through Metz." On June 5 the unsuspecting Montmorin issued the passports. He was later suspected of complicity, but was cleared after investigation.

13 The National Assembly ordered the *Déclaration* to be printed and distributed. There is a copy of the original in the Archives Nationales. Charavay, the Paris bookdealer, claimed to have sold the original to the Marquis de l'Aigle. See *L'Amateur d'Autographes,* 1902, 107-08.

> ... But to-day when the sole recompense of so much sacrifice is to see the destruction of royalty, all authority disregarded, property violated, the security of persons everywhere in danger, crimes going unpunished, and complete anarchy setting itself up above the laws, the king ... believes he should put before the eyes of the French and of the whole world, a record of his conduct. ...
>
> Frenchmen, above all, you Parisians, inhabitants of a city which the ancestors of His Majesty have pleased to call the good city of Paris, distrust the suggestions and lies of your false friends, come back to your king, he will always be your father, your best friend.

As night fell Louis was ready for the great adventure of his life. On a table near him lay a brown wig, a plain gray overcoat, and a big stick.

CHAPTER XX

"I have escaped from that town of Paris"

THE ACTORS in the curious drama, on that night of June 20, were all dressed for their parts as was provided in the passport issued to Madame de Korff, her daughters Amélie and Aglaé, the governess Madame Rochet, the nursemaid Rosalie, and the valet Durand.

Madame Tourzel, the governess of the royal children, dressed up as the Baroness de Korff. The twelve-year-old Madame Royale and her little brother the dauphin were put in girlish frocks to make them look like Amélie and Aglaé. Madame Elizabeth, the king's sister, wore a simple morning dress and a white cap, as befitted the plain *bonne* Rosalie. Marie Antoinette, in a severe black cloak, looked the dignified governess Madame Rochet. Louis XVI, in his heavy gray overcoat and round hat, resembled the burly valet Durand.

The palace was dark, the corridors deserted. Walking on tiptoe, hearts racing, the royal family assembled in the apartment of Madame Royale. Marie Antoinette woke the six-year-old dauphin and dressed him in girl's clothes. The child was sleepy; he could not understand what all these mysterious doings were about. "I asked him," his sister recalled years later, "what he thought we were going to do; he told me that we were going to play a comedy, because we were all disguised." The child spoke truer than he knew.

Madame de Tourzel led the children out of the Tuileries

by a small unguarded door. After a short interval, Madame Elizabeth slipped out, then the king. Silently they stole down to the small dark rue de l'Echelle—near what is the rue de Rivoli to-day—back of the stables, where stood a berlin with four horses. The driver was Count Axel Fersen, disguised as a *cocher.* They waited for the queen. Five minutes passed, ten, fifteen . . . Marie Antoinette did not appear. Louis was shaking. Suddenly a clatter of wheels on cobbles of the nearby rue St. Honoré. Louis and Fersen peered from the darkness and recognized Lafayette, the watchful commander of the National Guard, making a tour of inspection. Lafayette noticed nothing amiss, and Louis muttered, "The scoundrel!" [1]

At last the queen showed up—she had lost her way in the dark. It was now about half an hour after midnight. Quickly they drove through the dark deserted streets to the Porte St. Martin, where they arrived about two o'clock in the morning. The small berlin drew up alongside a big berlin with six horses, and the royal family transferred from one to the other without stepping on the ground. The smaller vehicle was pushed into a ditch.

At Bondy, about six miles outside of Paris, fresh horses were harnessed, and Fersen took leave of the royal family: *Au revoir à Bruxelles!*

They drove fast along the deserted highway. At Meaux, some twenty-six miles from Paris, the sun rose. Gloom lifted from the travelers. The children removed the veils from their faces and looked out upon the fresh landscape, bathed in the first rays of the sun. Louis suddenly broke his long silence. He grew talkative. "I have escaped from that town of Paris where I drank so much bitterness." He assured his sad and dubious wife, "Once in the saddle I shall be very different from what you have seen me up to the present moment." Then, as the sun rose higher and dispelled the chill of the night, Louis spoke gaily of the future happiness of France and the reëstablishment of the Catholic religion. About eight

[1] British Museum, ADD. MSS 34-438, p.66

in the morning they were about forty miles from Paris, and the king took out his bulbous watch, looked at it, and grinned:

"Lafayette is now in a terrible fix."

⚜

LAFAYETTE *was* in a fix, but it was not so terrible as Louis imagined. Paris heard of the king's flight almost at the very moment when Louis took out his watch and noticed that it was eight in the morning of June 21 and a warm day. The general alarm was given at nine-thirty. A furious mob attacked Lafayette and almost lynched him in front of the Hôtel de Ville. The National Assembly met instantly. "I have distressing news to give you," General Alexandre de Beauharnais, the husband of Josephine and president of the Assembly, said gloomily. "The king and the royal family have been *abducted* last night." Long silence—to let the fiction of *abducted* sink in. Then came a motion that Lafayette be censured for having permitted the king to get away. La Porte brought Louis' *Déclaration;* it was read to a stonily hostile Assembly.

The streets quivered. Portraits of the king were torn down and bespattered. The words *King* and *Queen* were blotted out on posters and signs. On the main entrance to the Tuileries was put up a sardonic sign: *House to Let.* The postman who delivered mail there was overcome with humor that morning; on the letters addressed to the king he wrote, "Left without forwarding address."

Marat's *Ami du Peuple* screamed, "Let the race of despots be annihilated forever." The Jacobin Club was jubilant. The municipality of Paris immediately closed all city *barrières,* arrested eminent persons of royalist connections, sealed the Tuileries and houses of the king's relatives, armed the sections and the market-places, suspended the bourse, redoubled the guards everywhere.

The Assembly issued an eloquent appeal to the nation:

> The king and the royal family have been abducted. . . . France wants to be free, and she will be free. They want to retrograde the

COUNT AXEL FERSEN

Aged 28. After a miniature painted in 1783.

MADAME ELIZABETH

Sister of Louis XVI (1764-1794).

revolution, and the revolution does not retreat.... Under the constitution, the king is the executive chief.... If he leaves his post, even though he be abducted despite himself, the representatives of the nation have the right to replace him....

Frenchmen, all the authorities are organized, all the public officials are at their posts, the National Assembly watches over the public safety.... Frenchmen, the absence of the king will not stop the activity of the government.

While the king was fleeing to the frontier, France was informed that she could get along without a king.

THE LUMBERING COACH rolling towards the Marne was not, despite the well-known gibes of Carlyle, a conspicuous vehicle or a slow one. The body was painted black and green, the wheels and perch were yellow, but these were colors common to stage-coaches and attracted no particular attention. Nor was there anything remarkable about the trunks piled on top and fastened in the back, or the bag of tools on the driver's seat, or the big lanterns in front, or the iron-tipped brakes near the wheels, or even the white-velvet portières over the doors. It was a vehicle like any other "ship of the road," perhaps somewhat bigger than the ordinary and possibly going faster than the common coach. The black-green-yellow berlin, pulled by six sturdy horses, averaged seven miles an hour, which was speed in those days.

Twice Louis was recognized. At Vieux-Maisons the postilion Picard saw the king's face and said nothing. At Chantrix, where the coach arrived early in the afternoon, Postmaster de Lagny, descendant of an impoverished noble family, and his son-in-law Vallet both recognized the king. They were agitated but loyal. They invited the royal family inside the posthouse and treated them with kindness and consideration. Even Marie Antoinette began to feel hopeful: Chantrix was eighty-eight miles from Paris, and so far no bad news had come from there. Grateful for the kind treatment they received, the king and queen gave de Lagny two silver plates—souvenirs still kept in that family.

Just outside Chantrix one of the wheels bumped against the side of a narrow bridge, the horses reared and broke the harness. An hour was lost in repairs. By the time they reached

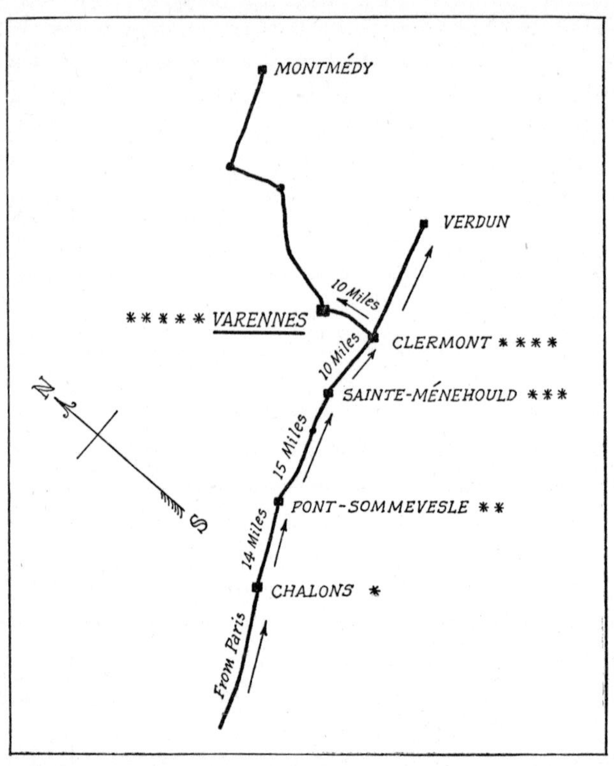

THE LAST STAGE OF THE FLIGHT TO VARENNES

* Arrived 5:00 P.M., June 21, after a breakdown of one hour.
* * Arrived 6:30 P.M.
* * * Arrived 8:00 P.M.
* * * * Arrived 9:30 P.M.
* * * * * Arrived 11:00 P.M.
Distances in English miles.

Chalons on the Marne it was already five in the evening. Again a postmaster recognized the king and kept silent. A number of other Chalons citizens saw the face of Louis XVI but were sympathetic. No one molested the coach as it left the town.

At this point Bouillé's loyal cavalry should have guarded the highway to Montmédy. But some one had miscalculated; there were no troops in sight. Louis and Marie Antoinette were disturbed, but they drove at great speed—at about nine miles per hour—to Pont-Sommevesle, the next station, where they arrived at six-thirty in the evening. Again no troops, but the town was in great agitation because strange things had been happening that day.

At noon on that day, while the coach was still forty miles away, a troop of forty hussars, commanded by the young Duke de Choiseul, had arrived at Pont-Sommevesle, and the excitable townsfolk, fearing that the soldiers had come to collect taxes, sounded the tocsin. Peasants from the neighboring villages came rushing to town armed with scythes, pitchforks, and old muskets. Choiseul, a young man whom Fersen called a "blunderer," was afraid of a collision between soldiers and people, and he told the good folk that the hussars had come simply to meet and conduct a treasure shipment to Sainte-Ménehould. After waiting until five in the afternoon, the aristocratic commander concluded that something had gone amiss with the coach—it was already two hours late—and ordered the hussars to ride back to Sainte-Ménehould. That miscalculation was to prove fatal.

The royal coach did not stop at Pont-Sommevesle but hurried to Sainte-Ménehould, a distance of fifteen miles which was covered in ninety minutes. "At Sainte-Ménehould," Louis comforted the agitated queen, "we shall find the first detachment of troops, and our trip is successful."

AT SAINTE-MÉNEHOULD there was a troop of dragoons, but it was of no help. The commander, Captain d'Andouins, leaned over from his horse and whispered to Moustier, the noble guard who was riding alongside the coach, "Leave at once, hurry, you're lost if you don't hurry." Then the captain put his head inside the coach: "Something has gone wrong; I'm leaving so as not to arouse suspicion."

The town was quiet in the dusk, and Louis did not heed the captain's warning. While the horses were being harnessed at the hostelry the Golden Sun, the king looked out of the window. Drouet, the postmaster, a tall and brisk young fellow who had served in the cavalry at Paris, thought that the brown-wigged traveler's face seemed familiar. Looking at the assignats with which he was paid, the postmaster was struck by the resemblance of the head on the money and that in the berlin. Again he looked at the face in the coach...: Surely in all France there was only one man with such a beaked nose, such a round chin, such a short-sighted look....

Drouet said not a word. As soon as the coach had departed in the direction of Varennes, twenty miles away, he dashed to the Town Hall with the electrifying news. In a few minutes the tocsin struck alarm throughout the quiet countryside, and Drouet was galloping by a shortcut through the woods to warn *les patriotes.*

The berlin rode fast through the Argonne Forest in a moonless night. At Clermont, where the roads to Verdun and Varennes forked, a detachment of cavalry was supposed to be waiting. No horse was in sight. Louis' hand shook as he took out a detailed plan and showed the queen that there should have been troops at the cross-roads.

It was midnight, a very black night, when the coach lumbered into the deserted little town of Varennes. "The inhabitants," Moustier recalls, "were shrouded in the profoundest slumber." The post-station in that seeming ghost-town had no horses, and Moustier argued with the postilions, offering them a heavy tip to continue with the worn animals. Suddenly shouts rent the air, and the clatter of hooves reverberated on the cobblestones. A *sous-lieutenant* with sixty hussars had at last come to guard the royal family. But at the same time the local National Guard had also come and surrounded coach and cavalry. The horsemen flashed their sabers. The guardsmen raised their muskets. Possibly the hussars could have fought their way out and given the berlin a chance to escape. But Montmédy, the fortress where Louis would have found shelter, was thirty miles away. The horses were too exhausted to make the dash. Worst of all, the king could not bear the sight of violence or the smell of blood. Wearily he ordered the cavalry not to resist. He admitted his identity to the clamoring guardsmen and townsfolk and gave himself up, himself and his wife and his children and his sister, as prisoners of the people.

⚜

TIRED from a twenty-four hour long ride in a springless coach, the royal family knew no sleep that night. At sunrise (Louis noted in his Journal that it was five or six A.M.) the National Guard ordered the prisoners to get ready for departure. Quietly they drove back to Sainte-Ménehould, where they lunched at the Town Hall. The people were silent, ominously silent, and the king and queen were in fear that at any moment fury would break loose, the silence being so unnatural. *"Sur ma tête,"* the mayor of Sainte-Ménehould had to swear to Louis and Marie Antoinette that he would protect them from any untoward "accident."

⚜

NEWS of the sensational "capture" reached Paris as if by telegraphy, and the people burst into hilarious gaiety. They sang in the streets, joked in the cafés, danced on the Champs Élysées.

More serious persons asked grave questions. Thomas Lindet, a priest and a member of the Assembly, asked his brother Robert, who was also a deputy, "Will France be a republic?" The Jacobins, who were the extreme radicals of the Revolution, in their famous Club, asked the same question in more heated words. During a debate on the subject of whether or not Louis had forfeited his crown, Danton shouted hotly: "The individual called king of the French fled after having sworn to uphold the constitution. . . . This individual signed a paper which declared that he went to seek means to destroy the constitution. . . . If he admits the authorship, *certes,* he is a criminal, unless one wants to call him an imbecile. . . . And an individual cannot be king when he is an imbecile."

The National Assembly debated the question of the king's fate until the early hours of the morning, when a resolution was passed to bring back the monarch, the dauphin, and "other persons"—the queen's name was studiously ignored—under heavy guard. Three prominent deputies, Latour-Maubourg, Pétion, and Barnave, were chosen as commissioners. General Mathieu Dumas (ancestor of the novelist) was appointed commander of the military guard.

About half-way between Varennes and Paris, in a little town near Épernay, the royal berlin was met by the three commissioners. Louis and Marie Antoinette were studiedly calm. They had been received so far with a marked lack of disrespect, and now they wondered how the commissioners, deputies of the nation, would treat them.

Pétion, a Paris demagogue, was brusque. Latour-Maubourg, a marquis and former friend of Madame de Tourzel, could not face the fallen monarchs whom he had come to guard, and he retired to a respectful distance behind the coach. Barnave, a handsome young lawyer, was an idealistic revolutionist whose animosity toward the monarchy was not personal.

Pétion and Barnave got into the already crowded berlin and sat down between the king and the queen. Now the two revolutionists and the two crowned heads had a chance to get acquainted. Pétion—Jerome Pétion de Villeneuve—did not make a good impression. He was a thirty-five year old lawyer from Chartres, an extreme radical with the austere and righteous views of the fanatic; in less than three years he was to be hounded to death by his own followers. Barnave, very boyish at thirty, was an altogether different type. Eloquent and courteous, he charmed the queen. He, too, was fascinated by Marie Antoinette, an attractive woman of thirty-six, an unfortunate queen, a tender mother; for Barnave had a romantic streak. Had he not written in 1788, one year before he was catapulted into that perilous revolutionary fame which ended on the guillotine, that "women are capable of all that is good and all that is evil"?

Pétion leaned back in his seat and pretended to be a greater boor than he really was. He ate and drank with deliberate *malpropreté,* hoping to annoy Their Majesties and perhaps also his fastidious colleague Barnave. With that curious relish which Charles Laughton displayed as Henry VIII, Pétion devoured a chicken and threw the greasy bones out of the window right in front of the king's face, making the short-sighted Louis duck quickly.

Barnave, sitting close to the queen, respectfully encouraged Their Majesties to talk, and Louis explained the reasons for his flight from Paris. The young deputy criticized his conduct. When the conversation languished, Barnave addressed himself to the dauphin who was sitting on his mother's knee, for the prince charmed the revolutionist with his liveliness and intelligence. "Isn't it true," Barnave asked the dauphin with a smile, "that you are sorry to return to Paris?"

"Oh," the child exclaimed, "I am well everywhere, provided that I am with my father and my mama-queen."

FEW noteworthy incidents occurred on the road. In one village a curé tried to approach the king and was beaten by the National Guard. This so enraged Barnave that he leaned out of the coach and cried, "Tigers, have you ceased to be Frenchmen? Nation of brave men, have you become a people of assassins?" In his fury he leaned out too far and would have toppled over had not Elizabeth seized him by the tail of his coat. The spectacle made Marie Antoinette laugh.

At another village peasants heaped insults on the king. "Oh, how fat he is, the bastard! We paid plenty to fatten him. *Vive la nation! Vive Barnave!* To hell with the rest of them!" When the queen offered the officer of the guard a drink, the crowd shouted, "Don't take it, she is a bitch of a poisoner!"

Near Paris, Louis said to Barnave, "This is a very sad journey for my children. What a difference between this and the trip to Cherbourg! At that time calumny had not yet misled public opinion. How prejudiced they are! They may disown me, but they will never change me; I shall always love the people."

His father's sad tone touched the little dauphin, who took the king's hand and kissed it. "Don't be sad, my papa, next time we'll go to Cherbourg."

PARIS was icily still as the coach entered the city in the evening of Saturday, June 25, the fifth day after the flight. The streets were lined with immense crowds of tight-mouthed people, grim and reproachful. On the walls placards warned: WHOEVER APPLAUDS THE KING WILL BE FLOGGED; WHOEVER INSULTS HIM WILL BE HANGED. Nobody applauded, nobody insulted. Despite the sultriness of the evening, the silent men kept their hats on. The National Guard stood at attention, rigid and mournful, holding rifles muzzles down, as was customary for a *convoi funèbre*. Not a human sound broke the silence as the "funeral procession" drove through the streets of Paris.

The iron gates of the Tuileries opened to receive the royal family and were instantly locked behind them. A tense and silent crowd on the other side of the fence watched the king and queen enter the palace.

"It's been hot to-day," Louis said as he entered his apartment; "this damned trip has worn me out. Bring me a *potage*. . . . Make my bed."

THE WHOLE EPISODE of the flight and the return stirred the country deeply. As yet there were few republicans in France, but Louis' behavior had alienated many of his sympathizers. The National Assembly in particular was in a state of perplexity. They distrusted *the* king, but they needed *a* king.

"AWAKENING OF THE THIRD ESTATE"
A cartoon contemporary with the fall of the Bastille.

"THE FAMILY OF PIGS BROUGHT BACK TO THE STY"
A cartoon contemporary with the return from Varennes.

There was no way of disposing of Louis XVI without destroying the constitutional foundations on which the new order was based and of which the king was an integral part. And yet Louis XVI had declared himself hostile to the revolution and had tried to run away from his "good people." He had lost public confidence; he had shown himself faithless, perfidious, perjured, so the Jacobins argued. To restore him to power would be sheltering a traitor. He had broken his word once, and he would do it again. At best he could never be anything but what Lamartine once called a "pardoned king," a paroled prisoner who could never be trusted.

Depose Louis XVI? Jacobins like Régnier argued in favor of deposition and of the establishment of a council of regency during the minority of the dauphin. This, however, entailed incalculable dangers. As Jean-Marie Roland de la Platière, a prominent radical deputy, said, "It is impossible to choose a regent without giving rise to factions among the various persons who could pretend to the title and without thereby furnishing pretexts for war." Public opinion, moreover, would not have supported such a step, for Louis XVI, despite his blunders and weaknesses, was still the most generally liked Frenchman in public position. Even many radicals regarded him as a good-natured and disinterested patriot, but a victim of a counter-revolutionary family. Certainly he was preferable to any other Bourbon. As Lafayette said on the day when Louis was brought back to Paris, "Despite everything, he is the best prince of his family and, taken all in all, the best in Europe."

The Assembly spent the night hoarsely debating the king's fate, while Louis slept calmly in the Tuileries. A motion to the effect that the royal family be placed under special guard aroused royalist wrath. "Unconstitutional," shouted Pierre-Victor Malouet, a monarchist deputy, "the constitution declares the king sacred and inviolable."

"It is simply," Pierre-Louis Roederer, who was destined to play a fateful part in Louis' life, defended the motion, "a question of keeping the king under provisional arrest."

"No, no, no," the monarchist deputies cried.

The motion was carried tumultuously.

SUNDAY morning the "provisional" royal prisoner received a committee of three (Louis Tronchet, Adrien Duport, Antoine d'André) and gave them a declaration of his conduct:

> The causes of my departure are the outrages and menaces perpetrated against my family and me on April 18.... The insults have gone unpunished.... There was neither safety nor decency for my family and for me in Paris. In consequence I tried to leave the city. Unable to do it openly, I resolved to leave at night.... It was never my intention to get out of the kingdom; *I have never had any understanding on this subject either with foreign powers or with my relatives.*... Lodgings for me and my family have been prepared at Montmédy. I chose that place because it was fortified, and my family would have been safe there; and being close to the frontier, I would have been in a position to oppose any kind of invasion of France.

This declaration was read in the Assembly, and the king's remaining friends were pained by such transparent untruths. The Jacobins gloated: Didn't we tell you that your precious king was a perjurer and a liar—? As if further to discredit the king, the National Assembly read a letter from General Bouillé, whose conscience stung because his arrangements for the flight of the royal family had miscarried, threatening the revolutionists with dire consequences:

> I tremble to think that the king's life is at the mercy of a people made ferocious by you.... All the princes in the world realize that they are menaced by the monster which you have brought forth, and soon they will burst upon our unhappy country.... Your chastisement will serve as a memorable example to posterity.... You will answer for the lives of the king and the queen to all the kings in the world. If a hair is touched on their heads, *not a stone will remain of Paris....*

The rodomontade was drowned in gales of sardonic laughter.

CHAPTER XXI

"The Assembly nailed him to the throne"

THE KING was a prisoner in the Tuileries, there was now no doubt about it. The fiction of royal liberty, so persistently kept up before the flight, was no longer maintained. Guards surrounded the Tuileries, and guards stood in all the royal antechambers. The doors of the king's apartments were always open and watched. Only when Louis put on his shirt and the queen her chemise were the doors shut for a moment. Four officers of the National Guard always accompanied Marie Antoinette, whose apartments were on the ground floor, when she went to visit her son upstairs; two men remained outside, and two watched her in the room while she talked to the boy. No one could enter or leave the Tuileries without a pass from Lafayette or Bailly. King and queen never left the palace.

Nevertheless Louis and Marie Antoinette managed to build up a line of communication with the outside world. This was done ingeniously by means of whispered phrases, disguised messengers, cryptic signs, and ciphered slips of paper. The king and the queen now gave themselves wholeheartedly to the counter-revolution, staking their future solely on foreign aid. Louis felt no loyalty whatever to a government that was his jailer. His one stipulation in coöperating with the émigrés and the foreign powers against the revolution was that no French blood be shed, for he did not remember the adage about the impossibility of making omelets without breaking eggs. In a secret letter to General Bouillé Louis wrote these characteristic words: "Civil war horrifies me, and I do not want to shed the blood of my subjects, whether misled or loyal. My fate is tied with that of the nation and *I do not wish to rule by violence.*"[1]

Such an attitude was rather futile, especially since the king's monarchist friends abroad were consumed with fierce hate for the revolution, ready to drown the rebels in blood and to reduce Paris, in the words of General Bouillé, to a heap of rocks. This was by no means a rare instance of one's friends being one's most dangerous enemies. In vain both Louis and Marie Antoinette pleaded caution and diplomacy. "The king," Marie Antoinette wrote to Fersen, "thinks that only by means of negotiation can help be useful. . . . The king thinks that overt force would be of incalculable danger." But the émigrés were starved for power and mad with hatred, envenomed by poverty and galled by inactivity. They were goaded by the hot-headed Gustave III of Sweden, who set himself up as Europe's champion monarch and swore to "annihilate the hydra" of revolution, even if he had to destroy Louis and Marie Antoinette in the process. This curious paladin of thrones frankly admitted that he cared nothing for the lives of the prisoners in the Tuileries; what mattered to him was the principle of monarchy. "It is all the same," he said, "whether it is Louis XVI or Louis XVII, or Charles X who occupies the throne, provided that there be a throne." The Swedish swashbuckler was moving heaven and earth to invade France (with the help of Louis' brothers and men like Breteuil, St. Priest, Calonne, Bouillé). "But," as Catherine II of Russia said cynically, "the king of Sweden has no money."

MOVED by Marie Antoinette's hysterical appeals, her brother, Emperor Leopold II of Austria, called upon monarchical

[1] *Fac-Simile de lettres de Louis XVI à M. le Marquis de Bouillé* (Paris, n.d.). This booklet contains photostats of eight genuine letters.

Europe to combine against the "hydra," even though it meant imperiling the lives of the royal prisoners. Strangely enough, the European monarchs did not display that "trade-union" feeling that one might have expected. They responded only with warm words. George III of England replied that he took the "liveliest interest" in the fate of Their Majesties of France. Charles IV of Spain wondered, Spaniard-like, why Louis XVI had not saved himself at Varennes by a "courageous death." The king of Sardinia said that he was "pained and indignant" at the plight of the French monarchs. The ruler of Naples promised to ban French newspapers from his duodecimo kingdom. The czarina of Russia wrote eloquently about the horrors of revolution. Only Frederick William II of Prussia was genuinely scared. "What a terrible example!" cried the nephew and successor of Frederick the Great, and offered to coöperate with Emperor Leopold.

But Marie Antoinette's imperial brother in Vienna, on whom Louis and his wife founded all their hopes, was not a type to leap into quixotic adventures like that "swaggerer" Gustave III of Sweden. Leopold, moreover, was weary of the importunities of the émigrés and contemptuous of their characters. "They think of nothing but their romantic ideas and their personal vengeances and interests, and believe that everybody should sacrifice himself for them." In any case Louis begged his brother-in-law not to precipitate any violent action. "If I am forced to be immolated on the scaffold like Charles I," Louis wrote, "I am ready. But no war! No war!"

Therefore Leopold and his Prussian ally contented themselves with issuing a declaration (the so-called Declaration of Pillnitz) to the effect that it was "in the common interest of all the sovereigns of Europe" to give Louis the means to establish a monarchical government in France. The declaration was harmless enough, but it caused indignation among the excitable patriots in France, and much of the resentment was turned against Louis.

⚜

In the meantime Louis received powerful assistance from an unexpected quarter in Paris. A strong faction in the National Assembly had come to the tardy realization that it was impossible to destroy the monarchy without at the same time opening wide the gates to anarchy. Whether Louis was deposed or merely stripped of all his powers, the result would be the same: France would be torn by civil strife. Already the extreme-radical Cordeliers Club and many of the Jacobins clamored for the king's deposition, and the capital was agitated by their unrestrained propaganda; on July 17, 1791, several people were killed on the Champ de Mars when the Cordeliers presented their petition for the suspension of the king. If the extremists were not checked, France, still largely monarchist, faced the possibility of sanguinary dictatorship (as was to happen two years later when the Committee of Public Safety was set up) and the certainty of foreign invasion. In this crisis a triumvirate of talents combined in the National Assembly; it was composed of Joseph Barnave, who during the return from Varennes had developed a great affection for the queen, Adrien Duport and Alexandre de Lameth. These chastened revolutionists had once been ardent antimonarchists, but now they joined forces with Lafayette and other moderate royalists to block the extremists and to stabilize the shaken royal power. This group came to be known as the Feuillants, called after the monastery (where they met) by that name.

On at least two occasions (and possibly more) Barnave managed to slip into the guarded Tuileries and have interviews with Louis and Marie Antoinette in a little room on the *entresol*. In thus establishing contact with the imprisoned royal family the handsome young deputy from Grenoble staked not merely his reputation but, as it turned out, his life. Mirabeau had once said of him prophetically, "That's a young tree that will grow tall, if they will let it grow." The sapling hoped to grow in the shadow of the throne, a forgivable miscalculation which older and more experienced men than Barnave had made to their sorrow. To obviate the hazards involved in per-

BARNAVE THE TRIMMER

A contemporary cartoon. Collection Liesville, Paris.

sonal meetings—for there were spies everywhere—Barnave and Marie Antoinette maintained contact by means of a cipher correspondence, the key to which was rather transparent. Barnave was 2:1, Alexandre de Lameth, 1:12, Duport 4:15, the Feuillants *"ces messieurs."* The carrier of these letters, the thin lifeline between the National Assembly and the Tuileries, was Count François de Jarjayes, a middle-aged compatriot of Barnave, whose wife held a position in the Tuileries. When Jarjayes visited his wife in the palace, the queen would unobtrusively slip a sealed letter into his pocket; then Barnave would get it. Jarjayes was never searched upon leaving or entering the Tuileries, and so the correspondence was not betrayed.[2]

⚜

BARNAVE's advice was this: that the king and queen accept the revolution, forget their grievances, and try to win back popular confidence. He explained that his own group, the Feuillants, together with the Fayettists and the moderate elements in the Assembly were forging a new constitution in which Louis would be granted considerable powers and dignities. If Louis knew how to play politics gracefully and honestly accept what was being given, and if the queen had no *arrière pensée,* then there was a chance to save the monarchy and to restore public order. In a letter to the queen Barnave wrote bluntly:

> The queen has misjudged the revolution . . . ; but it is useless to harp upon the past. One should examine the present and try to find what advantage one can draw from it. The queen would be very much deceived if she believed that her personal existence is lost forever in France. Informed persons will tell her that she is the object of profound resentment, but that there always remain great means for restoring opinion, so long as one has retained a reputation for character and courage. The queen has

[2] The queen used the same cipher in her correspondence with Fersen. The key to the cipher was not made public until almost a century and a half later. In 1934 Alma Söderhjelm, the decipherer of the correspondence, published her *Marie-Antoinette et Barnave. Correspondence secrète (juillet 1791-janvier 1792).*

stirred up deep grudges. . . . She has always been regarded as an enemy. . . . But soon the French people will become tired of hating.

Neither Louis nor Marie Antoinette, however, was psychologically able to accept the counsel of anybody remotely connected with the revolution. The king was unshakably distrustful and the queen irremediably embittered; both had suffered too many humiliations at the hands of the populace to have any confidence in either the people or their representatives. Marie Antoinette liked Barnave but was dubious of the cause he represented. She said that the constitution upon which he and the Assembly were working was a "tissue of impracticable absurdities" but would have to be accepted to gain time.[3] Louis was likewise contemptuous of the constitution-in-the-making. He considered it an instrument of "enslavement," a trap set by the revolutionists to discredit him in the eyes of Europe. "On the other hand," he concluded, "it would be even more dangerous to reject it."

THE IRONY was that the constitution which the queen vehemently denounced as "monstrous" and made by "monsters" was a much better instrument than either the king or the royalists had a right to expect. Far from being the work of "monsters," it was drawn up by some of the ablest men in the Assembly, such as Talleyrand, Clermont-Tonnerre, Sieyès, Target, Barnave, Tronchet, Duport, Lameth, Pétion, Thouret. The king, to be sure, was deprived of absolute power, but he was placed in a position of influence and dignity as head of the state and was granted sufficient leeway to exert considerable influence on affairs, if he wished. The point was that the constitution stabilized Louis' position and offered him the chance to serve his agitated country in the manner of his "cousin" the king of England. No more, but not less. Moreover, the instrument was elastic enough to enable a chief

[3] Marie Antoinette to Mercy, August 7, 1791; Bibliothèque Nationale, n.a.Fr.6968, p.448.

executive endowed with political ability to exercise those subtle and often great powers which were not expressly forbidden. As Barnave told the queen, "The root of his power is in the constitution; it will grow rapidly, if he does not provoke something that might destroy it."

Louis remained cold and Marie Antoinette angry and blind. She continued to rage against the deputies—"this race of tigers which inundates the kingdom"—and called for a war of extermination against the revolution. "For us," she wrote a few days before Louis solemnly swore to uphold the constitution, "it is only a question of lulling them, to give them confidence in us in order the better to foil them later. ... We have no other means left than the foreign powers. It is necessary that they come to our aid at any price."

She might have remembered the old adage that those whom the gods set out to destroy they first deprive of sight.

⚜

ON SEPTEMBER 3, 1791, Louis XVI was given his last chance. On that day the National Assembly crowned its two turbulent years with the completion of the *Acte Constitutionel* and made ready to submit it to the imprisoned king for acceptance, if not approval.

A deputation of sixty was empowered to carry the document to the Tuileries and present it to the king, without, however, making any speech. "It is sufficient," the proud Assembly decided, "that he be told simply the object of the mission."

Escorted by the National Guard and applauded by an enthusiastic populace, the deputation arrived in the palace at nine in the evening. It was an impressive committee. Not even Marie Antoinette could say that the archbishops of Paris and of Rouen, Brillat-Savarin, Malouet, Barnave, Duport, Lameth, La Rochefoucauld, Sieyès, Talleyrand, to mention but ten out of the sixty, were revolutionary "tigers." Louis received them standing in the great Council Chamber. He was cool and bland. In a few brief words he said that he would examine the constitution as soon as possible and give his decision. As if any one cared about his decision! In the meantime, he added without the slightest attempt at a smile, he had decided "to remain in Paris." If this was irony, the sixty deputies pretended not to notice it.

Louis' "acceptance" of the extremely democratic constitution was a foregone conclusion, but the speech was prepared by Barnave, Duport, Lameth, and Lafayette. The king was supremely indifferent. It was not his constitution, and he cared nothing for what was in it. Exigency compelled acceptance and he would accept. What difference did it make what was said in the speech? Or in the constitution, for that matter? He had reached such a point of frustration that nothing much mattered any more. If Barnave, the young fool, and Lafayette, the turncoat aristocrat, wanted a constitutional king, he would pretend to be a constitutional king. He had been brought up to think of himself as the sovereign of France who *granted* favors to his subjects; now he was *being granted* something by rebels. His personality, so excessively inflexible, revolted against an order of events which turned his world topsy-turvy, but to avoid conflict he was ready, in a forlorn fashion, to say *Yes* to those who held a whip.

This meekness drove Marie Antoinette, storm-tossed by emotions, to vocal exasperation. When she looked over the draft of the acceptance speech, written by strangers in her husband's name, she exclaimed, "But this is not the speech of a king who deeply resents his outrages!" Louis shrugged his shoulders. And while all France was waiting anxiously for the king's decision, the queen cried in anguish, "*Mon dieu!* Is it possible that I, born with character and sensing strongly the blood that courses in my veins, should be destined to pass my days in such a time and with such men?"

⚜

LOUIS sent his ghost-written letter to the National Assembly. It was an intelligent letter, an *apologia pro vita sua,* which impressed the deputies and infuriated the queen; it explained at length why His Majesty had decided to accept the constitution. "From the beginning of my reign, I wished to reform abuses, and in all the acts of government I liked to take public opinion for my guide." He pointedly reminded the Assembly that it was he who had convoked it to reform the finances which were in a bad state due to no fault of his. "At my accession to the throne the finances were deranged, and the immense expenditures of an honorable war, maintained for a long time without an increase in taxation, caused a considerable disproportion between revenues and expenditures." During the revolution, Louis stressed, he had loyally supported the Assembly's legislative program, always hoping that the "law would recover its sway." But the hope was vain. Violence was on the increase, and anarchy was king. Now, however, that the Assembly had come to the sobering realization that law and order were necessary in a civilized country and had embodied these principles in a written instrument, he would gladly coöperate again. "I accept the constitution; I promise to maintain it at home and to defend it abroad, and to execute it with all the means that it puts in my power."

The voice was the voice of Louis, the words those of Barnave, Lameth and Lafayette. But the nation liked the sound.

In the left-hand margin of the first page of the constitution an unsteady royal hand scribbled, *"J'accepte et ferai executer 14 7tembre 91. Louis."*

⚜

THE ACCEPTANCE of the democratic constitution by the king required a ceremonial setting. After the letter of acceptance was read before the Assembly, Louis and his family and ministers went thither to swear fealty to the representatives of the people of France; and the deputies, most of whom had read history, were embarrassingly aware that this was the crowning moment of the revolution.

The Assembly was debating the question whether to receive the king standing, in honor of Majesty, or sitting, as befitted free citizens, but the matter was still undecided when the usher announced dramatically, *"Voilà le roi!"* As Louis, without decorations and without the trappings of royalty, entered the Assembly, the deputies spontaneously rose in greeting and stood up while the king walked slowly to the platform and placed himself near President Thouret. Louis addressed the standing deputies:

"Gentlemen, I come here to dedicate solemnly the acceptance which I have given to the constitution. In consequence I swear—." A sudden shuffling and scraping drowned his voice. The king's hand shook visibly as the whole Assembly was seating themselves in the middle of his speech; Marie Antoinette gasped audibly at the unexampled insult. "—I swear to be faithful to the nation and to the law—." At this point Louis regained his poise and followed the example of the deputies by sitting down. This too was unheard of. Calmly the seated king concluded his oath: "—and to employ all the power delegated to me to maintain the constitution."

Louis' presence of mind aroused considerable admiration and his acceptance much enthusiasm. The Assembly applauded and accompanied Their Majesties back to the Tuileries. Martial music played and artillery thundered.

A NEW DAY dawned. The Assembly had completed its work by giving France an ardently desired constitution (as it had promised in the Tennis-Court Oath), and the king had cemented his ties with the nation by accepting it. France had little more to ask and the king nothing else to give. Surely the revolution had already accomplished its purpose; many hoped that it had run its course. Even Paris relented. For the first time since his captivity Louis was cheered by the populace; he and his wife were allowed to go riding in the Champs Élysées and permitted to attend the opera. The municipality, a city machine run by tough politicians, celebrated the end of the revolution with lavish displays of fireworks and costly illuminations. Palloy, a contractor who always signed his name "Palloy, Patriot," and who made a very good thing out

LOUIS XVI WEARING THE REVOLUTIONARY COCKADE
Portrait by Jean-François Carteaux, 1791. Musée de Versailles.

of being a revolutionary patriot, built an open-air theater on the place where the Bastille once stood (Patriot Palloy's company, by the way, got the contract for demolishing it and selling the stones at a profit), and the people came to enjoy scintillating spectacles. Louis added to the general feeling of well-being by giving fifty thousand livres to the poor. Everybody felt fine and brotherly. Elizabeth, the king's pious young sister, wrote ironically, "We've been to the opera; we're going to the comedy. *Mon dieu,* what pleasures!"

But Louis was placidly cynical about the whole matter. Since he was no longer free, he did not consider himself under moral obligation to the nation, and whatever he said or did was in the nature of a gesture made under compulsion. With the hopelessness of a weak man he felt his present situation to be permanent and that nothing really mattered. Moreover, he was contemptuous of all those who thought that the constitution was a magic key to salvation and guarantee of eternal unrestraint. In a frank letter to his intractable brother Artois he wrote: "The nation loves the constitution, because this word reminds the lower classes only of the independence which they enjoyed for two years and the classes above, of legality.... The lower people see that they are being reckoned with; the bourgeois sees nobody above him. Self-esteem is satisfied.... Time will teach them how much they deceive themselves." Time was also to teach Louis that the common people had no monopoly on self-deception.

THE EXCITING MONTH of September thus came to an end with the dissolution of the National Assembly. It left a great record behind it. It had regenerated France with five thousand ninety-three new laws passed in the course of two hectic years; it had steered through a great political upheaval. Now the deputies were going home (in a burst of generosity they had voted themselves ineligible for election to the next Assembly) to tell the citizens that the revolution was over, that what they had sworn in the summer of 1789 to achieve they had loyally fulfilled, and that now France could settle down to an era of happiness and prosperity, to a golden age of equality and liberty. The citizens throughout France were also to be reminded that they had a loving chief executive in the Tuileries, no longer an absolute monarch victimized by a degenerate court clique, but a constitutional king directly responsible to the people. Louis came to close the session of the Assembly and told the deputies, "Upon returning to your homes, gentlemen, you will tell your fellow-citizens that their happiness will be my sole occupation. Tell them that their king will always be their first and their most faithful friend."

The president of the Assembly said emotionally, "The revolution is at an end."

CHAPTER XXII

"It is fine to be king of a free people"

FRANCE was happy to hear that the king had sworn to coöperate loyally with the new order, and in the prevailing optimism Louis reaped a full harvest of popularity. He was free to move about Paris, and everywhere he went the sovereign people greeted him with extreme warmth. The good citizens had forgotten their past grievances against their good king and hoped that he too had interred the past. It had all been a family quarrel; now all the brothers and parents could live in harmony. At the Théâtre Italien Louis shared honors with the bright actors of *The Two Hunters and the Milkmaid* and received as much applause as the Thespians who gave *The Jealous Lover*. Popularity could go no further. "At the moment," Madame Elizabeth confided to a friend, "the king is the object of public worship. But how long will it last?"

A revolution, however, could not be liquidated by a constitution, and as the promised golden age did not come quickly, the mood of the nation underwent a change. Many causes combined to dispel the current of optimism. Economic conditions continued to be bad. The country was still suffering from two years of disorder and uncertainty. Since business was handicapped by political instability, the unemployed could not be absorbed. The assignats, the government's paper money (which bore the face of the king), began to drop catastrophically in value, good money became rare, and as usual prices soared. Much of the nation's cash and precious metals left the country via the pockets of the thousands of émigrés, most of whom were men of property. This combination of unemployment, disappearance of ready money, and high prices was a blight on the cities, especially Paris, where a new revolutionary situation was developing rapidly. In the country where the sentiment was largely Catholic and royalist, unrest was stimulated by nonjuring priests and fed by the peasants' traditional land-hunger. Jacqueries and riots in many rural areas showed that France was still speeding along a revolutionary road whose end was not yet visible.

In the storm that was obviously gathering, a wise king would have remained still as a mouse and unobtrusive. Louis, however, or rather his obdurate wife, was committed to a policy of active counter-revolution at a time when the nation was half-prepared to trust the king.

THE LEGISLATIVE ASSEMBLY which met early in October seemed to be a promise of political stability. Because the new deputies came from the well-to-do classes, they were not emotionally radical; in fact, they rather inclined to maintain the *status quo* and the constitution. A strong minority of some 260 deputies—more than one-third of the whole body—was organized to defend the monarchy against the 136 Girondins (including Jacobins) who were unfriendly to Louis XVI, although by no means republicans. The rest of the deputies—345 of them—sat in the center, both physically and politically, ready to be swayed either rightward or leftward as the occasion, or the orator, required. This Center was potentially royalist and potentially radical; it was to be "had" by any person or group clever enough to stir it.

The chances of the king's taking advantage of the favorably disposed Legislative Assembly were not great. Even if Louis had wanted to be loyal to the constitution and to coöperate with the legislature, the queen would not have allowed it.

In her overpowering bitterness she called the bourgeois-conservative Legislative Assembly a "collection of scoundrels, lunatics, and beasts." [1]

Friction between the king and the legislature could not long be delayed. In November the Assembly passed severe measures against the émigrés and the princes abroad who were tirelessly organizing an army on the French frontier. If they did not return to France within two months, the Assembly decreed, the émigrés were to be declared guilty of conspiracy, condemned to death, and their property confiscated. Louis promptly vetoed the laws as too harsh, understandably refusing to condemn his own brothers; but he made a public appeal to them to return to France.

To Artois, the most vocal and reactionary of his brothers, Louis wrote:

> Surely you must have knowledge of the decree issued by the National Assembly concerning the Frenchmen who have left their country. I did not think it my duty to give it my consent, wanting to persuade myself that gentler measures may achieve more efficaciously the proposed object. . . . The various steps I have taken should have left no doubt in your mind as to my intentions or wishes. Public tranquillity and my personal peace both demand your return. Without being amiss in your most essential duties, you could not prolong a conduct which disquiets France and afflicts me. Spare me the regret of having to concur in the severe measures against you. Consult your true interest, let yourself be guided by the attachment which you owe to your country and in the end yield to the wishes of Frenchmen and of your king.[2]

The letter, which Louis knew would be made public, was mainly remarkable for insincerity. For the king did not want his brothers to come back to what would have amounted to a prison. Secretly he continued his financial support of his counter-revolutionary brothers and other needy émigrés; be-

[1] October 31, 1791; in A. Geffroy, *Marie Antoinette et Fersen. Mémoire* (Rome, 1879), p.18-19.

[2] November 11, 1791; Bibliothèque Nationale, n.a.Fr.308, no.314; also Archives Nationales, AD I 74.

tween July, 1791, and February, 1792, he sent 665,000 livres to Artois.[3]

Louis' refusal to approve the laws against the émigrés created a painful impression. Many people said openly that the king actually encouraged the foreign powers and the émigrés in their designs against France; others felt that he deliberately did nothing to prevent the counter-revolutionary intrigues abroad. Mounting popular impatience drove the Legislative Assembly to rap the knuckles of a strangely undutiful monarch. "It is up to you, Sire, to put a stop to these hostile preparations; it is up to you to speak to the foreign powers in a language befitting a king of the French."

Louis murmured evasively that he would take the words of the Assembly into "very great consideration."

⚜

WHILE the Assembly and the nation were anxiously waiting for the chief executive to come out with a ringing declaration against the foreign powers that threatened to invade France in order to save Louis XVI, he, the king, wrote a secret letter to Frederick William II of Prussia that was, by any standard, treasonable.[4]

Monsieur my brother [Louis wrote], I have learned . . . of the interest which Your Majesty has shown not only for my person but also for . . . my kingdom. I claim it with confidence at this moment when, despite my acceptance of the new constitution, the factious openly show designs to destroy entirely the rest of the monarchy. I have just written to the emperor, the empress of

[3] Archives Nationales, F7 4390 A, c. no.23. A typical letter from an émigré, the Marquis de Beaupré, to the king reads: "By the most cruel of injustices the National Assembly has stripped me of all that I possessed in France. . . . My ruin is complete. Sire, I appeal to you with confidence when I have nothing." *Ibid.*, no.44aa cotte D, no.50. Louis could not resist such appeals.

[4] The letter may be found in Jules Flammermont, *Nègociations secrètes de Louis XVI et du baron de Breteuil avec la cour de Berlin, décembre 1791–juillet 1792* (Paris, 1885), 9-10. It made a long and circuitous route. Written on December 3, it did not reach Breteuil in Brussels until the end of the month. On January 4 Breteuil forwarded it to Berlin, where it arrived on January 12. On the 13th the Prussian king solemnly promised to keep it a secret: the promise was kept for decades.

Russia, the kings of Spain and of Sweden,[5] and proposed to them the idea of a congress of the major powers of Europe, supported by an armed force, as the best means of checking the factious here, of reëstablishing a more desirable order of things, and of preventing the evil which torments us from gaining hold in other states of Europe. I hope that Your Majesty will approve my ideas and will keep this step on my part in the most absolute secrecy.

After this letter was dispatched, Louis blandly informed the Assembly that he had done his best to stop foreign machinations against France and promised to continue the "constitutional line" in the future. "I feel profoundly," he concluded with an insincere compliment, "that it is fine to be king of a free people."

Such a contradictory course—pretended patriotism at home and intrigue abroad—necessitated considerably more agility than Louis XVI possessed, and so he gradually got himself into a tangle that only a knife could cut. Fatuously he hoped that both sides would believe him, but a double face usually carries one-sided conviction, often the least desired. In explanation, if not justification, of the king's conduct one may perhaps recall that he was as bewildered as any placid person is bound to be when tyrannized by a domineering wife, bullied by an unscrupulous family, and frightened by a revolutionary people.

⚜

IT WAS Marie Antoinette's novel idea that only war could solve their problem. War, she reasoned, would either destroy the constitutional government or make it so victorious that in gratitude it would restore Louis to absolute power. This curious female reasoning, which Louis obediently accepted, led to a policy of hunting with the hounds and running with the hares, of encouraging the rising pro-war sentiment in France and inciting belligerency abroad.

In a letter to Breteuil, his plenipotentiary abroad, Louis

[5] Actually these letters were written by Marie Antoinette.

elucidated at length that queer aberration which he called policy:

> In all established governments, if armed citizens show an inclination to reënter their country in order to destroy the government . . . , it would not be possible for the chief of the state to permit such a thing. . . . Such is precisely my case. I have many times written to the princes demanding that they separate the troops so as not to arouse anxiety which would force me to act directly against them. . . . It is necessary that you convince the powers that it is not I who want war against them, but that under the circumstances I could not act otherwise, and that I shall always receive with pleasure that which they can do for me.

Then the king proceeded to explain that if war broke out between France and the foreign powers, it was almost a certainty that France would be defeated. He pointed out that the country was in such physical and moral decline that it could not maintain even half a campaign. Should France, by some miracle, win—"such a hypothesis is the least likely"—then he, the king, would gain great prestige from having advocated war. In case of defeat—"you know how the French go from one extreme to the other"—the country would be so dejected that it would turn in fury against the "new edifice," the constitution, as the author of all misfortunes and destroy it by restoring the former royal power.

"My conduct," Louis concluded, "will be such as to remove all suspicion, and above all not to let any one suspect my relations with the foreign powers. It is necessary that my conduct be such that in misfortune the nation should see no other way out but to throw itself into my arms."

CHAPTER XXIII

"We are ready to purge the earth"

WOULD the throne, already deeply shaken by the revolution, be able to withstand the shock of a foreign war, especially an unsuccessful one? It did not seem likely. Louis and Marie Antoinette staked their future on a desperate gamble.

Both misread the national psychology and underestimated public opinion. Already the shortage of food and the high prices stirred latent antiroyalist animosities in the excitable populace. Early in the winter of 1792 Louis' popularity was steadily sinking. People began to call him *Monsieur Veto* on the streets, and journalists dubbed him *Louis Capet* in their publications. In the Legislative Assembly, Manuel, a vocal Jacobin, said bluntly, "I don't like kings," and around the Tuileries grim-faced, long-haired pikemen kept sullen watch. The hostile faces lurking everywhere near the palace frightened the king so that he sent for Pétion, and that queer man, who was then mayor of Paris, said ironically that the people were guarding His Majesty against abductors. And from the workers' Faubourg St. Antoine came a delegation of tough-fisted men to the Assembly and shouted, "We're ready to purge the earth of the king's friends and to stop him from deceiving us."

The clamor for war became deafening. From all over France came petitions for war against Emperor Leopold and offers to help the government. Soldiers, patriots, politicians, everybody wrote letters to the Legislative Assembly, letters of demand, of indignation, of threat. "Love of the fatherland and hatred of tyranny will easily make us brave all dangers," wrote a group of Paris citizens. A soldier stationed in Rheims boasted that soon he and other Frenchmen would show the tyrant Leopold the heroism of a nation which has "broken her chains and sworn rather to perish than to be enslaved." Two hundred and thirty-five citizens of Caën, in an unfriendly mood of theeing-and-thouing, warned Louis that it was time for him to declare war against Emperor Leopold and his German allies. "If the foreign enemies should enslave us with thy help, thou wilt not retain thy crown."

Louis waited for the Assembly to act. But the deputies were split into hostile groups whose programs were as confused as their rhetoric was sizzling. So-called Brissotins thought that war would cement the revolution, Girondins believed that war would weaken their enemies the Jacobins, Jacobins were for peace because Brissotins and Girondins were for war. In the struggle for position and prestige, the Girondins manœuvered the king into dismissing the unaggressive cabinet and appointing a more truculent ministry. The chief of the new cabinet, as minister of foreign affairs, was the blustering General Dumouriez, and the second important personality in this "Girondin Cabinet" was the pedantic Roland de la Platière, author of *The Art of Printing on Linen and of Manufacturing Fustian* and husband of a voluble ideologue who talked emotionally about liberty. Louis instantly disliked the black-gowned, unbending Roland with his ramrod strut and self-righteous platitudes; but the boisterous Dumouriez who talked boastfully and told wonderful stories won the king's admiration. "They told me that Dumouriez was a hot-head, but he gives me only good advice," Louis said to a friend.

The king wanted to take Dumouriez into his confidence and use him as he had once used Mirabeau, but the queen would have nothing to do with any one connected with the revolution, especially when help, in the form of the Austrian armies, was so near. That Dumouriez was no revolutionist but a clever soldier ambitious to help himself by helping the monarchy made no difference to Marie Antoinette, who saw in every non-aristocratic Frenchman an enemy. When Dumouriez entered the queen's apartment for the first time, he found her, flushed of face, pacing the room like a caged cheetah. "Take care!" she snapped. "This will not last." And she burst into a tirade against the revolution, mixing it with dire threats.

The veteran soldier was not easily browbeaten. "Madame, I am over fifty; my life has been exposed to many dangers." Then as the high-strung woman sat down limply, the General's features relaxed. "Believe me, Madame," he said softly, "I abhor anarchy and crime as much as you do.... I assure you this is no momentary popular movement, as you seem to believe. It is almost a unanimous insurrection of a great nation against deep-rooted abuses.... I will do what I can to bring together the king and the revolution; it is up to you to help me."

When Dumouriez had gone, the queen said to her lady-in-waiting Madame Campan that she did not believe the "protestations of a traitor." Anyhow, she added, it was a waste of time to bother with such fellows now, because the foreign powers were mobilizing and were going to be victorious for a king as "virtuous as Louis XVI and a cause as just as ours."

Suddenly a blow fell. While Louis was oscillating between fear and hope for the impending war with Austria and the Assembly was wrangling on the same subject, news came that Emperor Leopold had died in Vienna. White-faced, Louis locked himself in his apartment; Marie Antoinette took to bed with cramps.

The revolutionists celebrated the death of their imperial enemy. "The emperor is dead and soon M. and Mme. Veto will be too," so newsboys shouted in the streets. Parisians retailed gossip on the queen's illness, and rumors spread that the death of her brother had driven her mad. The Comédie Française played *The Death of Cæsar* to packed wildly cheering houses.

Leopold's death, however, did not deprive the revolution of a powerful enemy, for his successor, the twenty-four year old Francis II, was more belligerent than his cautious father had been. The young emperor sympathized with his aunt in the Tuileries and readily listened to the émigrés who urged war on France to forestall the Jacobins in their plans to destroy Louis XVI.

In Paris Marie Antoinette prepared for any eventuality by burning her secret correspondence and all evidence of her counter-revolutionary activities. Louis engaged François Gamoin, a smith whom he had known in his own locksmithing days at Versailles, to build a secret closet in the Tuileries as a hiding-place for valuable papers (his own papers were much more innocent than those of the queen). In the passage leading to the king's bedroom Gamoin broke part of the thick wall, covered it with a door of solid iron, and secured it with a heavy lock. In this secret *Armoire de fer,* which Gamoin was later to betray,[1] Louis deposited papers for which an historian must be grateful but which a biographer must deplore as an indiscretion.

THE CRISIS came to a head on April 20, 1792. As more and more Austrian and Prussian troops concentrated on the frontier, French patience gave way, and General Dumouriez decided it was time to accept the challenge. By one of those common ironies, it was Louis XVI's duty to declare war against his nephew Emperor Francis II who was undertaking a sanguinary struggle to save him.

In a tense atmosphere Louis took the floor and addressed

[1] Gamoin's autograph denunciation (in atrocious spelling) is in Bibliothèque Nationale, n.a.Fr.6241, no. 308.

THE DAUPHIN

MADAME ROYALE

Children of Louis XVI and Marie Antoinette. Portraits by Alexander Kucharsky; the dauphin, 1792.

the Legislative Assembly. "Gentlemen, my minister of foreign affairs will read a report on our political situation."

Dumouriez read a long list of grievances against Austria and concluded: "War."

Then Louis spoke again: "You have just heard the report. Its conclusions have been adopted unanimously in my council. They conform to the wishes often expressed by the National Assembly. I have exhausted all the means for maintaining peace. Now I come, in the name of the constitution, formally to propose war."

The words were cold and correct, hardly in keeping with the frenzy of a large part of the Assembly. There was a feeling of resentment against His Majesty's marked lack of enthusiasm. For to many deputies this was to be a holy war, a jehad against tyrants and a crusade against thrones. Such oratorical torrents as now poured from mighty throats under the gilded roof of the Assembly marked the dawn of a new age of political excitement. Cried the more than half-crazy Anacharsis Clootz:

> Here is the crisis of the universe. God entangled primitive chaos; the French will unravel the feudal chaos. God is powerful. . . . We are powerful. . . . Free men are the Gods of the earth. . . . They [kings] make impious war on us with serf soldiers and with extorted money; we make a holy war with free soldiers and contributions voluntarily consented. Our victories will be our banquets. Legislators, I place in the sanctuary, in the presence of my lares and my penates, in the sanctuary of the constitutional God, the sum of twelve thousand livres to dress, equip, arm, and pay forty to fifty fighters in the sacred war of men against crowns. . . . I present to you at the same time my last work whose very title makes the aristocrats tremble: *The Universal Republic.*

Another deputy, Merlin de Douai, hurled an infectious slogan at the heated heads in the Assembly:

"War on kings, peace to the nations!"

Against such fire and such fury Louis stood out conspicuously colorless—especially since circumstances called upon him to act as an ardent patriot at a moment when he was conspiring with the enemy against the patriots. The best he could do was to murmur phrases and hope for French defeat. To help the enemy as much as possible, Louis told Marie Antoinette the plans of the cabinet, and she in turn communicated them to the Austrians. One bit of such information was extremely useful. "The present ministers," the queen wrote secretly to Mercy in Brussels, "count upon a rising in the neighboring nations, upon the desertion of the foreign troops, upon the possibility of detaching Prussia from the other powers; and for this they have set aside millions."

As Louis expected, the campaign did not go well for France. The French volunteer army was inexperienced, possessed of more ardor than skill, and was led by officers whose aristocratic origins were no guarantee of revolutionary loyalty. As a result of the first defeat of the patriots in Belgium, an epidemic of fear seized France. Now that the frontiers lay open, nonjuring clergy and aristocrats, convinced that the revolution was collapsing, incited against the government. "Treason," cried the revolutionary patriots. Clever propagandists reiterated the accusation that the chief traitor resided in the heart of the capital, and a popular *chanson* entitled *À Louis Capet* asked the question that tortured the patriots: "Louis, are you French or are you Austrian?"

Dites-moi, Louis, est-tu français,
Ou né du sang d'Autriche?
Pouvons-nous combler de bienfaits
Un prince qui nous triche?

In the atmosphere of panic the Assembly acted to defend itself against internal enemies. It passed a drastic law against nonjuring clergy, making them liable to banishment at the request of any twenty citizens. The king considered this a violation of the constitution, and, encouraged by the Austrian victory, he was ill-advised to veto the law. A few days later the Assembly, under popular pressure, voted the formation of a camp of twenty thousand men near Paris to protect the capital. Again Louis exercised his constitutional right by vetoing the act.

The two vetoes unleashed a cyclone of denunciations. In the eyes of the patriots, the king, a pardoned king after all, stood out stripped of all his constitutional pretensions, an enemy of the revolution living in the heart of the capital of the revolution. There was a terrific clash in the Assembly. Deputy Ribes, who had secret financial dealings with the king,[2] made a bitter attack on Louis' critics. "The scoundrel Père Duchesne and the infamous Martel," he shouted, "vomit their atrocities, they call the king now M. Capet, now M. Veto, now Louis the Bloody; they call the queen, royal tigress—"

"You're a scoundrel," a voice interrupted.

Laughter from the Left benches.

"You're delirious," some one cried at Ribes.

"You rave."

"He's crazy," thundered Deputy Gossuin, "let us pass to the order of the day."

Nobody else defended the king.

At a cabinet meeting the righteous Minister Roland spoke blunt words to the silent king. "I know," the husband of Madame Roland said, "that the austere language of truth is rarely received on a throne, and this is why revolutions become necessary." Louis changed color, at the moment said nothing. Later in the day he dismissed Roland with contemptuous curtness and said to Dumouriez, "Do me the favor of getting rid of these insolent factious persons. My patience is at an end."

"Dangerous," muttered the general, but promised to do his best. On the following day the other Girondin ministers were dismissed, and Louis defied the country by appointing a royalist cabinet. France was in an uproar.

[2] Ribes' receipt for 800,000 livres is in the Archives Nationales, F [7] 4390 [a] C no.1.

⚜

THE ACTIVE CITIZENRY regarded the king's *coup* as a declaration of war against the revolution, an act of defiance against the nation at a time when foreign armies were on the frontier. The more extreme revolutionists called for drastic action. It was time, they insisted, that the nation put a traitorous king in his place. One of the popular orators, haranguing a crowd in the Tuileries garden, went so far as to advise murder. "This monster," the orator cried almost beneath the king's window, "uses his power and his treasury to oppose the regeneration of the French.... He wants to bring to France desolation and death. Cruel one, thy crimes will have an end.... Tremble, tyrant, there is among us a Scivola ... !"

Louis was upset by such oratory, but the queen persuaded him that the revolution was on the decline, beaten by the Austrians, and that he could now afford to rally royalist elements around him. One royalist newspaper advised Louis to dissolve the Assembly and make himself absolute ruler. To help along the process of disintegration the king untied the purse-strings of his secret funds, much of them deposited in London in the name of Septeuil, *premier valet de chambre,* and began a systematic distribution of large sums where they would do most good. La Porte, the intendant of the Civil List, acted as Lord Bountiful. The records are silent as to the recipients,[3] but occasionally there is a ray of light in the archives. It seems that a good deal of the royal moneys went to journalists and printers.[4] The editors of the *Logographe,* for example, received some ninety thousand livres for presenting the king's side. Much money went to politicians and revolutionists. Raimond Ribes, the deputy of Aude who defended the king in the Assembly, received eight hundred thousand livres, possibly for distribution among fellow-deputies. There is reason to believe that popular demagogues like Santerre and Pétion took the king's money. Months later,

[3] One day, June 16, Louis spent 377,000 livres; Archives Nationales, C187, 137, p.26. Between June 7 and 29 La Porte passed out 34,000 pounds sterling; Archives Nationales, F 7 4390, No.C7. Much of the money, possibly most, was of course handed out without receipts.

[4] Archives Nationales, C187, 137.

when Marie Antoinette was in prison, she pointed to Santerre and said bitterly:

"That man, whom you now see our jailer, has several times solicited and obtained of the king considerable sums from the funds of the Civil List. How many others, in the National Guard and even in the Assembly have under various pretenses obtained financial assistance . . . ! Of what use to us were the large sums distributed by our friends to Pétion, Lacroix, and other conspirators? They took the money and betrayed us." [5]

⚜

DESPITE the venality of many revolutionary leaders, the populace had an incorruptible revolutionary morality. The people did not want the king's money but his crown.

In the morning of June 20, men and women began to gather in the faubourgs to march to the Assembly and protest against the king's dismissal of the ministry. This was the third anniversary of the Tennis-Court Oath, and "all the friends of liberty" were determined to make it memorable.

Marat's sheet blazed: "A perverse queen fanaticizes an imbecile king. They are preparing a Saint-Bartholomew of the patriots." A colossal red flag in the Cordeliers section bore the proclamation, MARTIAL LAW OF THE PEOPLE AGAINST THE REVOLT OF THE COURT.

The streets filled. Marchers walked grimly behind cannon which bore engraved tablets of the Declaration of the Rights of Man. Streamers proclaimed, LIBERTY, EQUALITY. Hundreds of slogans pleased or stirred the spectators. Friends of the revolution delighted in WHEN THE COUNTRY IS IN DANGER ALL THE SANS-CULOTTES ARE ON THEIR FEET. Friends of the king trembled at ADVICE TO LOUIS XVI: THE PEOPLE, TIRED OF SUFFERING, WANT LIBERTY OR DEATH.

5 "To-night," La Porte wrote to Louis on June 18, "we will make an attractive proposition to Santerre." Archives Nationales, C187, 135, no.15. Santerre, the leader of the radical sections, later denied that he took the king's money.

They burst into the garden of the Tuileries and made for the unguarded palace. The king was alone with a few gentlemen and his sister in a locked room. "Gentlemen," Elizabeth cried, "save the king." Two gentlemen drew swords. Doors crashed and windows were being broken. Louis stood still and white. The door was wrenched open and in crowded hot-faced red-bonneted men. "Down with Veto!" "Recall the ministers!" The gentlemen and the intrepid Elizabeth formed a frail wall around Louis.

A gentle-eyed young revolutionist stepped forward and said softly, "We ought to slay the whole royal family." Another, whose red bonnet bore the inscription *La Mort,* stood staring at Louis with fixed murderous eyes. Some one put a Phrygian cap on the king's immobile head. A pike with a sharp blade was leveled at Louis' throat; it was parried by a guardsman with a bayonet, while Elizabeth said coolly, "Look out, Mister, you might hurt somebody." Louis stood stock still.

Down under the windows in the garden they were yelling, "When are we going to see the heads of the king and queen?"

But they had not come to kill the king: they came to warn him. Louis Legendre, a forty-year old butcher and friend of Danton, approached the king and said: *"Monsieur—"* His Majesty was startled by such familiarity. "Yes, *Monsieur,"* Legendre repeated, "listen to us. You are here to listen. You are a traitor. You have betrayed us again. But look out! The measure is quite full and the people are tired of your game."

In the queen's apartment a similar scene was enacted. Led by Santerre, a crowd of hot-eyed, dirty-bonneted women smashed their way into Marie Antoinette's presence, shoved a cap into her face, and ordered her to don it. "Give a bonnet also to the prince: tricolors to the Little Veto." The proud queen did not lift an arm. Baron Hue put the red cap on the boy's blond head. The prince, thinking it was a new game, laughed.

Fish-market words lashed at Marie Antoinette. She winced at some of the obscene names, tightened her grip on her son, stiffened. The canaille must not see a queen in pain. A pretty girl in the crowd, exclaimed, "My, but the Austrian is proud and spiteful!" Marie Antoinette looked at the girl, saw she was clean and good-looking, and said softly, "Why do you hate me? Have I, without my knowing it, done you any harm?" The girl: "Not to me, but to the nation." The queen replied: "Poor child, you believe what they tell you. You call me *l'Autrichienne,* but I am the wife of the king of France; I am the mother of the dauphin; I am French with all the feelings of a wife and mother. Never again shall I see the country of my birth."

So much dignity and pride touched the revolutionists. Santerre leaned across the table that separated him from the queen: "Madame, have no fear; we don't want to hurt you. But reflect that it is dangerous to deceive the people." Then he leaned closer and said in a low voice, "You have blundering friends, Madame; I know some who will serve you better." He straightened and bruskly ordered withdrawal. The crowd filed out, past the rigid queen, mutely carrying banners: *"Tremble, tyrant, thy hour has come." "Down with Veto and his wife."* A picture of the guillotine bore the words, *"National justice for tyrants."*

Mayor Pétion arrived tardily. He said to the king, "Sire, you have nothing to fear."

Louis: "Fear! A man of good will with a clear conscience has nothing to fear. *Tiens,*" he took the hand of a grenadier, "put your hand on my heart and tell this man if it beats any faster than usual."

This scene took place near the balcony where the red-capped king was conspicuous. Pétion turned to the people below: "Citizens, you have begun the day with dignity and wisdom; you have shown that you are free. Finish it in the same way, with dignity, and do as I do, go home."

The people, sure of their strength, obeyed.

In the crowd were two young men. They had been observing in silence the happenings in the Tuileries, and when they saw on the balcony the king wearing a red bonnet, one of them, a pallid, thin-nosed army officer, said hotly, "How did they ever let in that rabble? If four or five hundred of them had been swept away with cannon, the rest would still be running."

The speaker was an army captain named Napoleon Buonaparte.

THE LITTLE INSURRECTION on June 20 was a dress rehearsal. On the part of the extreme revolutionists it was an experiment in violence to determine how far they could go in breaking into the Tuileries and insulting the king. What they wanted to find out was to what extent the Legislative Assembly and the nation would allow insult and injury to be done to the constitutional chief executive. If the nation should protest, then the radicals would bide their time until the king had discredited himself further. If the attack of June 20 aroused no strong reactions, then the revolutionists were sure that the way was clear to abolish the throne and destroy the monarchy. But it took a little time before opinions could make themselves heard.

On the day following, many deputies, themselves intimidated by the populace, visited the palace, and Louis showed them the evidence of the mob's raid—broken furniture, smashed doors, shattered windows. The legislators were sympathetic but uneasy, for in the garden another crowd was gathering. The little dauphin, seeing more people, asked ingenuously, "Mama, is it still yesterday?" It was actually the anniversary of the king's flight to Varennes (June 21), and the crowd below cried, "Let's make him atone." From the city came the sound of mournful drum-beats.

Visitors came to express sympathy and offer aid. The one who made Louis most happy was Malesherbes, seventy-one and still hale, who had returned from retirement at the news of the king's plight. To hearten his royal friend he said, "The storm is too violent to last." Louis shook his head.

Another visitor was Mayor Pétion. He came to assure the

king that the people who were gathering in the garden were unarmed. Pétion apologized for yesterday's doings. "Anyhow," he concluded, "your person has been respected."

Louis was angry: "Entering my house with armed force, assaulting my guard, breaking my doors—do you call this respecting my person? What happened yesterday is a scandal!"

Pétion tried to defend himself, but Louis cut in: "Keep quiet! Go and do your duty. I will hold you personally responsible for the tranquillity of Paris. Adieu!" [6]

In a public statement Louis denounced the attack of the mob and virtually accused the municipality of Paris of breaking the constitution and of violating the peace. "The king," he concluded truculently, "wants to tell the French nation that violence will never wrest from him a consent which he considers contrary to the public welfare." Stung by the criticism, Mayor Pétion appealed to his constituents not to assemble under arms and not to attack the king's residence, but the faubourgs laughed at the mayor and sent a delegation to the Hôtel de Ville, denouncing "a false king, guilty of high treason" and demanding his instant suspension. If the authorities refused, the delegates warned in the simple language of men who know the value of guns, "our arms are raised, and we will strike down the traitors, wherever we shall find them, even among you." Constituted government was becoming a farce.

In the meantime the country had time to register its opinion of the attack on the Tuileries on June 20. Anxiously revolutionists and moderates scanned the reports and listened to the national voice; but the results were sufficiently inconclusive to intensify the current insecurity.

A torrent of petitions poured into the Assembly demanding the suspension of the king. Citizens from Lyons, Blois, Grenoble, Montpellier, Brest, Bordeaux, urged the *déchéance du roi* and threatened to march on Paris with armed force.

6 Archives Nationales, M655, no.3.

These petitions and addresses read curiously alike and used the same stereotypes, which shows that they were carefully organized and phrased by provincial revolutionary (mainly Jacobin) clubs. On the other hand, high public officials throughout the country appealed to the Assembly to protect the king and punish the radicals who disturbed the peace. Petitions to this effect came from the administrators of the departments, such as Eure, Somme, Seine-Inférieure, Indre, Ardennes, Pas-de-Calais. The administrator of the Somme, for instance, offered twenty battalions of National Guardsmen "to assure the preservation of the king." Even in revolutionary Paris no less than sixteen thousand citizens signed a complaint against the municipality, accusing it of responsibility for the outbreak of June 20; the city politicians, however, were strong enough to keep the accusation from being read in the Assembly.

The strongest protest came from Lafayette, who was with the army in the field. The general left the camp and hurried to Paris to deliver a bitter denunciation of the Jacobins. On the floor of the Assembly he cried indignantly that the violence done to the king "excited the indignation and alarm of all honest people" and demanded that the instigators of the insurrection should be "persecuted and punished as criminals."

This vehement attack on the revolutionists caused an uproar. "He should be guillotined," a Jacobin bellowed, "for having deserted his post in the field." The president of the Assembly moved that Lafayette's motion that the instigators of the insurrection be persecuted as criminals be adopted. "You're a scoundrel," the president was shouted down. "To prison with the president!"

Nevertheless a majority of the Assembly was with Lafayette, who planned to organize his partisans and rescue the king. Again, however, Marie Antoinette proved a stumbling-block. She refused to coöperate. To her the aristocrat who had espoused the popular cause in the revolution was as detestable as any wretched Jacobin. In her bitterness she is said to have betrayed Lafayette's plans to rally the National Guard to Mayor Pétion. It was hopeless to try to do anything with such people as Marie Antoinette, and the disgusted Lafayette left Paris.

⚜

Louis and Marie Antoinette, still convinced that the Austro-Prussian armies would save them and that the revolution was on the decline, continued to spend money trying to win over wavering revolutionary chiefs. According to the account of June 30, Louis had over 7,000,000 livres cash from his Civil List.[7] He also borrowed 1,050,000 livres from a M. Chavelet.[8] Several hundred thousand pounds came from the secret fund deposited in London. Some of this money, to be sure, went to pay the wages of the two hundred and forty persons who made up the royal household in the Tuileries (yes, the chief executive of a democratic nation still lived like a king!),[9] but most of the funds were otherwise spent. Danton was approached and probably accepted money—which explains his strange moderation vis-à-vis the king. Santerre, it seems, took fifty thousand livres.[10] Guadet, a prominent Girondin, haughtily refused to accept the king's money; but a secretary in the ministry of justice, for some unstated reason, was given forty thousand livres.[11]

The money did not help, because a determined minority of radicals, convinced that Louis was a traitor, was bent upon the abolition of the monarchy. On July 2 Vergniaud, a great Girondin orator, made an attack on Louis in classic rhetoric full of somber historical allusions. It was an ominous speech, showing the sharp drift of opinion. On July 7 came the news

7 Archives Nationales, F 7 4390 A, No.C7.

8 Ibid., C187, 137, nos. 67 and 68: August 7 and 9, 1792.

9 Among these 240 were 25 cooks, 12 porters, 14 stewards, etc. Archives Nationales, C222, 160 154-56, no.155.

10 He later denied it: "I replied that nothing in the world could corrupt me, that I never belonged to any faction, that my sole guides were reason, justice and law;" Santerre's statement to the Assembly, December 9, 1792: Archives Nationales, C187, 135, no.16.

11 *Ibid.*, C187, 137, no. 72-74.

of the Prussian army's approach to the frontier, and the Assembly, in a frenzy of excitement, declared *la patrie en danger* and called upon every patriot to defend his country. Roederer, a prominent deputy, appealed to the king to join the nation in this hour of crisis. Brissot, the Girondin chief, cried, "The country is in danger! If the king is really sincere, he will join you. If he refuses...."

⚜

LOUIS was conspicuously calm. Passionate debates tore the Assembly asunder. Was the king a traitor or was he a patriot? Few defended him, but many were unwilling to go the length of suspending him from office, for it meant destroying the constitution and laying the country open to fraternal strife. And yet, as anguished Jacobins cried, how entrust the defense of the country to a chief executive (commander of the army and navy) who hardly made an effort to deny his connections with the invading enemy? Meanwhile some fifty thousand Prussians (for whom Frenchmen had an unconquerable contempt) crossed the threshold of France, and the proud patriots, both in Paris and in the provinces, felt as if they were being branded with hot irons. Had it come to this, they asked bitterly, that servile henchmen of tyrants should threaten the home of liberty and try to destroy the cradle of revolution? France roared with accusations against the king. He had sold out to the hated German tyrants—he, the meek husband of a German woman—and in this supreme moment of crisis it was imperative that he be deprived of his high office.

On July 17 a petition signed by five hundred and ninety soldiers was read to a stormy Assembly: "We do not refuse obedience to a king, but we make a great distinction between a king and a conspiring and criminal court.... Deputies, listen to the voice of the nation.... Suspend the executive power.... Public safety demands it."

The words were echoed and reëchoed in a thousand clubs, sections, coffee-houses, homes. As yet the voices were not republican voices; as yet the demand was for a provisional sus-

JEAN SYLVAIN BAILLY

ANTOINE JOSEPH SANTERRE

pension of a *particular* king, and not of the monarchy as such. But the Assembly feared to undermine the throne.

It was Marie Antoinette who, as usual, blunderingly facilitated the work of the revolutionists. Frightened by the growing number of lawless individuals who were daily gathering in Paris from the provinces, the queen made hysterical appeals to her friends abroad. "A delay of one day," she wrote, "may produce incalculable misfortunes." She convinced herself that her and the king's lives were in danger and pleaded that the Duke of Brunswick, who commanded the invading Prussian army, issue a declaration warning Frenchmen that if further violence were committed against the royal family, Paris would be annihilated. Without such a manifesto, the queen wrote crazily, Louis would lose his life within twenty-four hours. "The throng of assassins," she concluded, "is swelling." So was, one might add, her lack of sense. The Duke of Brunswick stupidly heeded the queen and issued a manifesto warning Frenchmen against harming the royal family.

The Brunswick Manifesto hit France and exploded. Even moderate elements who had refused to believe their king a traitor were now convinced that Louis XVI was coöperating with the despised Prussians. The king's name was disgracefully connected with foreigners and armed enemies of the country at a moment when national feeling amounted to a religious passion. Nothing could save Louis now.

France seethed like a sea in storm. Clubs, societies, sections, and assemblies wrote petitions and letters, not merely of protest—the days of protest had passed—but of disobedience to the constitutional chief executive. Letter after letter, read before the Assembly, proclaimed, "We refuse to recognize Louis XVI as king of France." Other letters warned the Assembly, "If you refuse to suspend the king and save France, we will have the honor of doing it ourselves."

A large portion of the French people disowned the king in spirit. Action was bound to follow.

⚜

THE FURORE and indignation aroused by the Brunswick Manifesto made Louis realize that it was a bad mistake. Immediately he wrote a letter of justification to the Assembly, denying having anything to do with the matter and refusing to accept responsibility for the defeat of the French army.

"Never," he wrote, "will any one see me receive dictates from foreigners or from a faction: my duties are to the nation. ... I shall maintain the national independence until my last breath. Personal dangers are nothing compared to public misfortunes.... One day, perhaps, the people will know how much their happiness is dear to me." [12]

Deputies leaped to their feet and demanded to be heard. From all over the chamber came shouts of "Traitor," "Let him act, not talk," "I denounce...."

Mayor Pétion obtained the floor. He had come, he said, to denounce the king in the name of the city of Paris. He spoke quietly, passionlessly:

> We accuse Louis XVI without bitterness.... The most honorable passions should be silenced when it comes to saving the state.... The memory of a haughty and devouring dynasty, in which one counts one good king against twenty tyrants, hereditary despotism increasing from reign to reign ... —*voilà* the rights of Louis XVI to the constitutional scepter.... The chief executive is the first ring in the counter-revolutionary chain.... His name is a signal of discord.... His conduct is a positive and perpetual act of disobedience to the constitution.... Louis XVI constantly invokes the constitution. We invoke it in our turn, and we demand his deposition.

LONG and hotly the Assembly debated, and in the end it refused to vote the king out of office. The scholarly Condorcet, reporting for the Special Commission, proposed that the whole question be postponed; but this was no solution, for the armed sections demanded action. The next move belonged to the people.

From every part of Paris came reports that the sections

[12] August 3, 1792; Archives Nationales, AD I 99.

were planning to attack the Tuileries. Louis was agitated but refused his friends' plea to flee Paris. Marie Antoinette was equally stubborn. What good was life without a throne? "Far rather perish," she exclaimed, "than meet the fate of King James II."

The armed sections took over the streets and surrounded the palace with lynx-eyed spies. Terrorists paralyzed the Assembly, slugging deputies who were suspected of moderation. Terror ruled the city.

On the night of August 9, 1792, the sovereign people was ready to strike. That night the stillness was riven by the tocsins.

Aux armes, citoyens!

CHAPTER XXIV

"Down with the tyrant!"

THE REVOLUTIONARY SECTIONS had planned the assault on the Tuileries as meticulously as a general staff prepares a military campaign. Even the date—midnight of August 9-10—was set weeks in advance.

Louis had no appreciation of the perfection of the revolutionary technique, and, although he knew the attack was coming, he could not believe that it would take place at the scheduled moment. All day long on August 9 the royal family waited for the inevitable. There was not much the king could do in preparing a defense. Whatever was possible to do under the circumstances the court did during the day. Several volunteer nobles (among them the aged Malesherbes with his tiny sword), a few hundred Swiss guards, and a troop of National Guardsmen under command of Captain Mandat took up their stations at the gates, doors, and corridors of the Tuileries.

After supper the royal family gathered in the large Council Chamber. Together with a few friends they were going to pass the night, the last night of the monarchy, sitting up, a huddled group of scared men, women, and children.

An hour before midnight Mayor Pétion arrived and, after consulting with Louis, ordered Captain Mandat to dispose his small body of troops at various strategic points—in the courts, in the garden, and at the wickets.

At that moment a group representing the armed sections entered the Hôtel de Ville, threw out the legally elected municipal officers, and formally declared the insurrectionary *Commune du Dix Août* (it still lacked several minutes of midnight). Midnight struck, and the revolutionary commune gave the signal for the tocsins and the drums.

The tocsin of the Cordeliers led off. Then the chain of alarms spread from section to section until it embraced the whole city. From the bowels of the capital came the boom of cannon and the beat of drums. Paris was shuddering in the night.

Swift and precise orders poured from the light-flooded Hôtel de Ville. A messenger was dispatched to the Tuileries imperiously summoning Captain Mandat. The commander of the Guard replied that it was his sworn duty to defend the constitutional king. A second messenger came with threatening summons in the name of the government. Mandat turned pale, obeyed. "I shall never return," he said to the king. He got to the Hôtel de Ville, was accused by the insurrectionary officials of having planned to attack the sovereign people, and was promptly condemned to prison. The procedure was only a grim jest. As soon as Mandat stepped out of the chamber, a bullet crushed his skull, the mob fell on him, tore his body to pieces, and threw the fragments into the near-by Seine.

The Tuileries and its guards were now without a competent commander.

THE NIGHT was hot, and the windows in the big Council Chamber were wide open. The royal family and their friends listened with constricted hearts to the roar and clangor as they penetrated the room. They sat still and pale on the floor, on the edge of sofas, on the window-ledges, listening to the awakening of a city preparing for a pogrom. The sound-alarms spread, increased, thickened, blanketed the city in mass crescendo.

The beat of the tom-toms was nerve-racking, but Louis went calmly to sleep.

Armed men, in tightly packed columns, emerged from the dark streets and converged silently upon the Tuileries. By dawn the Place du Carrousel was occupied by a civilian army with gleaming pikes and cannon trained on the palace. The sky began to redden in the east, casting pale rays over the revolutionary bonnets, and the king's sister Elizabeth, thoughtfully looking over the scene, called over to Marie Antoinette: "My sister, come and see the sunrise."

Louis awoke, rubbed his eyes, and joined the group at the window. His clothes were awry and his hair disheveled. Thus at sunrise did the king of France face the sovereign people.

WATCHING the scene was Deputy Roederer, the representative of the Assembly who had spent the night shuttling back and forth between the palace and the Manège. He remarked in after years that Marie Antoinette was not the heroic woman that legend made her out to be later. On the contrary, she was a woman in despair, haggard, her eyes red from weeping. "She was a woman, a mother, a wife in peril." The queen looked at Roederer, who in his huge tricolor sash was the embodiment of Revolution, and asked him in a trembling voice what they should do. Roederer advised leaving the Tuileries and seeking refuge in the National Assembly. He was confident that the deputies were in a position to protect the lives of the king and queen. "Anyhow," he said, "it is the lesser danger."

"But, Monsieur," Marie Antoinette objected, "we have forces here."

"In which case, Madame, let us see what dispositions have been taken for resistance."

Sudden cries interrupted the conversation. They ran over to the window. "Good Lord!" one of the gentlemen in the room exclaimed, "it's the king in the garden. What the devil is he doing below?" Louis had simply gone out for air and was showered with abuse by the armed populace on the other side of the gate. He was brought back to the apartment, breathing fast.

⚜

Louis went down the corridors. Some of the soldiers dutifully cried *Vive le roi!* but without enthusiasm. Others exclaimed *Vive la nation!* and stared at the king with hostility. A few broke into the insulting *Down with Veto!* and muttered curses.

Slowly the sun lighted up every corner of the palace and yards, and the armed people outside began to force the big iron gates. The portals crashed, and the tide of revolution poured in the courtyards. "Deposition or death!" "Deposition or death!"

Into the royal chamber rushed a municipal officer. "Do you not hear? The people demand the abolition of the monarchy!"

Louis was impassive. He never even lifted his head. But the queen asked, "What will happen then?" She got no answer.

From below came the sound of clashing arms and of furious, panting voices. Several guardsmen were defending the outer doors. Roederer hurried in with a deputation from the Assembly. He was breathless, his voice shrill with terror. He found Louis sitting at a table, hands upon knees, head bowed —a figure of clay. "Sire," Roederer gasped, "you don't have more than five minutes to lose. There is no safety for you but in the National Assembly. You don't have enough men to defend the palace."

Louis lifted his head heavily. "But I didn't see such a large crowd on the Place du Carrousel."

Roederer, twisting his hands: "Sire, they have twelve cannon."

Gerdret, one of the deputation, a tradesman from whom the queen used to buy laces, broke into the conversation in support of Roederer. This infuriated the high-strung queen. "Silence, Gerdret! It is not for such as you to raise your voice here. Silence—!"

To Roederer she said, "But, Monsieur, we have forces!"

"Madame," said the excited deputy, "all Paris is on the march. Do you want them to massacre the king, your children, your servants?"

"God forbid! I wish I could be the only victim."

Roederer turned to the king. "Sire, time presses. It is no longer a question of begging you to come or giving you advice. There is only one thing to do: we demand permission to take you with us."

Louis at last looked up, stared fixedly at Roederer. Abruptly he rose, turned to the queen, and said one word:

"Marchons!"

⚜

HALTINGLY the French monarchy filed out of the apartment. They carried nothing but what they wore on their backs. A group of gentlemen wished to form a defending circle around the king, but Roederer warned against it. "Be calm," Louis told his friends.

They walked out into the garden preceded by Roederer who was conspicuous in his tricolor sash as a municipal officer. Louis was immediately behind him. Marie Antoinette led the dauphin. Elizabeth walked arm in arm with the king's daughter. In the rear marched the Swiss guard.

"The king walked straight ahead, his face calm, but engraved by misfortune," so writes La Rochefoucauld, one of the gentlemen in the entourage. The queen was in tears, drying them from time to time. She leaned on La Rochefoucauld's arm for a moment, and he felt her trembling. Her little daughter was crying too.

A jeering mass of humanity blocked the way. In the name of the government Roederer begged them to let the royal party pass, but the people shouted curses, screamed threats, brandished weapons. "Down with the tyrant!" "Death to the tyrant!" It was marvelous irony, this application of the word *tyrant* to the meekest of meek men by an armed mob bent upon murder!

After thirty minutes of agony, during which time Louis was a monument of white-faced patience, the family was allowed to go through. Near the Manège Louis stepped into fallen leaves. "The leaves are falling early this year," he said on this tenth of August.

The corridors of the Assembly were packed, and in the terrific crush the royal family was torn apart, shoved and buffeted. The dauphin was separated from his agonized mother but was picked up by a tall guard who carried him over his head and deposited him on the desk of the speaker—trophy of war. Louis squeezed his way through the milling fierce-tongued mass and walked up to the president. There was a stunned silence as the king of France addressed President Vergniaud of the Legislative Assembly:

"I come to prevent a great crime, and I believe that I could not be safer anywhere than in the midst of the representatives of the nation."

Vergniaud's voice trembled: "Sire, you may count upon the firmness of the National Assembly. It knows its duties; its members have sworn to die maintaining the rights of the people and the constituted authorities."

The words were brave but not relevant. On that day the Assembly was no more master of its destiny than the king was of his.

IN THE HALL of the Assembly a cubicle was assigned to the royal family. It was a tiny room, with bars, like a cell, originally the box of the reporter of the *Logographe* and comfortable enough for one person. The *loge* was so low that a grown man could not stand up in it.

Louis sat in front, facing the Assembly, and his family was squeezed on a bench back of him. From the floor of the Assembly, from the corridors and from the balconies, hot eyes and accusing fingers were pointed in the direction of the caged royal family. Men stood on chairs, women leaned over the balustrades, children climbed the columns to feast eyes on the captive "Monsieur and Madame Veto." Vainly Vergniaud, proud face sharply etched, beat the gong and pounded his fists for silence. The people could not be restrained in their hour of triumph. This was victory, revolution, drama, and war. Even humor, satiric humor, was not lacking in the spectacle, for, before the hungry eyes of this intoxicated mass, the king, driven by ferocious hunger, was gnawing ravenously at a boiled chicken. Like an actor in full view of the house, the king was chewing the fowl with the total concentration of the starved, oblivious to man and manners. Even Marie Antoinette, accustomed as she was to her husband's eating habits, could not hide her mortification. She turned away her white face, and she touched no food all day.

What a pig! the people muttered. Even friendly deputies were shocked at what they thought was callousness on the king's part. Such a lack of sensitiveness at such a moment was beyond the comprehension of excitable people.

SHARP DETONATIONS came from the direction of the palace. There a battle was in progress.

The Tuileries was defended by several hundred guards, mostly Swiss, and some gentlemen. As the mob, firing musket and cannon, approached, deadly fire from the upper windows raked its ranks. The undisciplined attackers recoiled, fell back on the Place du Carrousel. Within a few minutes the Swiss had cleared the immediate grounds of the palace.

But as the sound of firing penetrated the hall of the Assembly, Louis, always in terror of bloodshed, took a pencil and scribbled an order to the Swiss to cease firing: "The king commands the Swiss to withdraw to their barracks; he is in the midst of the National Assembly." In the confusion this order either never was delivered or reached only a few of the Swiss. At any rate, the fight began anew, and the Swiss fought with disciplined calm and a promise of victory.

Again Louis took a fateful hand in the matter. Though squeezed behind bars in a cubicle, he was still king, at least

THE GREAT SEAL OF THE MONARCH LOUIS XVI

After a cast from the original in the Archives Nationales, reduced one-quarter.

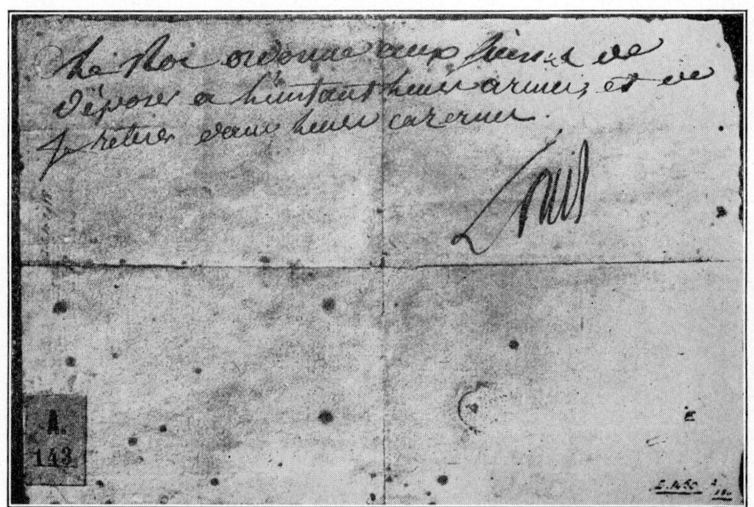

Le Roi ordonne aux Suisses de déposer à l'instant leurs armes, et de se retirer dans leurs casernes.

Louis

A.
143

LOUIS XVI'S LAST COMMAND

The order to the Swiss Guards to lay down their arms, August 10, 1792. Musée Carnavalet.

to his loyal guards, and he did not want them to die for him. Still less did he desire to see Frenchmen killed. Hastily he scribbled an order of three lines—the last order issued by Louis XVI:

"The king commands the Swiss immediately to lay down their arms and to withdraw to their barracks."

The three lines, signed in tall bold letters LOUIS, were a death-warrant to several hundred people.

Like true mercenaries, the Swiss obeyed their king. They evacuated the palace and marched out in two separate columns. One column reached the hall of the Assembly and there laid down their arms under the eyes of the king. Then they filed out, unarmed, and were attacked. Few escaped.

The second column marched down the garden toward the Place Louis XV. Here they were attacked from behind by the National Guard, which had joined the populace, and by the gendarmes on horseback. The Swiss were massacred and then cut to slices. Their heads and arms were severed from their bodies, their uniforms torn to shreds: the mobs fought each other for pieces of rags.

That day and night, while the king and his family were sardine-packed in a stifling cubicle, Paris felt the intoxication of blood-lust. "Men of blood," as young de Tocqueville who was in the National Guard recalls, hunted for hiding Swiss and killed them on the spot. There was a smell of burning flesh. Cadavers were piled in a heap and roasted in a gay bonfire.

Eight hundred Swiss and gentlemen lost their lives because Louis XVI could not bear the thought of violence.

And the people, drunk with blood, danced and sang the *Carmagnole* to celebrate the victory:

Madame Veto avait promis [*bis*]
De faire égorger tout Paris [*bis*]
Mais son coup a manqué,
Grace à nos canonniers.
Dansons la carmagnole,
Vive le son! Vive le son!

Dansons la carmagnole:
Vive le son du canon!

It was hot to suffocation in the hall of the Assembly. A fierce August sun was beating through the windows, and no breeze could penetrate the packed corridors and crowded doors. The faces in the hall were red with sweat and the voices hoarse with excitement. In their tiny cubicle the royal family could hardly breathe; the women were on the verge of prostration, but Louis was placid. From time to time he took out a lorgnette and looked through the barred aperture at the pandemonium in the hall below. His face expressed no emotion as he watched blood-bonneted men bring in six standards and deposit them triumphantly at the president's desk as trophies of victory over the Swiss. Imperturbably Louis observed grimy men, their necks exposed and red from sweat, bring in precious objects looted from the Tuileries. With fierce revolutionary probity the men laid down, at the foot of the platform, the property of the nation wrested from tyrants—candlesticks, buckles, spoons, chests, forks, tablecloths, plates, dishes and utensils.[1] Every piece of spoil was saluted as a trophy of war. Louis did not mind.

Deputations from the commune and the sections invaded the Assembly and demanded imperiously the formal deposition of the king. One spokesman shouted, "For a long time the people demanded that the king be deposed; you haven't even suspended him! We warn you that the fire is in the Tuileries and that we will not put it out until the people are satisfied."

From inside and outside the hall came such a protracted assault of yells and imprecations that steady men's nerves gave way. President Vergniaud, unable to stand the succession of shocks, dragged himself off the platform and gave the chair to Guadet. But the mob was out of control, and it seemed as if the royal family and every one of its sympathizers would be

1 Archives Nationales, C182, c.II, no.100; and F7 4390 A.

massacred unless something was done immediately. Guadet, strained beyond endurance, gave the chair to Gensonné. Gensonné pleaded for silence. After agonizing minutes he obtained silence and beckoned to Vergniaud.

It was painfully still, and even Louis leaned forward with a touch of curiosity as Vergniaud, his face drained of blood, rose to speak. In one unsteady hand he held a piece of paper. "I come to present to you a very harsh measure—"

Then he read the act of suspension of the monarchy which he, together with a handful of deputies, had hastily drawn up:

"The National Assembly decrees:

"The Chief of the executive power is provisionally suspended of his functions—"

It was signed, "in the name of the nation," by Gensonné and countersigned by Roland, the new minister of the interior, and by Danton, the new minister of justice. Terrified by the mob, the deputies voted the decree unanimously. Louis was unmoved as he heard himself legally suspended.

Now came commissioners from the commune and proposed that Louis and his family become hostages of the government and be "put in a state of arrest." The cowed Assembly voted everything the mob and its henchmen demanded. Louis was put under guard. The Civil List was abolished, but a *traitement* of half a million livres a year was provided for the support of the king and his family—which shows that at this time the Assembly was sympathetically inclined toward Louis and meant him personally no harm. The deputies, in fact, were themselves so frightened that they did not dare go home that night. They prolonged the session until two in the morning, although the acrid smoke from the Tuileries and the nauseating smell of burning human flesh made the air in the hall unbreatheable. Throughout all this fearful day and suffocating night the royal family remained cooped up in the foul cubicle of the *Logographe*. Life held no greater horrors afterwards.

⚜

At two in the morning relief came. Rooms were made ready for the royal family in the monastery of the Feuillants, across the yard from the Assembly. It was a short walk but an awful experience. D'Aubier, one of Louis' servants who was an eyewitness, described the scene:

> We crossed the yard through a mass of spears still dripping blood. The way was lighted by candles placed in the mouths of muskets. Ferocious cries demanding the heads of the king and the queen added to the horror. One madman, raising his voice above the others, cried that if the Assembly delayed delivering them to the people, he would set fire to their jail.

The temporary jail was composed of four small adjoining rooms, each giving on the corridor. A handful of servants and a dozen gentlemen were with the family, the gentlemen guarding the doors.

Gangs of armed men, loudly threatening murder, surrounded the monastery that night. A group of them invaded the corridor, banged on Louis' door, and cried that they would stay there all night and kill him if anyone made the slightest attempt to rescue him. In the courtyard, under the king's window, violent insurrectionists shouted, "Throw us down his head." Louis paled when the revolutionists demanded the queen's head. "What has she done to them?" he asked.

Marie Antoinette had no fear of death, but she was haunted with anxiety for her children. Convinced that they would all be massacred in their sleep, she went into Louis' room for a shadow of consolation, but such imperturbable resignation as his was no help in a crisis.

The queen returned to the children, and Louis went down on his knees. "Something may yet happen in our favor," D'Aubier said consolingly. Louis shook his head vigorously: "Charles I had more friends than we have. . . ." How the fate of Charles I haunted him! But it also kept him from worrying unduly: what was foreordained could not be helped. And,

DAVID'S "THI

This is a hitherto unknown drawing by the famous painter, Jacques Louis David, and has an interesting history.

In the autumn of 1792 the government offered a prize for the best work of art commemorating the founding of the First Republic. David's sketch (he never finished it), depicting the dramatic moment when the royal family sought shelter in the Assembly, won the prize. David, an active radical, may well have been an eye-witness of the event. Louis and Marie Antoinette are seen in the cubicle behind the bars. Note the horror and repulsion on Marie Antoinette's face.

OF AUGUST"

Originally the drawing showed Louis eating a chicken in full view of the shocked and accusing people (note the fingers of accusation). But when the Restoration of the Bourbons took place in 1815, David, then a famous and respected society painter, hurriedly erased the chicken.

This sketch cannot be seen in the Louvre. In fact, until this writer forced a search, the Louvre was unaware that it possessed the David treasure. It has never been reproduced. This is the first, specially arranged reproduction. Copyright belongs to the Louvre.

despite the queen's conviction that they would all be murdered that night, Louis went to bed and immediately fell into profound slumber.

TO D'AUBIER this sleep was wondrous. How could one sleep when outside, under the windows, armed *sans-culottes* were smoldering with murderous intentions and watching like vultures! The window was wide open; there were no bars or shutters. Such innocence, or insensitivity, impressed even the revolutionists. *Parbleu,* what a man!

Two of the amazed revolutionists climbed to the ledge of the window and looked in. Bearded men with reckless eyes they were, their faces distorted villainously by the flickering torch-light, and they stared at the stout man sleeping peacefully. They looked at each other, then grimly: "Let's shorten the fat Veto." But it was so funny they suddenly burst out laughing and got down. There was hilarious laughter below. The laughter rang through the garden. Louis awoke: "Are the queen and my children sleeping?"

They were not sleeping. They were on their knees praying.

Early in the morning Louis had a welcome visitor. It was his gentleman of the chamber, Baron Hue, who had saved himself the day before by leaping into the Seine, where a fisherman had picked him up. Now he returned to serve his captive master. "I found him in bed," Hue later related, "with a coarse cloth about his head. He looked at me piteously, called me to him, and, pressing my hand, desired me, with great eagerness, to give him account of what happened at the palace after he left it."

Hue burst into tears and informed Louis of the death of several friends. Louis felt the sting of guilt and the need of apology. To Hue and to the gentlemen standing around the bed he explained that it would have been hopeless to put up a fight.

"Apart from the fact that the National Guard would have

refused to attack in the name of the constitution, what end would it have served? The [revolutionists'] measures were too well planned for me to have been victorious, even if I had remained in the palace. The rebellious commune caused Mandat to be murdered; they frustrated all the dispositions of defense he had made."

IN THE MORNING of August 12, which was a Sunday, the royal family was brought to the hall of the Assembly and again shut in the cubicle of the *Logographe*. The Assembly was to decide the fate of the deposed monarch, or rather his last domicile. Louis was not yet certain that he was really a prisoner—after all, the Assembly had only deposed him—and nursed the illusion that perhaps the arrest was only temporary, a measure of safety. Now the debates on the floor of the Assembly came as a series of shocks, especially to Marie Antoinette, for the speakers expressed no doubt as to the status of the royal family. The majority of the deputies, to be sure, showed neither vindictiveness nor hostility, but it was obvious that the Assembly was not free. It was there simply to rubber-stamp the will of the insurrectionary commune, and the commune was lord of the city and dictator of France.

One deputy proposed that the comfortable palace of the Luxembourg be assigned to Louis and his family, but the representatives of the commune sneered, "The Luxembourg has underground passages which would make escape easy." Some one suggested the Ministry of Justice on the Place Vendôme, and again the commune rejected it as not being a prison but a palace. Then the phrase *Tower of the Temple* was thrown into the discussion.

At the word *Temple* Louis made a startled gesture and Marie Antoinette trembled. Surely they would not dare put them into that! "I have always had such a horror of that tower," the queen whispered to Madame Tourzel, "that a thousand times I begged to have it torn down."

The commune insisted that the Temple was the one place

where the royal prisoners would be sufficiently uncomfortable and absolutely secure. "The Temple offers," the commune wrote, "accommodations which Louis XVI, by his misfortunes, has a right to expect from a people which wishes to be severe only to be just." Deputies were shocked at the suggestion. After all, they argued, Louis XVI was guilty of no crime deserving a medieval stone dungeon. The Assembly, however, possessed no armed forces and therefore had no right to independent opinions. Bullied by the heavily armed commune, the deputies dutifully voted for the Temple. They also relinquished their prerogatives as representatives of the whole nation by handing over the constitutional chief executive to the mercies of the illegal city government. Danton, the idol of Paris and the head of the national government, promulgated and signed the decree that Louis and his family be "entrusted to the custody and the virtues of the citizens of Paris."

Louis listened to the reading of the decree with his customary passivity, but when the Assembly voted to remove all his friends, he rose in protest. "Charles I," he cried, "was more fortunate than I, for they left him his friends to the very end."

He never doubted that his fate was that of Charles I.

CHAPTER XXV

"This is how the people treat their kings"

SHOULD a modern visitor to Paris start at the Hôtel de Ville and walk in a northeasterly direction along the narrow, crowded, winding rue du Temple (virtually unchanged since the Revolution), he will reach, within about fifteen minutes, a charming little park called Square du Temple. On this peaceful green square, where children play around the statue of the poet Béranger and soldiers flirt with girls on the benches, once stood a colossal stone tower, topped by five turrets, as massive as the Bastille and much taller. It was one of those typical medieval structures designed to serve as a fortress, a castle, and a dungeon. For centuries the tower, which stood in its own grounds but was part of an enclaved complex of buildings belonging to the Knights Templar, remained uninhabited. Nor was it fit for human habitation. This Temple Tower the vengeful commune selected as the prison of Louis XVI.

On Monday, August 13, the Assembly informed Louis that he should make ready to leave for the Temple and asked him to prepare a list of servants he wanted to take with him, on condition that their "civism be beyond suspicion." Louis demanded four servants for himself, three for the queen, two each for the dauphin and Madame Elizabeth. The commune reduced the list to one servant per person.

The city of Paris took no chances. In fear of a possible uprising or an attempt to rescue the king, Claude Santerre, Lafayette's successor as commander of the National Guard, mobilized all the armed forces in the capital. Every company was at its post, and all the city gates were locked. Armed battalions covered every foot of the way from the Feuillants to the Temple—along the belt of the grand boulevards of to-day: Italiens, Montmartre, Poissonnière, Bonne Nouvelle, St. Denis, St. Martin, up to the Porte du Temple.

Three o'clock was set as the hour of departure, but the prisoners could not start until five. The crowd was so immense that it seemed impossible to break through. From all over Paris curious folk continued to pour in to see the never-to-be-forgotten spectacle of a king and a queen led to a dungeon. In this milling stream of human beings the two large coaches, filled with the royal family and their servants, looked like tiny immovable islands. Louis and Marie Antoinette occupied one coach, together with their old friend Mayor Pétion and City Procurator Manuel; both municipal officials kept their hats on as a sign of revolutionary independence.

With enormous difficulty the cavalry escort broke open a path for the slow-moving coaches. The surging mass of humanity was hurling insults and imprecations at the fallen royalty. Louis and Marie Antoinette sat tense and rigid, trying to seem unafraid in the face of thousands of enraged people. At the Place Vendôme the coaches stopped so that Louis could look at the demolished statue of his ancestor Louis XIV. "Voilà, Sire," Manuel sneered, "this is how the people treat their kings."

"Would," Louis replied, "that their fury confined itself to inanimate objects!"

It was already dark when they reached the Temple. The prisoners were led through the complex inner courts of the Priory until they got to the Tower which rose like a sinister apparition from obscurity. The silence was pervasive.

The main door of the Tower was of massive oak, about half a foot thick, encased in sheets of iron and held in place by enormous metal bolts. It gave way gratingly into a cavern of impenetrable darkness. A municipal officer stepped in, followed by Baron Hue with a lantern. They climbed a narrow winding stair leading to the second floor, about fifteen feet from the ground; here an iron door, with heavy locks and thick bolts, was almost as massive as the portal below. "Your master," the municipal officer broke the silence, "was used to gilt ceilings. He shall now see how the assassins of the people are lodged."

It was a dirty, foul-smelling, musty room, furnished in the most primitive fashion. The bed lacked linen and was verminous. The floor was dust-coated. While Hue and the valet Chamilly were cleaning up hastily, Louis and Pétion came in. Despite himself, the mayor was startled at the condition of the room. He muttered an apology, but Louis, according to Hue, "showed neither surprise nor displeasure." His eye fell on an obscene picture on the wall, and he removed it. "I cannot suffer such things to be seen by my daughter."

Then he lay down on the sheetless verminous bed and slept tranquilly.

⚜

"PATRIOT" PALLOY, the demolisher of the Bastille, arrived the next morning with a crew of wreckers, carpenters, masons, and laborers, to fortify the Tower and isolate it from the rest of Paris. Immediately they began to tear and hammer and dig. The wall surrounding the Tower was made thicker and doubled in height. Trees were uprooted, neighboring houses demolished, the grounds leveled. All windows in the vicinity facing the Tower were walled up.

While the Tower was hastily being made escape-proof, the commune supplied the prisoners with the necessary household goods and wearing apparel. From the National Storage, silver dishes and table-linen were selected with thoughtful care:

THE TOWER OF THE TEMPLE

A drawing of the late eighteenth century. Musée Carnavalet.

One soup-tureen
Eighteen sets of spoons and forks
Four spoons *à ragout*
One olla
Eight coffee-spoons
One spoon for powdered sugar
One coffee-pot for six cups
One coffee-pot for two cups
Twelve silver-handled knives
Five damask table-cloths
Twelve napkins
Two dozen hand-towels
Two dozen aprons
Six dish-cloths.[1]

For Louis' personal use the commune sent one morning jacket, two white jackets, one pair of silk hose, one pair of shoes, a sponge for the face, and a sponge for the teeth.[2]

⚜

PRISON LIFE soon fell into a routine that was not unpleasant. The family occupied two separate floors, Louis the second and the women the first, and contact between them was happily uninterrupted, although always under the careful supervision of the five commissioners appointed by the municipality. One of the commissioners was so placed that he always held Louis in view, another tasted his food, a third was outside; but Louis was indifferent to their presence so long as they did not interfere with him. Every morning the women went up to Louis' floor for breakfast, and afterwards all of them descended and passed the day in Marie Antoinette's

[1] Archives Nationales, AA53 plaq.1, nos.17-21. The furniture was supplied by the merchant Masson, at a cost of over 63,000 livres. It included 15 mattresses, 15 coverlets, 15 bolsters, 15 folding beds, and the proper number of pillows and sheets.

[2] Archives Nationales, AA53 plaq.1, no.2, In the Carnavalet Museum in Paris (Case 67) there is a list of Louis' laundry in the Temple, as of December 17: 15 shirts, 13 collars, 16 handkerchiefs, 4 neckties, 1 vest, 2 pairs of silk hose (white), 10 towels, 4 nightcaps, 8 napkins, 1 cotton cap, 3 pairs of underwear, 2 sheets. Later Louis was also supplied with various precision instruments for drawing and measuring, such as brass rulers, compasses, etc.

room, each doing something to while away the hours. Louis usually read or instructed his son.

Madame Royale, the king's young daughter, in later years recalled their first days in the Tower:

> We spent the day all together. My father taught my brother geography; my mother taught him history [!] and made him memorize verse. My aunt [Madame Elizabeth] instructed him in arithmetic. My father was fortunate in finding a library, which occupied him.[3] My mother worked on a tapestry. The municipal officers were very familiar and showed very little respect for the king.

The family, however, was in no way mistreated, although the guards were occasionally impolite and maliciously addressed the king as *Louis*. But they meant no harm. Some of them, in fact, were friendly and jolly. One or two of them were impressed by the king's tender solicitude for his children and openly expressed their doubts as to the correctness of the official propaganda that depicted him as a bloodthirsty monster. "A man who loves his children like that," a guard said, "could not have done all the evil they say he did." It was Mayor Pétion who was mainly responsible for the considerate treatment the family received. The mayor did what he could to soften the severity of the commune. He continued to address Louis as "Sire," signed himself "with respect," and offered every possible help: "If you have any needs, Sire, I beg you to let me know."

⚜

A GREAT REACTION was rolling over France—the revolution, indeed, was just beginning with the abolition of the mon-

[3] This library has been preserved and may be seen in the Carnavalet Museum in Paris; it belonged to the archivist Barthélemy, who gave Louis permission to use it. The books are bound in brown leather and have gilt backs. Among them are some twenty volumes of *Histoire du Bas-Empire*, about twenty-five volumes of *Histoire moderne*, some ten volumes of *Histoire de France*, ten *Histoire romaine*, ten *Hommes illustres*, ten *Histoire ancienne* —in short, an ideal library for Louis, who loved to read history.

Generally Louis left his family at about 9 in the evening and went up to his room where he read till midnight. In five months he read through the astounding number of 257 volumes.

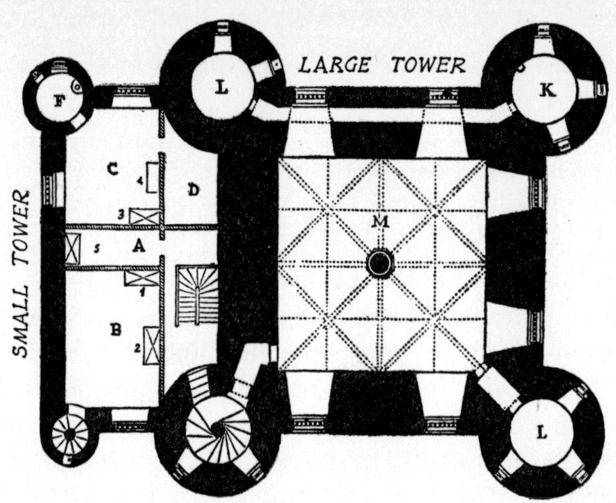

A, antechamber; *B,* queen's room; *C,* Madame de Tourzel's room; *D,* washroom; *K,* wardrobe; *L,* cabinet; *M,* guards' room. *1,* queen's bed; *2,* Madame Royale's bed; *3,* Madame de Tourzel's bed; *4,* dauphin's bed; *5,* Madame de Lamballe's bed.

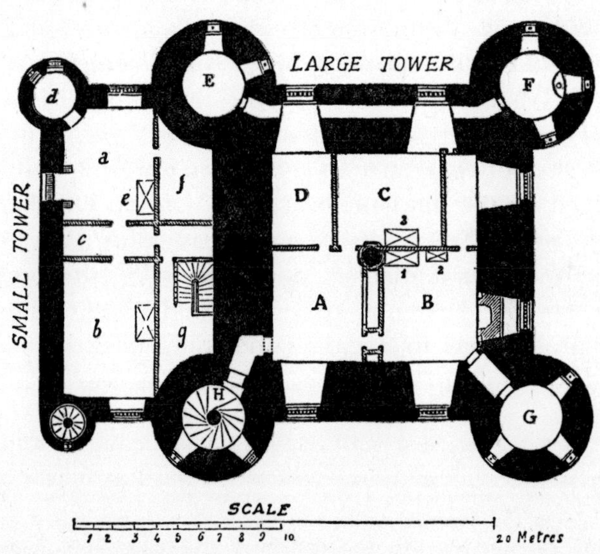

Small Tower, occupied by Louis from August 13 to September 29, 1792: *a,* king's room; *b,* kitchen; *c,* Hue and Chamilly's room; *d,* king's reading-room; *e,* king's bed; *f,* washroom; *g,* staircase.

Large Tower, occupied by Louis from September 29, 1792, to January 21, 1793: *A,* antechamber; *B,* king's room; *C.* Cléry's room: *D,* dining-room; *E,* wood-house; *F,* wardrobe; *G,* king's oratory; *H,* staircase.

FIRST AND SECOND FLOORS OF THE TEMPLE TOWER

archy—and the royal family was to experience its sting. News, mostly bad news, slowly percolated into the silent Tower. The imprisoned family would stand in the embrasures and try to catch the cries of the newsboys; in this way they learned of events that portended hopes and others that spelled disaster. They heard of the desertion of Lafayette, of the Prussian invasion of France, of the fall of Longwy—and their hopes were aroused. Then came more news, ominous news: even from the mere newspaper headlines (as cried by the boys) it was evident that terror was sweeping France. The guillotine went into action.[4]

Heads began to roll. La Porte, the king's friend and distributor of his moneys, was guillotined. The editor of the *Gazette de Paris* was guillotined. Others were being guillotined. The Jacobins cried, "To the scaffold with Louis the Traitor." Radicals demanded, "Death to the aristocrats." All the news bespoke death. The Tenth of August had abolished the monarchy and unleashed murderous instincts. As Paul Barras exclaimed on August 17 ("the eighth day of liberty"), "The epoch of great vengeance has come."

The epoch of vengeance was abroad in the land, and it was intensified by the news of the fall of Verdun. On that day, Sunday, September 2, Paris went mad with fear. While Danton, the virtual dictator, was electrifying the populace with his cry for "daring, more daring," and volunteers flocked to the tricolor eager to save the fatherland, embattled patriots decided to "mop up" the home front before leaving for the

[4] The guillotine was a new instrument and has a curious history. In October, 1789, Joseph Guillotin, a distinguished physician and humanitarian, proposed to the Assembly that a machine replace the crude executioner's ax. In March, 1792, the Assembly ordered Dr. Louis, the secretary of the Academy of Surgery, to supervise the construction of such a machine. The actual builder was a German mechanic named Schmidt, whose specialty was making harpsichords. Dr. Guillotin had nothing to do with the construction of the instrument, which was, in fact, at first called *Louisiette,* in honor of Dr. Louis. The machine claimed its first victim, a thief named Pelletier, on April 25, 1792. The first political victim was executed on August 21—when the Reign of Terror began. At this time the guillotine stood on the Place du Carrousel, within view of the Assembly, possibly to intimidate the deputies. A little later it was moved to what is now the Place de la Concorde.

THE CONTRIBUTION OF DOCTOR GUILLOTIN

A very early representation of the guillotine. Collection Liesville, Paris.

battle-field. A dreadful feeling had spread among the people that the royalists in the prisons and in hiding were waiting to rise as soon as the revolutionists had departed for the front. And so the tocsins began to ring, inviting the patriots with the long knives and sharp spears to come out and clean up. From prison to prison they went and systematically butchered about eleven hundred human beings in the course of five days and five nights.

⚜

WHILE the prisoners were being massacred in the city jails, bands of assassins gathered outside the walls of the Temple. There were not enough guards in the Tower to defend the royal family from the mobsters who had come to murder them. Anxiously Louis and Marie Antoinette stood at the unbarred windows, watching and wondering, for they had no precise information as to what was happening in the city. Suddenly from the massing mob flashed a severed blond head stuck on a blood-smeared pike, and Marie Antoinette collapsed as if struck with an ax: the gruesome head was that of her friend Madame de Lamballe. With blood-freezing yells the assassins rushed the outer yard of the Tower.

They halted before a flimsy tricolor banner, symbol of revolutionary authority, stretched across the gate leading to the inner Tower court, and one man among the municipal officials was quick to take advantage of the psychological moment. Seeing the mob hesitant, Jean Pierre André Danjou, an ex-priest and member of the commune, leaped on a heap of stones and flung his arms in a gesture demanding attention. He knew how to harangue crowds, this mountainous ex-priest with his powerful lungs, and he held them spellbound with flattery and cajolery.

"What do you want? What do you demand? The tyrant? He is here—who can doubt it? You would commit the greatest of crimes if you made an attempt on his life. He does not belong to you. He belongs to the law, which you have no right to violate...."

Won by the ex-priest's eloquence, the men promised to do no bodily harm to the tyrant on condition that they be allowed to send a deputation to see him in his dungeon. A dozen mobsters were selected and went in. One of them carried in his palm a piece of blood-soaked flesh—the heart of Madame de Lamballe. He was drunk and shouted that he wanted the heart cooked so that he could devour it. Marie Antoinette fainted. Another man cried at Louis, "Look at the head of de Lamballe and you will know how the people avenges itself on its tyrants." A third yelled, "The enemy is at Verdun; we shall all perish, but you will die first." Louis remained calm.

Later, when the mob left and a brooding silence settled over the Tower, Louis said to Danjou, "You have saved our lives; we thank you."

⚜

After the September massacres in the prisons of Paris, the country was gripped by a terror that also embraced the Tower. Barometrically reflecting the mood outside, guards and officers became ruder and harsher. Ugly drawings and ominous words were chalked on the prison walls and doors: "The guillotine is permanent; it awaits the tyrant Louis XVI." "The young wolf cubs should be strangled." Revolutionary songs full of threats were sung by the soldiers to annoy the prisoners. One of the guards, the shoemaker Simon, showed his contempt for the deposed king by refusing to speak to him directly. In the presence of Louis he would say to the royal valet, "Cléry, ask Capet if he wants anything." Cléry's answer was invariable: "He wants nothing." Another guard, Turlot, said to Cléry, "If the executioner doesn't guillotine this damned family, I'll do it myself." Most persistently insulting was the turnkey Rochez, a man with a sneering face, a sadist whose perpetual delight was to bait the helpless prisoners. He would take a long time fumbling with the keys, the while deliberately blowing smoke from his ill-smelling pipe into the faces of the king and queen. The guards sat around in chairs, watched the show, and laughed hilariously.

Only once did Louis show signs of annoyance, and that was when all the officials, obeying a new order of the commune, began to address him as *Capet*. He did not mind *Louis*. He did not mind *Monsieur*. But for some reason *Capet* upset him: he objected that his family had not used that name for centuries. After he got accustomed to *Capet,* they began to call him *Tyrant*. That really hurt him, and he never heard it without wincing. "I a tyrant! The whole concern of a tyrant is for himself. Has not my concern always been for my people?"

His people now began to show an unhealthy interest in his fate. On September 20, the fifth week of the imprisonment in the Tower, occurred two events that had a direct bearing on Louis' future. At Valmy, General Dumouriez, who gave up politics for the army, defeated the Prussians and checked their invasion. In Paris, the Legislative Assembly was dissolved and replaced by the National Convention.

This new Convention was destined to sit through the bloodiest period of the revolution, although the majority of its 783 deputies were far from radical. Most of them, in truth, were hostile to the Paris mob and its brutalities. But inevitably the National Convention became a fierce battleground on which two determined minorities, the propertied Girondins and the proletarian Jacobins, fought each other to annihilation. For the moment, however, all these hostile groups—Girondins from the provinces, Jacobins from the cities, rich men and poor men—were united on one subject, the abolition of the monarchy.

Formal abolition of the monarchy was the first act of the National Convention. So profound had been the transformation in French opinion in the last few months that a thousand-year-old institution was voted out of existence without the compliment of a debate, in an atmosphere of frivolity. This odd scene was devoid of solemnity. Abbé Baptiste-Henri Grégoire, a hothead, obtained the floor and spoke to a packed house: "We know very well that all these baleful dynasties have never been anything else than voracious races which lived on human flesh.... We must destroy this magic talisman.... I demand therefore that you formally abolish the monarchy."

Spontaneously the Convention raised hands in acquiescence. But one deputy protested that such an important act should not be passed without at least a show of debate.

Abbé Grégoire lashed out: "What's the use of debating when everybody agrees? Kings are the same in the moral order as monsters are in the physical. Royal courts are the workshops of crime and the dens of tyrants. The history of kings is the martyrology of nations. What's there to debate...?"

Again the deputies leaped to their feet and ardently acclaimed the sentiments of the speaker. Without further discussion they voted "unanimously that royalty is abolished in France."

That afternoon a municipal officer, accompanied by gendarmes and followed by a cheering crowd, marched up to the Tower. A trumpeter blew the bugle, and when silence was obtained, the officer shouted the proclamation:

"Royalty is abolished in France.... The seal of the state will bear the words *République de France*..."

Inside the Tower, where the words penetrated clearly, Louis pretended not to hear. While the guards were watching him keenly to note his reaction, the deposed king continued to read a book. He never even looked up.

⚜

Louis was not displeased at the news of the abolition of the monarchy. Often in the past he had wished he could resign with a clear conscience, and now that responsibility was taken off his shoulders, he felt, perhaps for the first time in his adult life, really serene. He had, moreover, cause to hope that he would no longer be molested, now that France was a republic and the ex-king safely in prison. Thus consoling himself, Louis settled down happily to a long period of reading.

Yet even behind thick walls Louis XVI was, as the Abbé Grégoire said, a "magic talisman," which had to be destroyed before the new order could feel itself secure. No one was more aware of this than the politically mature Jacobins who controlled the commune and the Paris mob. They were convinced, rightly enough, that so long as the king was alive the republic was in danger, and they began a ruthless campaign against "Louis the Last," as they now called him in official acts and propaganda leaflets.

The new agitation against the king was promptly felt in the Tower. A series of harsh acts reminded the royal prisoners that their enemies were vigilant. Louis was deprived of his sword, his stars, his *Cordon Rouge,* and "all other insignia of feudalism." Then all writing materials—pens, pencils, crayons, paper, and ink—were taken from the prisoners. All cutting instruments were likewise confiscated. But the worst blow was the decree of segregation of *Louis le dernier* from his family and his removal to the Great Tower. The separation, so cruelly felt by all the members of the family, took place at the end of September. Louis, his heavy face twisted in pain, held Marie Antoinette's hands, while she sobbed bitterly. She had at last, in the days of common terror, come to love that clumsy, kindly father of her children. Her son, the dauphin, was to stay with his father; the daughter was to go with the mother. The only consolation of the family was that they would be allowed to walk together daily for an hour after luncheon.

⚜

The Great Tower into which Louis was transferred was, from the point of view of physical comfort, an improvement over the small one. It was better furnished, had more light, and was spacious enough to permit partitioning into three or four rooms. Louis was especially pleased with a fireplace, because the autumn air was chilly and the dauphin had bad lungs and needed warmth. The beds of the king and the dauphin were placed near the fireplace. A four-foot-high mirror on the mantelpiece added cheer to the room.

After Louis and his son had settled down with their valet Cléry to lead a sort of studious existence, Procurator Manuel came to find out how things were. Louis received him with his usual cool dignity.

MANUEL: "How are you? Do you have all that you need?"

LOUIS: "I am satisfied."

"You have undoubtedly been informed of the victories of our arms, the taking of Speyer, the conquest of Savoy?"

"Yes, I heard one of these gentlemen speak of it."

"What, you get no newspapers?"

"No."

Manuel turned to the municipal commissioners: "We must give Monsieur here all the newspapers; he ought to learn about our successes..." Then to Louis: "Democratic ideas are gaining ground. You have heard of course that the people have established a republican government."

"Yes, I have heard, and I hope that the French will find that happiness which I have always wanted to procure for them."

"You are now a plain citizen, and you will be treated as such. If you need anything, let us know and we will get it for you."

"I thank you, I need nothing."

Manuel kept his word; he sent four or five newspapers to the Tower, but some higher authority soon stopped them.

Louis, however, had other reading materials to occupy him. When he was not giving lessons to his son,[5] he read

[5] On November 23, 1792, Louis demanded from the commune 33 Latin and French books for the education of his son. Among them were: *Appendix de diis et heroibus,* Jouvence's *Abrégé d'histoire politique,* Aurelius Victor, Eutropius, Fontaine's *Fables,* Florus, Horace, Justinius, Ovid's *Metamorphoses,* Quintus Curtius, Sallust, Suetonius, Tacitus, *Adventures of Télémaque,* Terence, Virgil, also a Latin grammar, a French grammar, a Bible, the Lives of the Saints. The total cost of these books was 180 livres.

The request for these books aroused a heated discussion in the council of the commune. One councillor said, "I do not see that we have any

"LOUIS THE LAST AND HIS FAMILY LED TO THE TEMPLE"
A contemporary cartoon.

"THE RARE ANIMALS"

"or the Translation of the Royal Menagerie to the Temple, August 20, 1792, the 4th of Liberty and the 1st of Equality." A contemporary cartoon. Louis is depicted as a turkey, Marie Antoinette as a she-wolf with snakes in her hair, the royal children and Madame Elizabeth as the wolf's cubs.

books—travel, history, politics, natural science, the Roman authors—and always ended the day with the *Imitation of Christ* in Latin. He was happy with his books, for they permitted complete relaxation of body and mild stimulation of mind. There were no demands on his time and no calls of duty, and he was sufficiently resigned not to worry about the future.

> We mounted to the second floor [so reads a report of a delegation of commissioners sent to the Tower on November 1] and entered the apartment of Louis Capet and his son. After having scrupulously visited all the rooms and examined all the furniture, we found that he was lodged wholesomely and comfortably; we also found no trace of pen or ink or pencil or paper. We asked him if he lacked anything for his convenience and if he had no complaints to make of his food, to which he replied that he was satisfied with the way he was being treated and that his only desire was to be given the satisfaction of living with his family.

Thus tranquilly passed the days in the Tower. October went and November came, and it seemed that life would go on like this, regulated, supervised, and secure. Louis was too absorbed in his books and too thoroughly cut off from the outer world to know that the final act of his life was being carefully constructed. He was unaware that the Jacobin agitation to have him tried and condemned was gaining ground, that more and more Frenchmen were being infected by the clever propaganda that branded him a "tyrant," "brigand," and "monster," and that finally a new catchphrase was making the rounds: "Liberty needs the blood of kings."

reason for refusing the demand of Louis Capet. He only tries to while away his hours, and we are in honor bound not to show him any animosity. I vote in favor of his petition." Others opposed the request on the characteristically French ground that since Capet had only a few weeks to live, why waste money on books? A few argued that such silly things as Latin books were unfit in this modern age and "contrary to morals," proposing, instead, histories of the American revolution, a life of Cromwell, the story of the Massacre of St. Bartholomew. In the end Louis' request was granted.

CHAPTER XXVI

"Louis, the French nation accuses you"

IN THE MIDDLE of November the Jacobins at last forced the issue of the king's fate upon the Convention, and once the matter was pushed, it had to reach bottom, like a stone rolling down hill. Only a handful of Jacobins knew what they wanted—the death penalty; the rest of the deputies were in a sea of confusion and did not even know how to proceed with the question. The debates, as reported in the official *Moniteur,* show a chaotic state of mind. There was first of all, a long argument on "How shall we discuss the question?" Pétion proposed the formula, "Can the king be judged?" Long and clashing discussions led to the conclusion that he could. Then the debate turned upon the query, "Is it in the interest of the nation to judge Louis XVI?" In other words, granting that the deputies had a legal right to act as the king's judges (which they had not), was it good policy to do so? The majority agreed that it was essential that Louis be tried.

Having thus cleared the decks, the deputies faced the central question: What kind of penalty should be imposed? Evidently the punishment depended upon the guilt. If Louis could be proven a traitor, then death was the inevitable penalty. And here the Jacobins showed what clever political manœuverers they really were. They organized petition-writers in all their clubs and flooded the Convention with demands for the condemnation of the "monster who wanted to devour us" and the annihilation of the "assassin of his people." An atmosphere of hate was thus created and subtly influenced the debates. On the floor of the Convention the Jacobin deputies persistently used phrases that were designed to give the impression that the prisoner in the Temple was nothing but a bloodthirsty ogre. "You wanted to butcher us," cried one, brandishing his fist in the direction of the Temple; "you merit death." Another shouted, "A drunken killer." Others argued that the trial of Louis would make all other kings tremble and thus hasten the world revolution. This view was best stated by Thomas Paine, the Anglo-American radical, in a letter to the Convention, of which he was an honorary member:

> France is now a republic.... She has finished her revolution. It is to her interest that all nations be as free as she is, that the revolution becomes universal; and because the trial of Louis XVI will prove to the world the villainy of governments in general and the necessity of revolution, France should not let such a precious opportunity pass....

While the debates were becoming acrimonious, the Jacobins played a trump card. On November 18 one François Gamoin, a locksmith, made a confession that earlier in the year he had constructed a secret *Armoire de fer* in the Tuileries at the express order of the king. The locksmith opined that Louis had stored important documents in that Iron Closet. The Convention was agog with excitement, and Roland, the minister of the interior, immediately rushed over to the palace to open the *Armoire*. It was packed with papers, which were promptly sealed and transported to the Convention. Here at last was a mine from which to quarry evidence against the king; the Convention thought it had proof of his guilt and voted that he should be charged with treason.

To prepare the case a Commission of Twelve was appointed. Day after day, while a sentinel guarded the room, the commissioners worked over the papers, examining, sorting, digesting, summarizing, annotating. Altogether there were over forty cartons of documents, and it took the Commission more than two weeks to digest them.[1]

Despite the excitement of the deputies and the assertions of later historians (who rarely took the trouble to look into the original documents), it is a curious fact that the papers found in the Tuileries were largely innocuous. The really treasonable letters, such as the correspondence of Louis and Marie Antoinette with the foreign courts, were not found in the Iron Closet. None of the 627 documents found in the *Armoire* struck this writer (who examined the papers in the Archives Nationales) as stuff that would move a really impartial jury to convict a man of treason. The bulk of the papers consisted of correspondence *received* by Louis. Of the 627 documents, no less than seventy-six were letters written by clerical folk in protest against the ecclesiastical laws that the king had signed. One such letter, written by a nun, read, "God and Cæsar are the sole masters whom we recognize as our legitimate sovereigns." This may have been counter-revolutionary, but it was not illegal, and, moreover, Louis was only the recipient, and not the writer, of such sentiments. Other letters contained appeals for charity, requests for jobs, offers of resignation; there were also bills, receipts, orders, drafts, petitions.[2] Everything, in short, but evidence showing treason to the state.

IN THE MEANTIME a mild reaction occurred in the Convention. During the breathing-spell allowed by the examination of the documents many deputies had time to cool off and get scared at the awful responsibility involved in judging and condemning a king. Some of them argued that the Convention was only a legislative body and had no constitutional right to act as a court of law. This bombshell set off many

[1] Archives Nationales, C187, 131: "Procès-verbaux de la commission des douze & des vingt un réuni, établi par decrets des 21 9bre & 6xbre, l'an 1er de la république." See also *ibid.*, C182 CII 88-92.

[2] Archives Nationales, C183, 107.

explosions and threatened to blow up the whole case built by the Jacobins. For a while it looked as if the majority would stampede out of the enclosure in which the Jacobins had corraled them. Then arose a prissy little man, a deputy from Arras named Robespierre, and spoke with the chilly logic of a Frenchman and the priggishness of a professional revolutionist:

You are not here to pass sentence for or against a man, but a measure of public safety. Louis has been dethroned for his crimes. Louis therefore can no longer be judged: he has already been condemned. . . . (*Applause*). To try Louis XVI is to retrograde towards despotism; it is a counter-revolutionary idea, for it puts the revolution itself on trial. For if Louis could be the object of a trial, he could conceivably be absolved, he might even be innocent. . . . And if Louis could be presumed innocent, what becomes of the revolution . . . ? If Louis is innocent, all the defenders of liberty, the *fédérés,* the people of Paris, all the patriots of France, are guilty.

The phrase *If Louis is innocent, the people are guilty* was like a scorpion's tail on the conscience of the deputies. Robespierre disdainfully reminded them that they had gone too far already and could not back out. It was either Louis or the revolution: either the king was innocent or the revolution was innocent. It could not be both. If he was innocent, he would never forgive the revolutionists for having dethroned and imprisoned him. If he was guilty . . . !

The Convention voted to constitute itself a special tribunal to sit permanently until the trial of the king was over.

THEY were eager to hurry with the trial, for the public mind was in turmoil and threatened to erupt. Everybody was writing letters to the Convention—pleading for the king, threatening the king, offering to die for the king.

Citizen President [wrote one Julie], I am not an aristocrat, but I am a woman, young and sensitive, and the misfortunes of Louis the Sixteenth tear my heart. If he is condemned, if he is to perish, I offer myself as victim in his place. Let me mount the scaffold in his stead. Vainly will you say that the blood of a woman is not equal to that of a king; we are all equal, and my soul is as pure as his.

On the margin the president wrote, "Ignore it."

I urgently beg the National Convention [wrote a doctor in the military hospital at Meaux] to accord me the head of Capet: it should be cut off for the good of humanity. I want to dry it and then engrave on it the most appropriate inscriptions to show the people all the horror which they should feel for such monstrosities.

Such letters came in hundreds, so that the Convention feared a popular explosion. Far too much feeling was aroused by the unprecedented news of a public trial of a monarch, and the anxious Convention appointed a Commission of Twenty-Four to draw up an *Act of the Crimes of which Louis Capet is Accused;* it was to be done in a hurry. Within four days the *Act* and the questionnaire (which Louis was to answer) were completed, and on December 10 Louis was suddenly informed that he would be brought before the bar of the National Convention to answer questions.

EARLY in the morning of December 11 Louis heard bugles and drums. He was much upset. The municipal officer said to him, "Monsieur, in a moment you will receive a visit from the mayor, but I must warn you that he will not speak to you in the presence of your son." He added that the dauphin must rejoin his mother. Louis said, "Kiss me, my boy, and kiss your mother for me," and stonily told Cléry to take the child downstairs. He strode up and down the room, curiously agitated. Uncertainty banished his usual calm. "Tell me," he said to the municipal officer, "this new mayor, is he young, old, big, small, fat, thin?" The officer did not know. "What is he going to tell me?" "I don't know, you will soon find out." Louis sat down, jumped up, walked a bit, sat down again, rubbed his hands against his thighs.

Officials and guards filled the room. Chambon, the new mayor, stepped forward: "I am charged to inform you that the Convention awaits you." He nodded to Coulombeau, the secretary of the commune, who unrolled an official document: "Louis Capet is to be arraigned before the bar of the Convention..." Louis interrupted impatiently, "My name is not Louis Capet. My ancestors once bore that name, but I have never called myself that." Suddenly he changed the subject. "Besides, for four months I have been exposed to arbitrary treatment. This morning they separated me from my son. He is my joy..."

Coldly the mayor asked if Louis Capet would come along. Louis went silently. In the courtyard he was scared by the unexpected sight of armed men, pikes, guns, cannon, blue-uniformed horsemen, and he fell into immobility. His coach was surrounded by infantry, preceded by cavalry, followed by artillery. They drove through a strangely silent city where every street, every boulevard, every square and public building, was heavily guarded.[3]

AT THREE in the afternoon the temporary president of the Convention rapped for silence. "Representatives, you are going to exercise national justice.... All Europe is watching us. History will record your thoughts and judge your actions. Incorruptible posterity will judge you with inflexible severity. ... The most profound impassiveness and silence is appropriate for judges.... You know that justice presides only over tranquil deliberations....

"Louis Capet awaits your orders."

All heads craned in the direction of the door, and in a

[3] *Le Moniteur,* December 11, 1792, reports: "Never was Paris more calm, never did the armed citizens show greater zeal than on the day when Louis XVI appeared before the bar of the Convention. The public establishments had a guard of 200 men; numerous and frequent patrols circulated on the streets...; reserve troops were stationed in each section; a powerful guard protected the National Convention.... All these measures were necessary, but to see the tranquillity of the capital, one would have almost thought them useless."

tomblike stillness Louis entered. He wore a brown overcoat, his face was unshaven, and he carried his hat in hand like a citizen coming to petition a court of law. But he walked with a curious dignity. There was an indefinable air of kingship about the stoutish prisoner, and for the first time in his life Louis as an individual, as an ordinary human being stripped of all the trimmings and trappings of royalty, impressed his fellow-citizens despite themselves.

The president's voice was magnified in the unnaturally silent hall: "Louis, the French nation accuses you. *The Act of Crimes* is going to be read to you. You may sit down."

Louis sat down, quietly listened to the list of his crimes. In front of him sat his cousin the Duke of Orleans, now Philip Égalité, insolently staring at the prisoner through a lorgnette. Marat was there too, washed and dressed in a new *soutane* for the occasion, glaring hatred at the "bloody tyrant." But Louis ignored them, he was absorbed in listening to the chain of his crimes against the revolution.[4] When the reading came to an end, every one held his breath as the harsh-voiced president began to fire questions at the prisoner.

"Louis, the French people accuse you of having committed many crimes.... In June, 1789, you ordered out troops against the citizens of Paris. Your satellites have shed blood."

Louis' voice was firm, pleasant and well modulated, so that the ladies in the balcony gasped with surprise. "In those days I was commander of the army, but I never had any intention of shedding blood."

President: "You permitted the national cockade to be trampled before your eyes."

[4] Archives Nationales, C187, 132: "Inventaire des pièces recueillies par la commission de 21 contre S.M.Louis XVI: ens[e] des 51 pièces qui lui ont été communiqués à la séance de la Convention Nationale du 11 décembre 1792." There were altogether 51 documents, including a letter of Louis to Lafayette (June 29, 1790) and to General Bouillé (December 15, 1791), Louis' expense accounts, showing sums of money distributed for bribery, and correspondence with La Porte about Mirabeau. These documents could be construed to prove conspiracy against the revolution, although they were not incriminating *per se.*

LOUIS, sharply: "This is false; it never happened before my eyes."

PRESIDENT: "You spent a fortune to corrupt the people, to win popularity."

LOUIS: "Nothing gave me greater pleasure than to give money to those who needed it; there was no question of plots."

PRESIDENT: "In June, 1791, you fled with a false passport."

LOUIS: "As regards my trip to Varennes, I have explained all that to the National Assembly."

PRESIDENT: "Later you spent money on pamphlets and newspapers in order to pervert public opinion."

LOUIS, hesitating, evidently evading: "I have no knowledge of this."

PRESIDENT: "You have done nothing to suppress the counter-revolution in the provinces."

LOUIS: "I have given all the orders that the ministers proposed."

PRESIDENT, sharply: "Septeuil's receipts show that you have given considerable sums of money to the émigrés."

LOUIS, insincerely: "I don't recall."

"Your brothers, enemies of the country, have rallied the émigrés, raised regiments, made loans, and you did nothing to disown them."

"I disowned all the steps taken by my brothers as soon as I knew about them."

"You ordered the generals to disorganize the army and make the troops desert to your brothers."

LOUIS, bruskly: "There isn't a word of truth in this accusation."

"You destroyed our navy by letting the officers emigrate."

LOUIS, coldly: "I could not stop them."

"In the colonies your agents fomented counter-revolutionary plots."

"I know of no agents in the colonies."

"You refused to sanction the law against nonjuring priests."

LOUIS, sharply: "I had a constitutional right to do so."

"In Paris you supported counter-revolutionary groups."

"I never did."

"You planned to bribe deputies of the National and Legislative Assemblies."

"Many individuals came with such projects, but I rejected them."

PRESIDENT, quickly: "Which persons?"

LOUIS, drily: "I can't recall."

"To whom did you promise to give money?"

LOUIS, curtly: "Nobody."

PRESIDENT, shifting ground: "Abroad you lowered French prestige by not protesting against maltreatment of French citizens."

"The diplomatic correspondence will prove the contrary; and anyhow this concerns the minister of foreign affairs."

"On the 10th of August you assembled troops in the Tuileries."

LOUIS, sharply: "Why not? The officials of the city, of the department, of the nation were there and saw that the palace was threatened, and as a constituted authority, I had a right to defend myself."

"You caused French blood to be shed."

"No, Monsieur, I did not."

"You vetoed the decree to establish a camp of twenty thousand men near Paris."

LOUIS, drily: "I had a constitutional right to veto decrees."

A WAVE of sympathy for the prisoner pervaded the packed and silent hall.[5] His voice was so warm and his answers so quick

[5] John Moore, *A Journal during a Residence in France,* II, 529: "The King's appearance in the Convention, the dignified resignation of his manner, the admirable promptitude and candour of his answers, made such an evident impression on some of the audience in the galleries, that a determined enemy of Royalty, who had his eye upon them, declared that he was afraid of hearing the cry of *Vive le Roi!* issue from the tribunes; and added that if the King had remained ten minutes longer in their sight, he was convinced it would have happened."

and apparently sincere that few in the audience could bring themselves to believe that this sad, stout man with the good-natured face was a tyrant and a plotter. His manner, so patient and generally courteous, contrasted strongly with the brusqueness of the president, who interrupted frequently, "Louder, Louis, they can't hear you." Moreover, there was a feeling in the hall that the case against the king was not very strong.

A fat secretary shoved a series of papers under Louis' nose and asked him to identify them, but the king refused to commit himself without a more careful examination and consultation with lawyers. His invariable answer was, "I don't recognize this." Then the president said, "Go into the waiting-room. The Assembly wants to deliberate."

Louis rose. "I demand counsel," he said, and went out of the hall.

A furious debate broke forth. Frantically the Jacobins, enraged that Louis had made a good impression, shouted that this was no ordinary trial and that the prisoner should not be allowed any defenders. Bitter words were hurled back and forth. Finally Pétion obtained the floor. "I say," he cried, "no one can refuse him counsel without at the same time attacking all the principles of humanity." The majority agreed and voted that Louis be allowed to choose his defenders.

All this time Louis was standing patiently in the reception-room, munching a piece of bread which a guard had given him. He tried to make conversation but was rebuffed: the "tyrant" was not safe company even for a humble soldier. So the prisoner took out a copy of the constitution which he carried in his pocket and read it quietly.

LOUIS RETURNED to prison without being informed of the Convention's decision. He was worried. "Monsieur," he said to Arbeltier, the municipal officer in his room, "do you believe they will refuse me counsel?"

Arbeltier was oracular. "Monsieur, if the Convention will allow it you will have it."

Louis consulted the constitution, which he knew by heart anyhow. "Yes, the constitution allows it. But do you think I may get in touch with my family?"

"I will ask the prison council."

Arbeltier came back with bad news. "Monsieur, I have to inform you that you will not be allowed to communicate with your family."

"That is pretty harsh," Louis exclaimed; "but what about my son—he is only a boy of seven."

"Your son is considered a member of your family."

Louis shrugged. "My supper?"

They brought in six cutlets, a chicken, several eggs; this he washed down with a glass of wine and promptly slept.

ON THE FOLLOWING DAY Louis was informed that he was allowed to choose counsel. He selected two able old jurists, Judge Target and Tronchet. Target promptly refused to accept the dangerous assignment, pleading illness;[6] but Tronchet gladly accepted a post which thousands of Frenchmen still considered honorable—that of defending their king. At the news of Target's refusal, hundreds of letters poured into the Convention, offering to defend Louis and even to die for him. Many of the champions were women.[7] Among

[6] But during the trial Target published a pamphlet, *Observations sur le Procès de Louis XVI,* in which he argued against condemnation.

[7] One letter was written by Olympe de Gouges, a middle-aged *femme de lettres:* "Let's leave out my sex; heroism and generosity are also shared by women.... I believe Louis imperfect as king; but stripped of this proscribed title, he ceases to be guilty in the eyes of the republic. His ancestors have heaped evils upon France... and all the thunder has rebounded on his head. ... He was weak, he was misled, he misled us, he misled himself.... It is not necessary to cut off a king's head to kill him...."

Another letter, more passionate than Olympe's, was written by *Citoyenne* Dupré of Lyons: "I am only a woman, but a friend of *la patrie,* and I dare say as good a patriot as a citizen, and mother of a family. I have been brought up to respect the laws and my superiors, and without swerving from these principles, permit me to tell you my feelings about the conduct of our *ci-devant* king. His crime? It was to support the hopes of the émigrés.

the numerous offers was one that moved Louis to tears; it was from his seventy-one year old friend and ex-minister Malesherbes. The king happily accepted his services.

When Tronchet, "the cold and virtuous," arrived at the Temple to meet his client, he was told that he could not get in unless he stripped naked and let himself be searched even "in the most intimate places." Such was the decree of the prison council. The chilly-tempered lawyer, who was destined to become one of Napoleon's Supreme Court justices, burst into Homeric wrath at such an arbitrary ruling and crude violation of the law. He was let in without being searched.

Despite the superior legal abilities of his defenders, Louis had no illusions as to his position or prospects. He knew that he was fated to die, like Charles I, but he wanted his exit to be dignified, worthy of a king of France. His chief interest was to leave the historic stage without a blot on his name.

> No sooner did he see me [Malesherbes described his meeting with Louis in prison] than he put away the Tacitus he was reading and took me in his arms. His eyes were wet, and he said: "Your sacrifice is so much the more generous as you expose your life without being able to save mine." I pointed out to him that there could be no danger for me and that it would be too easy to defend him successfully. He insisted: "I am sure of it, they will make me perish; they have the power and the desire. No matter. Let us occupy ourselves with my case as if I should win it, and in truth I will win it, for the memory which I shall leave will be stainless."

THE DEFENDANT and his counselors had to work fast, for the Convention was under tremendous pressure to finish the case. The longer the trial lasted the greater was the danger

That, citizens, is all that is reprehensible.... On the 10th of August the king and his family sought your hospitality. And... you have imprisoned him and his family, you are punishing him for the crimes of his aggressors, him who never shed a drop of blood." Archives Nationales, AA53, plaq.3, no.17. None of the letters was discussed in the Convention. The correspondence can be consulted in Archives Nationales, C243, 304; also AA53 plaq.3 and *passim.*

of a civil eruption. Already shots between republicans and monarchists were being exchanged in the provinces, and there was always the menace of a revolt of the countryside, which was Catholic and conservative, against "godless," mob-ruled Paris. The Jacobins deliberately kept the populace at fever heat and goaded the Convention into precipitous action, well knowing that France was by no means antiroyalist. Whatever the majority of the deputies thought of their self-imposed function as judges, the Jacobins had no doubt that the trial was to be a farcical stage-play with a preordained conclusion. Out of fear lest the country revolt against them, the Jacobins showed understandable impatience with all the legal folderol and hotly resented the suggestion that an expert examine the king's correspondence to determine its genuineness. "History will record this great trial," one deputy warned. "We need no such proof," sneered Camille Desmoulins; "we know he is guilty." Another Jacobin shouted that he was tired of this juridical chicanery: "The blood of our brothers demands vengeance."

The majority, however, wanted Louis tried as fairly as circumstances permitted and gave him a sporting chance to defend himself by allowing him to identify or reject the documents on which the case against him was based. The number of these papers appalled Malesherbes and Tronchet; weary old men, they feared they would not be able to examine the documents and prepare a defense in the brief time allotted to them. "It is physically impossible," both lawyers appealed to the Convention, "for two men, one of whom is a sexagenarian and the other more than a septuagenarian, to prepare a defense in such a short time." They asked for a third counsel, the younger De Sèze.[8] The Convention granted the request.

In the afternoon of December 15, four days after Louis' appearance before the bar of the Convention, a commission

[8] Archives Nationales, C243, 305, no.6. The letter and the signatures show that the hands that wrote them were indeed old, almost palsied: the words are unsteady and uneven.

of seven men came to the Temple with a portfolio full of documents for the prisoner to examine. It was all done in the strictest legalistic manner so dear to *fonctionnaires;* every scrap of paper was handed to Louis, then checked in an inventory, then shown to Tronchet, then to the commissioners. On each piece that Louis identified as his own he wrote an *L* in the margin, then the commissioners wrote their initials. In the inventory every page was countersigned by Louis, Tronchet, and the seven commissioners. They finished at midnight.

Altogether one hundred and eight documents were submitted to Louis. In the case of seventy-three of them he said, "I don't recognize this," "I don't recall this," "I have no knowledge of this," "This is not my writing." Of only thirty-five pieces he said, "I recognize my signature." Then all the papers, those Louis accepted as genuine (about one-third) and those he rejected, were packed together and taken back to the Convention.[9]

THE CONVENTION was in tumult. Jacobins yelled inside, the mob threatened outside, and the majority of the deputies were a flock of scared sheep. The sneering Robespierre threatened the hesitant Center, the ridiculous "legalists" who wanted the trial to have a semblance of legality, with dire vengeance if they ignored the will of the people. And the "people" were constantly incited by the agitators. In the sections they were sharpening pikes and muttering about another Tenth of August. A lynching spirit gripped Paris, and a sinister mob surrounded the Convention. Fierce and shrill were the cries that the "last king of the French" be instantly "punished for his crimes." A curt declaration was printed and distributed by the sections: "We swear, by the rights of the people, by the memory of the victims of the Tenth [August], by the need to be free, LOUIS WILL PERISH, OR NO REPUBLICAN WILL SURVIVE HIM."

[9] Archives Nationales, C138, no.2 and no.3.

That was on the 21st of December, which was an Ember-day and the birthday of Louis' daughter whom he had not seen for ten days. He rose early, went over to the fireplace, and began to read. This time it was not a history but a breviary. He did not touch food. "To-day," he said to the amazed municipal officer, "I fast."

Dorat-Coubières, the municipal officer, was a stout unbeliever with independent republican ideas. To his colleagues below he described Louis' fasting and added: "That seems to me to give the key to Louis' moral character; and *certes,* piety in a king is not a virtue but a very dangerous formidable vice. Louis XI, Charles IX, Philip II were all devout, and all three of them were also oppressors of the people, monsters."

The other officers of the prison council came up to see the fasting monster, and Louis asked them for news of his family. "My daughter," he murmured, "has her fourteenth birthday to-day." The officers stared in surprise as they saw his eyes fill with tears.

He asked Dorat for a razor, for he had not shaved for several days. Dorat said, "We will shave you." Louis replied, "I don't want anybody to shave me." The prison council refused him a razor; they also refused Marie Antoinette scissors for her finger-nails.

Later in the day Malesherbes arrived and told the prisoner that he would be brought before the Convention on December 26 and formally tried. Louis was serene. Even if his life were spared, he said, he would never accept a throne reconquered by force. He wanted always to rule by love, not by violence.

Then he spoke of his wife, how she had been calumniated and made to suffer cruelly. "She was little more than a child when she arrived at court. Mother and grandmother were both dead." There was no one to guide her, Louis said, and she "adopted a mode of life exempt from ceremony and restraint." Louis defended her warmly. She always remained

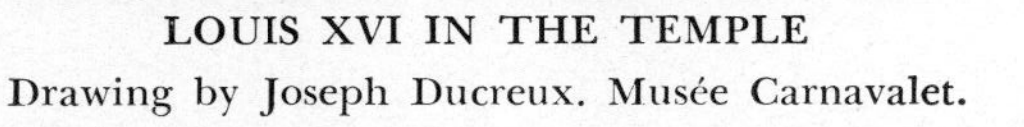

LOUIS XVI IN THE TEMPLE

Drawing by Joseph Ducreux. Musée Carnavalet.

THE WIDOW CAPET

By J. L. Prieur after Kucharsky. Musée Carnavalet.

good and virtuous, he said. "Unfortunate princess! My marriage promised her a throne; now what a prospect—!"

ON THE DAY before he was to go up for trial Louis prepared his Testament. Fearing that he might be killed on the way, he made two copies, one of which he kept in the room and the other he gave to Malesherbes.

The most surprising thing about the Testament is its quietly, unpretentiously dramatic quality. The sentiments are those of a man who knows he is going to die, is resigned to it, and has no doubt whatever about his innocence. A spirit of serenity pervades the document.[10]

He declared that he died in the Catholic faith and begged forgiveness for those who were in error, those whom he might have offended, and those who were his enemies. He recommended his wife and children and family to God. He asked his wife to bring up his children as good Christians and honest men and begged her to pardon him the suffering he had caused her. "I exhort my son, should he have the misfortune of becoming king, to remember that he owes himself wholly to the happiness of his fellow-citizens; that he should forget all hates and all grudges." He expressed deep gratitude to those who had been attached to him and reminded his son to remember their services.

"I end by declaring before God, and ready to appear before him, that I do not reproach myself with any of the crimes with which I am charged."

Now the burden was off his mind, and he could face the people, his accusers, with the poise and even the cheerfulness of a willing martyr.

IN THE MORNING of December 26 the mayor of Paris and his suite came to the Tower and found the prisoner talkative,

[10] The full text is given in Appendix I.

almost gay. He went with them gladly. Again the streets were packed and silent. Louis surprised the mayor and the secretary of the commune with his conversation on the Roman authors. At a time like this, with hundreds of thousands of cold hostile eyes following the prisoner's coach! "I thought it very curious," the secretary remarked later. One of the municipal officials in the coach said, with Gallic irony, that he thought Seneca a hypocrite for pretending to be a philosopher and at the same time defending Nero's crimes before the Senate. Louis replied spiritedly that the argument was spurious, that however Seneca behaved politically, it did not affect the value of his philosophy. Then he switched the conversation to Livy and criticized him for putting long speeches into the mouths of generals, which, Louis said, no commander would deliver at the head of an army. It was a neat point in historical criticism. Of himself Louis never said a word.

He met his three lawyers in the waiting-room of the Convention, and De Sèze showed him the defense speech he had prepared—a document fifty-one pages long. The peroration was a masterpiece of pathos. Louis said, "Cut that out; I don't want to arouse pity."

The hall was tensely silent as De Sèze began to read his speech: "The day of justice has succeeded the days of wrath. ... Louis is now no more than a man, a prisoner.... I beseech you, citizens, to hear me with indulgence."

For three long hours the lawyer spoke, and no one interrupted him. He was conscious that in the person of Louis XVI he was defending an ancient tradition before the people of France, and he read his words with gravity. Step by step he disposed of all the accusations, he cited facts and quoted laws; he argued that many of the charges had no validity because they were *ex post facto* (for acts anterior to the constitution), while others arraigned the misdeeds of the ministers and not of the king. It was a good speech, the best that could be made in Louis' defense, and the deputies listened earnestly. They were touched as De Sèze concluded on a personal note:

> Louis ascended the throne when he was a boy of twenty, and at the age of twenty he gave on the throne an example of morals; he had no criminal weaknesses nor corrupting passions. He was economical, just, severe; he showed himself always the constant friend of the people. . . . The people wanted liberty, and he gave them liberty—

The silence was broken by murmurs of approval and scattered applause—

> —And yet it is in the name of these very people that they demand to-day—. Citizens, I cannot complete it—. I pause before history; remember that it will judge your decision. . . .

Then Louis rose and said: "Citizens, you have just heard my defense. I shall add nothing to it. It is perhaps the last time that I speak to you, and I declare to you that my conscience has nothing to reproach me with. My heart is torn to hear myself accused of having shed French blood."

"You may withdraw," said the president.

On the way back to prison Louis was cheerful and joked with the secretary of the commune. "I see you wear a hat to-day; last time you forgot it." The secretary was embarrassed, and Louis shifted the conversation to the subject of hospitals. He said it would be a fine idea to establish hospitals in every section so that the poor might have good medical service. Then he asked the mayor personal questions —where he came from, what his profession was, whether he had a family, how long he had been married. An odd misunderstanding ended the talk. Seeing a threatening movement in the street, the guards outside the coach suddenly cried, *"Fermez les fenêtres!"* "That's abominable!" Louis exclaimed. "What's abominable about closing windows?" the mayor asked; "it's only a measure of safety." "Oh," Louis explained, "I thought they cried *'Vive Lafayette.'*"

CHAPTER XXVII

"Is Louis Capet guilty?"

SEVEN HUNDRED and forty-nine deputies were locked in debate on the question of what to do with Louis. They had seen the evidence and heard the king's defense, but the majority were no wiser than before. There was little in the evidence to convict Louis of high treason, and there was nothing in his conduct to persuade them of his innocence. But, as the Jacobins insisted, it was politically suicidal not to condemn Louis; matters had gone too far for backing out now. It was either Louis or the revolution—and the revolution was like Cæsar's wife.

But what to do, how to do it? Death! cried the Jacobins unanimously. The majority, however, felt repugnance against being the executioners of a man whose guilt was not absolutely established and who was evidently more of a victim than a transgressor. All willingly admitted that Louis had been weak, that he had made mistakes, even that he was no friend of the revolution; but such failings certainly did not deserve the guillotine. There were also political considerations; the responsible majority feared the appalling consequences, at home and abroad, of the execution of a king. Already half of monarchical Europe had mobilized against France, and the "armies of despotism" stood poised to strike down the home of liberty. For three weeks, therefore, the Convention was at loggerheads on the question, debating itself hoarse and fraying its nerves with the conflict of proposals and alternatives.

So deep was the ferment and so acute the realization of the historic crisis that hundreds of deputies thought it necessary to justify themselves in the eyes of the public before the judgment of history by publishing their considered opinions on the question of the king's fate. A few of these *Opinions* will show the confusion and bewilderment that reigned in the Convention, which in turn reflected the mind of the nation:

Albouys (deputy from Lot)	"Let the country decide"
Anthoine (Moselle)	"Let the Convention condemn the tyrant"
Andouin (Seine-et-Oise)	"Get rid of the royal family"
Dandenac (Loire)	"Let us exile Louis"
Artigoyte (Landes)	"Let us condemn the criminal"
Bailly (Seine-et-Marne)	"Let us banish him permanently"
Ballaud (Vosges)	"Let him be tried by a special tribunal"
Barrot (Lozère)	"Let him be deported to a distant island"
Baudin (Ardennes)	"Permanent expulsion"
Bayle (Bouches-du-Rhône)	"Let the nation vote on the sentence"
Derby (Aisne)	"Suspend judgment until after the war"
Debourges (Creuse)	"We have no right to judge him"
Delecloy (Somme)	"Six years' detention"
Desmoulins (Paris)	"Death to Caligula, the tyrant" [1]

From the welter of opinions it seemed that all the deputies were convinced that Louis was guilty of something (though not of high treason), or at least that he was not innocent, and that some punishment should be imposed, the penalty ranging from six years' imprisonment to decapitation.

And what was the opinion of the nation at large? From the letters that kept streaming into the Convention it appeared

[1] These pamphlets are to be found in Archives Nationales, ADI, 103 A, and also ADXVIII[e] 209.

that the question of Louis' fate shook the conscience of France. In the deepest sense this was a crisis of conscience; for thirty generations the nation had been welded by kings, for a thousand years its history had been monarchical. And now France stood before the gleaming knife of the guillotine and had to decide whether to let the knife drop, a bloody steel wall between her royal past and the uncertain future. Louis XVI, standing accused before the people of France, had been the sovereignty and the symbol of France, and the country was loath to convict him as a criminal.

The letters from the provinces revealed a more generous attitude toward the king than was shown by Paris. With the exception of the stereotyped communications from the Jacobin clubs (all of which clamored for "death for the tyrant"), the letters asked for mercy—imprisonment or banishment, but not death.

"If Louis has committed blunders," wrote a Bordeaux citizen, "he has been sufficiently punished by losing his throne and suffering a long imprisonment worse than death." [2]

A citizen from Rennes wrote: "Louis was weak, but he had delivered France from slavery. Should the country become the tyrant of its liberator? Let him be imprisoned until after the war. Then he should enjoy the same liberty as other citizens." [3]

The most interesting proposal came from Thomas Paine, who was a member of the Convention. Paine had urged that Louis be tried, but only to discredit the principle of monarchy. Now that the crown was in the gutter, he advised that Louis be banished. Whither? There was one country, the Anglo-American author of *Common Sense* wrote, that Louis XVI had helped to become free:

"Let the United States of America become the asylum of Louis Capet. There, under the shadow of the miseries and crimes of royal life, he will learn, from the constant con-

[2] Archives Nationales, C357, 1895, no.10.

[3] *Ibid.*, C357, 1895, no.11. A great many letters are kept in Archives Nationales, AA53, plaq.1, no.33, 37, etc.; and plaq.3, no.18, 21, 24, 25, 26, 27, etc.

templation of public prosperity, that the true system of government is not that of kings but of representation."

This letter, like the others, was read from the tribune but not discussed.

ON TUESDAY, January 15, 1793, the weary Convention decided to stop reading letters and to put an end to argument. The atmosphere had become unhealthy for debate, for the Paris mob was beginning to take the law into its hands. "I declare," shouted a burly leader of an armed gang from the sections, "that I am in a state of insurrection and that if I see an aristocrat, a Feuillant, a Rolandist, or any other cretinous creature, I'll kill him on the spot." Marat, who was a deputy, also called for blood. "Your primary duty," he told his fellow-citizens, "is to cement public liberty with the blood of the despot."

It was time to vote. There were three questions on which to vote. The first was formulated thus: "Is Louis Capet guilty of conspiracy against public liberty and of an attack upon the general security of the state?"

The roll-call began in an atmosphere vibrant with excitement. As the name of each deputy was called, he walked up to the tribune, was asked "Is Louis Capet guilty?" and said *Yes*. Of the seven hundred and twenty-one deputies present (twenty-eight were away), six hundred and eighty-three voted *Yes*. Thirty-seven qualified their vote. None voted *No*. The vote on guilt was thus unanimous.

The president of the Convention announced: "In the name of the French people, the National Convention declares Louis Capet guilty of conspiracy against public liberty and the general security of the state."

THEY PROCEEDED with the second question: "Should the sentence against Louis Capet be submitted to the people for ratification?"

Again the deputies walked up to the tribune, and again they voted, but this time with less unanimity. Many of them deposited small slips of paper qualifying their ballots. Deputy Lalande (de la Meurthe) wrote, "I declare that I am not a judge and in consequence I say neither *Yes* nor *No.*" Deputy Larailon wrote, "I am not here to judge criminals; my conscience makes me abstain from voting." Deputy Fauchet: "As a citizen, I say *Yes;* as a judge I have no right to vote." Deputy Mormon (Vendée): "I refuse to vote."[4] Others were not so scrupulous.

The total vote stood: two hundred and eighty-seven *Yes,* four hundred and twenty-four *No.*

It was ten o'clock at night when the president closed the session with the formal declaration: "The National Convention decrees that the sentence against Louis Capet will not be submitted to ratification by the people."

⚜

IN THE MORNING of January 16 began the final phase in the struggle over Louis' life. All Paris knew that the deputies had voted him guilty of conspiracy, and now the citizens streamed into the hall of the Convention for the last scene, more colorful than an opera, more exciting than a stage-play—the condemnation of a king. From early morning the galleries were packed with the curious and the cruel. Ladies *en négligée charmant* were squeezed tight against rough soldiers, workers craned heads over those of young girls, old women dug elbows into citizens. Some of the spectators were gay, a few were grave, all were silent. Many brought their lunches and dinners.

The Convention argued the phrasing of the question of penalty. One alternative was *Life or Death for Louis,* but it was rejected as not concrete. Another proposal was to split the question into three parts, each to be passed upon by a two-thirds vote: *Death?—Detention?—Deportation?* This mo-

[4] The minutes of the session and the vote-slips are in Archives Nationales, C243, 307, no.6; and C243, 313, nos.1-37.

tion was stormily debated and turned down as time-consuming.

The sun had already set when the deputies agreed upon a formula:

What penalty should be inflicted upon Louis?

And then began one of the most harrowing sessions in parliamentary history, lasting through the night, through the following day, through the night again, into the next day, uninterruptedly...

THE ROLL-CALL that night started with the names of the deputies of Haute-Garonne. There were nine deputies, and of them the first spoke the laconic *La Mort* that went through like an electric shock, and so did the second, and third, and fourth, and fifth.... It was breathlessly still in the hall. The first five for *Death*.

Then were called the seven deputies of Gers, and only one of them did not utter the words *La Mort*.

Now the famous representatives of the Gironde were called to the tribune, and every neck craned forward. Among these twelve Girondin deputies were some of the greatest leaders of the revolution (soon to lose their own heads), men of moderation, anti-Jacobins. Only yesterday their leader, Vergniaud, had sworn before friends that he would never vote for Louis' death. Now Vergniaud, at the tribune, made a little speech. "I was in favor of ratification by the people, but the Convention has decided otherwise. I obey: my conscience is clear. The law speaks—It is *Death*." And all his colleagues but two repeated "this terrible word."

The hours rolled heavily as seven hundred and twenty-one deputies, some ambitious and others patriotic, a few thoughtful and many impassioned, gave each his vote and cloaked it in a declaration of panic or principle.

The heaviest vote for death was piled up by the deputies of Paris. Only three of the twenty-four representatives of the revolutionary capital did not favor the death penalty.

The others voted *La Mort* to the accompaniment of harsh words.

Said Danton, who had promised to save Louis' life for a million francs (but had added, "I am quite willing to save his head but not to lose mine"), "I am not one of those who believe that one can make peace with tyrants without cracking their heads."

Danton's colleague, Billaud-Varenne, said curtly, "Death within twenty-four hours."

Camille Desmoulins spoke contemptuously: "I vote for death, perhaps too late to save the honor of the National Convention."

Marat orated: "Convinced that Louis is the principal author of all the massacres that have defiled France since the revolution, I vote for death within twenty-four hours."

The Parisian painter David said two words: "*La Mort*."

Robespierre delivered a long oration full of smugness: "I do not like long speeches. . . . I pride myself on understanding nothing of those logomachic principles invented to elude the evident consequences of a known principle. . . . All that I know is that we are the representatives of the people, sent by them to cement public liberty by the condemnation of the tyrant, and this is sufficient for me. . . . I vote for death."

The greatest sensation was caused by the Paris deputy Philip Égalité, ex-Duke of Orleans and cousin of Louis XVI. He had solemnly promised his friends that he would abstain from voting so as not to dishonor the family name. Now he walked up to the tribune, and every one was struck by his resemblance to his imprisoned cousin—the same moon face, the same bulging eyes, the same double chin, the same receding forehead and hooked nose. This replica of Louis XVI said in a firm voice, "Convinced that all those who have attacked the sovereignty of the people deserve death, I vote for death."

A gasp of indignation broke from the hall and the galleries. "Oh, the monster!" some one exclaimed. One deputy said

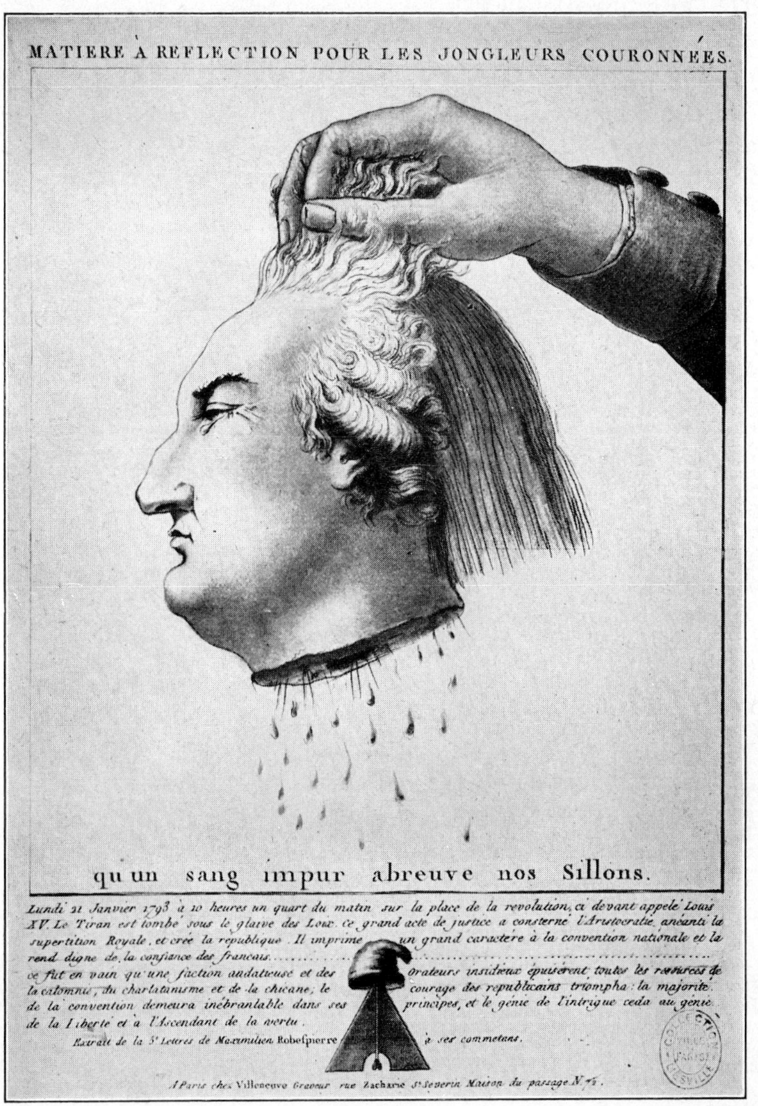

"A MATTER FOR CROWNED CHARLATANS TO PONDER"

An engraving issued shortly after Louis' execution. The text at the bottom is extracted from Maximilien Robespierre's letters to his constituents. Collection Liesville, Paris.

cynically to another, "Fortunately Louis is leaving us the one relative who can most disgust us with royalty." [5]

Comic relief was provided by the crazy Anacharsis Clootz, the self-styled Ambassador of Humanity and Orator of the Human Species, who thundered, "I also condemn to death the infamous Frederick William of Prussia."

⚜

THE VOTE was counted amidst scenes of tumult and hysteria, but when the president rose to announce the result, a pall of stillness fell over the hall.

The Convention had 749 members, the president said, and twenty-eight were absent. That left 721 voters, which meant that a simple majority should be 361.

The 721 ballots fell into four large categories: 288 voted for detention, banishment, or confinement; 46 voted for a suspended sentence of death; 26 voted for death but urged delay and public discussion; 361 voted for unconditional and immediate death.

Unconditional and immediate death had an absolute majority of one vote.[6]

"The penalty," the president announced laconically, "is *Death*." [7]

Louis' lawyers entered the hall and demanded to be heard. They carried a letter from their client protesting against the first vote, which had condemned him as guilty of conspiracy. "I owe it to my honor, I owe it to my family, not to consent to a sentence which accuses me of a crime of which I am not guilty; I shall appeal to the nation." To a Convention that

[5] Even before the revolution Parisian wits used to say that if the Duke of Orleans put up a throne in the Palais Royal and invited all those who despised him to come and pay one penny admission, he would become the richest man in the kingdom.

[6] But there were accusations of unfairness; in the confusion the clerk was inclined to register *La Mort* more frequently than it was uttered; see a protest in Archives Nationales, AA53, plaq.1, no.40.

[7] The minutes of the session are in Archives Nationales, C243, 307, no.7; and C243, 314.

had just voted the death penalty, Louis' words sounded flat, anticlimactic. De Sèze demanded a delay and protested that the penalty just voted was illegal and unconstitutional, since it was passed by a simple majority. He pointed out that the penal code required three-quarters of the vote for capital punishment.

The president replied drily, "As Louis' counsel it is your sacred duty to defend him." He promised that the Convention would take up the matter of delaying the execution.

⚜

MALESHERBES found Louis hunched over the mantelpiece. As Louis turned to see his visitor, the old man threw himself into the king's arms, sobbing, "You are condemned—."

Dry-eyed, Louis patted his friend's back. "I am not afraid of death," he said.

He asked the four commissioners in the room that he be left alone with his lawyer, and then he consoled the broken Malesherbes. "I haven't the slightest reproach to make. Do not worry. I am ready to appear before God, and I swear that I have always wanted the people's happiness." The soothed old man promised to come back to the Tower that night.

After Malesherbes had gone, Louis told his valet he wanted to shave. Suddenly, as he saw his head reflected in the basin, the thought of the guillotine overcame him; his hands trembled and his nose and ears turned white. *"Allons,"* he muttered, *"plus de courage."*[8] He steadied himself, finished shaving, and took up an old issue of the *Mercure*. Then he asked Cléry to bring him the volume of the *History of England* that described the execution of Charles I.

"To-morrow," Cléry said hopefully, "they are voting on your reprieve. Perhaps—."

"I am not hopeful," Louis said, "but what hurts me very much is that Orleans, my cousin, voted for my death."

That day the commune decreed that Louis should no longer be allowed to communicate with the outside world,

[8] Bibliothèque Nationale, MS n.a.fr., 11251, p. 11.

not even with his lawyers. When Malesherbes came to the Tower, he was not admitted. Louis was not informed of the new ruling, and he waited for his friend until late into the night. He was restless and read intermittently. Since he had been in the Tower, he told Cléry, he had read more than two hundred and fifty volumes. He wondered anxiously how many more he would have a chance to read.

⚜

ON SATURDAY, January 19, the Convention took up the question of the reprieve. The six hundred and ninety harassed deputies present were asked to decide whether it was desirable to stay the execution or not. Wearily they trudged up to the tribune and registered their votes. At three o'clock in the morning the final vote stood three hundred and ten for reprieve, three hundred and eighty against. Louis was to be executed within twenty-four hours.[9]

It rained all night and the streets were flooded. A hush of expectancy fell over the city. Some one distributed surreptitiously a few handbills on the boulevards: "People, thou art asleep! And thy king is going to die! People awake, save thy father!" Nobody paid any attention.

Sunday morning came sunless and dripping. Louis was still waiting for news and hoping to see Malesherbes when four municipal officers arrived and silently searched the room. The rain continued to fall, the hours passed. In the afternoon came General Santerre and said that Garat, the minister of justice, and Lebrun, the minister of foreign affairs, were coming up. "Good," Louis sighed, "it's my reprieve."

The members of the government were stiff and formal, wearing their hats as they faced the prisoner standing in the doorway. Garat said coldly, "Louis, the secretary will read you the minutes." At a nod, Secretary Grouvelle unrolled an official paper. "The National Convention declares Louis Capet, last king of the French, guilty of conspiracy"—Louis made a gesture of indignation—"against the liberty of the

[9] Archives Nationales, C243, 307, nos. 9-11.

nation. . . . The National Convention decrees that Louis Capet undergo the penalty of death." Within twenty-four hours.

"Monsieur," Louis spoke calmly, "I beg you to tell the Convention that I demand a delay of three days, and the right to see a priest. Wait, I shall write the request."

Hastily he scribbled on a sheet of paper:

> I demand [he crossed out "from the National Convention"] a postponement of three days in order to prepare myself to appear before the presence of God. For this I demand to see freely the person whose name I shall indicate . . . , and that this person should be protected from all trouble and all fear on account of this act of charity. . . . I demand to be delivered from the perpetual surveillance. . . . I demand during this interval to be able to see my family when I want to and without witnesses. I wish very much that the National Convention would immediately occupy itself with the fate of my family and permit them to leave freely.

Garat promised to deliver the request, and Louis handed him another slip of paper. It contained the name and address of a nonjuring Irish priest, Edgeworth de Firmont (Louis spelled it *Fermon*), 483 rue du Bac, a stone's throw from the Tuileries.

No sooner had the ministers left than Louis asked for dinner. His appetite was not blunted by the death sentence. "I see no knife," he said as he sat down at table. The municipal officer explained that he was not allowed to have any cutting implements. "Do they think me so eager to die," the prisoner asked indignantly, "that I would commit suicide?"

In the evening Garat came with an assortment of news, good and bad. He told the prisoner that he could see his family and have his confessor, but that a postponement of three days was out of the question. As for Marie Antoinette and the rest of the family, Garat explained in the pompous language of the period, "the French nation, always great, always just, will occupy itself with their fate."

ABBÉ EDGEWORTH DE FIRMONT

JEAN-BAPTISTE CLÉRY

"Take me downstairs to my family."

"We can't do that," Garat said, "but we can bring them up to you."

Louis asked the guards to move the table to the center of the chamber and the chairs to one side; he demanded a pitcher of water and glasses, in case any of the women should feel ill. The room was cleared of guards, commissioners, and even of the faithful valet. For the last time in their lives, Louis, Marie Antoinette, their children, and Madame Elizabeth were to be together, and alone.

They came up about seven o'clock. Louis waited for them at the door of the antechamber. Marie Antoinette, sobbing, embraced him. Then Louis led them into the big room and shut the door.

Husband and wife found each other changed. Marie Antoinette, although only thirty-seven, looked old, haggard, her hair gray and her skin pallid. Her eyes were filled with horror. She could not talk much. Louis' appearance also had altered. His skin had a sickly prison pallor, and he seemed hurt like a wounded animal that does not complain.

There were no witnesses to hear what was said, but Madame Royale later recalled that her father told them he was not afraid of death. He was only worried about the pain he caused his family. "He told my mother about his trial, excusing the scoundrels [Louis probably did not use that word] who made him die." He also explained that he was opposed to an appeal to the people, "because that would cause trouble in France." Then he spoke to the wide-eyed dauphin, who stood between the knees of his parents, and told him to pardon all those who were guilty of his death. The boy began to cry: he said he would go down on his knees before all the sections in Paris to obtain grace for his papa.

Two hours passed. Marie Antoinette wanted them all to spend this last night together, but Louis refused on the ground that he needed rest for to-morrow's supreme ordeal. In a choked voice she made him promise to let her come up early in the morning to say farewell. Abruptly Louis rose and opened the door. Guards and commissioners watched silently as Marie Antoinette and Madame Royale clung to Louis' arms, while the dauphin held his father's hand. "Promise," they begged, "that you will let us see you to-morrow." Louis was silent. Suddenly he turned and with a muttered "Adieu, adieu," hurried back into the room.

Marie Antoinette did not want to give the revolutionary officials the satisfaction of pitying her. She straightened up: "My son, learn from the misfortunes of your father not to avenge his death." Then she flashed a proud look at the municipal officers as if offering them royal clemency.

After the family had gone down, Louis told the guards not to let his wife and children visit him in the morning. The pain of final separation was unbearable, he said.

Abbé Edgeworth supped with Louis that night. Louis ate heartily. They talked about the morning mass and found that there were no ecclesiastical vestments and vessels in the Tower. The abbé made out a list of things he wanted, and Louis handed it to the commissioners with the request that they search the neighboring churches. And so, by a curious irony, godless revolutionaries were sent out in a rainy midnight to scour Paris for religious furniture to satisfy the soul of a condemned king. They succeeded in borrowing everything from the curé of the church of St. Francis of Assisi, and by early morning, while Louis slept soundly, the improvised altar was set up in the room.[10]

[10] Abbé Edgeworth's list called for a crucifix, a missal, a chalice, a communion cloth and pall, a paten, a purificator, an amice, an alb, a girdle, a lavabo, a maniple, a stole, a chasuble, two altar-cloths, one large and one small wafer.

CHAPTER XXVIII

"The blood of kings brings good luck!"

DURING THE NIGHT the council of the commune, sitting in a state of fear, was debating the novel business of executing and burying a king. Charles Henri Sanson, the executioner, asked, "I must know absolutely how Louis is to leave the Temple—in the ordinary tumbril? And what is to be done with the body?" It was a difficult problem to solve. The commune could not transport the king of France in a tumbril used for common criminals without cheapening the solemnity of the occasion; and there was no special tumbril for monarchs. Mayor Chambon, a physician by profession, refused to lend his coach for such a ghastly purpose, but Étienne Clavière, the minister of finance, had no objections to loaning his. As for burial, after some hesitation the commune decided that the body should be consumed in a grave of quicklime in the cemetery of the Madeleine de la Ville l'Évêque, a few minutes' walk from the place of execution.[1] When it came to the business of selecting delegates to attend the decapitation, all the councilors except an ex-priest named Jacques Roux showed their repugnance.

1 The cemetery of the Madeleine should not be confused with the Madeleine church. The latter is on the Place de la Madeleine, looking down upon the Place de la Concorde. The cemetery of the Madeleine is a small square on the rue d'Anjou (8e), near where the Boulevard Malesherbes runs into the Boulevard Hausmann; the Gare St. Lazare is only two blocks away. The whole square ("Square Louis XVI") is taken up by a chapel in memory of Louis XVI and Marie Antoinette.

The councilors were excessively jittery. They feared that on the morning of the execution some royalists would either abduct Louis or kill him to spare him the shame of public decapitation. Although there was no strong royalist party in Paris and despite the fact that the king's friends were neither organized nor otherwise active, the commune was too unsure of itself to forego an imposing military display. Perhaps it also wished to impress its power upon the waverers and political enemies. Virtually all the armed forces of the capital, some one hundred and thirty thousand men, were mobilized during the night and occupied the squares, boulevards, and bridges. The city gates were closed tight.

⚜

MONDAY MORNING, January 21, dawned wet and chilly. The air over the city was oppressive, a compound of dripping sky and emotional tension. Somewhere a humble citizen was writing to the Convention, begging for the privilege of taking the place of the king on the scaffold. In one of the workers' sections the butcher Louis Legendre demanded that Louis' body be cut into eighty-four pieces to be distributed to all the departments of France. In a Paris café a royalist named Pâris walked up to deputy Louis Lepeletier de Saint-Fargeau, who had voted for the immediate execution of the king, and stabbed him to death. Louis for Louis!

Louis woke at dawn after a good night's sleep and called for the valet to light a fire and raise the curtains. "I need daylight," he said; "the events of yesterday have fatigued me. Where is Abbé Firmont?"

"On my bed, Sire."

"Will you be able to serve at mass?"

"Yes, Sire."

The valet helped Louis dress and started to comb his hair. With a detachment that was terrifying, Louis told Cléry exactly how to do his hair—to raise it and braid it in such a way that the nape would be clear of hair. Satisfied

EXPIATORY CHAPEL OF LOUIS XVI AND MARIE ANTOINETTE

With the tombs of the Swiss guards killed on August 10, 1792. Completed in 1826, under the restored Bourbons. Square Louis XVI, on the site of the old cemetery of the Madeleine, rue d'Anjou, Paris.

that his neck was ready for the knife of the guillotine, Louis called for the abbé to begin the mass.

From the distance came the muffled beat of the tambours.

After communion Louis made his last arrangements as coolly as if he were clearing up before going on a little pleasure trip. He put aside his books, arranged his papers neatly, gathered all his money (about three thousand livres) in one pile, and emptied his pockets. On the money he carefully put a label: "For M. de Malesherbes." From the drawer he took a few locks of hair and wrapped them meticulously; on top he wrote, "Hair of my wife, my sister, and my children." He detached from the watch-chain the silver signet bearing the escutcheon of France and the initials LL and marked it for his son. Then he slipped his golden wedding-ring off his finger and summoned Cléry. "Give the ring to the queen. I part from it in grief."

The drum-beats were coming from the courtyard, and the commissioners were climbing the stairs.

"Tell the queen," Louis said to the valet, "that I beg her pardon for not having her come up. I wanted to spare her the pain of so cruel a separation."

It was 8:30 when General Santerre and the commissioners, among whom was the gloating Jacques Roux, came to fetch the prisoner. The tambours beat uninterruptedly.

Louis asked for three minutes to get ready. He wanted to have a few words alone with his confessor and to get his Testament. Jacques Roux refused to take the Testament. "I am here," he said brutally, "to conduct you to the scaffold, not to do your errands."[2]

"Quite right," Louis said, and gave the paper to another commissioner. He turned to Santerre: "Let us go. I am ready."

As they crossed the chamber, Louis said, "Gentlemen, I beg you to recommend to the commune all those in my

[2] These words have been disputed, yet they rest on good authority—that of Roux himself and of Santerre. Their report may be found in Arsenal MS 6943: "Derniers momens de Louis Seize." Also in Bibliothèque Nationale, n.a.Fr., 11251, p.36. See likewise *Le Moniteur* for January 23, 1793.

service, and especially to let Cléry serve the queen"—he checked himself and corrected—"my wife."

The carriage was waiting in the courtyard. Louis exclaimed in surprise: "It isn't a tumbril!"

⚜

In his brown overcoat and three-cornered hat, Louis looked like a placid, comfortable bourgeois as he mounted the carriage. On his left sat Abbé Edgeworth and in front were two gendarmes. Slowly, to the uninterrupted beating of the tambours, the coach rolled out into the rue du Temple and was instantly surrounded by twelve hundred grim-faced soldiers.

They drove through a ghost city. So far as the eye could see, through the whole length of the boulevards, walls of men, double and triple walls, stood silently under arms. Between the Tower and the Place de la Révolution there was not a foot of unguarded space. There were no other human beings on the streets—neither women nor children nor living animals. Doors were closed and windows shuttered. Nobody stirred, nothing was heard except marching feet and the funereal tom-tom of the tambours.

Even the stone walls of the city bore testimony that on this day a "tyrant" was being executed, for placards, posted at the order of the mayor, stared down upon the silent chain of guards and the slowly rolling solitary carriage:

> The sword of justice is going to strike the greatest and most guilty of conspirators. In the course of this long trial you [Parisians] have preserved the calm that befits free men; you will know how to keep it during the execution of the tyrant. You will prove by your behavior that an act of justice does not resemble an act of vengeance. This day will be a memorable example, for kings and for nations alike, of the just chastisement of despots and the dignity which a sovereign people ought to preserve in the exercise of its power.

The "tyrant" was as silent as the city, sitting still, looking neither to the right of him nor to the left of him, his fingers around a breviary. A momentary disturbance, like a pebble dropping into a lake, interrupted the awful stillness and was quickly drowned. As the coach passed the Porte St. Denis, the unbalanced Baron de Batz and two desperate young royalists broke through the guards and cried, "To us, Frenchmen! To us, those who want to save their king!" The words were received, by the few who heard them, in wooden silence. Swiftly the two royalists were hacked to pieces: not even their names have been preserved. De Batz escaped. It was all done with such cool efficiency that few noticed anything amiss. Louis himself was unaware that two young fools had given their lives for him. A carved image he sat, absorbed in wordless prayer.

AT A QUARTER PAST TEN the coach rolled down the rue Royale towards the Place de la Révolution. The enormous square was packed with armed men, standing shoulder to shoulder, in massive checkerboard squares.[3] They opened a narrow path to enable the coach to glide through to the guillotine, which stood solitary in the center of the square, facing the Tuileries—"so that in his last moments the criminal should contemplate the palace of his ancestors."

Not till the carriage halted at the foot of the platform did Louis look up. He closed the breviary, keeping one finger on the page, and said to the abbé, "We have arrived, unless I am mistaken." Calmly he reopened the book and finished reading the last prayer. Then he handed the breviary to the abbé and stepped out briskly. For the first time he looked around and saw a massed forest of heads without visible limit, and horsemen like statues guarding the immediate vicinity of the "machine." Louis glanced at the platform, which was

[3] Every approach to the great square was guarded by cannon. There were four cannon at the rue de la Révolution, four at the entrance to the garden of the Tuileries, four at the rue St. Florentin, one at the rue des Champs Elyseés (to-day rue Boissy d'Anglais: where the American Embassy abuts), four at the route de Neuilly (to-day Avenue des Champs Elysées), two in the garden of the Tuileries, two at the head of the Pont de la Liberté (to-day Pont de la Concorde).

a foot above his head, and then higher up, at the slender wooden rectangle standing upright and austere, holding a gleaming knife in its upper frame. He turned away and in a burst of imperiousness shouted at the drummers, "Shut up!" They stopped suddenly, while Louis coolly ascended the steps to the platform.

At the foot of the upright, near the wicker basket, three executioner's assistants tried to seize the condemned man's arms, but Louis pushed them aside and unaided removed his coat. Sixty thousand pairs of strained eyes watched as the prisoner untied his hair and undid his cravat. His *sang froid* was breath-taking, and every one held his breath as Louis unbuttoned his shirt and opened it wide to expose his neck and shoulders. One executioner gripped his wrist. "What do you want?" Louis shook him off with a flip. "To tie you." "Tie me?" he cried. "Never! What's more it's useless, I am sure of myself." The *bourreaux* surrounded him threateningly. "No, no, you are wasting your time. I shall never let you tie me." The executioners looked around for help, fearful of a tussle with the prisoner, whose physical strength was prodigious, but determined to do their duty. But already Louis was weakening. He looked appealingly to the abbé, and the latter, his eyes moist, nodded. "Do what you like," said the condemned man.

They tied his hands behind his back with a handkerchief and cut his hair. Abbé Edgeworth embraced him and told him to ascend.... Firmly Louis walked up the two or three rough-hewn steps leading to the *lunette* with its hollowed-out neck-rest. Just before he was to lie down, he hurled away the nearest executioner with a shove of his elbow and turned suddenly to the ocean of upturned strained faces. "Frenchmen," he cried in a voice vibrant with despair, "I die innocent—" [4] Madly Santerre ordered the drums to drown out his

[4] There are many versions of Louis' last appeal. Some accounts have it as: "I am lost; I die innocent; I forgive my enemies." Other versions say: "I am

THE EXECUTION OF LOUIS XVI IN THE PLACE DE LA RÉVOLUTION

After an engraving by Monnet.

voice. As they fitted the neck into the groove, directly under the patient knife,[5] Louis cried chokingly, "May my blood cement the happiness of the Fr—"

The tambours beat uninterruptedly.

The executioner leaned over the basket and firmly picked up the severed head. He raised it on high and walked along the four sides of the platform, showing it to the sovereign people. And then, as the blood dripped slowly to the ground, a terrifying shout broke from thousands of throats:

Vive la république!

And they rushed to the platform and fought wildly for every drop of blood oozing from the still warm body, to dip their handkerchiefs and scarves and even pieces of paper. Some one raised the shrill cry:

"Republicans, the blood of kings brings good luck!"

The dam of hysteria broke loose, and men embraced, and they sang intoxicating songs of liberty and danced riotously around the guillotine.

An hour later the commissioners appointed by the commune to attend the execution and witness the burial made their dry report:

In our presence the corpse of Louis Capet was brought to the Madeleine cemetery by the gendarmes. We have recognized the corpse in all its members; the head was separated from the trunk. We observed that the hair back of the head was cut, and that the corpse was without a necktie,[6] without a coat and without shoes. For the rest, he was dressed in a shirt, a stitched waist-

innocent; posterity will avenge me." All eyewitnesses agree upon the words, "Frenchmen, I die innocent." As for Abbé Edgeworth's famous last words to Louis, "Son of St. Louis, ascend to heaven!" that is a legend manufactured by the royalists. The abbé himself later denied the phrase, and no contemporary witness recorded it.

5 An Associated Press dispatch of February 4, 1936, told that the guillotine knife that killed Louis XVI was sold at auction in Paris for 2,500 francs (then about $167). However, the Tussaud Museum in London also claims to possess the original knife—and there was only one knife.

6 It is not certain whether the commissioners were indulging in irony at the expense of the beheaded man—"without a necktie"!—or whether they were just thoughtless.

coat, breeches of gray cloth, and stockings of gray silk. Thus clad, he was laid in a coffin, which was put in the grave, and immediately covered [with quicklime].[7]

Twenty-two years later, when the Bourbons were restored to the throne, they tried to give their brother decent burial. But all that could be found of Louis XVI was a handful of chalky mud.

[7] Archives Nationales, C182, CII, no.103.

APPENDICES

APPENDIX I

Louis XVI's Testament[1]

IN THE NAME of the very holy Trinity, Father, Son and Holy Ghost—. To-day, the 25th day of December, 1792, I, Louis XVI, king of France, being for more than four months imprisoned with my family in the Tower of the Temple at Paris, by those who were my subjects, and deprived of all communication whatsoever, even with my family, since the eleventh instant; moreover, involved in a trial, the end of which it is impossible to foresee, on account of the passions of men, and for which one can find neither pretext nor means in any existing law, and having no other witness for my thoughts than God to whom I can address myself—

I hereby declare, in His presence, my last wishes and feelings.

I leave my soul to God, my creator; I pray Him to receive it in His mercy, not to judge it according to its merits but according to those of Our Lord Jesus Christ who has offered Himself as a sacrifice to God His Father for us other men, no matter how hardened, and for me first.

I die in communion with our Holy Mother, the Catholic, apostolic, Roman Church, which holds authority, by an uninterrupted succession, from St. Peter, to whom Jesus Christ entrusted it; I believe firmly and I confess all that is contained in the creed and the commandments of God and the Church, the sacraments

1 The original is displayed in a glass case in the Museum of the Archives Nationales at Paris. Written on December 25, 1792, it was handed by Louis to Baudrais, a municipal officer, on January 21, 1793, a few seconds before he left for the guillotine. Baudrais immediately signed his name to it and in the afternoon of the same day deposited it with the commune, where it was signed and certified by Coulombeau, the secretary, and Durouet, the vice-president. These signatures are visible in the accompanying illustration.

and the mysteries, those which the Catholic Church teaches and has always taught. I never pretended to set myself up as a judge of the various way of expounding the dogmas which rend the church of Jesus Christ; but I agree and will always agree, if God grant me life, with the decisions which the ecclesiastical superiors of the Holy Catholic Church give and will always give, in conformity with the discipline which the Church has followed since Jesus Christ.

I pity with all my heart our brothers who may be in error; but I do not claim to judge them, and I do not love them the less in Christ, as our Christian charity teaches us, and I pray to God to pardon all my sins. I have sought scrupulously to know them, to detest them and to humiliate myself in His presence. Not being able to obtain the ministration of a Catholic priest, I pray God to receive the confession which I have made, and above all the profound repentance which I feel in having put my name (although this was against my will) to acts which might be contrary to the discipline and the belief of the Catholic church, to which I have always remained sincerely attached. I pray God to receive my firm resolution, if He grants me life, to have the ministrations of a Catholic priest, as soon as I can, in order to confess my sins and to receive the sacrament of penance.

I beg all those whom I might have offended inadvertently (for I do not recall having knowingly offended any one), or those whom I may have given bad examples or scandals, to pardon the evil which they believe I could have done them.

I beseech those who have the kindness to join their prayers to mine, to obtain pardon from God for my sins.

I pardon with all my heart those who made themselves my enemies, without my having given them any cause, and I pray God to pardon them, as well as those who, through false or misunderstood zeal, did me much harm.

I commend to God my wife and my children, my sister, my aunts, my brothers, and all those who are attached to me by ties of blood or by whatever other means. I pray God particularly to cast eyes of compassion upon my wife, my children, and my sister, who suffer with me for so long a time, to sustain them with His mercy if they shall lose me, and as long as they remain in this mortal world.

I commend my children to my wife; I have never doubted her maternal tenderness for them. I enjoin her above all to make them good Christians and honest individuals; to make them view the grandeurs of this world (if they are condemned to experi-

Première Archives Nationales

Reg.e A.2. f.o 17. N.o 103. +

Au nom de la tres Sainte Trinité du Pere du Fils et du S.t Esprit. Aujourd'hui vingt cinquieme jour de Decembre, mil sept cent quatre vingt douze. Moi Louis XVI.e du nom Roy de France, etant depuis plus de quatre mois enfermé avec ma famille dans la Tour du Temple a Paris, par ceux qui etoient mes sujets, et privé de toutte communication quelconque, mesme depuis le onze du courant avec ma famille. de plus impliqué dans un Procès, dont il est impossible de prevoir l'issue a cause des passions des hommes, et dont on ne trouve aucun pretexte ni moyen dans aucune Loy existante, n'ayant que Dieu pour temoin de mes pensées, et auquel je puisse m'adresser. je declare ici en sa presence mes dernieres volontés et mes sentiments.

Je finis en declarant devant Dieu et prest a paroitre devant Lui que je ne me reproche aucun des crimes qui sont avancés contre moi. Fait double a la tour du Temple le 25 Decembre 1792.

Louis

Paraphé et Vû au conseil ce 21 Janvier 179

LOUIS XVI'S TESTAMENT

The opening paragraph and the last three lines. Archives Nationales, Paris.

ence them) as very dangerous and transient goods, and turn their attention towards the one solid and enduring glory, eternity. I beseech my sister kindly to continue her tenderness for my children and to take the place of a mother, should they have the misfortune of losing theirs.

I beg my wife to forgive all the pain which she suffered for me, and the sorrows which I may have caused her in the course of our union; and she may feel sure that I hold nothing against her, if she has anything with which to reproach herself.

I most warmly enjoin my children that, after what they owe to God, which should come first, they should remain forever united among themselves, submissive and obedient to their mother, and grateful for all the care and trouble which she has taken with them, as well as in memory of me. I beg them to regard my sister as their second mother.

I exhort my son, should he have the misfortune of becoming king, to remember that he owes himself wholly to the happiness of his fellow-citizens; that he should forget all hates and all grudges, particularly those connected with the misfortunes and sorrows which I am experiencing; that he can make the people happy only by ruling according to the laws; but at the same time to remember that a king cannot make himself respected and do the good that is in his heart unless he has the necessary authority, and that otherwise, being tangled up in his activities and not inspiring respect, he is more harmful than useful.

I exhort my son to care for all the persons who were attached to me, as much as his circumstances will allow; to remember that it is a sacred debt which I have contracted towards the children and relatives of those who have perished for me and also those who are wretched for my sake. I know that there are many persons, among those who were near me, who did not conduct themselves towards me as they should have and who have even shown ingratitude; but I pardon them (often in moments of trouble and turmoil one is not master of oneself), and I beg my son that, if he finds an occasion, he should think only of their misfortunes.

I should have wanted here to show my gratitude to those who have given me a true and disinterested affection; if, on the one hand, I was keenly hurt by the ingratitude and disloyalty of those to whom I have always shown kindnesses, as well as to their relatives and friends, on the other hand I have had the consolation of seeing the affection and voluntary interest which many persons have shown me. I beg them to receive my thanks.

In the situation in which matters still are, I fear to compromise them if I should speak more explicitly; but I especially enjoin my son to seek occasions to recognize them.

I should, nevertheless, consider it a calumny on the nation if I did not openly recommend to my son MM. de Chamilly and Hue, whose genuine attachment for me led them to imprison themselves with me in this sad abode. I also recommend Cléry, for whose attentiveness I have nothing but praise ever since he has been with me. Since it is he who has remained with me until the end, I beg the gentlemen of the commune to hand over to him my clothes, my books, my watch, my purse, and all other small effects which have been deposited with the council of the commune.

I pardon again very readily those who guard me, the ill treatment and the vexations which they thought it necessary to impose upon me. I found a few sensitive and compassionate souls among them—may they in their hearts enjoy the tranquillity which their way of thinking gives them.

I beg MM. de Malesherbes, Tronchet, and De Sèze to receive all my thanks and the expressions of my feeling for all the cares and troubles they took for me.

I finish by declaring before God, and ready to appear before Him, that I do not reproach myself with any of the crimes with which I am charged.

Made in duplicate in the Tower of the Temple, the 25th of December, 1792.

LOUIS

APPENDIX II

Pamphlets and Public Opinion

THE FRENCH being an articulate people, they fought their great Revolution also with the sharp pen. From 1787 on, the country was flooded with pamphlets on every problem that confronted the nation. Although poorly printed and crudely stated, these brochures had the force and passion of a powerful cause. They varied in size from four pages to forty and in method from persuasion to frenzy. As a barometer of public opinion the pamphlets, taken in the large, are uncannily reliable: they enable one to measure the crest and the trough of popular feeling. For example, when Louis XVI was put on trial there promply appeared about ninety pamphlets (at least the Bibilothèque Nationale, LB 39f, lists that number only), most of them favoring execution. An analysis of four hundred and fifteen pamphlets that appeared between 1787 and 1793 gives some interesting results: Until 1790 the pamphlets are almost all favorable to Louis XVI; in 1790 opinion was beginning to shift against the king; in the latter part of 1791, after Varennes, the pamphlets voice loud distrust; in 1792 the volume of criticism swells, until early in 1793 there is an almost universal clamor for death of the "tyrant."

Below are listed some of the pamphlets, together with an occasional quotation to illustrate the savor and the mood.

1789

"Un petit mot à Louis XVI sur les crimes de ses vertus" (30 pp.), by the counter-revolutionary journalist F. L. Suleau.

"Louis XVI le bienfaisant" (20 pp.).

"Générosité du Roi envers les citoyens" (7 pp.).

"L'aventure extraordinaire, arrivée à notre bon Roi Louis XVI."

1790

"Peuple François, vous êtes trompé" (39 pp.).
"Qu'ils sont bêtes ces français!" (75 pp.), by Comte Du Prat.
"Les imitateurs de Charles Neuf, ou les conspirateurs foudroyés" (127 pp.).
"Résurrection de Louis XVI, roi des juifs et des françois" (30 pp.).
"Le roi trompé et détrompé, ou les bonnes leçons, Histoire Indienne" (42 pp.).
"La passion et la mort de Louis XVI, roi des juifs et des Chrétiens" (Jerusalem, 1790).
"La passion de 1790, ou Louis XVI sacrifié pour et par son peuple" (24 pp.).

1791

"Le roi traité comme il le mérite."
"Louis XVI, roi des français, detroné par lui-meme."
"Sera-t-il roi, ne le sera-t-il pas?"
"Les régicides."
"Lettre d'un homme libre à Louis XVI, premier agent de la nation française," contains the following conclusion:

"Formerly, although endowed with some virtues, you have been nothing but the oppressor of a people, whose father you wanted to be. Henceforth, without any talent, you will become the protector of a nation, of which you will be only an agent.... Renounce, therefore, the imposing titles, odious titles of monarch and tyrant; exchange, if necessary, the royal purple for the mantle of the philosopher; leave the crowd of kings for the seat of the sages.... Renounce for ever the desire to command subjects...."

"Louis XVI et Antoinette, traités comme ils le méritent" (16 pp.) is an unrestrained attack on both Louis and Marie Antoinette ("the shame of her sex"). It was written after the return from Varennes:

"O cowardly deserter! We forced thee to return. Come before the bar of the Assembly, come to hear your sentence. O traitor and perjurer, thou hast violated the most sacred oaths! Thou hast condemned thyself.... O Henri IV, shade of a beloved king! Thy successor Louis XVI has become in our eyes a new Caligula. They say, he knows not what he is doing! Until when ought we to have a king so imbecile?... Until when ought we to suffer by his side that Messalina, that tigress thirsty for blood... who enjoys washing her hands in the blood of the subjects of her husband.... Think, unbridled Megara, that thy pride, thy rage and thy infernal projects will be nothing but smoke to us.... O Louis XVI! vain ghost of a king, colossus too imposing, whose head was once hidden in the clouds and whose feet were often covered with blood, fall never to rise again...."

1792

"Adresse urgente aux habitans de Paris. Sur le projet de déchéance du roi" (4 pp.).

"Reproches de Louis XVI à son peuple" (16 pp.).

"Popule meus! Quid tibi feci?" is a desperately pathetic pro-royalist cry:

"O my people, what have I done to you, and why do you overwhelm me with bitterness? Is it because I recalled the Parlements...? Is it because I surrounded myself with honest ministers ...? Is it because I, a grandson of Louis XV, lived in the greatest frugality...? Is it because I protected American Liberty...? Is it because I gave you liberty by doubling the Third Estate...? Is it because I came to Paris, without guard...? Is it because I sanctioned all the decrees of your representatives...? My people, open your eyes...."

1793

"Républicains, guillotinez-moi ce Jean-Foutre de Louis XVI, et cette putain de Marie Antoinette" (8 pp.).

"Prière pour le roi" (4 pp.). This was distributed shortly before Louis XVI's execution; but the watchful agents of the Surété Générale confiscated all the sheets.

"Save the king, O my God, from the hands of his enemies and deliver him from those who rose against him.... Save him from the men who are hungry for his blood, who seek to devour him.... Rise, O my God, and fly to his aid..."

APPENDIX III

Bibliography

THE BULK of this book is based upon materials drawn from the archives of Europe, especially France. The most valuable information was derived from the Archives Nationales in Paris, although this great depot of documents possesses but few of the private papers and official letters of Louis XVI, most of which seem to have been somehow destroyed in the turmoil of the Revolution. In the Bibliothèque Nationale in Paris (Salle des Manuscrits), as well as in the Bibliothèque de l'Arsenal, the author found much material on the personal life of Louis XVI. The archives of Vienna and London likewise contributed their quota. Altogether the MS stuff in Paris was difficult to locate but not hard to obtain once it was located. In the archives of Vienna and London the task was made easier by the generous coöperation of the archivists, and the author wishes to take this opportunity to express his warm appreciation of the courtesy shown him by the Austrian and English archivists.

Below are listed the titles of the MSS, their reference numbers, and comments on their contents.

I. BIBILIOGRAPHIC GUIDES

Archives Nationales.—*État sommaire par séries des documents conservés aux archives nationales* (Paris, 1891).

—*Inventaires et documents. Inventaire sommaire et tableau méthodique des fonds conservées aux archives nationales.* Ier partie: *Régime antérieur à 1789* (Paris, 1871).

Bibliothèque Nationale.—*Catalogue de l'histoire de France* (Département des imprimés de la Bibliothèque Nationale, 12 vols., Paris, 1855-95). Vol. II: *Louis XIV à Louis XVI.*

——*Catalogue de l'histoire de France. Table générale alphabétique des ouvrages anonymes.* I: *Table des noms de personnes;* III: *L-M* (photostat).

CARON, P.—*Manuel pratique pour l'étude de la révolution française* (Paris, 1912).

*Catalogue d'une collection révolutionnaire, formée par feu M. le Marquis D'A * * * ** [*lbon*]. *Pièces historiques, ouvrages, pamphlets, almanachs, journaux et estampes, relatifs à la révolution, à Louis XVI, à Marie-Antoinette, et à la famille royale.* (*Vente des 19 au 23 novembre 1917, Hotel Drouot.*)

FORTESCUE, G. K.—*List of the Contents of the Three Collections of Books, Pamphlets and Journals in the British Museum Relating to the French Revolution* (London, 1899).

GRANEL, A.—*Louis XVI et la famille royale. Catalogue annonçant les titres de 3,000 volumes* (Paris, 1905). (Mainly sermons, martyrologies, verse, funeral orations, prayers, etc.)

LADOUÉ, P.—*Les panégyristes de Louis XVI et de Marie-Antoinette depuis 1793 jusqu'en 1912* (Paris, 1912). (A bibliographic essay without plan or method.)

Les manuscrits relatifs à l'histoire de la révolution et de l'empire dans les bibliothèques publiques des départements (Société de l'histoire de la Révolution Française, XXXIV, 1913).

TOURNEUX, M.—*Marie-Antoinette devant l'histoire. Essai bibliographique* (2d ed., Paris, 1901). (Lists 459 titles.)

II. DOCUMENTS

Archives Nationales, Paris

"Documents sur le séjour de Louis XVI au Temple, sur divers personnages ayant figurés dans son procès, sur plusieurs membres de la Convention nationale et sur certains événements de la Révolution à Lyon." (Seven fascicles in one box.) —AA53

"Bibliothèque Administrative. Louis XVI et famille royale. A. Actes et discours du Roi. B. Adresses et pétitions au Roi." (Printed pamphlets, laws, etc.) —AD^{I} 74-76

"Bibliothèque Administrative. Régime administratif et politique. Lettres du Roi et des Ministres, 1789-1790." (Printed letters and declarations.) —AD^{I} 98-99

"Bibliothèque Administrative. (Septembre 1792): Procès de Louis XVI (Opinions des députés A-F). —AD^{I} 103-06

"Procès de Louis XVI: Opinions des députés." (Fourteen bound volumes.) —ADXVIII^{e} 209-22

"Archives Nationales: Armoire de Fer. Inventaire, 1884." (A list of the contents in the *Armoire de Fer.*) —AE^{I}

"Procès-verbaux des assemblées nationales et pièces annexes. Convention nationale." (Papers seized in the Tuileries and other documents used in the trial.) —C182-87

"Convention nationale. Lettres et papiers trouvés... dans l'appartement de... Sainte Foy." —C219

"Convention Nationale. Papiers des Tuileries." (Four boxes of letters from and to Louis XVI.) —C220-23

"Convention Nationale. Papiers des Tuileries." Letters, addresses, and petitions on the subject of the king's trial.) —C243

"Comité de sûreté générale. Procès de Louis XVI." —F^7 4388

"Comité de sûreté générale. Pièces sur la famille royale." —F^7 4389

"Comité de sûreté générale. Pièces trouvés chez La Porte." —F^7 4390^3

"Police Générale. Comité de sûreté générale. Commission des 24: Prison du Temple." —F^7 4391

"Cartons des rois: Louis XVI." (Letters, bills, reports.) —K 159-62

"Cartons des rois: Correspondance de M. le Comte de Vergennes... 1774-87." —K 163-64

"Monuments historiques. Lois et arrêts: Quittances, mandements, ordonnances..., Louis XVI, 1774-92." (Formal laws and decrees.)—K 2425

"Mémoirs et plans pour servir au voyage du roi en Cherbourg, 1786." (A MS of 86 pp., containing the itinerary and six maps.)—KK 1085

"Mélanges: Guerre." (A letter from Louis XVI to Pétion.)—M 655, no. 3

Bibliothèque de l'Arsenal, Paris

"Recueil d'extraits pour l'éducation du comte d'Artois." (Two small volumes of extracts from Artois' private library: used by Louis XVI and his brothers.) —2324-25

"État des chasses de la Reine et Monseigneur comte d'Artois pour le sanglier pendant l'année 1784, 1785, 1786, 1787, 1788." (Five booklets, containing detailed accounts of the chase.) —2712-15

"Catalogue de livres, provenant de chez Louis Capet condamné, District et commune de Versailles, Dépot C." —5389-91

"Pièces relatives à l'histoire de Paris pendant la Révolution 1787-1800." (Miscellaneous documents and songs.) —6316

"Recueil de pièces relatives à l'époque révolutionnaire, à l'Empire et au gouvernement de Juillet." (Contains, among other things, a copy of Louis XVI's Testament, his last-moment conversation, as well as a list of the Conventionnels who voted for his death.)—6943

"Pièces fugitives composées sous le règne du parlement de 1771." (Miscellaneous stuff, especially on public opinion.) —7590

Bibliothèque Nationale (Salle des Manuscrits), Paris

"Recueil de pièces originales comptables ordonnées par le trésorier général de la liste civile." (Mainly financial bills.) —Fr. 10418

"Procès verbal des grâces accordées par Sa Majesté [Louis XVI] à l'occasion de son sacre, 1775." (A bound MS of 477 leaves.)—Fr. 10983

"Journal des événements survenus à Paris, du 2 avril au 8 octobre 1789; analyse des comptes rendus des séances de l'Assemblée nationale..., par un clerc du procureur au Châtelet." (419 pp.) —Fr. 13712

"Essay sur la vie de Monseigneur Louis Dauphin mort à Fontainebleau le 20e de décembre en 1765, par M. l'Abbé Soldini, confesseur de Mme la Dauphine." (72 pp.) —Fr. 13784

"Mémoire sur la suspension faite dans la Maison du Roy, décembre 1780." (77 pp.) —Fr. 14130

"Instructions, sous forme de lettre, adressées au duc de Berry, plus tard Louis XVI, par son confesseur, l'abbé Soldini." (30 pp.) —Fr. 14714

"Première conversation avec Mgr. le duc de Berry [Louis XVI], le 1er avril 1763, et le plan général des instructions que je me propose de lui donner, par l'abbé Soldini." (54 pp. At the bottom of the title-page Soldini wrote: "Ces conversations m'ont été communiquées par M. l'abbé Berthier frère du P. Berthier son héritier, lequels Berthiers les avoit reçues du m. le duc de la Vauguyon 1784.) —Fr. 14715

"Quittances et pièces diverses: mandements royaux, quittances, mémoires, comptes, etc." (271 leaves, mainly bills.) —Fr. 26262

"Catalogue alphabétique des 'Livres du boudoir' de la reine Marie Antoinette." (19 pp.) —N.a.fr. 1699

"Catalogues de la bibliothèque de la reine Marie Antoinette (1792): Livres de la Reine. Noms des auteurs avec le titre de leurs ouvrages." (2 vols., 42 pp. and 102 pp.) —N.a.fr. 2512-13

"Analyses, inventaires et extraits des dépêches des ambassadeurs impériaux en France (1486-1793), conservés aux archives impériaux de Vienne et recueillies par Jules Flammermont." —N.a.fr. 6946

"Extraits des dépêches des ambassadeurs impériaux en France (1715-1792)." (Copies of Mercy's dispatches in the Vienna archives, made by Jules Flammermont; eight volumes of this collection deal with the reign of Louis XVI. This is by far the richest source on the politics and personalities of the reign.) —N.a.fr. 6957-64

"Analyses de dépêches de Mercy-Argenteau (1766-94)." (425 pp.). —N.a.fr. 6966

"Documents relatifs à Florimond de Mercy-Argenteau." (88 pp. Papers dealing with Mercy's family.) —N.a.fr. 6965

"Dépêches de Mercy-Argenteau (1766-94)." (275 pp.)—N.a.fr. 6967-68

"Dépêches de Goltz et Alvensleben (1777-88)." (613 pp. The dispatches of the Prussian ambassadors in Paris.) —N.a.fr. 6969

"Journal et correspondance de l'abbé Louis-Nicolas Maudoux, confesseur de Louis XV et de Marie-Antoinette (1776-78)." (3 vols., but not very important.) —N.a.fr. 10852-54

"Appel nominal. Extrait du Procès verbal de la séance permanente de la Convention nationale des 16 et 17 janvier 1793, l'an 2me de la République sur cette question: Quelle peine sera infligée à Louis?" (154 pp., containing names, votes, and comments of each deputy.) —N.a.fr. 11250

"Derniers moments de Louis XVI. Détail de ce qui s'est passé depuis sa communication avec sa famille jusqu'à son exécution." (74 pp., probably written by Cléry.) —N.a.fr. 11251

"Dépenses de la cour, 1776: Ce compte de la cour de France et de l'ancienne cour de Pologne a été parafé apostillé par Louis XVI." (110 pp.) —N.a.fr. 21206

"Journal des principales époques du règne de Louis XVI: Papiers de Lefèvre d'Amércourt." (2 vols., beginning July, 1774.) —N.a.fr. 22110-11

British Museum, London

"Description et relation de tout ce que a été fait et de ce que s'est passé à l'occasion du mariage de Louis Auguste Dauphin de France avec Marie-Antoinette . . . , par De La Ferté, Intendant des Menus." (A bound MS of 223 pp.) —Add. MSS 20707

"Royal Autographs: Letter of Louis Augustus, Dauphin, to ?, 23 August, 1765." —Add. MSS 21509, fol. 58

"Copies of Official Letters . . . enclosed in Dispatches of English ambassadors to . . . Duke of Leeds, Secretary of State, 1782-1794: 1, Papers relating to the negotiation with France and Spain, 1782, 1783; 2, 'Memoire secret' on the state of France, and the projects of the comte d'Artois, 14 December, 1789." —Add. MSS 28068

"Relation de Monsieur de Durler capitaine au Regiment des Gardes-Suisses et commandant environ 500 hommes qui se sont défendus sur l'escalier de la Chapelle et dans l'interieur du château, le 10 août 1792." (8 pp.) —Add. MSS 32168

"Song, 'Amour, fuis loin de moi,' with pianoforte accompaniment by Marie Antoinette," (Holograph, 2 quarto pp.)—Add. MSS 33966

"The Auckland Papers; correspondence and papers, political and private, of William Eden, First Baron Auckland."—Add. MSS 34-438

Public Record Office, London

"State Papers: Foreign. Lord Stormont, April, 1774-1778." (15 vols. of extremely important dispatches of the British ambassador in France.) —SP 78, vols. 292-306

Haus- Hof- und Staats-Archiv, Vienna

"Reisen S(ein)er Majestät nach Paris und durch die Schweiz von 1777. Journal." (3 folio volumes.)

"Frankreich, Hofcorrespondenz, 1716-1791, faszikel 6
" " 1715-1792, faszikel 7
" " 1716-1792, faszikel 8

III. BOOKS

There is no pretense to completeness in this list of published books. The author has consulted only a small number of the books on the Revolution, mainly those which in his opinion contained new or illuminating information. Needless to add, only those books which have actually been used are listed below.

ALBINI, F. de.—*Marie Antoinette and the Diamond Necklace, from Another Point of View* (London, 1900). (A rather worthless and credulous story.)

ALIONVILLE, A. F. d'.—*Mémoires secrets de 1770 à 1830* (Paris, 1838). (Only the first two volumes are pertinent.)

ANCÉLON, E. A.—*La vérité sur la fuite et l'arrestation de Louis XVI à Varennes* (1866). (One version of this subject.)

ARGENSON.—*Journal et mémoires du Marquis d'Argenson* (9 vols., Paris, 1865-67). (Vols. IV, VII, VIII, IX have some information on Louis XVI's childhood.)

ARNAUD-BOUTELOUP, Mme.—*Le rôle politique de Marie Antoinette* (Paris, 1924). (A good study of a neglected subject.)

ARNETH, A. v.—*Maria-Theresia und Marie Antoinette, Ihr Briefwechsel während der Jahre 1770-1780* (Paris and Vienna, 1865). (One of Arneth's indispensable works.)

——— *Maria-Theresia und Joseph II. Ihre Correspondenz* (Vienna, 1867-68). (An important source.)

——— *Marie Antoinette, Joseph II und Leopold II. Ihr Briefwechsel* (Leipzig, 1866). (An important source.)

———and FLAMMERMONT, J., ed—*Correspondance secrète du Comte de Mercy-Argenteau avec l'Empereur Joseph II et le Prince de Kaunitz* (2 vols., Paris, 1889). (Indispensable.)

——— and GEFFROY, A., ed.—*Correspondance secrète entre Marie-Thérèse et le Comte de Mercy-Argenteau, avec les lettres de Marie-Thérèse et de Marie Antoinette* (3 vols., Paris, 1874). (Invaluable.)

AUGEARD, J. M.—*Mémoires secrets de J. M. Augeard, secrétaire des commandements de la reine Marie-Antoinette, 1760 à 1800* (Paris, 1866). (Informative, but exaggerated.)

AULARD, A.—*Histoire politique de la révolution française, 1789-1804* (Paris, 1901). (A standard history.)

———, ed.—*La société des Jacobins. Recueil de documents pour l'histoire du club des Jacobins de Paris* (6 vols., Paris, 1889-97). (Contains valuable materials.)

BACHAUMONT.—*Marie-Antoinette, Louis XVI et la famille royale. Journal anecdotique tiré des mémoires secrets pour servir à l'histoire de la république des lettres, 1763-1782* (Paris, 1866). (Based on the first nineteen volumes of Bachaumont's *Mémoires secrets*—amusing anecdotes.)

BACOURT, A. de, ed.—*Correspondance entre le Comte de Mirabeau et le Comte de la Marck pendant les années 1789, 1790 et 1791* (3 vols., Paris, 1851). (An invaluable source.)

BAILLY.—*Mémoires de Bailly* (3 vols., Paris, 1821-22). (Not very coherent and extremely sketchy.)

BAPST, G.—*Inventaire de Marie-Josèphe de Saxe, Dauphine de France* (Paris, 1883). (Contains some interesting facts.)

BARBIER.—*Journal historique et anecdotique du règne de Louis XV* (4 vols., Paris, 1847-56). (Anecdotal.)

BARENTIN, C. L. de.—*Lettres et bulletins de Barentin à Louis XVI, avril-juillet, 1789* (ed. by Aulard, 1915).

——*Mémoire autographe de M. de Barentin, chancelier et garde de sceaux sur les derniers conseils du roi Louis XVI* (Paris, 1844). (An attack on Necker.)

BARRIÈRE, F.—*La cour et la ville sous Louis XIV, Louis XV et Louis XVI* (Paris, 1830). (Anecdotes.)

——*Tableaux de genre et d'histoire peints par différents maîtres, ou morceaux inédits sur la régence, la jeunesse de Louis XV, et la règne de Louis XVI* (Paris, 1828). (Anecdotal fragments from memoirs.)

BEAUCHESNE, M. A. de.—*Louis XVII, sa vie, son agonie, sa mort; captivité de la famille royale au Temple* (2 vols., Paris, 1866). (Despite the title, a good collection of important documents.)

——*La vie de Madame Élizabeth, sœur de Louis XVI* (2 vols., Paris, 1869). (Contains excellent documents.)

BEAUCOURT, Marquis de.—*Captivité et derniers moments de Louis XVI. Récits originaux et documents officiels* (2 vols., Paris, 1892). (An indispensable collection of source materials.)

——*Étude sur Madame Élisabeth, d'après sa correspondance, suivie de lettres inédites et autres documents* (Paris, 1864).

BECKER, O.—*Die 'Séance royale' am 23 Juni 1789* (Berlin, 1909). (A Ph.D. dissertation, based on secondary sources.)

BERTRAND DE MOLLEVILLE, A. F.—*Mémoires particuliers pour servir à l'histoire de la fin du règne de Louis XVI* (2 vols., Paris, 1816). (There is also an English edition, London, 1797, of these Memoirs; de Molleville was Louis XVI's minister of state.)

Beschreibung der Feyerlichkeiten, welche bey Gelegenheit der Durchreise Ihrer Königlicher Hoheit der Durchleuchtigsten Frau Dauphine, Marien Antonien ... von den Vorderöstreich-Breissgauischen Landständen veranstaltet worden (1770). (An official account of Marie Antoinette's journey to France.)

BEUGNOT, Comte Albert.—*Mémoires du Comte Beugnot ancien ministre, 1783-1815* (2 vols., Paris, 1866). (Not very informative.)

BISSING, F.—*Frankreich unter Ludwig XVI* (Freiburg, 1782). (A secondary study.)

BOURNISEAUX, P. V. J. de.—*Histoire de Louis XVI, avec les anecdotes de son règne* (2 vols., Paris, 1829). (Pious royalist drivel. The Preface says: "God and the king are in my heart; God and the king guided my pen.")

BOUTRY, M.—*Le mariage de Marie-Antoinette* (Paris, 1904). (A good study.)

BROGLIE, E. de.—*Le fils de Louis XV, Louis dauphin de France, 1729-65* (Paris, 1877). (One of the few books on a neglected subject.)

BROWNING, O.—*The Flight to Varennes and Other Historical Essays* (1882). (A good essay on an exciting subject.)

——, ed.—*Dispatches from Paris, 1784-1790* (2 vols., Camden 3d series, 1909-10). (Official British ambassadorial reports.)

CABANÈS, Dr.—*The Secret Cabinet of History* (Paris, 1897, tr. by W. C. Costello). (Somewhat sensational exposé of Louis XVI's physiology.)

CAMPAN, Mme. de.—*Mémoires sur la vie privée de Marie Antoinette* (3 vols., Paris, 1823). (The discredited gossip of an imaginative lady-in-waiting.)

CAPEFIGUE, M.—*Histoire de grandes opérations financières* (Paris, 1855). (A rather shallow study of the farmers-general.)

——*Louis XVI, son administration et ses relations diplomatiques avec l'Europe* (3 vols., Paris, 1844). (Contains excellent documents from the archives.)

Cérémonial du Sacre des Rois de France, avec le formulaire en Latin et en Français. Tel qu'il fut suivi au Sacre de Louis XVI (Édition Rupella, La Rochelle, 1931). (A rare manual of an unusual subject.)

CHAUMETTE.—*Mémoires de Chaumette sur la révolution du 10 août 1792* (ed. by Aulard, Paris, 1893). (The brief memoirs of a revolutionist who was active during some exciting days.)

CHÉRON, F.—*Mémoires et récits de Chéron* (Paris, 1882). (Unimportant memoirs of a member of Louis XVI's court in 1792.)

CLÉRY.—*Journal de ce qui s'est passé à la Tour de Temple pendant la captivité de Louis XVI* (Paris, 1814). (The justly famous memoirs of Louis XVI's valet in the Temple prison. An English translation was published at London in 1910.)

COMBES, L.—*Épisodes et curiosités révolutionnaires* (Paris, 1872). (Repeats the senseless gossip about Louis' impotence.)

CONSTANT, L., ed.—*Louis XVI d'après les documents authentiques* (1869). (A short and not at all "authentic" or "documentary" book.)

CROY.—*Journal inédit du duc de Croy, 1718-84* (2 vols., Paris, 1906). (Some useful details on the reign of Louis XV.)

DECHÊNE, A.—*Un enfant royal: Louis-Joseph-Xavier Duc de Bourgogne, 1751-61* (Paris, 1933).

DESJARDINS, G.—*Supplément à l'histoire du Petit-Trianon* (Versailles, 1894).

DONIOL, H.—*Histoire de la participation de la France à l'établissement des États-Unis d'Amérique* (Paris, 1886). (Diplomatic documents.)

DROZ, J.—*Histoire du règne de Louis XVI* (3 vols., Paris, 1839-42). (A dry, political, legalistic history.)

DRUON, H.—*Histoire de l'éducation des princes dans la maison des Bourbons de France* (2 vols., Paris, 1897). (A good study in a neglected field.)

DUTEMPLE, E., ed.—*Ordres du Jour inédites de Santerre, commandant des Gardes Nationales Parisiennes en 1792 et 1793* (Paris, 1875). (Very important documents.)

ECKARD, M.—*Mémoires historiques sur Louis XVII, roi de France et de Navarre* (Paris, 1818). (A mediocre book on a useless subject.)

Edgeworth de Firmont.—*Mémoires* (Paris, 1815). (The unimportant memoirs of Louis XVI's last confessor.)

Elliott, Grace D.—*Journal of My Life during the French Revolution* (London, 1859). (The curious journal of the mistress of the Duke of Orleans—and others—not devoid of breathless fabrications.)

Feuillet de Conches.—*Louis XVI, Marie Antoinette et Madame Élisabeth. Lettres et documents inédits* (6 vols., Paris, 1864-73). (This is one of the most famous documentary collections on the subject—and largely discredited. Critics are agreed that only the fifth volume contains authentic letters; the other volumes must be used with the utmost caution, if at all. A careful analysis of the collection, probably by Lord Acton, may be found in *North British Review*, LII [1787], 259-62.)

Fischbach, G.—*La fuite de Louis XVI d'après les archives municipales de Strasbourg* (Paris, 1879). (A too detailed study based on archive materials; excellent, but limited.)

Flammermont, J.—*Les correspondances des agents diplomatiques étrangers en France avant la Révolution, conservées dans les archives de Berlin, Dresden, Genève, Turin, Gênes, Florence, Naples, Simancas, Lisbonne, Londres, La Haye et Vienne* (Paris, 1896). (A superb collection of choice documents, indispensable to the student of history and diplomacy.)

——*Études critiques sur les sources de l'histoire du XVIIIe siècle*. I: *Les Mémoires de Mme Campan* (Paris, 1886). (A surgical operation skilfully performed on the body of once-famous memoirs.)

——*Négociations secrètes de Louis XVI et du baron de Breteuil avec la cour de Berlin, décembre 1791-julliet 1792* (Paris, 1885). (Flammermont was the first to publish this correspondence.)

Flassan, M.—*Histoire générale et raisonnée de la diplomatie française* (Vol. 6, Paris, 1809). (Still reliable.)

France d'Hézecques, F. de.—*Souvenirs d'un page de la cour de Louis XVI* (Paris, 1873). (Interesting memoirs.)

Frénilly.—*Souvenirs du Baron de Frénilly pair de France, 1768-1828* (Paris, 1908).

Funck-Brentano, J. C. F.—*The Diamond Necklace* (1911). (Good for its bibliography, pp. 1-10.)

Garat, D. J.—*Mémoires sur la révolution, ou exposé de ma conduite dans les affaires et dans les fonctions publiques* (Paris, An III). (Confused bombast.)

Garrett, M. B.— *The Estates General of 1789. The Problems of Composition and Organization* (New York, 1935). (A fine study of the pamphlets; bibliography, 222-64.)

Gauthier, L.—*L'histoire de France par le document. Reproductions de pièces originales tirées des collections des Archives Nationales et accompagnées de notices* (Paris, n.d.). (The first fascicle contains ten photostats of documents about Louis XVI.)

Geffroy, A.—*Gustave III et la cour de France* (2 vols., Paris, 1867). (A first-rate study based on original sources.)

—— *Marie Antoinette et Fersen, Mémoire* (Rome, 1879). (A brief but critical essay.)

GIRARD, G., ed.—*Correspondance entre Marie-Thérèse et Marie-Antoinette* (Paris, 1933). (Includes 167 authentic letters, drawn from the collections of Arneth and Geffroy, as well as two letters from the Vienna archives never published before. Altogether a complete collection of the letters passing between mother and daughter which are known to be authentic.)

GOGUELAT, M. de.—*Mémoire de Goguelat, sur les événemens relatifs au voyage de Louis XVI à Varennes* (Paris, 1823). (Goguelat participated in the military arrangements for the flight to Varennes; this is his personal justification for the failure—a polemical and worthless pamphlet.)

GORET, Ch.— *Mon témoignage sur la détention de Louis XVI et de sa famille dans la Tour du Temple* (Paris, 1825). (Goret was a member of the Commune of the 10th of August, and this booklet gives some extremely interesting facts.

HAGGARD, A. C. P.—*Louis XVI and Marie Antoinette* (2 vols., London, 1909). (Lieutenant-Colonel Haggard, D.S.O., has pasted together a lot of episodes, incidents and anecdotes.)

HALE, E. E. and E. E., Jr.—*Franklin in France. From Original Documents* (2 vols., Boston, 1887-88). (Poorly written, badly edited and wretchedly translated documents.)

HEIDENSTAM, O. G., ed.—*The Letters of Marie Antoinette, Fersen and Barnave* (tr. from French by W. Stephens and W. Jackson, London, 1926). (Originals on a fascinating subject.)

HOUSSAYE, A.—*Louis XVI* (Paris, 1875). (A worthless essay.)

HUE, F.—*Dernières années du règne et de la vie de Louis XVI* (An English edition appeared at London in 1806, long before the French original was published. Baron Hue was an officer of the king's chamber during the fateful days of August, 1792; his memoirs are inevitably interesting.)

ISAMBERT, ed.—*Recueil général des anciennes lois françaises* (Paris, n.d.). (Vols.XXII to XXIX contain the laws passed under Louis XVI.)

Journal général de la cour et de la ville. (An anti-revolutionary journal, published between September 16, 1789, and August 10, 1792. For a critique of this interesting publication, see L. Monraysse in *Révolution Française,* LXI [1911], 385-427.)

Journal de Paris. (An impartial daily, four pages long, beginning January 1, 1777, and ending in the same year.)

KAGENECK, General de.—*Lettres au Baron Alströmer sur la période du règne de Louis XVI de 1779 à 1784* (Paris, 1884). (Interesting from the point of view of court affairs, for Kageneck was commander of the Royal Guard.)

KLINCKOWSTROM, R. M. de.—*Le comte de Fersen et la cour de France* (2 vols., Paris, 1877). (Based on Fersen's correspondence, but now somewhat out of date.)

LAVISSE, E.—*Histoire de France* (Paris, 1910). (The first part of Vol. 9 of this excellent history deals with the period of Louis XVI.)

LEGG, L. G. W.—*Select Documents Illustrative of the History of the French Revolution. The Constituent Assembly* (2 vols., Oxford, 1905).

LESCURE (pseudonym).—*Correspondance secrète inédite sur Louis XVI, Marie-Antoinette, la cour et la ville, de 1777 à 1792* (2 vols.; Paris, 1866). (Extremely interesting and valuable information gathered from the Russian archives and compiled anonymously.)

—— *Marie-Antoinette et sa famille, d'après les nouveaux documents* (Paris, 1866).

LESER, E.—*Necker's Zweites Ministerium* (Mainz, 1871). (A Ph.D. dissertation based upon opinion rather than primary facts.)

LÉVIS, Duc de.—*Souvenirs et portraits, 1780-89* (Paris, 1815). (Keen character sketches by a sharp observer.)

LOMÉNIE, L. de.—*Beaumarchais et son temps. Études sur la société en France au XVIIIe siècle d'après des documents inédits* (2 vols., Paris, 1856). (A scholarly work, especially valuable for the student of the American Revolution.)

LOUIS XVI.—*Collection des meilleurs ouvrages qui ont été publiés pour la défense de Louis XVI* (2 vols., 1793. Ed. by A. J. du Gour). (A rather sketchy bibliography.)

—— *Comptes de Louis XVI* (Paris, 1909). (The complete financial accounts of Louis XVI, edited by Beauchamp, from MSS in the Archives Nationales.)

—— *Correspondance politique et confidentielle inédite avec ses frères et plusieurs personnes célèbres, pendant les dernières années de son règne et jusqu'à sa mort* (2 vols., Paris, 1803). (This work, edited by Helene Maria Williams, is altogether spurious. A criticism of it, by Beaucourt, may be found in *Extrait de la Revue Bibliographique et Littéraire*, 1865.)

——*Description de la forêt de Compiègne, comme elle étoit en 1765; avec le guide de la forêt* (Paris, 1766). (This booklet was composed by Louis when he was a boy of twelve; a copy may be consulted in the Reserved Room of the Bibliothèque Nationale.)

——*Études du Télémaque, imprimées en 1766 par Louis-Auguste . . ., réimprimées en 1814; présentés à Madame, duchesse d'Angoulême* (A reprint of Louis XVI's own little anthology.)

—— *Exposé des motifs de la conduite du roi, relativement à l'Angleterre* (Paris, 1779). (The pamphlet justifying the American war.)

—— *Fac-Simile de lettres de Louis XVI à M. le Marquis de Bouillé. Suivis d'un plein pouvoir de Monsieur depuis Louis XVIII* (Paris, *ca.*1840). (Photostats of six genuine letters written by Louis XVI.)

—— *Journal* (ed. by L. Nicolardot; Paris, 1873).

—— *Lettre du roi* (Paris, January, 1793: the letter, published by Louis' lawyers, protests against the death penalty.)

—— *Lettres et preuves de leur authenticité* (ed. by B. Chauvelot, 1864). (Another spurious collection.)

——*Louis XVI peint par lui-même ou correspondance et autres écrits de ce monarque* (Paris, 1817). (Another apocryphal collection, probably invented by Babié de Bercenay and Imbert de La Platière.)

——*Œuvres de Louis XVI, précèdées d'une histoire de ce monarque et d'une lettre de M. Berryer* (2 vols., Paris, 1864). (This collection contains 80 letters by Louis, many of which are apocryphal. Most of the "works" herein compiled should be viewed with suspicion.)

——*Réflexions sur mes entretiens avec M. le duc de la Vauguyon* (ed. by de Falloux; Paris, 1851). (These *Reflexions* are genuine.)

——*Procès de Louis XVI. Recueil de pièces originales* (n.d.). (Seven volumes of documents.)

——*Procès de Louis XVI, ou collection complète des opinions, discours et mémoires des membres de la Convention Nationale* (Paris, An III). (Nine volumes of opinions and speeches.)

——*The Testament of His late Most Christian Majesty Louis XVI* (tr. by H. C. E.; London, 1793).

MALESHERBES.—*Vie de Chrétien-Guillaume Lamoignon Malesherbes, ancien premier président de la Cour des Aides* (Paris, 1802). (A study that is more edifying than critical.)

MALLET DU PAN.—*Mémoires et correspondance* (vol. I, Paris, 1851).

MALOUET.—*Mémoires* (2 vols., Paris, 1868).

MONIN, H.—*L'État de Paris en 1789. Études et documents sur l'ancien régime à Paris* (Paris, 1889). (Important data.)

MONITEUR.—*Reimpression de l'ancien Moniteur, depuis la réunion des États-Généraux jusqu'au consulat, mai 1789—novembre 1799* (32 vols., 1840-45). (The indispensable newspaper of the French Revolution; it carried official decrees as well as complete reports of the parliamentary debates.)

MONTBAREY.—*Mémoires autographes de M. le prince de Montbarey, ministre secrétaire d'état au département de la guerre sous Louis XVI* (Paris, 1826). (The dull memoirs of a dull bureaucrat.)

MONTIER, A., ed.—*Correspondance de Thomas Lindet pendant la constituante et la législative, 1789-92* (Paris, 1899). (Valuable for public opinion.)

MOREAU, J. N.—*Leçons de morale, de politique et de droit public* (Versailles, 1773). (This was the textbook used by Louis XVI: it is dedicated to him.)

——*Mes souvenirs, 1717-1803* (2 vols., Paris, 1898). (Marie Antoinette's librarian, and the historiographer of France, tells some dull incidents.)

MORRIS, G.—*The Diary and Letters of Gouverneur Morris, Minister of the United States to France* (ed. by A. C. Morris, New York, 1888, 2 vols.). (Morris makes some keen observations on the course of the Revolution.)

MOUSTIER, Comte de.—*Relation du voyage de Sa Majesté Louis XVI, lors de son départ pour Montmédi et de son arrestation à Va-*

rennes, le 21 juin 1791 (Paris, 1815). (An addition to the Varennes literature, by an eye-witness.)

Musée des archives nationales. Documents originaux de l'histoire de France (Paris, 1872). (Contains 1,200 facsimiles and reproductions of documents, many of them on the French Revolution.)

NOLHAC, P. de.—*Études sur la cour de France. Marie-Antoinette dauphine* (14th ed., Paris, 1901).

NOUGARET, P. J. B.—*Anecdotes du règne de Louis XVI* (6 vols., Paris, 1791). (Interesting anecdotes—for what they are worth.)

OBERKIRCH.—*Mémoires de la Baronne d'Oberkirch* (2 vols., Paris, 1853). (Interesting for glimpses of the French court.)

OELSNER, K. E.—*Flucht, Verhör und Hinrichtung Ludwigs XVI, Nach der Schilderung eines deutschen Beobachters* (*Konrad Engelbert Oelsner*) (Leipzig, 1911). (Oelsner lived in Paris from 1789 to 1793, and his reports on revolutionary events have the freshness and immediacy of an excited eye-witness.)

ORLEANS, L. P. J. duc de.—*Correspondance avec Louis XVI, la reine, Montmorin, Liancourt, Biron, Lafayette...* (Paris, 1801). (Of scant value.)

PADOVER, S. K.—*The Revolutionary Emperor: Joseph II* (London and New York, 1934). (The only biography in English.)

PAPILLON de la FERTÉ.—*Journal de Papillon de la Ferté, Intendant et controleur de l'argenterie, menus-plaisirs et affaires de la chambre du roi, 1756-80* (ed. by E. Boysse, Paris, 1887). (Contains illuminating and curious details on wardrobe, fêtes, furniture, balls, etc.)

PAROY, Comte de.—*Souvenirs d'un défenseur de la famille royale pendant la révolution* (Paris, 1895). (Moderately interesting.)

PARTON, J.—*Life and Times of Benjamin Franklin* (2 vols., Boston, 1864). (Still useful.)

PIMODAN, Comte de.—*Le comte F.-C. de Mercy-Argenteau, ambassadeur impérial à Paris sous Louis XV et sous Louis XVI* (Paris, 1911). (A fine biography, based upon primary sources.)

PINGAUD, L.—*Correspondance intime du Comte de Vaudreuil et du Comte d'Artois pendant l'émigration, 1789-1815* (2 vols., Paris, 1889). (More useful for Artois than for Louis XVI.)

Procès-verbal de la Convention Nationale, Tome cinquième, contenant les séances depuis et compris le premier janvier 1793... (Imprimerie Nationale, 1793). (The official publication of the sessions during Louis XVI's trial.)

RAUNIE, E., ed.—*Chansonnier historique du XVIII*[e] *siècle* (Vols.IX-X, Paris, 1884). (An excellent collection of contemporary songs and rhymed satires.)

RENÉE, A.—*Louis XVI et sa cour* (2d ed., Paris, 1858). (A rehash of second-rate materials.)

Revue des autographes, des curiosités de l'histoire et de la biographie. (A monthly, edited by G. Charavay, from January 15, 1868, to March, 1868, containing a number of reproductions of rare documents.)

ROCHETERIE, M., and BEAUCOURT, ed.—*Lettres de Marie-Antoinette. Recueil des lettres authentiques de la reine* (2 vols., Paris, 1895). (A splendid collection of 386 authentic letters, introduced by a critical bibliographic essay, pp.vii-cxxvi.)

ROEDERER, P. L.—*Chronique de cinquante jours, du 20 juin au 10 août 1792* (Paris, 1832). (Written by the man who played a significant rôle during the exciting days of August, 1792.)

SALAMON,—*Correspondance secrète de l'abbé de Salamon chargé des affaires du Saint-Siège pendant la révolution avec le cardinal de Zelada, 1791-92* (Paris, 1898). (Interesting observations on the course of the Revolution.)

———*Mémoires inédits de l'Internonce à Paris pendant la Révolution* (Paris, 1890). (Has virtually nothing on Louis XVI.)

SÉGUR, P. M. M. H.—*Au couchant de la monarchie: Louis XVI et Turgot, 1774-76* (Paris, 1910).

SÉMALLÉ, Comte de.—*Souvenirs du Comte de Sémallé* (Paris, 1863). (Not very exciting memoirs of one of Louis XVI's pages.)

SÉNAC DE MEILHAN, G.—*Le gouvernement, les mœurs et les conditions en France avant la révolution. Portraits des personnages distingués de la fin du 18ᵉ siècle* (Paris, 1862). (Much keen observation on eighteenth-century morals and manners.)

SODERHJELM, A.—*Marie-Antoinette et Barnave. Correspondance secrète (juillet 1791-janvier 1792)* (Paris, 1934). (The newly discovered correspondence; of unusual value.)

SOREL, A. E.—*La princesse de Lamballe, une amie de la reine Marie Antoinette* (Paris, 1933). (Sentimental nonsense.)

SOULAVIE, J. L.—*Mémoires historiques et politiques du règne de Louis XVI* (6 vols., 1801). (Soulavie was a famous forger, and everything that bears his name should be regarded with distrust. For a criticism see J. Flammermont, "Les papiers de Soulavie," in *Revue Historique,* XXV [1884], 107-15.)

SOURIAU, M.—*Louis XVI et la révolution* (Paris, 1893). (A shallow study.)

STRYIENSKI, C.—*La mère des trois derniers Bourbons, Marie Josèphe de Saxe, et la cour de Louis XV* (Paris, 1902). (A useful book on a neglected subject.)

TARENTE.—*Souvenirs de la Princesse de Tarente* (Nantes, 1897). (The princess was one of Marie Antoinette's ladies-in-waiting.)

TOCQUEVILLE, A. de.—*Episodes de la Terreur, extraits des mémoires du Comte de Tocqueville* (Compiègne, 1901). (A brief but extremely graphic account of the Terror by a young and intelligent eyewitness.)

TOURZEL.—*Mémoires de la duchesse de Tourzel, 1789-95* (2 vols., Paris, 1883). (She was the governess of the royal children.)

TUETEY, A.—*Répertoire général des sources manuscrits de l'histoire de Paris pendant la révolution française* (11 vols., Paris, 1892-1914). (A thorough summary of archival documents; each volume has an index.)

Vaissière, P. C. de.—*La mort du roi* (*21 janvier 1793*) (1910). (A brief account.)

Vast, A.—*Sur le chemin de Varennes* (Paris, 1907). (An account based upon documents.)

Véri.—*Journal de l'abbé de Véri* (2 vols., Paris, 1928-29). (Considering the important position of the abbé, who was a friend of Turgot, his journal is disappointing.)

Vizetelly, H.—*The Story of the Diamond Necklace* (2 vols., London, 1867). (A rather pedestrian account.)

Welvert, E.—*L'Éminence grise de Marie-Antoinette* (Versailles, 1922). (A brief study of the queen's confessor.)

——*Le secret de Barnave; Barnave et Marie-Antoinette* (Paris, 1920). (A good short account; see the review by Aulard in *Révolution Française,* LXXIII [1920], 275-79.)

IV. ARTICLES

d'Agours, B., ed.—"La baronne de Korff et sa participation à la fuite de Louis XVI," *Revue de la Révolution,* VII (1886), Document Section, 77-82. (Lists eight letters from the Moscow archives.)

L'Amateur d'Autographes. (A monthly edited by Charavay, founded in 1862: the issues for 1862-63, 1864-65, 1866-67, 1898-99, 1902-03, contain articles or documents on Louis XVI or Marie Antoinette.)

Amiable, L.—"Les Bourbons francs-maçons," *Révolution Française,* XXIX (1895), 526-33. (Guesses that Louis XVI was a Mason.)

——"Louis XVI et les Noeuf Sœurs," *Rév.Fr.,* XXXI (1896), 225-60. (Tries to prove that Louis XVI and his two brothers were Masons, members of the lodge La Militaire des Trois Frères-Unis. If true, it is unimportant; but it is probably not true.)

Aulard, A.—"Le détronement de Louis XVI (1792)," *Rév.Fr.,* XXXVI (1899), 25-69. (A political essay.)

——"La dette américaine envers la France. Comment elle fut contractée sous Louis XVI. Comment elle fut remboursée sous la révolution française," *Revue de Paris,* May 15 and June 1, 1925. (A good study.)

——"L'exécution de Louis XVI et la presse française," *Rév.Fr.,* LXXXII (1929), 65-76, 153-62. (A study of public opinion.)

——"La fuite à Varennes et le mouvement républicain, 21 juin-juillet 1791," *Rév.Fr.,* XXXV (1898), 385-436. (One of Aulard's comprehensive political studies.)

——"Patrie, patriotisme sous Louis XVI et dans les cahiers," *Rév.Fr.,* LXVIII (1915), 301-39.

——, ed.—"Lettres et bulletins de Barentin à Louis XVI. Avril-juillet 1789," *Societé de l'histoire de la Rév.Fr.,* XLI (1915).

Bart, P.—"La mort du roi et l'opinion (document inédits)," *Revue des Curiosités Révol.,* III (1912-13), 78-82. (Scanty.)

Beaucourt, G. du Fresne de.—"Une supercherie littéraire. Les lettres de Louis XVI," Extrait de la *Revue Bibliographique et litteraire,* 1865.

(A criticism of the spurious letters of Louis XVI published by Helene Maria Williams, Chauvelot, etc. The author, however, makes the unfortunate mistake of accepting the Feuillet de Conches collections as genuine.)

BINET, M.—"Les répercussions de la fuite de Louis XVI en Bretagne (23 juin—1er juillet 1791)," *Bulletin historique et philosophique,* 1911, 93-122. (Unimportant.)

BIRÉ, E.—"Les défenseurs de Louis XVI," *Revue du monde catholique,* October-December, 1894. (Based on material from the Archives Nationales.)

BORD, G.—"Les prisonniers enfermés à la Bastille sous Louis XVI." *Revue de la Rév.,* I (1883), Documents Section, 61-64, 92-96, 123-28, 156-60, 190-92; II (1883), 31-32, 60-64, 90-96, 123-28, 151-59. (A comprehensive analysis, based upon documents, of the prisoners in the Bastille, showing their number was vastly exaggerated.)

——"La vérité sur la condamnation de Louis XVI," *Revue de la Révol.,* III (1884), 152-62.

BRETTE, A., ed.—"Lettres de Thiroux de Crosne lieutenant-général de police, à Louis XVI (20-30 avril 1789)," *Rév.Fr.,* XXVIII (1895), 161-81. (From the archives.)

BUFFENOIR, H.—"Louis XVI et la boisson," *Rév.Fr.,* LXXIX (1926), 326-29. (A repetition of the long-discredited canard that Louis XVI was a drunkard.)

"Les Conventionnels régicides après la Révolution," *Archives historiques, artistiques et littéraires,* II (1890-91). (An unprofitable study of what happened to those who had voted for the death of Louis XVI—many of them likewise died under the guillotine....)

CORRE, A.—"Le procès de Louis XVI et la révolution du 31 mai, d'après la correspondance de Blad, deputé..., avec la municipalité de Brest," *Rév.Fr.,* XXIX (1895), 534-57. (The reverberations of Louis' execution.)

DEJEAN, E.—"Un projet de discours de Louis XVI par Necker." *Rév. Fr.,* LVI (1909), 193-98. (A good analysis of Necker's draft of the speech which the king made on May 5, 1789.)

DREYFUS, J.—"Le manifeste royal de 20 juin 1791," *Rév. Fr.,* LIV (1908), 5-22. (An analysis of Louis' motives in escaping from Paris.)

FAGNIEZ, G.—"La politique de Vergennes et la diplomatie de Breteuil, 1774-87," *Revue Historique,* CXL (1922), 1-71. (A good study of diplomacy.)

FEUILLET DE CONCHES.—"Les lettres de Marie-Antoinette," *L'Amateur d'autographes,* 1865, 116-19. (Argues that Arneth's collection of the queen's letters is hardly half complete, and that Marie Antoinette used to sign her name both *Antoinette* and *Marie Antoinette.*)

FLEISCHMANN, H.—"Louis XVI franc-maçon," *Revue des curiosités révolutionnaires,* I (1910-11), 335-43, 368-74, 415.

GAULOT, P.—"Un épisode de la captivité du temple, l'anneau et le cachet de Louis XVI," *Revue des questions historiques,* XLV (1889), 219-33.

GRANEL, A.—"Condamnation de Louis XVI par les loges allemandes. Documents et controverses," *Revue catholique et royaliste,* June-August, 1912. (The usual trash about the Mason-Jewish conspiracy.)

LACOUR-GAYET, G.—"Voyage de Louis XVI à Cherbourg (1786)," *Revue des études historiques,* March-April, 1906.

LARCY, R. de.—"Louis XVI et les successeurs de Turgot jusqu'en 1789," *Correspondant,* March 25, 1867.

—— "Louis XVI et Turgot, d'après des documents inédits," *Correspondant,* 1866.

LAURENT, G.—"La fuite de Louis XVI," *Bulletin Amicale de la Marne,* nos.19-21 (1925-26). (Documents from the provincial towns through which the king passed.)

LE VERDIER, P.—"Les reliques de la famille royale et les descendants de Cléry," *Revue des questions historiques,* LX (1896), 264-80.

LIMBURG, J.—"Die Schmähschriften auf Marie Antoinette," *Neue Freie Presse,* January 31, 1909. (A brief summary of some pamphlets against the queen.)

LOUISY, P.—"Louis XVI," *Nouvelle biographie générale* (1862), 858-99. (Probably the best short account of Louis XVI.)

MATHIEZ, A.—"Quelques anecdotes de Mme Campan sur Louis XVI," *Annales historiques de la Rév.Fr.,* new ser., III (1926), 190-91. (Insignificant.)

—— "Les tentatives de corruption de l'Espagne pour sauver Louis XVI," *Annales historiques de la Rév.Fr.,* new ser., III (1926), 179-83. (A document on Ocariz' attempt to save the king.)

MAUTOUCHET, P.—"Une lettre de Condorcet sur le procès de Louis XVI," *Rév.Fr.,* LXIV (1913), 220-24. (The letter was written on December 11, 1792; it is now in the Archives de la Sarthe.)

MORÈRE, J.—"Le manuscrit du mémoire de Louis XVI du 20 juin 1791," *Rév.Fr.,* XXXIV (1898), 318-21.

PINGAUD, L.—"Le commerce du Levant sous Louis XVI," *Revue des questions historiques,* XLI (1887), 150-82.

PINON, R.—"Louis XVI, Vergennes et la grande lutte contre l'Angleterre," *Revue d'histoire diplomatique,* 1929, 37-64. (A rehash of secondary materials.)

SAGNAC, P.—"Marie Antoinette et Barnave d'après leur correspondance secrète," *Rév.Fr.,* 1935, 207-41. (A critical review of Söderhjelm's book.)

SANTERRE.—"La journée du 10 août racontée par un révolutionnaire," *Revue de la Révolution,* VII (1886), Documents Section, 161-63. (The account of an eye-witness.)

—— "Rapport de ce qui s'est passé au faubourg Saint-Antoine, le 28 février 1791," *Revue de la Révolution,* XIII (1888), Documents Section, 92-96. (A document written by Santerre.)

SELIGMAN, E.—An untitled communication on the trial of Louis XVI, in *Rév.Fr.,* LXI (1911), 564-68.

TOURNEUX, M.—"La genèse du discours de Louis XVI aux états généraux, 1789," *Rév.Fr.,* LVI (1909), 318-29.

Vauthier, G.—"Palloy et l'ameublement de la tour du Temple," *Annales Révolutionnaires,* X (1918), 684-85. (The cost of furnishing the Temple prison.)

"Vie privée de Louis XVI aux Tuileries," *Revue de la Rév.,* XVI (1889), 213-18. (A summary of various memoirs, such as D'Hézecques, Weber, and some newspapers.)

Welvert, E.—"Procès-verbaux originaux de la Convention," *Archives historiques, artistiques et littéraires,* I (1889-90), 455-59. (A critical analysis of the minutes of the Convention, pointing out that there are errors and omissions in the original: the printed editions are more accurate than the original.)

——— "Projets de mariages princiers. Le dauphin (Louis XVI) et Amélie de Saxe. L'électeur de Saxe et Clotilde de France," *Archives historiques, artistiques et littéraires,* I (1889-90), 193-203, 341-58. (The little-known episode of the attempt to find a Saxon wife for Louis XVI.)

V. PAMPHLETS

"Adresse de 150 communes de Normandie à la Convention Nationale sur le jugement de Louis XVI" (Rouen, 1793), 15 pp.

"Bulletin du roi du 8 mars 1791" (Imprimerie Royale, March 8 to 16, 1791), 10 bulletins.

"Convention Nationale, Opinions . . ." (1793).

"Le cri du coeur, dialogue sur l'édit du roi du 30 mai 1774" (Paris, 1774), 16 pp.

Destainville, H.—"Le sacre et le couronnement de Louis XVI" (Troyes, 1923), 8 pp.

"Détails de tout ce qui s'est passé au Champ-de-Mars à la cérémonie de la Fédération, le 14 Juillet 1790" (Paris, 1790), 8 pp.

Duchesne, L. H.—"Comparaison des finances de la France en 1715, après la mort de Louis XIV, et vingt ans de guerre, avec celle du règne de Louis XVI en 1791, après vingt ans de paix" (Paris, 1791), 8 pp.

"Fête à la place de Louis XV, pour le mariage de Monseigneur le Dauphin: avec des inscriptions latins et françoises" (Geneva, 1770), 30 pp.

Hennet de Goutel.—"Vergennes and the American Independence" (tr. by L. Ensor, Paris, 1918), 41 pp.

"Journée du 10 avril 1791" (n.p., n.d.), 13 pp.

"Lettre sur le mariage de Monseigneur Louis Auguste de Bourbon, dauphin de France, avec l'archiduchesse Marie Antoinette" (Amsterdam, 1770), 32 pp.

Lévy, A.—"La culpabilité de Louis XVI et de Marie Antoinette" (Paris, 1907), 74 pp.

Necker, J.—"Réflexions présentées à la nation française sur le procès intenté à Louis XVI" (Paris, 1792), 32 pp.

"Pétition d'un grand nombre de citoyens de la section de la Halle au Bled" (n.d., n.p.), 8 pp.
"Rapport fait à l'Assemblée Nationale, par le commandant de garde au poste des appartements du traitre Louis XVI, depuis le Jeudi 9, jusqu'au Vendredi 10" (August, 1792).
"Relation de la journée du 10 août 1792. L'original est déposé dans les Archives de la Confédération Helvétique" (Versailles, n.d.), 24 pp.

INDEX

(1)